Recreating Japanese Women, 1600-1945

Recreating Japanese Women, 1600-1945

EDITED WITH AN INTRODUCTION BY

Gail Lee Bernstein

UNIVERSITY OF CALIFORNIA PRESS

Berkeley   Los Angeles   Oxford

University of California Press
Berkeley and Los Angeles, California
University of California Press, Ltd.
Oxford, England
© 1991 by
The Regents of the University of California

Library of Congress Cataloging-in-Publication Data

Recreating Japanese women, 1600–1945 / edited
with an introduction by Gail Lee Bernstein.
　p.　cm.
Includes bibliographical references and index.
ISBN 0-520-07015-1.—ISBN 0-520-07017-8 (paper)
1. Women—Japan—History.　2. Feminism—
Japan—History.　3. Women—Employment—
Japan—History.　I. Bernstein, Gail Lee.
HQ1762.R43　1991
305.42′0952—dc20　　　　　　　　　　　90-11194
　　　　　　　　　　　　　　　　　　　　　CIP

Printed in the United States of America

9　8　7　6　5　4　3

The paper used in this publication meets the
minimum requirements of American
National Standard for Information Sciences—
Permanence of Paper for Printed Library
Materials, ANSI Z39.48-1984. ∞

To the memory of Dr. Sharon H. Nolte (1948–1987), whose sudden death at the age of thirty-eight deprived the field of Japanese history of one of its most promising young scholars, and the contributors to this book of a respected and cherished colleague and friend

Contents

Preface / *ix*

Introduction
Gail Lee Bernstein / 1

PART ONE · WOMEN AND THE FAMILY: 1600–1868

1. Women and Changes in the Household Division of Labor
   Kathleen S. Uno / 17

2. The Life Cycle of Farm Women in Tokugawa Japan
   Anne Walthall / 42

3. The Deaths of Old Women: Folklore and Differential Mortality
   in Nineteenth-Century Japan
   Laurel L. Cornell / 71

4. The Shingaku Woman: Straight from the Heart
   Jennifer Robertson / 88

5. Female *Bunjin*: The Life of Poet-Painter Ema Saikō
   Patricia Fister / 108

6. Women in an All-Male Industry: The Case of Sake Brewer Tatsu'uma Kiyo
   Joyce Chapman Lebra / 131

PART TWO · THE MODERN DISCOURSE ON FAMILY, GENDER, AND WORK: 1868–1945

7. The Meiji State's Policy Toward Women, 1890–1910
   Sharon H. Nolte and Sally Ann Hastings / 151

8. Yosano Akiko and the Taishō Debate over the "New Woman"
   Laurel Rasplica Rodd / 175

9. Middle-Class Working Women During the Interwar Years
    Margit Nagy / 199

10. Activism Among Women in the Taishō Cotton Textile Industry
    Barbara Molony / 217

11. The Modern Girl as Militant
    Miriam Silverberg / 239

12. Doubling Expectations: Motherhood and Women's Factory Work Under
    State Management in Japan in the 1930s and 1940s
    Yoshiko Miyake / 267

13. Women and War: The Japanese Film Image
    William B. Hauser / 296

Afterword
Jane Caplan / 315

Glossary / *323*

Contributors / *325*

Index / *329*

Preface

This multidisciplinary collection of studies based on original research by Japan specialists focuses on the definition of Japanese women's roles over the last three hundred and fifty years, from the Tokugawa era to the end of the Second World War. Contributors to the volume have drawn on a rich and varied body of primary source materials, including poetry, folklore, oral history, religious teachings, screenplays, government publications, newspapers, and popular magazines, to describe the various forces and agents of change in the construction of Japanese women and to explore the gap between the feminine ideal and the reality of women's lives in that country. Organized chronologically and centered specifically on the cultural construction of gender, the thirteen chapters constitute a history of the evolution of female roles and feminine identity in Japan.

Our book originated in a three-hour panel on Japanese women's history held at the annual meeting of the Western Conference of the Association for Asian Studies in Park City, Utah, in the fall of 1986. The common themes that emerged from that panel encouraged us to expand and elaborate on our research at the following year's meeting in Tucson, Arizona. By the time we left Park City, we had already discussed putting out a book centered on changing definitions of Japanese womanhood, and we even had a tentative title: *Recreating Japanese Women*.

At the Tucson conference in 1987, the original group of panelists—Bernstein, Lebra, Molony, Rodd, Silverberg, Uno, and Walthall—were joined by Cornell, Hastings, Miyake, and Nagy. In an afternoon workshop following panel presentations, several other Japan scholars, women's history specialists, and advanced graduate students participated in an extensive critique of all the papers and worked to sharpen the thematic focus of the book. Although Robertson was unable to attend, she later sent her paper to the others for their comments.

We acquired two more contributors the following year when we invited William B. Hauser to share his work on women in wartime films and Patricia Fister to discuss one of the women artists represented in her exhibit "Japanese Women Artists, 1600–1900," which many of us had the good fortune of seeing at the University of Kansas Spencer Museum in April 1988 while attending the Rocky Mountain/Southwest Japan Regional Seminar meeting. The final contributor, European historian Jane Caplan, joined our project at the end of 1989, when she graciously agreed to provide an Afterword that would help integrate our research findings with theories developed in the study of women in the Western world.

Our common endeavor greatly benefited from the support of the University of Arizona. A grant from the Social and Behavioral Sciences Research Institute helped defray the considerable photocopying and postage costs. The Department of History's manuscript typist, Mary Sue Passé-Smith, applied her genius to the task of merging thirteen chapters typed on various disks into one unified manuscript, enhanced by her typing and editing skills. And Shizuko Radbill, the Japan librarian in the Oriental Collection, placed her expert research skills and the resources of the Collection at our disposal. As always, Michael Patrick Sullivan stood ready to provide practical, emotional, and intellectual support.

We owe a special word of thanks to Irwin Scheiner for his thoughtful, perceptive reading of the entire manuscript and his valuable recommendations for revision. The staff of the Press gave us the advantage of expert editing, helping pull together the style and substance of this book. In the end, of course, any errors are our responsibility.

We should also like to express our appreciation to the people who participated as discussants in the Tucson workshop: Robert J. Smith, Goldwin Smith Professor of Anthropology at Cornell University, and Stefan Tanaka, then Japan Staff Associate of the Social Science Research Council, offered many helpful suggestions. University of Arizona historians Tessie Liu and Karen Anderson lent a valuable comparative perspective. We benefited from criticisms made by Betty Brummal and Barbara Mori, and from the minutes prepared by rapporteur Pamela Gilbreath.

One other Japan specialist who had planned to join us for the workshop was Sharon Hamilton Nolte. She contributed a paper to our first conference in Utah, though at the last minute she was unable to attend. During the summer of 1987, shortly before the workshop, she died suddenly from an aneurism of the brain.

Sharon's husband, Reid Nolte, entrusted her academic papers to her friends and colleagues Ann Waltner, Anne Walthall, and Sally Hastings. The one unpublished manuscript that Sharon left was the chapter she intended to contribute to this volume. It was agreed that Sally Hastings should revise the manuscript for publication. The Midwest Japan Seminar, for which Sharon had been scheduled to write a paper, discussed the draft at its meeting on September 21, 1987. Sally Hastings presided at that meeting and attended our workshop in Sharon's place. In order to answer criticisms raised in those two discussions and to relate Sharon's manuscript to the others in the book, Sally added more material and rewrote the paper: essentially she recast and expanded the material to make Sharon's major points clearer and more convincing. Because Sally Hastings's contribution exceeded that usually encompassed by the term "editor," we thought it appropriate that she add her name as co-author of the paper.

Sharon Nolte's academic work was of very high quality, and it was central to her life. Had she lived, she undoubtedly would have produced a pioneering book on women and the state in modern Japan. It is altogether fitting that we honor her by dedicating this volume to her memory.

Introduction

Gail Lee Bernstein

Japanese women's lives, like those of women everywhere and in every time, have been shaped by a multitude of factors. The many forces that have affected their fate include their position within the family (and the nature of the family system itself); their social class standing; the predominant religious and social values of their society; and the prevailing legal, economic, and political institutions. These have changed continuously over the course of Japanese history, altering women's status and the roles they were expected to play. It makes little sense, therefore, to talk about Japanese women as though they formed a monolithic, unchanging group. Even within one historical time period, the lives of an upper-class woman, a merchant woman, and a female servant in a wealthy farm family were worlds apart in terms of work, clothing, norms of behavior, and the countless other indicators of standard of living, status, position—in short, life experience. Indeed, the distinction between femininity and masculinity itself has varied. Gender has been continuously recreated.

We are specifically concerned here with the creation of female gender. How has womanhood been defined and redefined over the past 350 years? Who did the defining? What gave femaleness its meaning? And what caused changes in the common understanding of differences between femininity and masculinity? Our underlying assumption is that

Following East Asian practice, Japanese surnames precede given names in this book, except in cases of Japanese scholars whose English-language works are cited or who reside in the West and observe the Western practice of giving surnames last. Unless otherwise indicated, Tokyo is the place of publication of all Japanese references.

1

gender, unlike sex, is not a biological given but is, in the words of Evelyn Fox Keller, "a socially constructed and culturally transmitted organizer of our inner and outer worlds."[1] Whereas sex roles refer merely to the fixed range of capabilities of female and male genitalia,[2] gender roles are sociohistorical conventions of deportment arbitrarily attributed to either females or males. "Women" and "men" are culturally created categories.[3] Our goal is to understand continuity and change in Japanese ideals of femininity, in the processes by which women were trained to approximate these ideals, and in the ways their actual roles diverged from these ideals.

Our starting point, the Tokugawa or Edo period (1600–1868), is variously viewed as the traditional, late feudal, or early modern period of Japanese history. During this time the Tokugawa military house, which had its capital in Edo (present-day Tokyo), monopolized the title of shōgun and ruled over lesser military houses. Below the hereditary military (samurai) class were three other fixed social or occupational classes— peasant, artisan, and merchant (in descending order of social status)— as well as numerous other groups, such as physicians, artists, and a court aristocracy, who did not fit precisely into any of these four official classes. Members of one class could not legally intermarry with members of other classes or change their occupational status. Thus, merchants could not become samurai, and samurai could not farm; peasants were forbidden from leaving their land and migrating to the cities to engage in trade.

By the eighteenth century, many of these restrictions were honored more in the breach. Nevertheless, the hierarchical social class system, reinforced by Confucian philosophical thought, dominated people's thinking about social relations and elevated elders, males, and officials above other members of society. Even after the abolition of feudal class distinctions in the late nineteenth century, an age- and gender-based hierarchy still held to varying degrees, both in society at large and within the family.

Because Japanese society, unlike American society, has been relatively homogeneous but highly rank-conscious, especially in the Tokugawa period, Japanese women's experience of womanhood historically had more to do with social class and biological age than it did with race,

1. Evelyn Fox Keller, "Making Gender Visible in the Pursuit of Nature's Secrets," in *Feminist Studies/Critical Studies*, ed. Teresa de Lauretis (Bloomington: Indiana University Press, 1986), 67.
2. See Carol Vance, "Pleasure and Danger: Toward a Politics of Sexuality," in *Pleasure and Danger: Exploring Female Sexuality*, ed. Carol Vance (Boston: Routledge & Kegan Paul, 1985), 9.
3. Linda Gordon discusses the history of women's history, including the notion of gender, in "What's New in Women's History," in de Lauretis (ed.), *Feminist Studies/Critical Studies*, chap. 2.

religion, or ethnicity. A woman's socioeconomic position, in turn, was determined by her family's social standing. Most people lived and worked within the family, which remained the basic unit of society. Therefore, any discussion of women and gender construction must center on the family system.

The ideal family in the Tokugawa period, as Uno (chapter 1) describes it, was the *ie*, the stem-family household, which retained only one child as heir in each generation. More than a biological unit, the *ie* is frequently defined as a corporate entity in the sense that it embraced nonkin (servants, adopted heirs, and the like) as well as blood relations (grandparents, their married heir, and his or her unmarried children). The *ie* also connoted household property, domestic animals, ancestors, and such intangibles as family reputation. Like a well-established business, the *ie* was devoted to its own perpetuation.

Although most, but not all, households were headed by a male as dictated by custom and law, Confucian teachings about filial piety gave older women a full measure of respect and care from junior household members, male as well as female. That respect was rooted not only in the older women's seniority but also in the influence and authority they earned during their life by demonstrating loyalty to the family and competence in the performance of household tasks and the preservation of harmony among family members. Hard physical labor in the fields and in the kitchen, an accommodating nature, and good relations with in-laws: these were the qualities expected of young wives in Japan's largely agrarian society.

Although all women were expected to marry, childbearing was not necessarily a woman's primary obligation. While children, and especially sons, were essential to the continuity of the *ie* and the care of the elderly, the Japanese family system had ways to compensate for infertility and infant mortality. Adoption of sons, of sons-in-law, and even of married couples guaranteed heirs, as did the custom of designating daughters as heirs. Thus, from the Tokugawa period and earlier to well into the twentieth century, womanhood was not primarily equated with motherhood, and motherhood was not necessarily defined biologically.

Nor was childrearing the "fundamental determining experience of womanhood."[4] Uno argues that older women, such as grandmothers, and younger children, wet nurses, and servants all participated in childrearing, as did fathers and grandfathers. Since the household was an economic unit of production, both the family's business and its reproductive functions took place at home, where several generations living

4. See ibid., 26–27. In contrast, motherhood was the "fundamental defining experience of womanhood" for late-nineteenth-century feminists in the West.

together under one roof participated in tasks crucial to the household's survival.

Walthall (chapter 2) confirms Uno's claim: at least for rich peasants, a woman's "womb was . . . less significant than the ability to maintain the family's fortune and reputation," and the Japanese woman did this in part by serving as a competent household manager. Indeed, Confucian ideology discouraged the active participation of young mothers in their own children's upbringing on the grounds that they were morally unsuited to such a serious role or were likely to spoil their children. Women were thus valued as workers, wives, and especially daughters-in-law, not solely as mothers.

Of course, we cannot always assume that official teachings concerning gender were reflected in social reality, as Walthall's copious documentation of peasant women's activities warns us. What women did (and what they got away with) was very different from socially prescribed norms, which usually were observed, if at all, by the small minority of women in the upper classes. The peasant women in Walthall's study experienced lives of much greater freedom and diversity than the official ideology would lead us to believe. Depending on their economic circumstances, family composition, and myriad other factors, they might go to school, travel, work for wages, choose their own marriage partners, enter into matrilocal marriages, marry men who were not heir to existing households and so help to found new households, divorce, remarry, engage in adulterous affairs, and serve as household heads. Promiscuous girls, barren wives, willful daughters-in-law, and divorcées all managed to survive relatively unstigmatized by village social sanctions. In fact, Walthall argues that precisely this flexibility in women's roles ensured the survival of the family itself and its individual members.

Nevertheless, the importance of women as wives and daughters-in-law is a repeated theme in Japanese history since 1600, with demographic implications that Cornell spells out in her discussion of mortality rates for elderly women in Tokugawa Japan (chapter 3). Despite the inevitable tensions between the young wife and her mother-in-law, this dynamic relationship was crucial to the life expectancy of women. Elderly women living with a daughter-in-law, Cornell finds, were more likely to live longer, especially if the daughter-in-law was young and had produced grandchildren. Those without family fared less well. The giving of care to the elderly thus becomes an enduring theme in the definition of womanhood. The dutiful daughter-in-law appears in many guises throughout the pages of this volume, but whether breadwinner, farm laborer, or simply household manager, she typically engaged in these activities to support her husband's family, including her long-lived mother-in-law.

What of women who did not marry out? Under what circumstances could a woman resist becoming a daughter-in-law? And what were the consequences of such unconventional behavior? Three examples of such women in the Tokugawa period appear in this volume: Robertson's Shingaku (Heart Learning) teacher, Fister's poet-painter, and Lebra's sake brewer (chapters 4–6).

Although the Shingaku movement carefully prescribed how women should behave to overcome congenital moral infirmities, not all Shingaku women performed according to their proper role. This role consisted of acquiring such virtues as obedience, frugality, modesty, and purity, and was best done in the context of marriage—that is, in service to her husband's family. "Marriage," in Robertson's words, "made possible a woman's achievement of 'female' gender": her female-likeness was premised and contingent on the marriage institution.

Jion-ni Kenka, an eighteenth-century disciple of Shingaku, illustrates a successful departure from the insistence that the only female-like woman was a married one (or a male Kabuki actor impersonating a woman). Resisting marriage, Kenka became first a Buddhist nun and then a disseminator of Shingaku teachings. Other female proselytizers spreading moral teachings about women's proper role followed in her footsteps. But, as Robertson observes, "female disciples and teachers of Shingaku did not epitomize the Shingaku Woman, even though they participated in her construction." A female-like woman was not supposed to be traveling around the country, even if her mission *was* to preach that the only female-like woman was a married one who stayed at home to serve her husband's family!

The religious life represented one legitimate alternative to marriage in the Tokugawa period, but there were others as well. Talented women could support themselves as professional entertainers, or geisha. A few gifted women were supported by their natal families. One example is the poet-painter Ema Saikō. A distinguished nineteenth-century *bunjin*, or scholar of Chinese studies, Ema was celebrated for her Chinese-style verse, calligraphy, and ink paintings. Throughout her life she remained under the wing of her doting father, himself a noted scholar and physician, and enjoyed the patronage of leading male artists of the day. By staying single, she avoided the strenuous obligations incumbent upon married women. As Fister points out, "The freedom from childbearing, conjugal domestic responsibilities, and manual labor allowed her to mature fully as an artist." Nonetheless, as an adult this brilliant woman suffered pangs of regret for missing out on a "normal" married life.

To the extent that Japanese women had a choice between pursuing a vocation or marrying, it was a painful one. Nevertheless, not all women had to make such an either/or decision. By entering into matrilocal, matrilineal marriages that enabled their families to "take a son-in-law," the female sake brewers in Lebra's study managed to become wives while avoiding the domestic duties imposed on daughters-in-law. The traditions of the merchant class, especially in the Kansai area, apparently encouraged women to be active in their natal family's business. Lebra provides several examples of such female entrepreneurs, perhaps the most outstanding of whom was Tatsu'uma Kiyo, whose "management strategies made her a pioneer in the [sake-brewing] industry during its period of most rapid growth and prosperity."

Kiyo circumvented customary constraints on active female participation in business by hiring male brewmasters and managers and by arranging marriages for her daughters that maximized the interests of the family business. "The practice of relying on wives and daughters to run the venerable family business," Lebra reminds us, "was already well established by the time Kiyo was born. Rather than automatically entrusting the business to a son with questionable ability, merchant houses could select the most talented apprentice-clerk as an adopted husband for their daughter, thus ensuring the success and continuity of the family business."

Once again we see how preservation of the *ie* took precedence over all other considerations. We also see, however, that although family interests could and did severely restrict women, under certain circumstances, as the case of Kiyo illustrates, it could also justify the transgression of customs and laws that favored men, such as marital residence patterns, primogeniture, and head of household succession. To be sure, women who became famous and powerful in their own right were not necessarily recognized or appreciated as such by their families or by society. Indeed, if, like Kenka, they succeeded by violating gender roles, they might be seen as dangerous. Tokugawa authorities regulated such roles and punished women who violated them. Kenka's own father was dismayed by her transgression of feminine norms of behavior. Whereas the family of Ema Saikō to this day proudly honors its talented ancestor by preserving her artwork in their family collection, later generations of Kiyo's sake-brewing family seem to have been embarrassed by her spectacular success in outwitting all other competitors. Their reticence to discuss this entrepreneurial matriarch and their failure to preserve records documenting her business achievements suggest a lingering ambivalence toward women who succeeded in unconventional, nonprescribed ways.

With the defeat of the Tokugawa regime in the middle of the nineteenth century and the establishment of a centralized nation-state, the new Meiji leadership ushered in a host of changes designed to rid Japan of its feudal past and to set a course toward "enlightened civilization." Thrown open to Western commerce and diplomatic contact, the long-isolated island country underwent a bewildering series of reforms, including the dismantling of the four-class system, the abolition of feudal privileges, the introduction of universal compulsory education, and the promotion of industrialization. The Meiji period (1868–1912) was a time of questioning old customs and practices and of experimenting with new forms, frequently under Western influence.

In this era of rapid change, it is not surprising that the question of women's roles should come under scrutiny. The Meiji government, in its efforts to remake Japan into a modern state, tried to take an active role in the creation of a new citizenry dedicated to the nation and loyal to the emperor. One aspect of this reformation was gender construction.

The aim of remaking Japanese women as part of the remaking of Japan was captured in the slogan "Good Wife, Wise Mother" (*ryōsai kenbo*) promoted by bureaucrats in the new government. Here for the first time, the definition of womanhood at least partly in terms of motherhood gained legitimacy. The words "wise mother" signaled the newly recognized importance of educating all women so that they could better perform their home duties, and in particular childrearing in accordance with "the latest scientific knowledge and practice." In a significant departure, the new state's pronouncements on gender, by addressing all women, "gradually replaced the premodern differentiation of women by class." The new ideal woman represented a composite of the "cardinal feminine virtues of the various Japanese classes." All women, for example, were enjoined to practice frugality in order to contribute to the nation's savings for investment in modern industry. This "constellation of virtues"—modesty, courage, frugality, literacy, hard work, and productivity—was "so appropriate for economic growth" that Nolte and Hastings (chapter 7) call it a "cult of productivity."

Still, Nolte and Hastings warn us that it would be wrong to confuse the "Good Wife, Wise Mother" slogan still current in Japan with the cult of domesticity popularized in present-day Japan and in Victorian England. Not all Meiji women were necessarily expected to confine themselves to kitchen and nursery. Middle- and upper-class women ideally engaged in charitable and patriotic activities as well, and lower-class women of necessity worked outside the home in factories vital to the nation's economic development. Indeed, the state's view of the family as "an essential building block of the national structure" in effect turned the home into a "public place"—the state writ small, blurring distinctions between public and private. Women's vital function as cornerstones of the family made them civil servants of sorts.

Legal support for this view of women and the family came from the Meiji Civil Code of 1898, which established the samurai ideal of the *ie* as the national standard for the family and reinforced the legal authority of the household head, who was usually male. The code legally subordinated women to men in a number of ways: A wife needed her husband's consent before entering into a legal contract. In cases of divorce, the husband took custody of the children. A wife's adultery (but not her husband's) constituted grounds for legal divorce and criminal prosecution. The household head's permission was required before women under twenty-five (and men under thirty) could legally marry.

Enforced until the end of the Second World War, the Meiji Code in its treatment of women as wives reflected not so much the Confucian belief in a wife's ineptness as the Meiji leaders' efforts to "ensure the smooth operation of a male-centered, authoritarian traditional family"; it did so by assuring that the family would not have two masters, just as "in the heavens there are not two suns."[5] Thus a woman's role, not her sex, mandated her subordinate position. Indeed, precisely because women were so important to the family, and the family to the state, women were excluded from participation in politics on the grounds that, as in the case of public officials and schoolteachers, partisan politics was an inappropriate activity for them. They needed to concentrate all of their energies on the management of the household, the education of their children, and the promotion of economic development. Yet as late as the end of the Meiji period, Nolte and Hastings remind us, the slogan "Good Wife, Wise Mother" connoted "Japanese state policy [that] placed much more importance on a woman's responsibilities as a wife [and as a kind of public servant] than on her function as mother."

In the First World War era, increasing numbers of literate women graduating from Japan's newly established national education system lent fresh voices to the national discourse on gender in Japan. The privilege of defining femininity—which through most of world history has been limited to "priests and philosophers, physicians and politicians"[6]— was now seized by Japanese women themselves. By encouraging women's creative talent, literary genius, and female sexuality, the "Bluestockings" (Seitō) group described by Rodd (chapter 8) necessarily confronted the new ideology of the proper female role. Although these women did not consciously set out to be political, various organs of the

5. Margit Maria Nagy, "How Shall We Live? Social Change, the Family Institution, and Feminism in Prewar Japan" (Ph.D. diss., University of Washington, 1981), 41, quoting Ume Kenjirō, *Minpō yōgi* (Yūhikaku Shobō, 1908), 1:39.

6. Marilyn J. Boxer and Jean H. Quataert, eds., *Connecting Spheres: Women in the Western World, 1500 to the Present* (New York: Oxford University Press), 5.

state, such as the Ministry of Education, the Home Ministry, and even the Metropolitan Police, accused their literary magazine, *Seitō*, of "corrupt[ing] the virtues traditionally associated with Japanese women" and undermining the concept of "good wife, wise mother."[7]

The state's "ongoing 'management'" of issues related to women and the family inevitably raised the question of the state's role in protecting mothers and children.[8] If the positive valuation of motherhood in the debates over state protection seems conservative to Western feminists today, it was certainly novel to early Taishō (1912–26) society. The traditional Japanese family had never stressed women's mission as mothers (and certainly had not argued for their biological superiority), but rather had stressed their duties as wives and daughters-in-law. And the Meiji government, its slogans notwithstanding, had not actually called for state support of mothers but, on the contrary, had solicited mothers' support of the state.

Not all Taishō feminist writers, to be sure, considered motherhood to be "women's heaven-ordained occupation." The poet Yosano Akiko, herself the mother of ten, argued that, in Rodd's words, "any human being should be allowed to take on as many roles as she or he can manage."

What is remarkable, however, in all these women's discussions of womanhood, is their contemporary ring: whether demanding state welfare to support the family or insisting on female suffrage, equal economic opportunity, freedom of education, and the right to express their individuality, feminists in early Taishō Japan boldly explored the full range of possibilities for the "new woman." Regardless of their particular point of view, women themselves, and not male sages or the state, actively engaged in a lively discourse on the meaning of female gender.

This discourse on gender did not take the form of words alone: women helped stretch and shape the boundaries of socially sanctioned female behavior by their deeds as well. During the 1920s an increasing number of women entered the workplace. Not only the unmarried daughters of the rural poor, but also the wives and daughters of the urban middle class—"respectable women"—appeared at train stations on their way to jobs in department stores and office buildings, occasioning the alarm of bureaucrats concerned about the social implications of a growing female labor force. As Nagy (chapter 9) reports, "The phenomenon of the middle-class working woman created profound anxi-

---

7. Sharon L. Sievers, *Flowers in Salt: The Beginnings of Feminist Consciousness in Modern Japan* (Stanford: Stanford University Press, 1983), 180.

8. Ibid., 226n.32.

eties about the future of family life and national unity, especially since the middle class was viewed as the bastion of social stability in an era of social and political turmoil."

Married working women struck at the heart of family-state nationalism, the ideology that subsumed the interests of women within the family and linked family stability to the preservation of national unity. Of course women, married and single, had always done productive work. But in the largely agrarian society of pre-twentieth-century Japan married women had worked on family farms or in family businesses, and single women had worked in factories on a temporary basis until marriage, in a pattern of labor known as "life-cycle service."[9] Now even middle-class married women still in their childbearing years were working for pay outside the home. Could working wives and mothers continue to sustain family stability? Conversely, could the middle-class family in a decade of economic dislocation survive without the wife's supplemental earnings? The outpouring of articles, surveys, and governmental studies on this subject in the 1920s testified to the importance of "women's issues": the nature, status, and proper sphere of women in this decade became the preoccupation of bureaucrats, journalists, and women alike.

Women's entrance into urban public space inevitably forced redefinitions of the bounds of proper decorum traditionally associated with female gender. Nagy's survey data on midde-class working women show that they still wanted to live up to traditional role expectations: they feared sacrificing their femininity, and they hoped "not to lose their special virtue as females" and to "cultivate accomplishments as a future housewife." Yet these surveys also indicate that at least some middle-class working women welcomed employment as both a guarantee of economic independence and an opportunity to develop themselves as individuals.

Further evidence for this emerging autonomy among working women in the interwar period is presented in Molony's chapter on activism among women in the Taishō cotton textile industry (chapter 10). The factory workers' decision to leave their rural families for employment in the mills shows that they refused to be passive victims; similarly, their agitation for better work conditions and participation in strikes belie the standard portrait of them as docile. Molony concludes that female factory workers by the 1920s and 1930s had developed considerable self-confidence and a sense of themselves as workers rather than simply as wives and daughters. Influenced by their education and by the activism of male workers, and hardened by their own work experiences,

9. L. L. Cornell, "Hajnal and the Household in Asia: A Comparativist History of the Family in Preindustrial Japan, 1600–1870," *Journal of Family History* 12, nos. 1–3 (1987): 155.

they increasingly learned how to make rational choices and to "determine their own economic and social conditions."

The growing sense of women's empowerment alluded to in the chapters by Nagy and Molony may help explain the public's fascination with the "modern girl" (*moga*) of 1920s media. This multivalent symbol, as Silverberg describes her (chapter 11), captured all the ambiguity associated with the emergence of autonomous, liberated working women in that decade. Depending on the perceiver, the *moga* was either the model of the very modern woman or the epitome of moral decadence. She challenged age-old definitions of femalelikeness with her open sexuality, her public flirtatiousness, and above all her independence from family—all by-products of her income-earning ability: if this "free-living and free-thinking" modern girl was making history, Silverberg suggests, it was "partly because she was making her own money."

The emergence of the modern girl symbolized the crisis in the traditional family, or *ie*, and the emergence of the smaller nuclear family that Nagy's survey data also disclosed. Women's newly expanded economic roles, writes Silverberg, called into question provisions of the Meiji Civil Code and other laws from that era which had denied women their political and legal rights because their place was within the Japanese family.

It is interesting that a female symbol came to portray all the contradictory values that were pulling Japanese society apart in this interwar period. The modern girl, half Japanese but also vaguely Western, highlighted the message that had first gained currency in the Meiji era—namely, that as women go, so go the "traditional family," Japanese values, and national unity. The modern girl was an "emblem for threats to tradition," Silverberg concludes, "just as the 'good wife and wise mother' had stood for its endurance."

The tension between the ideal of women's domestic role and the reality of their work and life outside the home has been an ongoing theme of Japan's last hundred years. It exploded under the strain of wartime, when the state again tried to appropriate women and the family as public institutions, part of the "state apparatus." Now, however, in order to shore up the old Meiji family-state ideology of nationalism, government leaders in their propaganda and legislation specifically underscored women's role as mothers. As a consequence of the state's pronatalist policy, women achieved what some feminists had been calling for since the early Taishō period: state protection of motherhood, however meager, legislated in the form of ordinances requiring employers to provide day-care facilities in plants with over two hundred workers. Miyake (chapter 12) argues that the celebration of female fecundity made government leaders reluctant to draft married women of childbearing age for military service or factory work, despite the urgent need for labor to replace conscripted males. And the women who were drafted—mainly young, unmarried women—enjoyed none of the protections extended to women of childbearing age. While mothers were glorified, female workers were exploited. The family again became part of the public sphere, producing, reproducing, fighting, and dying for the state.

The ideological insistence that women be not only pillars of the family but also housebound, even in the face of national need, social reality, and historical experience, is captured in the wartime films reviewed by Hauser (chapter 13). In these films, women "are background figures, holding the family together, supporting their husbands and sons when they are called into the military, and preserving family solidarity when the menfolk go off to war." The only women in these cinematic depictions who legitimately serve outside the household are single women not needed at home—entertainers, nurses, and prostitutes who volunteer to go to the front or to work in the war industries.

The wartime division of labor between single and married women described by Miyake is thus echoed in Hauser's study. Even the women in postwar films who are cast as critical of the war and of Japanese society remain essentially apolitical homebound domestics absorbed in the preservation of their families. It is as though the female factory workers, office workers, artists, teachers, preachers, entrepreneurs, volunteers, and political activists—all the women who appear on the pages of this book—never really existed, and the *moga* was nothing but a figment of media imagination.

Postwar Japanese society, reviving the gender construct of wartime Japan, recreated woman as mother. This time, however, she was the urban mother of the small conjugal family, removed from farming and factory or office work, separated from her in-laws, and, thanks to the state's postwar promotion of birth control, freed from excessive childbearing responsibilities. Conforming to the pattern of labor force participation in existence since the Tokugawa period, she worked for pay before marriage and was therefore treated as a temporary worker. After marriage, ideally, she focused entirely on her family's welfare and especially on her children's education, though she may have returned to work in an unskilled, part-time position after her children were grown. The postwar Japanese woman thus helped to perpetuate the myth that Japanese women never "worked" and have always been mothers first and foremost.

The thirteen essays in this volume, to the contrary, speak to the diversity that has characterized the lives of Japanese women and the discourse on them in the past four centuries. They illustrate how the meaning and proper role of woman have changed over time and among classes, differing in such essentials as the importance of biological mothering, the place of the mother in childrearing, the nature of women's work, the extent to which women should be educated, and the range of their sexual license. Whether women should focus on childrearing, how many children they should have, whether they should receive education and for what purpose and how much, whether they should or should not work for pay outside the home, whether they should participate in political matters or serve as household heads or run family businesses— these questions have been formally addressed in moral tracts and laws and played out in changing customs among various classes over the course of Japanese history. Numerous participants have shaped this discourse: the state, the scholarly community, the media, society at large, and women themselves. Indeed, Japan may be unique in having waged such a conscious discourse on women for such a long period of time, for since the early days of the Tokugawa rulers the "woman question" has engaged political leaders and the intellectual and moral elite alike. The issue of how women should behave and what they should and should not do has rarely been left either to chance or to individual choice.

If official ideology has been remarkably consistent in defining women in terms of certain traditional virtues and in assigning them the task of preserving the family, the way women were expected to perform their role, as well as the way they actually did so, has not been immutable. According to Tokugawa teachings, women served the family best by being uneducated, whereas in the Meiji period just the opposite was the case. In Tokugawa times they were expected to contribute mainly as farm laborers and household managers, yet in the Meiji era their place was either in the home, raising good disciplined citizens, or in the factories, supplementing household income and providing cheap labor for Japan's industrial effort. In wartime Japan they were called on to raise large families to contribute to Japan's imperialist efforts, while in postwar Japan they were enjoined to raise small families to foster Japan's economic prosperity.

The need to link women and the family to the new nation-state has been a major preoccupation of political leadership in the past century: excluded from politics, women have rarely been excluded from political considerations or bureaucratic concerns. Since the Meiji period both economic imperatives and nationalist ideology have catapulted women, figuratively if not always physically, out of their homes. Urged to serve as "good wives and wise mothers," as "public-spirited rational homemakers," and, in recent times, as "education mamas," Japanese women have also had other demands placed on them, ones going beyond simple piety and devoted nurturing. Organized into relief organizations, patriotic associations, textile factories, and defense industries, women have been variously valued not only for their management of the home, the education of their children, and their fecundity, but also for their productivity. The state has eulogized them for their contributions to war relief, to savings, and even to capital formation. As testimony to their deemed importance, bureaucrats have studied women's work conditions, their health, and their family relations and, with varying degrees of success, have tried to draft legislation to protect them as workers, mothers, and wives in the service of the state.

This vigilant concern with the scope of Japanese womanhood also characterized the pre-Meiji era, when the meticulous definition of femalelike behavior absorbed the minds of political authorities and the literati. Far from being invisible or ignored, Japanese women have captured the attention of moralists and the state for well over three hundred years. With their gender roles publicly prescribed, scrutinized, lauded, or condemned in government edicts, law codes, moral tracts, slogans, short stories, theatrical performances, folk tales, family histories, magazines, and films, Japanese women have never been without clear role models. Put another way, they have never been left alone.

Still, some women managed to steer courses for themselves around officially prescribed or socially sanctioned standards of femalelikeness. Since most of the published material in English on Japanese women has treated the women's movement, focusing on what women tried to change, we have tended to lose sight of what women could already do. In the period between 1600 and 1945, women asserted their autonomy in a variety of ways: through divorce and remarriage, wage work, business acumen, or artistic talent, and by participation in strikes, the modern suffrage movement, and literary publications that coined or advertised new slogans for themselves, such as "bluestockings," "new woman," or "modern girl." But they also achieved a measure of independence and influence in more socially acceptable, traditional ways, for example as matriarchs of successful families. In all these ways, women participated in the discourse on female gender and helped shape its contours.

The definition of womanhood is an ongoing process in Japan (and elsewhere in the world). Women in Japan today may very well be as Nagy's concluding quote suggests, "the most dynamic sector of the population," whose changing role can help "predict the shape of Japanese society in the twenty-first century."

PART ONE

Women and the Family:
1600-1868

ONE

Women and Changes in the Household Division of Labor

Kathleen S. Uno

In present-day Japan two domestic activities, motherhood and house-hold management, define the core of women's familial and social obligations. This model of womanhood, enshrined as a cultural ideal, guides the multitudes of urban women, who now greatly outnumber their country cousins.[1] Yet only a century ago, among the farmers who

I am indebted to Yasuko Ichibangase, Kazuyo Yamamoto, Kuni Nakajima, Hiroko Hara, Kaoru Tachi, Takeo Shishido, Yoshiko Miyake, Masako Ohtomo, Miharu Nishimura, Keiko Katoda, Michiko Mabashi, Keiko Kawaii, Kiyoko Tani, Teruko Inoue, Kazuko Tanaka, Mitsue Yoneda, Sachiko Kaneko, Jeff Hanes, Linda Angst, Miriam Silverberg, and Gerry Harcourt for encouragement and assistance during the initial stages of research. Fellowships from the Japan Foundation and the American Association of University Women funded early research and writing on this topic. Thanks for insightful comments to Gail Lee Bernstein, Christine Gailey, Peter Gran, Matthews Hamabata, Laura Hein, Dorinne Kondo, Barbara Molony, and Stephen Vlastos.

1. In 1980, 68 percent of the Japanese population resided in cities of more than 50,000 inhabitants, with 47.8 percent residing in the three great metropolitan areas of Tokyo, Osaka, and Nagoya; Tadashi Fukutake, *The Japanese Social Structure* (Tokyo: University of Tokyo Press, 1982), 100–102. Regarding contemporary urban new middle-class wifehood and motherhood, see Anne Imamura, *Urban Japanese Housewives* (Honolulu: University of Hawaii Press, 1987); Merry White, "The Virtue of Japanese Mothers: Cultural Definitions of Women's Lives," *Daedalus* 116, no. 3 (Summer 1987): 149–63; Suzanne Vogel, "Professional Housewife: The Career of Urban Middle Class Japanese Women," *Japan Interpreter* 12, no. 1 (1978): 16–43. Glenda Roberts's *Non-Trivial Pursuits: Japanese Blue Collar Women* (forthcoming), pt. 3, suggests that contemporary lower-class women also accept the centrality of household management and mothering in their lives, but that they fulfill their obligations to their families by different means than middle-class women. Some of Roberts's respondents justified their wage work as a contribution to family life because it contributed to the household economy.

17

made up roughly 80 percent of the population, peasant mothers in poor and middling households spent more time at productive than reproductive labor. Although village mothers toiled at domestic tasks such as cooking, cleaning, and child care, they also spent long hours cultivating fields and practicing sidelines such as silk reeling.[2] If one juxtaposes a portrait of prewar farm women planting seedlings and carrying rice sheaves with one of postwar housewives tending toddlers, cooking, and shopping, the contrast is striking. Two key questions for modern Japanese women's history are how this new urban middle-class womanhood emerged as a cultural norm, and how Japanese womanhood came to be defined solely in terms of reproduction—budgeting, buying, housekeeping, and childrearing.

In this chapter, I argue that the emergence of a postwar domestic conception of womanhood is related to early-twentieth-century changes in the household division of labor. In early-modern enterprise households, it was relatively easy for men, women, and children to participate both in productive work such as agriculture, handicrafts, sales, and customer service and in reproductive work such as childrearing, shopping, cooking, and cleaning.[3] After the Meiji Restoration (1868), state promotion of industrialization and education encouraged men and schoolchildren to depart daily from the home to engage in production and study, respectively. By default, women and small children remained at home. As employment in workplaces outside the home swelled during the twentieth century, the number of wives specializing in childrearing and housekeeping also increased, although even in 1930 a majority of the labor force still worked in household enterprises.[4] The emergence

2. Accounts of the lives of rural women in Robert J. Smith and Ella Lury Wiswell, *The Women of Suye Mura* (Chicago: University of Chicago Press, 1982), suggest that this was true during the 1930s as well. The sketches of village women's lives in Gail Lee Bernstein, *Haruko's World: A Japanese Farm Woman and Her Community* (Stanford: Stanford University Press, 1983), suggest that this was still the case during the early years following World War II.

3. Although I distinguish between these two types of activities, the fact that both took place at home and both were essential to the survival of the household tends to blur the distinction.

4. Regarding the growth of salaried and factory employment, see Earl Kinmonth, *The Self-made Man in Meiji Japanese Thought: From Samurai to Salary Man* (Berkeley and Los Angeles: University of California Press, 1981), 278–89; and Robert E. Cole and Kenichi Tominaga, "Japan's Changing Occupational Structure and Its Significance," in *Japanese Industrialization and Its Social Consequences*, ed. Hugh Patrick (Berkeley and Los Angeles: University of California Press, 1976), 59, 64–65. Information regarding employment in household enterprises between 1920 and 1940 is calculated from data in William W. Lockwood, *The Economic Development of Japan: Growth and Structural Change, 1868–1938* (Princeton: Princeton University Press, 1968), 464–65, 205, 111–12. Even in 1950 and 1970, the

of domesticity as a cultural ideal can be traced to the turn of the century, when a new division of labor arose in the households of public officials, professors, teachers, journalists, engineers, and white-collar workers, members of an elite who shaped public culture through their roles in policymaking, education, and the media.[5]

The starting point for this study is women's household activities in the preindustrial Tokugawa period (1600–1868),[6] which have received less scrutiny than those of the modern (1868–1945) and postwar eras. Previous studies of Tokugawa women, moreover, have largely employed legal and structural approaches to analyze customs and laws regarding marriage and succession. While works on historical demography by Japanese and Western scholars have probed household composition and the

proportion of employed persons in "self-employed" and "family worker" categories totaled 59 percent and 35 percent, respectively; see Cole and Tominaga, "Japan's Changing Occupational Structure," 76.

5. Western-influenced visions of female domesticity appeared in Japan in the 1870s, but their implementation in policy and the beginning of widespread dissemination date from the final years of the nineteenth century; see Keiko Fujiwara, "Introduction," in *Fukuzawa Yukichi on Japanese Women*, ed. and trans. Eiichi Kiyōka (Tokyo: University of Tokyo Press, 1988), vii–xv; Sharon Sievers, *Flowers in Salt: The Beginnings of Feminist Consciousness in Modern Japan* (Stanford: Stanford University Press, 1983), 22–24; Kathleen Uno, " 'Good Wives and Wise Mothers' in Early Twentieth Century Japan," unpublished paper presented at a joint meeting of the Pacific Coast Branch of the American Historical Association and the Western Association of Women Historians, San Francisco, August 11, 1988, 6–15; Fukaya Masashi, *Ryōsai kenboshugi no kyōiku*, expanded ed. (Nagoya: Reimei Shobō, 1981), 94–153. Translations of articles containing some early Meiji ideas regarding womanhood appear in William Braisted, trans., *Meiroku Zasshi* (Cambridge: Harvard University Press, 1976).

6. In English, full-length works containing extensive treatments of pre–World War II Japanese women include Smith and Wiswell, *Women of Suye Mura*; Sievers, *Flowers in Salt*; Mikiso Hane, *Peasants, Rebels, and Outcastes: The Underside of Modern Japan* (New York: Pantheon Books, 1982); and Dorothy Robbins-Mowry, *The Hidden Sun: Women of Modern Japan* (Boulder, Colo.: Westview Press, 1983). Shorter but useful discussions can be found in Joyce Ackroyd, "Women in Feudal Japan," *Transactions of the Asiatic Society of Japan*, 3d ser., 7 (1959): 31–68; Marjorie Wall Bingham and Susan Gross, *Women in Japan from Ancient Times to the Present* (St. Louis Park, Minn.: Glenhurst Publications, 1987); and Joyce Lebra, Joy Paulson, and Elizabeth Powers, eds., *Women in Changing Japan* (Stanford: Stanford University Press, 1976). In Japanese, among many existing works one might mention Takamure Itsue, *Josei no rekishi*, 3 vols. (Kōdansha, 1954–58; reprinted in 2 vols., Kōdansha, 1972; and in *Takamure Itsue zenshū*, vols. 4–5, Rironsha, 1966, 1971); Joseishi sōgō kenkyūkai, ed., *Nihon joseishi*, 5 vols. (Tokyo Daigaku Shuppankai, 1982), esp. vols. 3: *Kinsei* and 4: *Kindai*; Kinsei joseishi kenkyūkai, ed., *Ronshū kinsei joseishi* (Yoshikawa Kōbunkan, 1986); Seki Tamiko, *Edo kōki no joseitachi* (Aki Shobō, 1980); and Murakami Nobuhiko, *Meiji joseishi*, 4 vols. (Rironsha, 1969–72; reprint Kōdansha, 1977). Important source books and reference works include: *Fujin mondai shiryō shūsei* (Domesu Shuppan, 1977–78); Mitsui Reiko, *Gendai fujin undōshi nenpyō* (Sanichi Shobō, 1974); Joseishi sōgō kenkyūkai, ed., *Nihon joseishi kenkyū bunken mokuroku* (Tokyo Daigaku Shuppankai, 1983).

life course of early-modern villagers and, to a lesser extent, town dwellers,[7] only a handful, in English notably those of Thomas C. Smith, have considered the early-modern household division of labor by gender.[8]

More recent works by Japanese scholars range beyond household norms and structure, attempting to recreate the lived experiences of Tokugawa women, but much of this newer scholarship is narrow in focus.[9] In the early 1980s, Wakita Osamu, in the path-breaking series *Nihon joseishi* (Japanese women's history), called for fresh approaches to the history of early-modern Japanese women.[10] In his view, an overriding emphasis on oppression has retarded investigation of the limited but real power and prerogatives of Tokugawa women. Although Wakita did not explicitly problematize gender dichotomies such as public/private, public/domestic, or productive/reproductive, his treatment of early-modern female inheritance and political participation implicitly questions such dualisms.[11] In 1986, specialists still expressed dissatisfaction with the state of research on early-modern women and sought to move beyond themes of women's subordination, as this statement suggests: "Among the ordinary people (*shominsō*) the producers, men and women, helped one another and worked together. . . . They nurtured a *mentalité* (*ishiki*) which differed from that of the samurai class. Yet their image of woman has not yet fully come to light in research."[12]

7. In English, see Ackroyd's fine treatment of women in the medieval and Tokugawa eras, "Women in Feudal Japan." In Japanese, major works include Takamure, *Josei no rekishi*; Kawashima Takeyoshi, *Ideorogī toshite no kazoku seido* (Iwanami Shoten, 1957); Ōtake Hideo, *"Ie" to josei no rekishi* (Kōbundō, 1978); Ishii Ryōsuke, *Nihon sōzoku hō shi* (Sōbunsha, 1980). See notes 5, 6, 13, and 17, and Cornell's chapter in this volume (chap. 3). For further references, see Susan Orpett Long, *Family Change and the Life Course in Japan*, Cornell East Asia Papers no. 44 (Ithaca, N.Y.: Cornell University, Japan-China Program, 1987), 19–31, esp. 28; and Kathleen Uno, " 'Children Are Treasures': A History of Children in Modern Japan," in *Children in Historical and Comparative Perspective: An International Handbook*, ed. Joseph Hawes and N. Ray Hiner (Westport, Conn.: Greenwood Press, 1990), nn. 12, 15, 25, 26–29, 37.

8. Thomas C. Smith, *Nakahara: Family Farming and Population in a Japanese Village, 1717–1830* (Stanford: Stanford University Press, 1977), 79, 91–117, 127–30, 143–56, esp. 95, 144, 152–53; Gail Lee Bernstein, "Did Women Work in Old Japan?", unpublished paper presented at the East Asian Conference of the American Historical Association annual meeting, San Francisco, December 29, 1983; Miyashita Michiko, "Nōson ni okeru kazoku to kon'in," in Joseishi sōgō kenkyūkai (ed.), *Nihon joseishi* 3:31–62, esp. 31–53.

9. In addition to works cited above, see also the titles of women's history articles in recent Japanese historical and university journals. Specialized works such as these will establish a basis for fresh interpretations of the history of early-modern women.

10. Wakita Osamu, "Bakuhan taisei to josei," in Joseishi sōgō kenkyūkai (ed.), *Nihon joseishi* 3:2.

11. Ibid., 2–14.

12. Kinsei joseishi kenkyūkai (ed.), *Ronshū kinsei joseishi*, 2. Subsequent major works such as Wakita Haruko, ed., *Bosei o tou: Rekishiteki hensen*, 2 vols. (Jinbun Shoin, 1985); and

In response to this challenge issued by Japanese scholars, I contend here that analysis of changes in the household division of labor from the early-modern to the modern era offers a useful approach to Japanese women's history and gender studies. To illuminate this approach, I outline the early-modern household division of labor and suggest how it shifted in the modern era, drawing on a limited amount of evidence concerning the participation of women in production, men in reproduction, and children in both sorts of household activities. This interpretive sketch of the household division of labor is tentative, and is intended to spur further research. I do not dwell on women's participation in agriculture, for that has been treated elsewhere.[13] Rather, I touch on two less explored topics: artisan and merchant women's work in household enterprises,[14] and men's participation in housework and childrearing.[15]

A major objective of this chapter is to take issue with the framework for scholarly investigation of the preindustrial household division of labor. Scholars have often employed dichotomies in considering women's estate.[16] These categories are useful; however, they function ideologically rather than analytically when researchers mechanically relegate women and their activities to a private/domestic/reproductive sphere and men to a public/productive sphere. Such categories can obscure rather than clarify the range of attitudes and behavior open to women.[17]

Wakita Haruko, Hayashi Reiko, and Nagahara Kazuko, eds., Nihon joseishi (Yoshikawa Kō-bunkan, 1987), have explored the nature of motherhood and women's diverse experiences from ancient times to the present, rather than focusing on issues of concept, theory, or approach.

13. See notes 2, 33, 34, and 36, and Walthall's chapter in this volume (chap. 2).

14. See notes 41, 43, and 44. For discussion of women in the modern sake-brewing industry, see Lebra's chapter in this volume (chap. 6).

15. Additional discussion of men's role in childrearing appears in Uno, "Day Care and Family Life in Industrializing Japan, 1868–1926" (Ph.D. diss., University of California, Berkeley, 1987), 15–60.

16. Examples of works employing such categories are Linda Kerber, Women of the Republic: Intellect and Ideology in Revolutionary America (Chapel Hill: University of North Carolina Press, 1980); Mary P. Ryan, Cradle of the Middle Class: The Family in Oneida County, New York, 1790–1865 (Cambridge: Cambridge University Press, 1981); Joan Landes, Women and the Public Sphere in the Age of the French Revolution (Ithaca, N.Y.: Cornell University Press, 1988); Martha Vicinus, A Widening Sphere: Changing Roles of Victorian Women (Bloomington: Indiana University Press, 1977); Jean Bethke Elshtain, Public Man, Private Woman (Princeton: Princeton University Press, 1981); Mary O'Brien, The Politics of Reproduction (Boston: Routledge & Kegan Paul, 1981).

17. Assumptions regarding women's domesticity muddy otherwise useful discussions of women's work in households in Jill Kleinberg, "Where Work and Life are Almost One," in Work and Lifecourse in Japan, ed. David Plath (Albany: State University of New York Press, 1983), 215–47, esp. 226–28; and Miyashita Michiko, "Kinsei 'ie' ni okeru boseizō—nōson ni okeru haha no jittai to jokunshu no naka no haha," in Wakita (ed.), Bosei o tou 2:9–40.

Here I attempt to go beyond this standard dichotomous formula to focus on how women performed productive work and men performed
reproductive work, in order to gain a wider view of women's preindustrial household roles and the society enveloping them.

A household division of labor approach has several advantages. First,
by illuminating the actual conduct of women, it helps to recreate their
lived experiences within the context of the early-modern household.
This method complements earlier structural and normative approaches,
which lend themselves most easily to the study of elites; because explo-
rations of the household division of labor chronicle daily activities and
interactions, they can be applied to the study of rich and poor alike. (To
be sure, at present historical evidence concerning the mundane activities
of poor women, especially among artisans and merchants, seems sparse,
but perhaps this is because our way of phrasing questions has tended to
render certain facts invisible to the eyes of the beholder.) Second, studying the household division of labor sheds light on the history of children. Youngsters were not simply household dependents requiring female nurture; rather, as we shall see, they were helpers to their mothers
and other household members. In sum, through analysis of the household division of labor, we can gain a fuller view of the lives of women
and children, as well as men, and a richer sense of Japanese society as a
whole.

WOMEN, MEN, AND CHILDREN IN THE
EARLY-MODERN HOUSEHOLD DIVISION OF LABOR

Four main features of the preindustrial Japanese household, or *ie*,[18] exerted a great influence on the family division of labor: its corporate nature, its composition, its structure of authority, and its function as the
site of both productive and reproductive processes. These features were
designed to maintain household status and wealth, especially among the
samurai; however, no one has yet demonstrated conclusively that *ie* ideals had diffused widely among rural and urban commoners during the

18. In *Kinship and Economic Organization in Rural Japan* (New York: Humanities Press,
1967), the prominent Japanese anthropologist Chie Nakane asserts that the *ie* is a corpo-
rate group rather than a kinship unit. This view is shared by Jane Bachnik, "Recruitment
Strategies for Household Succession: Rethinking Japanese Household Organization,"
Man 18 (1983): 160–82; Matthews Hamabata, *For Love and Power: Family Business in Tokyo*
(Ithaca, N.Y.: Cornell University Press, 1990); and Dorinne K. Kondo, *Crafting Selves:
Power, Gender, and Discourses of Identity in a Japanese Workplace* (Chicago: University of Chicago Press, 1990). While it is true that *ie* members share affective ties, recruitment to *ie*
membership is not restricted to kin. For this reason, in this chapter I refer to the *ie* as a
"household" rather than a "family." Occasionally I have employed "family" in referring to
ie as "house," as in House of Windsor.

Tokugawa period. Class differences in household goals, as well as other attitudes and practices, deserve further investigation.[19]

The corporate nature of the *ie* shaped household priorities. Preservation of household property, occupation, name, and status in the local community were vital concerns. The fundamental goal was household continuity, not the well-being of individual members. Adults tried to train young female members, such as brides (*yome*) and daughters, and male members, including servants, sons, and even the heir, to subordinate their personal hopes for occupation, education, or marriage to *ie* needs.[20]

Structurally, the Japanese *ie* resembles a form of stem family: only one child remained in the household with the parents after marriage.[21] Generally a son succeeded to the headship, but if a household lacked sons, a daughter's husband (*muko*) might be adopted to serve as the next head.[22] When deficiencies of temperament, constitution, or talents made succession by natural offspring unfeasible, households again turned to adoption to secure a new head.[23] The successor and his or her spouse in turn produced children (preferably at least one son) to assume responsibility for the household in the next generation.

Household size also affected the division of labor. During the late Tokugawa and Meiji eras, the mean household size in many regions

19. Two works suggest the range of the debate: Fumie Kumagai, "Modernization and the Family in Japan," *Journal of Family History* 11 (1986): 375, claims that *ie* consciousness did not spread to propertyless rural and urban commoners in the early-modern period; in contrast, Irokawa Daikichi, *The Culture of the Meiji Period* (Princeton: Princeton University Press, 1985), esp. 19–35, 280–93, suggests that by the 1880s *ie* values had diffused among peasants.

20. For example, the handsome youth Yutaka married disfigured Tetsu because his father wished to save her household from extinction, but the result was an unhappy match for both parties; see Edwin McClellan, *Woman in the Crested Kimono: The Life of Shibue Io and Her Family, Drawn from Mori Ōgai's "Shibue Chūsai"* (New Haven, Conn.: Yale University Press, 1985), 41–42, 44, 114–15, 133–35.

21. Frequently, but not always, the oldest son remained to succeed to the headship. Variations in succession to headship are described in Nakane, *Kinship and Economic Organization*, 8–16; Harumi Befu, *Japan: An Anthropological Introduction* (San Francisco: Chandler, 1971), 41; Akira Hayami, "The Myth of Primogeniture and Impartible Inheritance in Tokugawa Japan," *Journal of Family History* 8 (1983): 3–29; and William B. Hauser, "Why So Few? Women Household Heads in Ōsaka Chōnin Families," *Journal of Family History* 11 (1986): 343–51.

22. For a glimpse of the diversity of Tokugawa urban family types, see Robert J. Smith, "The Domestic Cycle in Selected Commoner Families in Urban Japan, 1757–1858," *Journal of Family History* 3 (1978): 219–35. Here Smith also suggests that Tokugawa Japanese may have prized household continuity but not idealized a specific household form, e.g., the three-generation stem family.

23. Nakane, *Kinship and Economic Organization*, 4–5. For examples, see McClellan, *Woman in the Crested Kimono*, 41–44, 89–90, 92, 122, 131; Katsu Kokichi, *Musui's Story*, trans. Teruko Craig (Tucson: University of Arizona Press, 1988), 12–14.

hovered around five persons.[24] When these small households lost a member through death, desertion, or divorce, others had to assume the tasks of the departed. While prosperous households could augment family labor power by hiring servants, members of poor families simply had to exercise greater flexibility and take on additional responsibilities.

Cultural norms designated authority within the household, but the principles of gender and seniority legitimizing authority were somewhat ambiguous. The househead (*koshu*), usually a male,[25] possessed the greatest nominal authority, though it was tempered by the need for co-operation with other household members to attain the goal of *ie* continuity.[26] The head, like the others, had to engage in various tasks to maintain the household. Moreover, filial piety, which enjoined respect for and obedience to one's elders regardless of sex, tended to undercut the head's sole authority. Filial sons, for example, might bow to the wishes of female elders, especially their mothers, even though in principle women submitted to father, husband, and sons (the three obediences). Thus older women, as well as servants of both sexes, who had faithfully and ably labored long years for the household could gain a measure of authority and respect.[27] In the absence of an appropriate male, too, a woman could serve as househead. Among women, the spouse of the current head, or housewife (*shufu*), usually had the most authority, though her sphere of influence varied among the four classes. At a minimum she had jurisdiction over housekeeping, laundry, provisions, meals, and some social relations. In some regions the symbol

24. Akira Hayami and Nobuko Uchida, "Size of Household in a Japanese County Throughout the Tokugawa Era," in *Household and Family in Past Time*, ed. Peter Laslett (Cambridge: Cambridge University Press, 1972), 490; Chie Nakane, "An Interpretation of the Size and Structure of the Household in Japan over Three Centuries," in ibid., 519–20, 527–28, 531; Robert J. Smith, "Small Families, Small Households, and Residential Instability: Town and City in 'Pre-Modern' Japan," in ibid., 445–55.

25. During the Tokugawa period women served as househeads under certain circumstances, most often during the period a male heir was growing to maturity; see Hauser, "Why So Few?"; and L. L. Cornell, "Retirement, Inheritance, and Intergenerational Conflict in Preindustrial Japan," *Journal of Family History* 8 (1983): 63.

26. These other members included the current househead and housewife and the retired househead and housewife. If the older couple was still househead and housewife, son and young wife (or adopted son and house daughter) made up the second set of adults in the household.

27. An aging househead might step aside in favor of the heir; however, if the retired head and his successor disagreed, faithful conformity to the norm of filial obedience would have decreased the younger man's autonomy in managing household affairs. One also finds cases of male househeads deferring to their mother's directives; see Etsu Inagaki Sugimoto, *Daughter of a Samurai* (Garden City, N.Y.: Doubleday, Doran, 1928), 17: despite her father's reluctance, Sugimoto received a boy's education in accord with her grandmother's wishes.

of her authority was the rice scoop (*shamoji*), which she passed to her successor when she retired.[28]

From the Tokugawa period into the mid–twentieth century, both productive work, which sustained the *ie* by producing essential goods and income, and reproductive work (childrearing, cooking, and housekeeping), which maintained *ie* members, took place at home. The proximity of production and reproduction allowed men, women, and children alike to participate in tasks crucial to the household's survival. The full significance of this unity of production and reproduction for the division of labor in the small preindustrial Japanese household is not easily comprehended by scholars who assume the physical separation of work and home life. For example, participation in *ie* economic activities did not preclude helping with cleaning, cooking, or child care. Today the long workday and grueling commute allow salaried male workers scant time to spend with their children, but during the Tokugawa and Meiji periods the workplace of most fathers was near their children. Furthermore, the househead's obligation to maintain *ie* continuity gave many men a vital stake in the birth and successful rearing of at least one child.

The unity of production and reproduction also facilitated women's participation in productive labor. There was, of course, little need for women in wealthy households to labor at the family trade; but without women's agricultural and handicraft work, the majority of rural households could not survive. In towns and cities it seems likely that women's economic participation in merchant and artisan households was more extensive than scholars have previously imagined.[29]

Children, too, toiled at productive and reproductive work, in poor households often beginning at age four or five. We have already noted the general need of small households for extra workers; in addition, because the househead successor took up his father's occupation and girls' duties as wives resembled their mothers', parents were encouraged to begin children's vocational training at home at an early age. Thus household children as well as young servants and apprentices worked alongside adults in the preindustrial *ie*. Although schools of various types flourished during the late Tokugawa period, much of children's

28. Ueno Chizuko, "The Position of Japanese Women Reconsidered," *Current Anthropology* 28 (1987): 575–84, esp. 577–79; Segawa Kiyoko, "Japanese Women in the Last Century," in *Proceedings of the Tokyo Symposium on Women*, ed. Merry I. White and Barbara Molony (Tokyo: International Group for the Study of Women, 1978), 1–9.

29. See chapters by Lebra and Robertson in this volume (chaps. 6 and 4, respectively). For examples of the Meiji era, see Alice Mabel Bacon, *Japanese Girls and Women* (Boston: Houghton Mifflin, 1902), 223–24, 232; Akemi Kikumura, *Through Harsh Winters: The Life of a Japanese Immigrant Woman* (Novato, Calif.: Chandler & Sharp, 1981), 16–17.

education, in terms of both vocational training and socialization, took place in the household of either their parents or an employer.[30]

In sum, early-modern household goals, composition, authority, and activities argue against a rigid pairing of women with reproductive ("inside") work and men with productive ("outside") work in preindustrial Japan. Although a division of labor according to seniority and gender existed, women in ordinary households engaged in many forms of productive work and men performed some types of reproductive work. Because the household combined work and residence, performance of the myriad daily tasks of cleaning, consumption, childrearing, and production contributed to the primary goal of household survival. Furthermore, since learning by doing constituted crucial preparation for adult life, in all but the wealthiest households youngsters of both sexes participated in both productive and reproductive household tasks.

Women and Productive Work

While the *ie* household structure permitted the co-residence of several adult women—daughter-in-law (the young wife, or *yome*), mother-in-law, unmarried sisters of the head, and female servants[31]—existing demographic studies suggest that this residential pattern did not occur in the majority of households.[32] Whether *yome* or *shufu*, a young married woman in a poor or average household faced a formidable range of household tasks, as a bearer and rearer of children, as a domestic worker, and as a contributor to the household economy. Although a young wife living with her mother-in-law lacked autonomy in managing

30. Ronald P. Dore, *Education in Tokugawa Japan* (Berkeley and Los Angeles: University of California Press, 1965), 252–70; Tokiomi Kaigo, *Japanese Education: Its Past and Present* (Tokyo: Kokusai Bunka Shinkokai, 1968), 39–48. It is difficult to calculate Tokugawa school attendance rates owing to regional variation and lack of information regarding the numbers of schools, though clearly private academies and commoners' schools proliferated during the late Tokugawa. It seems reasonable to conclude that "somewhat under half" of ordinary commoners attended school, with the highest rates in districts close to major cities and "the north and Kyūshū falling badly behind"; Ototake Iwazō, *Nihon shomin kyōikushi*, vol. 3 (1929), 926–28, cited in Dore, *Education in Tokugawa Japan*, 322. See also Walthall's chapter in this volume (chap. 2).

31. After her mother-in-law retires the *yome* is referred to as "housewife" (*shufu*), and after the male heir marries she becomes "mother-in-law" (*shūtome*).

32. The proportion of households with two or more couples for four rural districts in the first half of the eighteenth century ranged from 19.5 to 30.2 percent; Hayami and Uchida, "Size of Household," 498, 504; see also Susan B. Hanley, "Family and Fertility in Four Tokugawa Villages," in *Family and Population in East Asia*, ed. Susan B. Hanley and Arthur P. Wolf (Stanford: Stanford University Press, 1985), 207–10. In urban areas, the proportion of elementary families (married couple or couple and children) ranged from 39–42 percent among owners to 53–60 percent among tenants in late Tokugawa Tennōji-mura; Robert J. Smith, "Transformations of Commoner Households in Tennōji-mura, 1757–1858," in ibid., 255; see also R. J. Smith, "Domestic Cycle," 222–23.

household affairs, the assistance of a second adult woman offered her some advantages. Even without a mother-in-law's coercion, the fact that a young wife's own future and that of her children depended on the household's wealth, property, and status could drive the *yome* to diligent efforts for the *ie*.

In city and countryside, rich women of all classes largely escaped the physical drudgery of productive and reproductive work; poor women, however, toiled to earn a living and to manage daily tasks. In ordinary farm households, the *yome* performed productive tasks requiring skill and strength, and did not devote extensive time to childrearing. While the farm wife's work varied according to locality, it invariably encompassed planting, cultivating, weeding, and harvesting paddies and vegetable fields;[33] in economically advanced regions women also cultivated cash crops such as vegetables or tobacco, raised silkworms, spun thread, or wove cloth for market. The peasant wife's duties included reproductive chores as well: doing laundry, scrubbing pots, sewing garments, and preparing meals. With all these tasks, a woman's workday lasted from before dawn to after nightfall. Because her productive work was vital to the maintenance and livelihood of the ordinary farm *ie*,[34] other household members—older children or the mother- and father-in-law—minded infants and toddlers in order to free the *yome* to engage in strenuous, skilled, or remunerative activities.[35] Maids and *komori* (part-time or live-in nursemaids) assisted wealthy peasant women with domestic tasks, but even prosperous rural wives apparently were not altogether exempt from farm work.[36]

Samurai women were barred from regular stipended posts, although some held nonhereditary positions as ladies-in-waiting, maids, wet nurses, or governesses in the households of feudal lords. Wives of high-ranking warriors employed servants, including full-time nannies, to do most of the reproductive work in their households. (By the late Toku-

33. Bernstein, "Did Women Work?"; Nagashima Atsuko, "Kinsei josei no nōgyō rōdō ni okeru ichi," *Rekishi hyōron*, no. 383 (March 1982): 48–65; T. C. Smith, *Nakahara*, 152–53. Also see Walthall's chapter in this volume (chap. 2). For the early twentieth century, see Hane, *Peasants, Rebels, and Outcastes*, 79–101, 233–36.

34. T. C. Smith in *Nakahara* discusses the work of rural female household members. As women could perform both reproductive and productive tasks, one might surmise that all-female households were less likely to become extinct than all-male households, because women could cook and manage the household as well as engage in economic activities—farming and by-employments.

35. See Uno, "Day Care and Family Life," 26–29.

36. Even in elite village families women helped with agricultural work, particularly during the spring planting and fall harvest seasons; see Hyman Kublin, *Asian Revolutionary: The Life of Sen Katayama* (Princeton: Princeton University Press, 1964), 11–17; Nagashima Atsuko, "Bakumatsu nōson josei no kōdō no jiyū to kaji rōdō," in Kinsei joseishi kenkyūkai (ed.), *Ronshū kinsei joseishi*, 146; Uno, "Day Care and Family Life," 34–36.

gawa period, however, some spouses of impoverished, low-ranking warriors engaged in secondary occupations to supplement the household's
meager income.)[37] Nonetheless, the better-off samurai wife was not
completely idle. She waited on her husband and in-laws, prepared special foods, entertained guests, inventoried household goods, decorated
the home, sewed clothing, and managed servants. As a girl she had also
labored at more menial, taxing chores, including sweeping the yard,
pruning bushes, cooking, sewing bedding quilts, and weaving mosquito
nets.[38] Society scorned idleness in women of all ages, save perhaps the
wives of nobles, feudal lords, and their top retainers. But even though
upper-level samurai women engaged in many household tasks themselves rather than leaving reproductive work entirely to servants,[39] they
were not criticized if they left child care almost completely to their servants.[40]

While feudal laws did not bar merchant women from assisting in the
household occupation, over time wives seem to have become less active
in the business affairs of the great merchant houses.[41] Nonetheless,
wives' careful supervision of many nominally domestic activities, including shopping, cooking, sewing, cleaning, entertaining guests, and exchanging gifts, could advance the fortunes of the enterprise. Like up-
per-echelon samurai women, the wives of rich merchants left
childrearing and menial household chores to servants,[42] whereas wives

37. Ōtake, "*Ie" to josei*, 220–23; Torao Haraguchi, Robert K. Sakai, et al., *The Status
System and Social Organization of Satsuma* (Honolulu: University Press of Hawaii, 1975), 10–
11, 48–51, 24–25, 63–64; Chikamatsu Monzaemon, "Yosaku of Tamba," in *Major Plays of
Chikamatsu*, trans. Donald Keene (New York: Columbia University Press, 1961), 91–130;
Uno, "Day Care and Family Life," 39–40; Shinmi Kichiji, *Kaitei zōho kakyū shizoku no kenkyū*
(Maruzen, 1965), 312.

38. Sugimoto, *Daughter of a Samurai*, 21, 23, 46–47, 92–95; Shidzue Ishimoto, *Facing
Two Ways: The Story of My Life* (New York: Farrar & Rinehart, 1935), 80–86, 134–39.

39. Of course, having young women do housework, cooking, serving, and sewing
served a second purpose: without firsthand knowledge of these domestic tasks, mistresses
would have had difficulties properly supervising their servants. The *Onna daigaku*
(Greater learning for women), an advice book for women (see below), prescribed physical
labor even for wealthy women: "It is in accordance with the manners of woman to do her
manual work though she may have many servants in her employment"; Atsuharu Sakai,
"Kaibara-Ekiken [*sic*] and 'Onna-Daigaku,' " *Cultural Nippon* 7, no. 4 (December 1939): 55.
Sakai, ibid., 43–56, has translated the *Onna daigaku*, as has Basil Hall Chamberlain in
Things Japanese: Being Notes on Various Subjects Connected With Japan (Tokyo: Hakubunsha;
London: Kegan, Paul, Trevich, Trebner, 1890), 67–76.

40. McClellan, *Woman in the Crested Kimono*, 44; Sugimoto, *Daughter of a Samurai*, 3, 70.

41. Hayashi Reiko, "Chōka josei no sonzai keitai," in Joseishi sōgō kenkyūkai (ed.), *Nihon joseishi* 3:96–108; Hauser, "Why So Few?" The parallel with the wives of entrepreneurs in early modern France is striking; see Bonnie G. Smith, *Ladies of the Leisure Class:
The Bourgeoises of Northern France* (Princeton: Princeton University Press, 1981).

42. Uno, "Day Care and Family Life," 36–38.

in lesser households did some or all of the domestic tasks themselves. Regardless of who actually performed the work, a woman's skill in social relations and in providing food, clothing, fuel, and other daily necessities benefited the business. Savings from frugal consumption could be invested in the enterprise. Thoughtful entertaining maintained clients' goodwill. Since apprentices lived with their masters, the household atmosphere, including the quality of room, board, and clothing, could affect employee morale as well as productivity and turnover. In smaller enterprises, merchant wives kept books, waited on customers, and took care of personnel matters, such as hiring and employee welfare.[43] However, when income fell short, in desperation the wives of the poorest merchants turned to employment outside their own household.[44]

The scant available evidence concerning the wives of indoor artisans[45] suggests that they assisted in the manufacture and sale of goods. A woman with a baby strapped to her back helping her husband make clay cooking stoves appears in one Tokugawa woodblock print, illustrating a wife's simultaneous participation in productive and reproductive work in an artisan enterprise. Similarly, a print of a bean-curd maker's shop showed the wife, also with an infant on her back, assisting in household production.[46] Even less is known about the economic role of the wives of rugged outdoor artisans, such as carpenters, sawyers, and plasterers. Although they probably had fewer opportunities to par-

43. Hayashi, "Chōka josei," 108–24; Charles J. Dunn, *Everyday Life in Traditional Japan* (Rutland, Vt.: Charles E. Tuttle, 1969), 153; Ihara Saikaku, *Some Final Words of Advice*, trans. Peter Nosco (Rutland, Vt.: Charles E. Tuttle, 1980), 148–56; Ihara Saikaku, *The Japanese Family Storehouse, or the Millionaires' Gospel Modernised*, trans. G. W. Sargent (Cambridge: Cambridge University Press, 1969), 42–43.

44. Ihara Saikaku, *Some Final Words*, 155–56, 185, 228–29; Ihara Saikaku, *This Scheming World*, trans. Masanori Takatsuka and David C. Stubbs (Rutland, Vt.: Charles E. Tuttle, 1965), 71, 50, 228. In the modern era, wives received clients at the office, kept the books, handled transactions with subcontractors, and managed the room, board, and welfare of employees; see Mary Lou Maxson, "Women in Family Businesses," in Lebra, Paulson, and Powers (eds.), *Women in Changing Japan*, 91–99. Since World War II employees are less likely to reside with their employers, but wives of small entrepreneurs still participate in business affairs; see ibid., 99–105; John C. Pelzel, "Factory Life in Japan and China Today," in *Japan: A Comparative View*, ed. Albert Craig (Princeton: Princeton University Press, 1979), 393, 399, 401.

45. Indoor artisans (*ishokunin*) such as smiths, lacquerers, and makers of fans, clogs, umbrellas, and furniture, produced their wares in workshops; outdoor artisans (*dejokunin*) worked outside in the building trades.

46. Dunn, *Everyday Life*, 154; Ozawa Hiroshi, "Kinsei no shokunin fūzoku," *Rekishi kōron* 9, no. 8 (August 1983): 7. Haruko Sumii, "We Switched from Being Drapers to Farmers," in *Widows of Hiroshima: The Life Stories of Nineteen Peasant Wives*, ed. Mikio Kanda, trans. Taeko Midorikawa (New York: St. Martin's Press, 1989), 79; and Kleinberg, "Where Work and Life Are Almost One," 226–28, describe wives' participation in the drapery and pottery trades of Taisho Japan.

ticipate in the household than did the wives of indoor artisans, they still may have kept the accounts or dispensed food, clothing, and emergency assistance to the workers under a labor boss (*oyakata*).

Ideology sanctioned women's participation in the economic life of households. Popular moral tracts, such as Kaibara Ekken's *Onna daigaku* (Greater learning for women), strongly colored by the neo-Confucianism of the ruling samurai class, emphasized women's responsibility to the *ie*, their duty to obey husbands and seniors, and their innate inferiority.[47] Although at first the circulation of these works was limited to educated women of the warrior class, the spread of literacy during the late Tokugawa period undoubtedly increased the influence of didactic tracts among rural and urban commoners, especially among rich farmers and merchants. The pamphlets instructed brides to serve their in-laws faithfully, to practice frugality and modesty, and to learn to manage household and servants well—advice that was on the whole more useful to women of propertied than propertyless households.

The lengthy sections on the *yome*'s duty to husband and in-laws and the supervision of servants contrast sharply with the very brief treatment of mothering, suggesting that the primary duty of a young wife was not child care but obedience to her seniors and training for eventual management of household affairs. Overall, the advice books encouraged women to perform whatever type of work the authorities in her household requested. In fact, some even argued that women's extensive moral deficiencies made mothers ill suited for contact with impressionable children; thus childrearing assistance by siblings or in-laws in the lower classes and by servants in the upper classes would enable them to concentrate on other types of productive and reproductive work for the household.[48]

Men and Reproductive Work: Childrearing

Men's contribution to childrearing in preindustrial Japanese households of all classes is easily overlooked, as it is often assumed that the upbringing of children fell wholly within women's domain. Yet descriptions of home life in autobiographies, travelers' accounts, and fiction attest to the participation of men in this crucial type of reproductive work. In fact, such activity is entirely consistent with household structure and ideology.[49]

47. Sakai, "Kaibara-Ekiken."

48. Uno, " 'Good Wives and Wise Mothers,' " 4–5.

49. For example, one propertyless charcoalmaker took time to catch and carefully roast rabbits, fish, and wild fowl to supplement his young son's meager diet; see Takai Toshio, *Watashi no jokō aishi* (Sōdo Bunka, 1980), 8–9. The discussion here focuses on

Tokugawa fathers apparently played an important role in educating their children, especially their sons. This was particularly true of men in the middle and lower orders of society, those whose trades did not require extensive formal education. Farm, merchant, and artisan fathers could train their own sons or, alternatively, send them out as apprentices to learn a trade; merchants also sent sons (and sometimes daughters) to school to acquire vocational skills, namely writing and arithmetic.[50] Warrior fathers, however, were less likely to educate their own sons. The official duties of high-ranking samurai took them away from home for extended periods of time, which prevented them from tutoring their sons in the required Confucian classics and martial arts. As the Tokugawa era progressed, feudal authorities provided instruction at domain academies; thus formal education became increasingly important for the appointment and advancement of samurai sons. At school, the judging of abilities and achievements by critical standards rather than by a father's fond eye prepared the youths for evaluation by superiors in the domain bureaucracies. Although some fathers attempted to mold their daughters' character and intellect, in general girls learned womanly virtues as well as specific vocational and household skills by observing and imitating female models.[51]

The role of fathers in the physical care of children is also evident. Responsibility for continuity of the family name, occupation, and status led households to want one child to survive to maturity. Furthermore, it behooved the conscientious head to make sure that the heir was carefully groomed to shoulder the household's social obligations and ply its trade. This concern applied especially to eldest sons, but fathers may have devoted attention to other children as understudies to the heir. Clearly, fathers sometimes lavished attention on a noninheriting girl or boy owing to personal qualities such as intelligence, alertness, tractability, diligence, or vocational aptitude.[52]

---

fathers; Uno, "Day Care and Family Life," 24–26, 29–32, treats the role of boys and grandfathers in child care.

50. Dore, *Education in Tokugawa Japan*, 266–68.

51. Mothers, grandmothers, older sisters, and female servants served as exemplars and teachers. If a girl received formal instruction from a tutor or at a commoner's school (*terakoya*), she was quite likely to have a male teacher (although according to Ishikawa Ken, *Terakoya* [1960], 132, cited in Dore, *Education in Tokugawa Japan*, 257, in Edo (Tokyo) one-third of *terakoya* teachers were female.

52. Fister's chapter on Ema Saikō in this volume (chap. 5) provides an early-modern example, and the lives of Takai and Higuchi Ichiyō do so for the prewar era. Although Takai's father had no property to pass on to his heir, he nonetheless tenderly cared for his son; Takai, *Watashi no jokō aishi*, 8–9. Higuchi's scholarly father gave her much attention and a first-rate education despite her mother's objections, for his son lacked the intelligence and disposition to apply himself to advanced learning; see Robert Danly, ed.

There is a fair amount of evidence documenting fathers' participation in child care during the late Tokugawa and early Meiji. Shikitei Sanba's *Ukiyo buro* (Bathhouse of the floating world) offers a glimpse of paternal child care among urban commoners of poor to average means during the late Tokugawa period: "A man in his forties arrived, holding by the hand a boy of five or so and carrying on his back, like a monkey trainer carrying his pet, a little girl of about two, who in turn was clutching a toy bucket made of bamboo and a ceramic baby turtle." In the bath, it is obvious that the father, Kinbei, is practiced at undressing his children, cajoling his son into entering the hot water, and washing the two. He even sings songs to distract the boy so that he will not mind the hot bath. The scene ends with Kinbei telling his children, "Mommy's waiting for us, and she'll probably have something nice for you if you're good."[53] Another account describes an impoverished samurai father, ordinarily a ruffian and womanizer, who nursed his gravely ill nine-year-old son day and night for seventy days; during this time he also dashed buckets of cold water on himself and prayed for his son at a local shrine.[54]

Isabella Bird's description of ordinary families encountered in her 1878 travels through northern Japan provides further evidence that fathers' productive labor and authority did not preclude involvement in child care during the early Meiji period. She found rural men to be very affectionate with children and noted that fathers as well as mothers cared for infants:

> I never saw people take so much delight in their offspring, carrying them about, or holding hands in walking, watching and entering into their games, supplying them constantly with new toys, taking them to picnics and festivals, never being content to be without them, and treating other people's children also with a suitable measure of affection and attention. Both fathers and mothers take pride in their children. It is most amusing about six every morning to see twelve or fourteen men sitting on a low wall, each with a child under two years in his arms, fondling and playing with it, and showing off its physique and intelligence. . . . At night, after the houses are shut up, looking through the long fringe of rope or rattan which conceals the sliding door, you see the father who wears [nearly] nothing . . . in the "bosom of his family," bending his ugly, kindly face

and trans., *In the Shade of Spring Leaves: The Life and Work of Higuchi Ichiyō, A Meiji Woman of Letters* (New Haven, Conn.: Yale University Press, 1981), 11–15.

53. Robert W. Leutner, *Shikitei Sanba and the Comic Tradition in Edo Fiction* (Cambridge, Mass.: Harvard University Press, 1985), 150–53; *Ukiyo buro* was published between 1809 and 1813, during the Bunka era (1804–18).

54. Katsu, *Musui's Story*, 88–90. See Leutner, *Shikitei Sanba*, 153, for post-Restoration examples. See Higuchi Ichiyō, "Troubled Waters," in Danly (trans.), *In the Shade of Spring Leaves*, 228; and Kashima Kōji, *Taishō Shitayakko* (Seiabō, 1978), 103–9.

over a gentle-looking baby, and the mother . . . enfolding two children destitute of clothing in her arms. For some reason they prefer boys, but certainly girls are equally petted and loved.[55]

Prosperous urban fathers also devoted time and attention to their children. Although her child had a wet nurse, when Umehara Miki's husband "returned late at night, the child would wake up and come out to play with both parents."[56] The spontaneity of this father-child relationship is striking. Both the father and mother responded to their offspring's freely expressed wishes with affectionate indulgence rather than stern discipline. In addition, this merchant father was willing to spend time with his child even after a long day's activities.

Men and Reproductive Work: Housework

It is also possible to reconceptualize male household members' relationship to a second type of reproductive work: housework. Male householders—householders, fathers, boys, and grandfathers—engaged in such chores as shopping and housework. Since household needs took priority over individual preferences, men and boys did these tasks if their efforts promised to enhance household prosperity. In 1610, for example, one prudent well-to-do merchant, Shimai Sōshitsu, left a set of written injunctions instructing his son to avoid luxury, entertainment, and religion; to stay at home; and to practice frugality in order to guard the family's riches. Thriftiness included painstaking attention to menial household tasks:

With your own hands kindle the fire under the stove, for breakfast and dinner, damping the embers afterwards. . . . Going out behind the house, collect all the bits and pieces of rubbish: small lengths of rope should be cut up for mixing in cement, . . . fragments of wood or broken bamboo, even as small as half an inch, should be stored, cleaned, and used as fuel for watch-fires; . . . when buying things for the first time . . . go out and buy for yourself. Buy at the cheapest rates, and make careful note of the prices. Afterwards . . . you will know whether the articles he [the servant] brings are too expensive or not. . . . Housekeeping may be said to be a matter of firewood, charcoal, and oil. . . . No matter what his calling, *if a man does not take these troubles upon himself, he can never run a household successfully.* . . . Scrape the bean-paste morning and night. . . . [Mix this together with bits of vegetable scraps and] give this to the serving-maids for breakfast and dinner as a side-dish. (emphasis added)

55. Isabella Bird, *Unbeaten Tracks in Japan* (New York: G. P. Putnam, 1880; reprint Rutland, Vt.: Charles E. Tuttle, 1984), 74.
56. Hayashi, "Chōka josei," 116.

No task was too lowly for the househead if its proper completion augmented the well-being of the *ie*. A man's solicitude for household consumption, seemingly a part of women's domain, helped maintain the family fortune by conserving capital. In fact, Shimai seemed not to conceive of the division of labor between husband and wife in rigid terms, writing that "husband and wife should live in lifelong harmony. They should love each other, feeling a common concern for household and business problems and striving together to be thrifty and unremitting in effort."[57]

Likewise, a successful peasant entrepreneur named Suzuki Bokushi (1770–1842) also exhibited great concern for domestic affairs. "Unless everything in his store, in the house, in the dressers, even in the needle cases was in its proper place, he could not relax. No matter how late guests stayed, he insisted that the house be put in order before anyone went to bed. If the cleaning was not done to suit him, he would pick up a broom or dust rag and start sweeping himself. Hating waste, he carefully preserved bits of lumber and bamboo splits."[58] In other words, for a household to prosper, fathers needed to pay attention to management of the hearth, just as mothers had to think about the family enterprise.

Children's Work

Although the wealthy could maintain children as dependents, children of poor and middling farmers and merchants (and probably of artisans as well) helped to sustain the household. Farmers' children gathered grass, plaited ropes, weeded fields, and picked mulberry leaves; they also gathered firewood for hearth and bath and babysat by carrying infants on their backs. Households gained income by indenturing children as apprentices or servants in others' establishments. Young employees, both boys and girls, performed a variety of menial tasks for their employers—cleaning, stoking fires, cooking, minding infants, run-

57. Ihara, *Japanese Family Storehouse*, 247–48, 249.

58. Suzuki Bokushi, *Snow Country Tales: Life in the Other Japan*, trans. Jeffrey Hunter with Rose Lesser (Tokyo: John Weatherhill, 1986), xl. In contrast to patriarchal Confucian ideology, some of the new religions, such as Kurozumikyō, which gained adherents among commoners after the late Tokugawa period, emphasized harmony and cooperation between spouses in its teachings. Kurozumi Munetada (1780–1850), the founder of Kurozumikyō, stressed a "spirit of 'mutuality and reverence' " in marital relations; Helen Hardacre, *Kurozumikyō and the New Religions of Japan* (Princeton: Princeton University Press, 1986), 72. See also Walthall's chapter in this volume (chap. 2). If their station in life required it, even samurai men engaged in housework, in their own household or another; see *The Autobiography of Yukichi Fukuzawa*, trans. Eiichi Kiyooka (New York: Columbia University Press, 1966), 11, 23; and Katsu, *Musui's Story*, 20.

ning errands, or working some aspect of a craft—depending on their masters' trade and instructions.[59]

Parents put children to work not only because the household needed their labor but also to instill good work attitudes in their children from an early age. One Tokugawa peasant offered advice on how to make a child into a good farmer:

> From the age of 8 boys should gather grass for the animals, pick up horse dung from the road, make rope, and help with other light work. When they work well, they should be praised and given a coin. When coins accumulate to a sufficient sum, the children should be allowed to buy something they want. Thus their childish hearts will develop the spirit of industry and perseverance. If they are given suitable work in this way when young and taught farming skills as they get older, by age 14 or 15 they will be industrious and meticulous farmers.[60]

The early training of children through work was not restricted to rural areas, however. In the urban bathhouse tales cited above, a well-to-do matron of "a refined appearance" informs a friend that she has placed her five-year-old daughter, Onabe, in service with a samurai household. Since a nurse accompanied Onabe to her master's house, and the cost of the elegant clothes required for her position was "hard on Papa's wallet," the mother's motive was neither to receive income nor to reduce the number of mouths to feed in the household. Rather, it was for Onabe to learn proper behavior. The mother confided, "If they're at home, they simply won't straighten out, no matter how you scold them. But when you send them off to live in a good household, everything begins to change."[61] Note that this mother believed her young daughter's education was best left to outsiders of a higher class.

POST-RESTORATION CHANGE

After the 1868 Meiji Restoration, new political and economic policies fostered a greater separation of public and private spheres, which impinged on the household division of labor. The separation of school and workplace from the home affected increasing numbers of children, then men, and finally women. Although early policies did not aim specifically to alter the family roles of children and men, by the end of the nineteenth century private educators and government officials deliberately sought to reshape conceptions of womanhood. The cumulative effects

59. Uno, "Day Care and Family Life," 30–32, 34–37.
60. T. C. Smith, *Nakahara*, 109.
61. Leutner, *Shikitei Sanba*, 183–85.

of all these changes slowly became visible by the early decades of the twentieth century, reshaping the daily lives of women, particularly among the new urban middle class.

The new government's policies had a substantial impact on children's place in the household. In 1872 the regime founded a nationwide school system and instituted universal compulsory education as part of its nation-building program. Yet because school attendance disrupted work patterns, many families regarded these policies as unwarranted interference in household affairs. Not only did schooling transform children from producers into dependents, but the loss of children's labor at domestic, farm, and shop chores also jeopardized income by reducing productivity, while expenses mounted owing to new expenditures for tuition, educational supplies, and school taxes (these amounted to as much as 10 percent of household income during the early Meiji).[62]

Indeed, parents in many localities during the early Meiji resisted compulsory schooling through nonenrollment, truancy, and the burning and razing of elementary schools;[63] eventually, however, compliance with the law induced a shift in the domestic division of labor, making more children dependents for a longer time and diminishing their contributions to productive and reproductive activities at their natal or master's household.[64] In urban areas, attendance figures suggest that most lower-class children under thirteen years of age had largely become dependent students by the mid-Taishō.[65] To the distress of educators, though, large numbers of rural households were unable to dispense altogether with child labor until after World War II.[66]

Promotion of commerce and industry also impinged on the household division of labor. The destruction of old trades, the expansion of wage labor, and the rise of salaried workers created large-scale organizations—offices, government bureaus, and factories—that split the former unity of production and reproduction in growing numbers of

62. Michio Nagai, "Westernization and Japanization: The Early Meiji Transformation of Education," in *Tradition and Modernization in Japanese Culture*, ed. Donald Shively (Princeton: Princeton University Press, 1971), 58.

63. Ibid., 54–55.

64. Children had been dependents in some wealthy families during the Tokugawa era, but the proportion of dependent children now increased. Furthermore, this form of childhood began to take hold among the urban lower classes during the Taishō era. See also note 65.

65. Former residents and observers of poor urban districts noted that more parents began to enroll children in school over time; see Kashima, *Taishō Shitayakko*, 82–84; Tomita Ei, "Hinmin kutsu no sannen," *Katei shūhō*, no. 604 (March 11, 1920): 4; Katoda Keiko, "Waga kuni ni okeru hinji kyōiku," *Shakai fukushi*, no. 23 (1982): 89.

66. Ushijima Yoshitomo, *Nōson jidō no shinri* (Iwamatsudō Shoten, 1946).

households.[67] As greater numbers of people marched out to work all day at places distant from their homes, wage-earning household members—primarily adult males, but also children and some married women—had fewer hours to spend on reproductive work at home.[68] Furthermore, because positions at nonfamilial enterprises, especially in technical and managerial positions, could not be passed on to sons, fathers had less incentive to socialize and care for their offspring. For new middle-class fathers, both proximity to children and motivation to engage in childrearing began to decline by the end of the nineteenth century as new forms of employment and economic organization proliferated.

These changes did not immediately influence the attitudes or behavior of the great majority of Japanese women. Although a handful of women boldly assumed new roles in the larger society as teachers and political activists,[69] most women labored at productive and reproductive tasks in the private world of the household as before. Nevertheless, early Meiji policies promoting *fukoku kyōhei* ("rich country, strong army") and *bunmei kaika* ("civilization and enlightenment") did have an indirect impact on women's roles, for the departure of men and children from the home for much of the day irreversibly reshaped the daily lives of women in growing numbers of households.

As in the case of children, post-Restoration policies affected urban women to a greater extent than rural women, and influenced the lives of middle- and lower-class women in different ways. The salaries earned by upper-middle-class males sufficed to support a wife and children as dependents. Children in these families received good educations, both

67. For more on these economic trends, see Nagy's essay in this volume (chap. 9); and Kinmonth, *Self-made Man.*

68. Assuming that women constituted a constant 40 percent of industrial operatives (a rather low estimate), one can estimate that male blue- and white-collar workers made up roughly 13 percent, 20 percent, and 27 percent of the labor force in 1909, 1920, and 1930, respectively, and that a high proportion of these male workers commuted to their workplace. Corresponding estimates of the proportion of female wage-earning operatives in the labor force for those years are 5 percent, 10 percent, and 12 percent; these percentages exclude women working in rural and household enterprises who did not commute to their workplace. Estimates are derived from figures in Tadashi Fukutake, *The Japanese Social Structure* (Tokyo: Tokyo University Press, 1982), 58; and Lockwood, *Economic Development of Japan,* 184n.54. Furthermore, few female operatives were married. Regarding Meiji female operatives, see Sievers, *Flowers in Salt,* 63; Hane, *Peasants, Rebels, and Outcastes,* 173–93; Gail Lee Bernstein, "Women in the Silk-reeling Industry in Nineteenth-Century Japan," in *Japan and the World: Essays on Japanese History and Politics in Honour of Ishida Takeshi,* ed. Gail Lee Bernstein and Haruhiro Fukui (New York: St. Martin's Press, 1988), 59–63, esp. 62. For the Taishō–early Shōwa period, see the chapters by Nagy, Molony, and Silverberg in this volume (chaps. 9–11, respectively).

69. Sievers, *Flowers in Salt,* 26–53, 87–188.

as a means of upholding the family status and to enable the sons to enter nonhereditary occupations as government officials or corporate managers and technicians. Since productive work and most education of children over six years of age took place at specialized institutions, wives took charge of the home, performing the unpaid activities of consumption, housework, and care of young children. Thus compulsory education and industrialization transformed the upper-middle-class urban woman into a private domestic laborer.

These changes affected the home lives of lower-class women differently. The separation from productive work was less complete for women whose husbands could not support the entire household, and so, to supplement the low, irregular income of unskilled and semi-skilled male occupations,[70] women (and sometimes children) continued to work. Some wives assisted their husbands at petty trades, while others took in piecework such as assembling straw sandals or matchboxes at home; still others plied trades ranging from street vending to scavenging for salable scraps and dressing hair.[71] In any case, neither lower-class urban women nor women in average and poor rural households could afford to specialize solely in reproductive work.

These results of policies implemented to strengthen the nation were unintended; the effort to reshape women's roles that commenced around the turn of the nineteenth century, in contrast, was wholly deliberate. Professional educators, including bureaucrats at the Ministry of Education, created a new prescription for Japanese womanhood, *ryōsai kenbo* ("good wife, wise mother"), in the wake of the 1894–95 Sino-Japanese War.[72] After 1899, *ryōsai kenbo* became the cornerstone of women's education, beginning with a handful of girls' higher schools and extending to the ordinary coeducational curriculum in 1911.

At first glance, *ryōsai kenbo* may seem to resemble early-modern elite views of womanhood, but in fact it constituted a new view of womanhood presented in the guise of tradition. Gone were the old congenital vices that had justified withholding familial and social responsibility from women. *Ryōsai kenbo* presumed a greater degree of female competence; if properly educated, mothers could prepare their children to be good subjects of the emperor by instilling in them diligence, loyalty, and patriotism. Mothers thus would render service to the nation from the home. Perhaps the daytime departure of growing numbers of men

70. The lower reaches of prewar Japanese society included petty craftsmen and merchants.

71. Uno, "Day Care and Family Life," 70–72.

72. See, for example, Nakajima Kuni, "Boseiron no keifu," *Rekishi kōron* 5, no. 12 (December 1979), 62–66; Fukaya, *Ryōsai kenboshugi no kyōiku*, 138–72; Uno, "Good Wives and Wise Mothers."

necessitated this new appreciation of feminine abilities. Certainly women's participation in unprecedented activities while their men were away fighting in the Sino-Japanese War contributed to the rising estimates of women's capabilities.[73]

CHANGES IN THE HOUSEHOLD DIVISION OF LABOR
AND WOMEN'S HISTORY

The study of women in the household division of labor in preindustrial Japan should begin by questioning assumed links among production, reproduction, and gender predicated on conditions of industrial societies. Freed from the two-part assumption that men engaged exclusively in productive tasks and women labored exclusively at reproductive chores—a distinction more suited to our own than to a preindustrial society—we can better appreciate the toil of *ie* members, the relationships between them, and their *mentalité*. It may prove equally profitable to question the equation of women with the domestic realm and men with the public realm. Women did face political and economic restrictions in their attempts to venture outside the home, but if one assumes that women had no role outside the household, almost inevitably female participation in public activity will be overlooked.[74]

This chapter has suggested the utility of the household division of labor in the study of women's history. By investigating the role of men in childrearing and household management in preindustrial households, we may better understand how women's (and men's) roles changed as new social organizations—government bureaus, factories, and corporations—proliferated in the decades following the Meiji Restoration. An awareness of the changing patterns in children's activities can illuminate women's history as well. By starting with the preindustrial role of children as productive and reproductive workers, we can see the impact of modern education on women's place in the household division of labor.

A household division of labor approach has implications for the study

73. Regarding women's production for the nation, see the essay by Nolte and Hastings in this volume (chap. 5); Miyake's chapter in this volume discusses the evolution of motherhood in the 1930s and 1940s as Japan mobilized for war (chap. 12).

74. For example, Nagashima, "Bakumatsu nōson josei," 167, points out that the grandmother in the wealthy, influential Sekiguchi house personally delivered gifts from the household and that the young wife, not the male household, negotiated her daughter's service contract with a prosperous family in Edo. These peasant women traveled out of their village overnight to represent their household in the great capital. Ishimoto, *Facing Two Ways*, 138–39, discusses the role of wealthy urban women as representatives of their households in giving and receiving gifts and attending funerals and memorial services. See also Wakita Osamu in Joseishi sōgō kenkyūkai (ed.), *Nihon joseishi* 3:11–14.

of gender and manhood as well. It leads to questions regarding noninheriting adult male household members who were not householdheads, for
instance, for the early-modern household controlled not only their subsistence and livelihood, but their political and sexual life (at least the
right to marry) as well. One might ask what, if any, were the similarities
in the situations of economically, socially, and politically subordinate
men and women, and whether reconsideration of relationships between
gender, status, dependence, and hierarchy in early-modern Japan is
called for.

The evidence presented here regarding changes in women's work in
households from the Tokugawa period to the late Meiji suggests that
the origins of the intensive style of mothering characteristic of the postwar urban middle class can be traced to the early twentieth century. It
also suggests that Japanese conceptions of womanhood as motherhood
and of childhood as a lengthy period of economic dependence are social
constructs that emerged in modern times. Moreover, the evidence presented concerning the division of reproductive labor in Tokugawa and
early Meiji households implies that to view mothering as woman's universal and natural destiny is to deny history.

Joan Kelly has argued that the histories of men and women sometimes diverge and that progress for men does not always constitute
progress for women.[75] The changes in the family division of labor and
in women's roles that occurred during the formation of the Japanese
industrial nation-state may further exemplify the divergence of the histories of the two genders. When workplace and home were one, women
labored at a variety of productive and reproductive tasks; with the
emergence of new specialized institutions that removed men and children from the home for long hours each day, women alone remained
bound to the home in middle-class twentieth-century Japan. The situation of lower-class women was also in flux, and their energy was taxed
more than ever in their efforts to obtain adequate incomes and to maintain a decent home life.

The new order offered women unprecedented educational and vocational opportunities. But did these opportunities offset new constraints in the household division of labor and the state's attempt to redefine women as *ryōsai kenbo*? At first glance, only the gains stand out.
Compulsory education was required for girls as well as boys, and conceptions of female inferiority lessened as mothers were accorded
greater responsibility for childrearing. Yet closer scrutiny reveals that,
by 1900, women had been barred from politics, virtually stripped of
property rights and the right to serve as family heads, and nearly ex-

75. Joan Kelly, "Did Women Have a Renaissance?" in *Women, History, and Theory: The
Essays of Joan Kelly* (Chicago: University of Chicago Press, 1984), 19–51.

cluded from universities, the gateways to leading corporate and bureau-cratic positions.[76] The emerging division of labor assigned work in the household strictly to women; the new legal system made their access to commanding positions outside the home more difficult. Of course, it is fair to ask to what extent men profited from the new division of labor. Perhaps the greater rigidity in family roles engendered by the separation of workplace and home in the modern age has been disadvantageous to men (and perhaps children) as well. After all, if Japanese women became trapped in the home, Japanese men became locked out of the home.

76. Murakami, *Meiji joseishi*, vols. 2 and 3.

TWO

The Life Cycle of
Farm Women in Tokugawa Japan

Anne Walthall

*Among the peasantry of Japan one finds the women who have the most freedom
and independence. . . . The Japanese peasant woman, when she marries, works
side by side with her husband, finds life full of interest outside of the simple
household work, and as she grows older, her face shows more individuality, more
pleasure in life, less suffering and disappointment, than that of her wealthier
and less hard-working sister.*

ALICE MABEL BACON[1]

Peasant women in Tokugawa Japan grew up, married, gave birth,
and died in generally obscure circumstances. Little is known of
them as individuals, and the emotional content of their lives remains
largely unrecorded. The accounts women themselves left molder
in family archives, and aggregate data can scarcely provide insights
into the nature of their childhood experiences, their relations with
their husbands and their husband's family, and their later years.
It is only by piecing together a variety of different sources that
we can begin to perceive, in patchwork, a pattern to these women's
lives.

One source is village records, such as the population registers
(*shūmon aratamechō*), petitions, passports (*mura-okuri issatsu*), promissory notes for brides, and deeds of inheritance, which, although their
main purpose was to promote social stability, tell us something about
women's experiences. In addition, agricultural handbooks describe
the kinds of work women performed, and precepts for women tell
us what they were expected to do. Early-nineteenth-century family
histories and diaries kept by wealthy peasant entrepreneurs are a

1. Alice Mabel Bacon, *Japanese Girls and Women* (Boston: Houghton, Mifflin, 1891; reprint 1902), 218.

third, more vivid source for the historian interested in exploring the fabric of Japanese women's lives. Those kept by Suzuki Bokushi from the snow country of Echigo, by the Sekiguchi family from Namamugi village near Yokohama, and by Suzuki Heikurō from a village in the Tama region that is now part of greater Tokyo are particularly rich sources, and I have used them extensively for this chapter.

The major conclusion we can draw from these materials is that social relationships between the sexes varied much more than historians have previously thought possible. Opportunities for women, like those for men, were largely a function of economic class and social status: the lives of impoverished peasant women bore little resemblance to those of their wealthy farm neighbors, and a rich peasant's wife, sister, or daughter experienced a much more agreeable existence than many a male from a poor peasant family.

The picture is further complicated by regional differences that produced a variety of social arrangements. In some regions but not in others, for example, women might serve as household heads, even though the designated roles for women presumably required that daughters obey their fathers, wives their husbands, and mothers their sons. Historians trying to make sense of this diversity might well be tempted to agree with one major figure in the preparation of the late-nineteenth-century Meiji Civil Code, who suggested that the customs of farmers were not really customs at all.[2] Put another way, it is impossible to establish a single portrait of rural women. The view that emerges from available sources suggests that, like all people who shape their lives around the rhythms of agricultural cycle, Japanese peasants were accustomed to responding flexibly to the vagaries of their existence. They had to deal with what David W. Plath had defined as the life-course problem—that is, "how to adapt one's personal trajectory and tempo of biographical events" to the preindustrial order.[3] Deciding when and whom to marry, for example, was not simply a function of tradition but necessitated real choices on the part of the woman and her family. Although every woman was a daughter, and almost all became wives, not all became mothers. For the women involved, each stage in their lives thus became increasingly problematical, and for historians today each step opens up more opportunities for debate and controversy: indeed, *was* there a typical or "normal" pattern of existence?

2. Carol Gluck, *Japan's Modern Myths: Ideology in the Late Meiji Period* (Princeton: Princeton University Press, 1985), 182.

3. David W. Plath, *Work and Lifecourse in Japan* (Albany: State University of New York Press, 1983), 4,17.

DAUGHTERS

Parents appear to have made few distinctions between boys and girls in infancy. Soon after birth both sexes observed the rites of passage through which they became members of their communities. Parents marking the arrival of a child had a variety of ceremonies from which to choose. Those that they deemed important seem to have varied more according to their economic standing, the time period, the region, and the life course of the other family members than to the sex of the newborn child.

In the case of wealthy families, the ceremonies marking the birth of a child of either sex were often elaborate. Thus, two weeks after Fute was born in 1783 to the Nomura family from Hitachi province, her grandparents held a banquet for 120 people to celebrate her birth.[4] To announce the birth of Ai in 1835, the Sekiguchi family from Namamugi waited only seven days but also celebrated rather lavishly, sending trays containing sake, pickles, radishes, mushrooms, and fish to everyone in the neighborhood. A month later they took their newborn daughter to the family shrine, paid a fee of two hundred *mon*, and distributed balls of red beans and rice to the neighbors. The poor could hardly afford such elaborate celebrations for any of their children.

Gender distinctions became more apparent in naming customs, gift giving, and ritual observances as infants grew into young children. Names distinguished girls from boys soon after they were born: while Ai's brothers were given names derived from ancient military terms, the character *Ai* means "beloved." Her first bath was not an important event, whereas her older brother's was. At Ai's first New Year, thirty-three neighbors and five relatives sent money, and her maternal grandparents sent her a doll; her parents reciprocated with rice cakes and held a banquet for family members. More people attended her brother's first New Year, however, and fancier presents were sent to the neighbors. At their third birthday, most girls were allowed to receive a new hairdo; Ai's was ignored because it conflicted with her brother's fifth birthday. For her seventh birthday, which marked her formal introduction into her peer group, she donned the Japanese woman's wide sash (obi), and her family held a party for children in the neighborhood, giving them all balls of red beans and rice. Yet these festive foods were presented to the neighbors at all of her brother's birthdays, and his fifth birthday was marked with an elaborate celebration with his peers.[5]

4. Ibaraki kenshi hensan kinseishi dainibukai, *Ibaraki-ken shiryō: Kinsei shakai keizai hen*, vol. 1 (Mito-shi: Ibaraki-ken, 1971), 198.

5. In Namamugi, celebrations for the boy's fifth and the girl's seventh birthday centered on parties, while in Edo the child would be dressed in bright clothing and taken first

Although boys may have received more attention at the major milestones of their early childhood, the upbringing of both sexes in their early years, as far as we can tell, was otherwise fairly equal. The way parents indulged infant boys and girls worried educators. According to Yamana Bunsei, a peasant from Kii province, "husband and wife raise the child. During the day it receives its father's caresses and affection, at night it enjoys its mother's milk."[6] Like most writers on the subject of childrearing, Yamana saw no need to differentiate between young boys and girls. But parents had to be careful. Precepts still in the possession of the Matsushita family in the Ina valley warned, "If the parents indulge in their love for their children and allow them to grow up as they please without discipline, when the children reach adulthood they will hate to work, they will delight only in evil things, . . . they will run away, and they will end their lives as outlaws."[7] Believing that children are innately good but have to be molded by their environment into social beings, other writers stressed the importance of observational learning and good role models. Although the evidence is inconclusive, it appears that the first five years of any child's life were made as pleasant as family circumstances permitted. When the child showed sufficient maturity, he or she was assigned age- and gender-appropriate tasks and treated more strictly.[8]

A host of factors—geographical location, economic opportunity, and historical change—made a difference in how a girl became a young woman. Yet girls everywhere were expected to be obedient and gentle, discreet in speech, clean and tidy, and industrious in women's tasks. Their education in practical skills was acquired in needle shops (*ohariya*) and girls' rooms (*musume yado*), which paralleled young men's associations and like them were established village by village. Attendance was compulsory (though perhaps not for the rich and prestigious) from age fourteen to marriage, and in some regions a girl was not considered a respectable, marriageable adult until she had been a member for several years. During the day she would help with the work at home, but at night she would go to the *musume yado*, where she would learn handicrafts, talk with other girls and the older women

to visit a shrine and then to neighbors and relatives; see Hisaki Yukio and Mita Sayuri, "Jūkyūseiki zenpan Edo kinkō nōson ni okeru joshi kyōiku no ichi kenkyū," *Yokohama kokuritsu daigaku kyōiku kiyō*, no. 21 (November 1981): 72–77.

6. Yamana Bunsei, "Nōkakun," in *Kosodate no sho*, ed. Yamazumi Masami and Nakae Kazue, vol. 2 (Heibonsha, 1976), 205.

7. Ōshika sonshi hensan iinkai, *Ōshika sonshi*, vol. 1 (Nagano-ken, Ōshika-mura: Ōshika Sonshi Kankōkai, 1984), 778.

8. Kojima Hideo, "Japanese Concepts of Child Development from the Mid-seventeenth to the Mid-nineteenth Century," *International Journal of Behavioral Development*, 9, no. 3 (September 1986): 315–29.

who supervised work and play, and perhaps sleep, although some historians have argued that the chief purpose was to provide a place for common study. Needle shops, which were open only during the winter, likewise concentrated on the skills required for everyday life. A farm wife skilled at sewing and other crafts became the "little mother" to her students, teaching them sewing and perhaps flower arranging, tea ceremony, gift wrapping, and music.[9] In the girls' rooms and needle shops, poorer farm women learned from other women, an opportunity unavailable to women from wealthier farm households who were discouraged from mingling promiscuously with ordinary peasants.

In some areas of Japan by the early nineteenth century, families might invest enough money in their daughters' educations to allow them to attend temple schools, or *terakoya*. Although Ronald P. Dore estimated that about 43 percent of all boys and 10 percent of all girls attended school, there was considerable regional variation: the impoverished Tōhoku region educated far fewer children of either sex than the more flourishing areas around Edo and Kyoto.[10] It is difficult to determine how many girls had schooling; one rural school near Okayama, for example, as encouragement to female students, kept no records of their attendance, since the teachers assumed that girls would be embarrassed to have their names called in public.[11] Nevertheless, we can assume that most girls who attended school came from middle-level peasant families and above because schooling was expensive: costs included lunch, clothing, shoes, and rainwear, in addition to the loss of a valuable labor source.

Girls studied for two to five years—not enough time to learn difficult Chinese characters, even had they been thought capable of it, but long enough to absorb moral instruction. Popular texts, like *Jokun* (Precepts for women), were based on Chinese classics that taught the virtue of obedience. Transposed into the Japanese syllabary and supplemented with biographies of exemplary women, these texts provided practice in reading and writing that enforced the code of behavior

9. Higuchi Kiyoshi, *Nippon joseishi hakkutsu* (Fujin Gahōsha, 1979), 220; Shiga Tadashi, *Nihon joshi kyōikushi* (Tamagawa Daigaku Shuppanbu, 1960), 276–81; Hiratsuka Ekitoku, *Nihon kyōikushi* (Kyōiku Kaihatsu Kenkyūjo, 1985), 134–35.

10. Ronald P. Dore, *Education in Tokugawa Japan* (Berkeley and Los Angeles: University of California Press, 1965), 321; Herbert Passin, *Society and Education in Japan* (Tokyo: Kodansha International, 1965), 44–46.

11. Shibata Hajime, *Kinsei gōnō no gakumon to shisō* (Shinseisha, 1966), 200–201. See also Shibata Hajime, "Nōmin ishiki to nōson bunka no dentō," in *Chihō bunka no dentō to sōzō*, ed. Chihōshi kenkyū kyōgikai (Yūzankaku, 1976), 191–92. This school was established by the poor peasants (*komae byakushō*) in 1782 to improve public morals through study by men and women alike.

thought appropriate for women by their authors, male members of the ruling class.[12] *Miscellaneous Lessons on Filial Piety*, a textbook written by Sekiguchi Tōemon, a wealthy rural entrepreneur from Namamugi, admonished girls to "do their housework, look after their in-laws and their husbands, and teach their children accounting, reading, etiquette, and handwriting."[13] Tōemon taught whoever was willing to come to his house, including the daughters of his tenants. In the early Meiji period, such informal opportunities for schooling disappeared, and the public institutions that replaced them may well have made education less available to the daughters of the poor. In villages where the male elite was uninterested in improving public morals, poor women remained illiterate.

Wealthy families, however, devoted a surprising amount of income and energy to the upbringing of their daughters. The Suzuki family from Echigo demanded much more than the simple skills learned by ordinary peasants. Taka, born in 1777, went to a temple school to learn penmanship at age eight and, together with her niece Shin, then studied the Chinese classics, selections of Chinese poetry, and correspondence. Her sister Fuji, like some other wealthy rural women, became an accomplished poet, leaving over a thousand poems at her death. But it was her brother Bokushi's granddaughter, Suwa, who seems to have been the most diligently schooled. Suzuki Bokushi served as his granddaughter's private tutor, teaching her everything he taught his son. She began to read and write by the age of seven, and she was already helping to record transactions in the family pawnshop when she was ten years old. By his own account, Bokushi believed in teaching his children to value practical learning, especially the techniques of accounting, and not to waste their time studying the classics. In the case of his granddaughter, however, he gave instruction in painting and poetry writing as well. From a young age, Suwa was also expected to perform certain public roles, representing the family at important ceremonial occasions. At twelve she and her cousin Tsune spent several days kneeling while a priest read from esoteric Pure Land texts. At sixteen she represented her family at the funeral of her great-grandfather in a nearby village.[14]

12. Shiga, *Nihon joshi kyōikushi*, 282–88. In Tochigi prefecture, Usui Sei had 120 to 130 students, both boys and girls. She taught the boys reading and the girls reading, sewing, and painting.

13. Nagashima Atsuko, "Bakumatsu nōson josei no kōdō no jiyū to kaji rōdō," in *Ronshū kinsei joseishi*, ed. Kinsei joseishi kenkyūkai (Yoshikawa Kōbunkan, 1986), 149.

14. *Suzuki Bokushi no shiryō shū* (Niigata: Niigata-ken Kyōiku Iinkai, 1961), 7, 26, 46, 207. Bokushi is famous for his ethnographic description of life in the snow country, orig-

In the villages near Edo, wealthy peasant entrepreneurs bent on acquiring the best and most expensive education available for their daughters had them become servants in the homes of daimyō and *hatamoto* (high-ranking retainers in the shōgun). Here, at no small cost to their families, they learned feminine deportment: good posture and graceful movement, elegant and deferential language, appropriate dress and bodily care, and techniques of managing a household. They might even move from one post to another to learn different forms of etiquette. Although the girls received nominal wages, their parents had to provide all of their daily necessities, bedding, pillows, mirrors, shoes, pocket money, and clothing—three changes a year— as well as presents and fees for the go-betweens and the employers. In 1812, the Sekiguchi family had three daughters in service. The average cost per daughter was about 5 to 6 percent of the family's household budget, not including emergency expenses, preparations made before the girls went into service, or presents upon entering and leaving a household.[15] According to a guide to service in samurai households, the costs were evidently worth it, for "if a girl remains with her parents she will never know how to deal with misery. If she has not suffered, she will not make a good bride, so girls apprentice themselves to learn self-discipline."[16] Today the pampered daughters of the upper middle class still go to finishing schools—the most prestigious women's colleges.

For the daughters of wealthy peasants who lived too far from samurai households and the educational opportunities they offered, costly pilgrimages functioned more or less as finishing schools. The pilgrimage both strengthened faith and provided an occasion for sightseeing and observation; it was a learning experience that took young women outside their home communities and forced them to interact with strangers. Taken usually a year or so before marriage, the pilgrimage made it possible for teen-agers to travel with their friends and female relations largely apart from male society, except for one companion-escort. Suzuki Toyo, mother of Taka and Fuji, never forgot her pilgrimage to the Ise shrine in 1752 when she was fourteen, and even at seventy she could recite the names of every inn she stayed at en route. All of her daugh-

---

inally published in 1835; see Suzuki Bokushi, *Snow Country Tales: Life in the Other Japan*, trans. Jeffrey Hunter with Rose Lesser (Tokyo: John Weatherhill, 1986).

15. The Sekiguchi family spent much less than Shibue Io's father, who paid four hundred *ryō* a year to keep her in service at the Tōdō mansion; see Edwin McClellan, *Woman in the Crested Kimono: The Life of Shibue Io and Her Family, Drawn From Mori Ōgai's "Shibue Chūsai"* (New Haven, Conn.: Yale University Press, 1985), 23.

16. Hisaki and Mita, "Edo kinkō nōson ni okeru joshi kyōiku," 83–85, 90. See also Kawano Junichirō, "Kōshi nikki ni miru bakumatsu-ki nanushi no tsuma," *Tama no ayumi*, no. 27 (November, 1984), p. 21.

ters made the pilgrimage to Ise, at a cost of five to ten *ryō* apiece, paid by their family.[17]

Of course, not everyone could afford a pilgrimage. Helen Hardacre has argued that "by the end of the [Tokugawa] era, there was a popular explicit understanding that all persons, male or female, had a patriotic duty to make the pilgrimage [to Ise] at least once. In fact, the pilgrimage became associated with coming of age rites and acquired an air of custom and duty rather than individual faith."[18] Nevertheless, Shinjō Tsunezō has noted that long-distance pilgrimages were an option only for wealthy women, not for the poor. Even the so-called escape pilgrimages (*nuke-mairi*) were never so prevalent as to allow every Japanese the opportunity to pray at Ise.[19]

By the early nineteenth century, wealthy peasant families believed it necessary to make truly remarkable investments in their daughters' schooling. Girls learned more than their mothers had, and they learned it from strangers at enormous expense. Why did peasant families invest so much time and money in training female members who would leave upon marriage? Was it simply to increase their value in the marriage market? Was it to add luster to the family's reputation? Or did bonds of affection lead parents and grandparents to spend money on what would rationally seem to be a poor economic investment?

While the reasons differed according to family circumstances, there is no doubt that wealthy peasants enhanced their family's reputation by investing in their daughters. A well-dressed, well-traveled, well-educated, and well-mannered girl was a family asset. Perhaps for this reason, even ordinary peasants indulged their daughters whenever they could. In fact, in 1841 Sata, daughter of Sajiemon from the Tsukui district in Sagami, was arrested for wearing clothes above her station.[20]

The poor usually could not afford to lavish resources on daughters, however. When girls from ordinary peasant and tenant farm families

17. *Suzuki Bokushi no shiryō shū*, 12–13, 199.

18. Helen Hardacre, *Kurozumikyō and the New Religions of Japan* (Princeton: Princeton University Press, 1986), 40.

19. Shinjō Tsunezō, *Shaji sanshi no shakai keizai shiteki kenkyū* (Hanawa Shobō, 1964), 988–89; Shinjō Tsunezō, *Shaji to kōtsu* (Shibundō, 1960), 158. The *nuke mairi* was a pilgrimage taken without permission of one's parents or other people in positions of authority.

20. Sata was wearing a crepe-lined under-kimono, the collar of which had large dapples, a handwoven wadded silk over-kimono, a jeweled pongee silk jacket with an under-collar of black satin, and a handwoven satin obi faced with crepe. She carried a small crepe wrapper for holding tissue paper and in her hair were two ornamental hairpins, one silver and one Korean; see Kanagawa-ken kikaku chōsabu kenshi henshūshitsu, *Kanagawa kenshi shiryōhen 7: Kinsei*, vol. 4 (Yokohama: Zaidan Hōjin Kanagawa-ken Kōsaikai, 1975), 780.

began to leave their homes and villages in the latter half of the Tokugawa period, they went to work as indentured servants (*hōkōnin*). Studies of polder villages in central Japan show that three-fourths of the daughters of tenants in one village left home in search of work, and nearly two-thirds from another were sent into service outside the village at least once in their lifetimes.[21]

Sending a young unmarried girl out to work for the sake of the rest of the family could have dire consequences. Parents worried that their daughter might be mistreated or sold into prostitution. Worse yet, once freed from her parents' supervision she might run away to the city, causing them embarrassment and financial hardship.[22] Many girls left their families at the age of twelve to serve strangers, receiving as payment two changes of clothing and yearly salaries remitted to their fathers in amounts ranging from one to two and a half *ryō*—half the cost or less of a pilgrimage to Ise. Children even younger could often find work as nursemaids.[23]

Factors such as the spread of indentured servitude (which took girls out of the village), the growing emphasis on education, and the opportunity to go on pilgrimages conceivably influenced sexual practices preceding marriage, the choice of marriage partner, and the age of marriage, perhaps reducing the community's ability to control its women through the old custom of *yobai* (night visits). Here, too, the evidence frequently is contradictory or varies according to a family's socioeconomic standing. There is also a discrepancy between official samurai ideology and actual peasant behavior.

Official samurai teachings frowned on premarital sexual promiscuity. The "Instructions for Women" sent to peasant villages by the lord of Matsumoto in 1793 announced that "after a girl is ten, she should not

21. Hayami Akira, "The Myth of Primogeniture and Impartible Inheritance in Tokugawa Japan," *Journal of Family History* 8, no. 1 (1983): 9–11; Saito Osamu, "Population and the Peasant Family Economy in Proto-Industrial Japan," ibid., 41.

22. In 1808 the peasant Magohachi, from a village near Hachiōji, sued to have his daughter returned to him. He claimed to have been assured by middlemen that she was working as a maid for the lord of Owari. Only when he fell ill and wanted to see her did he discover that she had been sold to a brothel in Shin Yoshiwara. See Osada Kanako, "Kinsei nōson josei no ichidanmen," *Tama no ayumi*, no. 27 (November 1984): 33. Examples of women who ran away without fulfilling their contracts may be found in Ōguchi Yūjirō, "Gejo hōkō to nōsagyō: kōshi nikki yori mita," ibid., 11; and Sakurai Masanobu, ed., *Shin Nihon joseishi* (Yūhō Shoten, 1979), 255–56. In 1859, destitute parents from a village near Osaka agreed to sell their daughter Hisa, then eighteen, for seventy *ryō* (formally called an adoption) and promised not to object to anything her new family might require of her; see Dan Fenno Henderson, *Village "Contracts" in Tokugawa Japan* (Seattle: University of Washington Press, 1975), 149–59.

23. Osada Kanako, "Onna no kurashi," in *Edo to chihō bunka*, ed. Kimura Motoi, vol. 2 (Bun'ichi Sōgō Shuppan, 1978), 126; Shiga, *Nihon joshi kyōikushi*, 281.

mix with boys. After she is twelve or thirteen, she should not come near men. It is best to be modest and discreet."[24] Yet evidence gathered by folklorists and historians, while sketchy and not altogether in agreement, suggests that peasants generally ignored these precepts.[25]

Several historians believe that premarital sex among village girls and boys was common. In Louis Frederic's words, "Boys and girls could have amorous intrigues as it suited them and these did not necessarily lead to marriage."[26] Meiji ethnographer Yanagita Kunio further argued that the young men's associations of each village, and not parents, actually controlled the selection of marriage partners by means of night visits. The boys would spend evenings with members of the girls' groups, working, singing, and chatting before pairing off and sleeping together. They would then tell their parents whom they had chosen as a marriage partner.[27]

Evidence from other areas, however, suggests that sexual relations were permitted only after the couple became engaged. In the mountains of Shikoku, young men visited girls in villages as far distant as twenty to thirty kilometers, where they helped in paper making and tried to ingratiate themselves with the girls' families, but they were watched so closely that they seldom managed to become intimate. In other areas, both boys and girls were criticized only if they had sex with more than one partner.[28]

24. *Ōshika sonshi* 1:779.

25. Robert J. Smith and Ella Lury Wiswell, *The Women of Suye Mura* (Chicago: University of Chicago Press, 1982).

26. Louis Frederic, *Daily Life in Japan at the Time of the Samurai, 1185–1603* (New York: Praeger, 1972), 58. Richard Varner, "The Organized Peasant: The Wakamonogumi in the Edo Period," *Monumenta Nipponica* 32, no. 4 (1978): 480, asserts that a man had to have many short-term sexual encounters before he could think of marriage. Thomas Elsa Jones found that in Namase in Ibaraki prefecture not more than 2 percent of the unmarried young women were virgins, and all married women had had sexual relations before marriage; quoted in Robert J. Smith, "Making Village Women into 'Good Wives and Wise Mothers' in Prewar Japan," *Journal of Family History* 8, no. 3 (1983): 74. In the villages of Higashi Matsuyama in Saitama prefecture, the sons and daughters of ordinary peasants were comparatively free in their sexual experiences, and for them marriage had the meaning of settling down; see Shishi Hensanka, *Higashi Matsuyama–shi no rekishi*, vol. 2 (Saitama-ken, Higashi Matsuyama–shi: Higashi Matsuyama–shi, 1985), 366.

27. Hirayama Kazuhiko, "Seinendan to sonraku bunka," in *Chihō bunka no dentō to sōzō*, ed. Chihōshi kenkyū kyōgikai (Yūzankaku, 1976), 246–49. That this view is still prevalent may be seen in an article by Ueno Chizuko, "Genesis of the Urban Housewife," *Japan Quarterly* 34, no. 2 (April–June 1987): 133. It has been said that in some villages, these night visits were made to widows or women whose husbands were away from home.

28. Hirayama, "Seinendan to sonraku bunka," 247; Ikegawa chōshi henshū iinkai, *Ikegawa chōshi* (Kochi-ken, Agawa-gun, Ikegawa-chō: Ikegawa-chō Kyōiku Iinkai, 1973), 590–91; Ōshika sonshi hensan iinkai, *Ōshika sonshi*, vol. 3 (Nagano-ken, Ōshika-mura: Ōshika Sonshi Kankōkai, 1984), 309–12.

Diverse courtship practices make it difficult to determine in specific cases the exact age of marriage. In areas where night visits were customary, the line between the role of daughter and the role of wife became blurred. This is also true in cases where married daughters of the poor continued to work for their natal families until their mid to late twenties or even older before moving to their husband's home. In some instances, marriages were not officially registered until after a trial period of a year had elapsed.

For all these reasons, one cannot say with certainty what the average age of marriage was for couples in preindustrial Japan. Although Carl Mosk and Saito Osamu think that women married young, Hayami Akira has suggested that, when daughters of tenant farmers migrated in search of work, they tended to marry late.[29] Miyashita's study of villages near Osaka showed that the wealthier the family was, the earlier their womenfolk married.[30] In general, then, a woman's age at marriage, like so many other aspects of her life, appears to have been determined by the socioeconomic standing of her family.

WIVES AND DAUGHTERS-IN-LAW

Under ordinary circumstances, marriage marked the major metamorphosis in a woman's life. Not all women had either the desire or the opportunity for married life, however. For the daughters of wealthy peasants, spinsterhood or divorce made it possible to live for oneself, not for others. For the poor, however, life without a husband was a matter not of choice but of necessity. In one household in the Hino region in the early 1800s, a mature unmarried woman continued to live in her natal home with her married brother (the family heir) because her father demanded her labor.[31] Constrained by the family's

29. Carl Mosk, "Nuptiality in Meiji Japan," *Journal of Social History* 13, no. 1 (1980): 475, 484; Saito, "Population and the Peasant Family Economy," 34–35; Hayami, "Myth of Primogeniture," 9–11.

30. Miyashita Michiko, "Nōson ni okeru kazoku to kon'in," in *Nihon joseishi*, ed. Joseishi sōgō kenkyūkai, vol. 3: *Kinsei* (Tōkyō Daigaku Shuppansha, 1982), 47–50. See Susan Orpett Long, *Family Change and the Life Course of Japan*, Cornell East Asia Papers no. 44 (Ithaca, N.Y.: Cornell University, China-Japan Program, 1987), 28, for a summary of the literature. The three daughters of Sekiguchi Tōemon all married at age eighteen; see Nagashima, "Bakumatsu nōson josei no kōdō," 151. In Higashi Matsuyama from 1777 to 1877, age at marriage varied between fourteen and the early thirties; see *Higashi Matsuyama–shi no rekishi*, 364. Mori's detailed study of women in Taishidō found that the youngest woman married at fifteen, the eldest at thirty-eight; see Mori Yasuhiko, "Bakumatsu ishin-ki sonraku josei no life cycle no kenkyū," pt. 2, *Shiryōkan kenkyū kiyō*, no. 17 (September 1985): 159–61.

31. Itō Yoshikazu, "Shūmon ninbetsu-chō ni awareta kinsei Tama no josei," *Tama no ayumi*, no. 27 (November 1984): 9. In the novel *The Doctor's Wife* (Tokyo: Kodansha In-

need for income, such women missed their chance for a family of their own.

Demographers debate the extent to which women married outside their natal village and the age difference between husband and wife. Here again, historical processes, regional variation, and diverse economic circumstances produced a number of peasant strategies for adapting personal trajectories to the rhythm of the preindustrial agricultural order. Regarding the first question, Richard Varner has argued that "spouse selection was restricted to within the village, for the peasants were generally opposed to marriages contracted with outsiders." If the young men's associations were to be strong, they had to enforce endogamy.[32] Laurel Cornell, in contrast, has shown that in one area in central Japan, most women went as brides to villages other than their own.[33] Mori Yasuhiko's study of a village near Edo and Miyashita Michiko's study of a village near Osaka demonstrate that the circle from which marriage partners were chosen depended on the family's economic interests: wealthy and influential peasants sought partners from far away, while poor peasants made more informal connections within the village, connections perhaps arising out of the nights when the young men's associations and the girls' room were allowed to merge.[34]

Age differences between husband and wife also vary considerably. Near Osaka the difference was nearly ten years, a finding that supports the arguments of Cornell, among others.[35] In contrast, the average age difference between husband and wife in one village near Edo was five years, and in the villages of Sagamihara it was almost nil. Among the poor at the end of the Tokugawa period were couples where the wife was older.[36]

If the ideal marriage did not necessarily link couples who were close in age, it did link families of equal status and class. Detailed studies of marriage patterns show that rich married rich, poor married poor,

ternational, 1978), Ariyoshi Sawako describes two sisters who sacrifice themselves for their brother's education.

32. Varner, "Organized Peasant," 481.

33. L. L. Cornell, "Old Age Security and Fertility: A Microdemographic Analysis of the Difference Between Men's Motives and Women's," Working Paper Series WP #7 (Indiana University, Population Institute for Research and Training, 1987).

34. Mori Yasuhiko, "Shūmon-chō ni miru kinsei josei no life cycle," *Rekishi hyōron*, no. 431 (March 1986): 35. Mori suggested that most marriages took place between families living within ten kilometers of each other, the distance that could be traveled both ways in a day; see Mori, "Bakumatsu ishin-ki sonraku josei no life cycle (pt. 2)," 171–73. See also Miyashita, "Nōson ni okeru kazoku," 51.

35. Cornell, "Old Age Security"; Mosk, "Nuptiality in Meiji Japan," 475.

36. Mori, "Bakumatsu ishin-ki sonraku josei no life cycle (pt. 1)," 159–61; Osada, "Onna no kurashi," 123–24. In between 18 and 19 percent of the families in the new field villages of Sagamihara, the wives were older than their husbands.

sometimes kin married kin, and families with sidelines that contributed significantly to the household economy found brides skilled in business management.[37] Marriage thus tended to reinforce economic divisions and social distinctions.[38] This fact may have been advantageous to Japanese women, who, although typically entering their husband's family as strangers and needing to be trained in the ways of their new home, may not have been as intimidated and unprepared to assume new household responsibilities as Chinese women, who tended to marry into families of higher status than their own and to be overawed by the power and wealth of their in-laws.[39]

Futhermore, not all daughters left their natal families upon marriage. We have already seen instances of women from poor families staying with their parents even after marrying in order to help with the farm work. In cases where a family had sufficient property but lacked an heir, it readily adopted a son-in-law or even a daughter to carry on the lineage, for the continuity of the family name and the worship of family ancestors was deemed more important than the perpetuation of bloodlines. Of the marriages in the area around Higashi Matsuyama, 15 percent involved the groom moving into the bride's home, a figure compatible with the rates found in other areas.[40]

Adopting a son-in-law was often the first response to a crisis caused by the death of a family's males.[41] Male adoptions were far less likely to result in a permanent union than taking in a bride, perhaps because males were less willing to adapt themselves to the customs of a different household, or perhaps because any man willing to be adopted already had flaws in his character that prevented him from maintaining an independent livelihood. As Jane Bachnik has pointed out, an adopted husband faced many of the same difficulties as a young bride coming into a house. If he did not get along with his new family, he was the

37. Mori, "Shūmon-chō ni miru kinsei josei no life cycle," 34–36; Long, *Family Change and the Life Course*, 24. Kumagai Kumie, "Modernization and the Family in Japan," *Journal of Family History* 11, no. 4 (1986): 373, has asserted that people who married across status lines were ostracized and transferred to the eta class. In one village near Edo, however, four women married samurai during the early nineteenth century without penalty; see Mori Yasuhiko, "Bakumatsu ishin-ki sonraku josei no life cycle no kenkyū," pt. 1, *Shiryōkan kenkyū kiyō*, no. 16 (September 1984): 168–71, 181–85; and pt. 2, 192–99.

38. Miyashita, "Nōson ni okeru kazoku," 52–53.

39. Judith Stacey, *Patriarchy and Socialist Revolution in China* (Berkeley and Los Angeles: University of California Press, 1983), 42, repeats the conclusions developed by Martin C. Yang from his prewar fieldwork in China in A *Chinese Village* (New York: Columbia University Press, 1945), 107.

40. *Higashi Matsuyama–shi no rekishi*, 360–66; Miyashita, "Nōson ni okeru kazoku," 44.

41. Ōguchi Yūjirō, "Kinsei kōki ni okeru nōson kazoku no keitai," in Joseishi sōgō kenkyūkai (ed.), *Nihon joseishi* 3:209–10, 220.

one to leave, even if he had already become the titular head of the family.[42]

Records from other parts of Japan suggest that when a daughter stayed in the family, she functioned as the househead even though her husband might be given the formal title in official records. Hirose Chiyo from Eshima in Harima had an adopted husband, and she knew more about what was going on than he did. Like a modern career woman, she found herself holding down two jobs: domestic work and the family cloth-making business.[43] She clearly had authority to make decisions in both realms.

Although concern for the family's future was the usual reason for bringing a groom into the family, in wealthy peasant families more emotional factors might also play a role. The Suzuki family in Echigo, for example, obviously used adoption to secure the future of its women. The family head in the early nineteenth century, Bokushi, adopted an heir and a husband for his daughter Kuwa and jettisoned his son Yahachi, born to his fifth wife late in his life. Before Suwa, his deceased son's daughter, was twelve years old, she had received a number of marriage proposals, but her grandfather refused all of them. Then Kichisho, the third son from a prominent family a few villages away, was apprenticed to the Suzuki family. He helped out in the store and generally made himself agreeable. A year later he married Suwa when she was just sixteen years old, and a few months later Bokushi drew up a contract to establish Kichisho and Suwa as a branch family. Rather than allow his beloved granddaughter to suffer the vicissitudes of leaving the family, Bokushi sought to guarantee her future at the expense of the main house and his officially designated heir. Unlike her female relatives, Suwa had a chance to get to know her husband before the wedding. As Bokushi said, "He suits the family and harmonizes well. Since last spring we have drawn closer together."[44]

What did harmony mean in peasant families? Harmony was usually the bride's responsibility and meant that she had to refrain from quarreling with the members of her new household, do the work expected of her position, and conform to family customs. Yet according to the precepts written for peasants by samurai intellectuals and the peasants themselves, the basis for harmony lay in the connubial relations of the couple itself. "The married couple is the foundation of morality. A couple is basically lustful, and if they get along, they produce a righteous

42. Jane Bachnik, "Adoption," in *Kodansha Encyclopedia of Japan*, vol. 1 (Tokyo: Kodansha International, 1983), 14–15; Miyashita Michiko, "Kinsei ie ni okeru boshinzō," in *Bosei o tou*, ed. Wakita Haruko, vol. 2 (Jinbun Shoin, 1985), 28.

43. Miyashita, "Nōson ni okeru kazoku," 60–61.

44. *Suzuki Bokushi no shiryō shū*, 26, 52, 60, 61, 62, 63.

harmony, but if they do not, everything falls apart."[45] Thus affection and social necessity went hand in hand, and herein lay the possibility of intimate space for the married couple apart from the family. The author of *Nōyaku kikō* (Observations of agricultural practices) suggests as much in his account of an overnight stay at a farmhouse in the Kiso valley. The newlyweds in his host family went to bed early and, separated from the others by only a screen, began noisy lovemaking. "Outrageous," exclaimed the guest, whereupon the old woman of the family got angry. "Harmony between the husband and wife is the basis of prosperity for the descendants. Rather than not have this auspicious intimacy, I permit their coupling day and night. People who laugh at their passion are themselves outrageous. Get out!"[46]

Japanese peasant households may have maintained an intimate space for young couples even when no privacy existed because satisfaction of the couple's needs was deemed the necessary basis for the harmonious maintenance of family and household. In cases of arranged marriage, a woman met her husband for the first time on her wedding day; if they were to work together for the rest of their lives and perpetuate the family, it was important to come to an understanding of each other as quickly as possible.

The mediating factor here was lust, a passion validated in the practice of premarital night visits and evidently given greater latitude within the Japanese peasantry than the military aristocracy, or, for that matter, the French peasantry. In France, there was not only no physical space for privacy (as in Japan) but also no intimacy. The married couple did not feel the need to be isolated in a room, nor was bed the place for sex. For French peasants, Martine Segalen has argued, sexuality was "less fundamental than it is today. . . . the success of sexual relations was less important than the success of the farm." Therefore, "the notion of the couple has no great meaning in the nineteenth-century [French] rural family."[47] Ironically, while sexuality seems to have become more important for a successful marriage in contemporary France, the reverse is true for Japan, at least in urban areas.[48]

45. Shiga, *Nihon joshi kyōikushi*, 289.
46. Ibid., 292.
47. Martine Segalen, *Love and Power in the Peasant Family: Rural France in the Nineteenth Century*, trans. Sarah Matthews (Chicago: University of Chicago Press, 1983), 49–50, 132.
48. Samuel Coleman, "The Tempo of Family Formation," in *Work and Lifecourse in Japan*, ed. David W. Plath (Albany: State University of New York Press, 1983), 192, points out that the current Japanese marital life-style places little emphasis on sexuality. Compare contemporary mores to the enjoyment with which rural men and women discussed sex in Smith and Wiswell, *Women of Suye Mura*, 61–67.

In addition to preserving family harmony, married women also bore a responsibility comparable to their husband's for the family's economic survival. Unlike samurai women whose sideline industries, if any, were always subordinate to and separate from their husband's official duties, in peasant families women and men worked closely together. Generally women did the tedious and time-consuming work, whereas men did the work that was heavy and dangerous.[49] Agricultural development in the eighteenth century required peasant women to add handicrafts and field work to their domestic chores. According to a "Record of Customs" ("Fūzoku-chō") written in Aizu in 1807, "within the last thirty years women have taken hoes and dig in the fields alongside the men, . . . and a really strong woman can work harder than a man." Because women who worked in the fields dressed like men and left their hair unkempt, the sexes could not be told apart.[50]

Although women worked alongside men in the fields, they were not paid equal wages. "A Painstaking Record" ("Ryūryū shinkuroku"), written in Echigo in 1805, shows that in the eighteenth century women were paid half or less what men made, but by the nineteenth century their pay increased to two-thirds that of men. At rice transplanting time, when female labor was at a premium, they received almost a man's wages. Even when women did the same work as men, however, their pay was less, possibly because the supervisors were male. Household work, including cottage industries that produced a cash income, was always valued less than a man's work.[51] Despite regional differences and variations in the scale of the family enterprise, the opportunity for women to work alongside their men simply meant that they worked more.

Women from wealthy peasant families, which tended to have more members, did little or no field work, but they were expected to assist their husbands, supervise the maids, and look after the children and dependent siblings. They also produced cloth and worked in the family business. Suzuki Kayo, from a village near Tachikawa, spun silk and acted as a moneylender, even loaning sums of ten to twenty ryō to her own husband.[52] Suzuki Toyo, from Echigo, helped her husband in the crepe trade and spun thread whenever she had free time. When she was past sixty years old she made a piece of cloth and put the profits from

49. Nagashima Atsuko, "Kinsei josei no nōgyō rōdō ni okeru ichi," *Rekishi hyōron*, no. 383 (March 1982): 53.

50. Sugano Noriko, "Nōson josei no rōdō to seikatsu," in Joseishi Sōgō Kenkyūkai (ed.), *Nihon joseishi* 3:63, 92.

51. Ibid., 68, 69, 76, 80–81, 86–87.

52. Kawano, "Kōshi nikki ni miru bakumatsu-ki nanushi no tsuma," 21–22.

its sale into a revolving credit association (*tanomoshikō*). Her earnings of five *ryō*, which she turned over to her son, Bokushi, helped him pay for a new storehouse. "My old mother never used anything but the roughest of bedding," he wrote, "but since the most important thing for business is a storehouse, she wanted it to be a success."[53]

Committed to the prosperity of her family and her descendants, a farm woman expected no less than to work long, hard hours. But in the culture of marriage, a woman was more than a beast of burden; she was the helpmate of her husband. The precepts handed down from the ruling class may have emphasized a wife's subordination to her husband and his family, but among the peasantry women held a more equitable position, one that even enabled them to talk back to their husbands, as did Tomi from Sagamihara in 1846. Her husband came home one night to find her absent, and when she appeared and he asked her what she had been doing, she replied, "None of your business." They then started shouting so loudly that the neighbors interfered.[54] In a mountain village of central Japan, Ken, who had the reputation of being "strong-willed and selfish," brought suit to investigate the murder of her brother by her relatives and village officials.[55] Thus, although examples can surely be found of battered and downtrodden wives, there were also wives who might be educated and independent, women who expected to be treated with respect. As Suzuki Bokushi wrote in his family history, "My beloved mother had great integrity and quarreled with no one. Indeed, she never got angry but devoted herself to my father, and they worked together like the two wheels of a cart."[56]

Most marital relations were so unremarkable as to pass almost unnoticed in the records; only descriptions of problem marriages expose the assumptions regarding the expected role of wives. One example is the marriage of the wealthy Suzuki Bokushi in 1792 to a seventeen-year-old girl named Mine. Although good-natured and well liked, Mine had been separated from her mother while still young and grew up without any training in the art of household management. Her deficiencies in this area led the Suzuki family to return her and her baggage to her

53. *Suzuki Bokushi no shiryō shū*, 21, 290.

54. Osada, "Kinsei nōson josei no ichidanmen," 29. For arguments supporting the position that women talked back to their husbands, see Kumagai, "Modernization and the Family"; and Smith, "Making Village Women into 'Good Wives and Wise Mothers.'" In *Snow Country Tales*, Suzuki Bokushi asserted that "unless from time to time [a wife] speaks up in place of her husband, family affairs will be a mess" (50). Yajima Tetsu, a member of the samurai class, despised her husband, scolded him, and called him stupid; see McClellan, *Woman in the Crested Kimono*, 114.

55. Ozaki Yukinari, "Shinshū Saku-gun Makibuse-mura kenjo ikken," *Rekishi hyōron*, no. 419 (March 1985): 45–66.

56. *Suzuki Bokushi no shiryō shū*, 21.

Fig. 2.1. Suzuki Bokushi. Portrait of his mother and father. The mother has a book in front of her, while the father has writing brushes at his side. Hanging scroll. (Suzuki Bokushi Shiryōkan, Niigata pref.) (Photograph by author)

natal home, even though she had given birth to a boy within the first year of marriage.[57] We can surmise from this case that the ability to bear sons was not the only or even the most important test of a daughter-in-law's acceptability: skill in running a household, at least among wealthy families, was possibly even more important.

57. Ibid., 13, 14. In this region, a bride's dowry consisted of personal possessions; in contrast, one document from Echizen shows a dowry of twenty-eight *ryō*; see Henderson, *Village "Contracts,"* 141.

This conclusion is also suggested by the case of the Yoshimura family, a peasant entrepreneurial household from the Kinai region, which included the following statement in a marriage contract drawn up in 1749: "Because we are a farming family, the household enterprises are very important. Managing the household and instructing the maids is crucial for the bride. If she cannot do that, she will not suit our social standing."[58] For wealthy peasants (though probably not for the poor), the fertile womb was indeed less significant than the ability to maintain the family's fortune and reputation.

The question of divorce highlights further differences between samurai morals and customs on the one hand and diverse peasant practices on the other. According to samurai teachings, widows and divorcées were not expected to remarry. Tales of virtuous women recount how they committed suicide rather than accept a second marriage—behavior praised also in China, where chastity was the crucial expression of female fidelity.[59] Only a man, furthermore, could initiate divorce, either by copying a prescribed three and one-half lines telling his wife to leave, or simply by sending her baggage back to her natal home. A woman could do nothing to prevent the divorce or to protect her access to her children.

Peasant practices, in contrast, often ignored the norms of the military aristocracy. For one thing, the divorce rate, according to one study of village ledgers near Osaka, was at least 15 percent (possibly even higher, since these documents include only cases where the marriages had lasted over a year).[60] In addition, peasant women as well as men initiated divorce. The eldest daughter of Sekiguchi Toemon married and had three children before deciding to live alone in a temple. In 1857, a woman named Nobu, claiming "disharmony in the household," appealed to the local government office for a separation from her husband. He was a heavy drinker, and her father paid him one *ryō* to agree to a divorce.[61]

One way for a woman to get a divorce was to go to an "enkiridera," a

58. Miyashita, "Nōson ni okeru kazoku," 54–55. Miyashita, "Kinsei ie ni okeru bo-shinzō," 25, has also pointed out that most divorces occurred within the first three years of marriage, which suggests that the inability to have children was not the cause.

59. Stacey, *Patriarchy and Socialist Revolution*, 40.

60. Miyashita, "Nōson ni okeru kazoku," 49–50. In Taishidō, the average length of marriage in fifteen divorce cases was seven years, the shortest period being nine months, the longest eighteen years. Divorce was likely to take place earlier than it does in modern Japan (where most women who are divorced are in their forties and fifties); see Mori, "Bakumatsu ishin-ki sonraku josei no life cycle (pt. 2)," 164–70.

61. Osada, "Onna no kurashi," 111. A woman named Sato left her husband after six months of marriage in 1816 because she did not want to do agricultural work; see ibid., 115–16.

temple for severing marital connections. In the last half of the Tokugawa period, some two thousand women apparently sought the services of such a temple, Tōkeiji, in Kamakura.[62] According to custom, if a married woman entered this temple and performed its rites for three years, the bond between her and her husband was broken. For women in a hurry, Buddhist temple officials served as divorce brokers. They would go to the husband's village and camp at the headman's door until he summoned the husband and forced him to agree to an amicable divorce. In most cases, just the news that the temple officials were coming was enough to produce a letter of separation. For their services the officials charged a stiff ten ryō.[63] Mantokuji in Kōzuke was another refuge for women who wanted a divorce. According to its records, Iku found her husband's violent behavior so intolerable that she sought shelter there. She had to convince both her father and her husband to let her have a divorce, and the temple offered her the only haven from which to do so.[64]

For poor women, divorce was simply a matter of leaving the husband's home. Where children were concerned, however, it was more complicated. Wealthy peasants usually kept all the children born into the family: Suzuki Bokushi's three children were raised by him after he divorced their mothers. But when Riyo, wet nurse to his first son, left her husband because he had pawned her clothes, she took her daughter with her. Riyo had been married previously, then divorced, and then had lived with another man before this second marriage. Her third husband had turned out to be a thief who absconded to avoid being arrested. "She had worked diligently at her chores, and she had taken good care of our son. How regrettable her fate despite her admirable spirit," wrote Bokushi.[65] Scattered throughout the village records are references to women who took both sons and daughters with them at divorce.[66] While it was relatively easy for a poor woman to leave her husband, opportunities for a good remarriage, not to mention financial security for her children, were considerably more limited than those for a wealthier woman.

62. Kaneko Sachiko and Robert E. Morrell, "Sanctuary: Kamakura's Tōkeiji Convent," *Japanese Journal of Religious Studies* 10, nos. 2–3 (1983): 214.

63. Higuchi, *Nippon joseishi hakkutsu*, 223–24. Osada, "Onna no kurashi," 110–11, has evidence of two cases in which the temple forced men to agree to divorce. One couple had been so passionately in love that they had eloped, but later the wife changed her mind.

64. Sakurai (ed.), *Shin Nihon joseishi*, 262.

65. *Suzuki Bokushi no shiryō shū*, 15.

66. *Higashi Matsuyama-shi no rekishi*, 364–67; Mori, "Bakumatsu ishin-ki sonraku josei no life cycle (pt. 2)," 164–70. At the end of the Tokugawa period, even the wife of a samurai who left her husband might keep her children; see McClellan, *Woman in the Crested Kimono*, 101.

Peasants did remarry, however, sometimes as many as three or four times. Some members of peasant society practiced what can only be called serial marriage. As Alice Mabel Bacon, a traveler to Japan in the late nineteenth century, observed, "Until very recently, the marriage relation in Japan was by no means a permanent one. . . . It was not an unusual occurrence for a man to marry and divorce several wives in succession, and for a woman to marry well a second or even a third time." Even in the 1930s, the men and women of Suye divorced and remarried at a rate that astonished contemporary observers.[67]

Among peasants, remarriage did not necessarily incur the stigma for divorcées or widows that it did in samurai society. Even after Suzuki Bokushi's young bride Mine was sent back to her parents, the Suzukis maintained an interest in her affairs, and her son and granddaughter occasionally visited her. At her second marriage, Bokushi acted as her patron (*oyabun*). When that marriage soon ended in divorce, she married a third time, having two children before the family broke off relations. Finally she married a widower, the headman of a nearby village.[68] Years later Bokushi proposed to remarry her, but the negotiations came to naught.

Curiously, divorce and remarriage were especially prevalent among the wealthier families, who otherwise were most likely to imitate samurai customs. The wealthy married at a younger age than poorer peasants, a practice that may have led to greater marital discord. Then, too, they could afford to be more selective in arranging marriages for their children. In addition, wives had greater autonomy in matters of divorce and remarriage. Suzuki Bokushi's sister Taka married Matsunaga Hyōshi when she was nineteen years old, but less than a year later she was back home. Her husband explained that his father's stinginess had depressed the young bride and therefore Hyōshi had decided to send Taka back to her parents for a while. Two weeks later came the news that Hyōshi had smallpox and was calling for Taka. She returned to nurse him until he died. Having lost his sole heir, her father-in-law proposed that Taka succeed him, but she adamantly refused and eventually married into another family.[69] In another example from the Suzuki family, four years after the death of Bokushi's son his daughter-in-law Yasu married Miya Kizaemon, recently a widower and at least twenty years her senior. He died eighteen months later, and the family asked her to remain

67. Bacon, *Japanese Girls and Women*, 57; Smith and Wiswell, *Women of Suye Mura*, 130, 149, 151, 152, 168, and passim.

68. *Suzuki Bokushi no shiryō shū*, 22.

69. Ibid., 7, 16, 17, 20, 27, 45, 63, 81.

as the widow in the main house, promising that as soon as her mother-in-law died she would become the *oyabun* (family head). At that point she could make up her own mind whether to marry again or retire. Although she recognized her ethical obligation to remain as a matter of form, Yasu nevertheless refused and returned to the Suzuki family.[70]

Wealthy peasant women thus could manipulate their marital relations to protect their own best interests. In contrast to China, where authority over a widow's fate remained with her husband's family,[71] in Japan no customary provisions seem to have been made for the wife; consequently, both the natal and marital families of a well-connected Japanese woman might quarrel over her future. By taking advantage of the conflict, a woman could decide for herself which family offered the best conditions or play one off against the other, as Yasu did by moving back and forth. No one disapproved of Yasu's willfulness; indeed, her third husband, who waited four years for her, was an extremely prestigious figure in local affairs.

While peasants apparently set little store by chastity, illicit affairs and adultery presented a more serious threat to the fabric of community life. In 1821 Suzuki Bokushi heard that the Yawata widow, after having committed adultery with her adopted grandson, had given birth to a boy. A relative agreed to take the baby and find a wet nurse for him, but even so her situation became so difficult that she ran away. After she had apologized to her natal family and her in-laws, she was allowed to return to the Yawata house in the middle of the night.[72] Despite the shame she brought on her family, however, she does not appear to have been punished in any way. Indeed, the type of scandals recorded by Bokushi were still rocking villages one hundred years later, according to the accounts in *The Women of Suye Mura*.[73] What is remarkable is the relative lenience with which they were treated, given the standards of behavior idealized by the samurai and, later on, by government bureaucrats.

In the records of villages in the Sagamihara region, Osada Kanako found seven incidents concerning adultery. In one, the husband, who was the grandson and heir of a village official, killed his wife and her lover, a servant, when he caught them together. Perhaps it was the difference in status that propelled him to this act, or perhaps

70. Ibid., 26, 28, 35, 37, 40, 42. Out of fifty-seven marriages in Taishidō, five women returned to their natal family at the death of their husband; see Mori, "Bakumatsu ishin-ki sonraku josei no life cycle (pt. 2)," 170.

71. Stacey, *Patriarchy and Socialist Revolution*, 34.

72. *Suzuki Bokushi no shiryō shū*, 42, 49, 56.

73. Smith and Wiswell, *Women of Suye Mura*, 111–15, 186, 190, and passim.

he was simply short-tempered. In the other instances, even when the women had eloped with their lovers they were forgiven by their husbands and neighbors upon their return. The original marriage brokers for one marriage wanted the wife to be divorced because she had committed adultery, but her husband replied that as far as he was concerned, that was only a rumor.[74] Once a woman gave up her unlicensed sexuality and returned to her social role as a wife, not only her family but the community as well seems to have been willing to accept her back.

On another plane, scandals point to the ambivalence that characterizes sexuality and the feminine personality in rural society generally, and the fear in which these are held. In Japan, as in France, the concept of woman exerted a twofold power over both household and husband. At the material level, a woman maintained the family reputation and managed everyday affairs, but at a symbolic level she was a sorceress, and her body was seen to be the site of taboos that, if broken, brought misfortune on the farm and its inhabitants.[75] Thus, although the Shintō emphasis on fertility gave special value to women and religious significance to their labor in transplanting rice, Shintō ideas of pollution required menstruating women to eat and sleep apart from their families.[76]

To circumscribe the power of mature female sexuality, men tried to direct it either to the confines of the red light district or to marriage. In 1846, the men of Inoshikakata village (now part of Komae city) made a public appeal to the intendant concerning the woman Rika, who had appeared six or seven years earlier. "She associates with gamblers and the young men of the village," they complained, "and she has made herself quite popular with them. At her drinking parties, she meddles in all sorts of proposals. . . . She is leading the youth of this village astray, and this will cause the village to decline. She has used evil tricks to ingratiate herself with village officials, and no one will stand up to her openly. We think she should be expelled."[77] The men behind this appeal clearly saw themselves as victims. Here, and in the scandal of the widow recounted by Suzuki Bokushi, the implication is that sexual misconduct was the woman's fault: she was the seductress and the instigator in any affair. This assumption that the woman is always guilty is not unique to Japanese society, and as the gossip repeated in *The Women of Suye Mura* indicates, even women themselves often blamed the female in illicit affairs.

74. Osada, "Kinsei nōson josei no ichidanmen," 31, 32; Osada, "Onna no kurashi," 100–108.

75. Segalen, *Love and Power in the Peasant Family*, 116, 125–26.

76. Segawa Kyoko, "Menstrual Taboos Imposed upon Women," in *Studies in Japanese Folklore*, ed. Richard M. Dorson (Bloomington: Indiana University Press, 1963).

77. Osada, "Kinsei nōson josei no ichidanmen," 29.

MOTHERS

Of the three stages in the lives of rural women, that of mother was the most problematical. The fundamental responsibility of the respectable married woman was to produce heirs who would carry on the family line (and care for her in her old age). Yet not all women were able to produce children. Moreover, every mother would probably experience the loss of at least one child. As Yamana Bunsei wrote, "When a wife first realizes she is pregnant, she worries day and night whether she will have a safe birth. Nothing can be done if the birth is difficult."[78] In one village, over 20 percent of children under age five died, and only 64 percent survived to maturity.[79] The Suzuki family history from Echigo shows that even the wealthy were plagued with miscarriages, stillbirths, and infant deaths. Of Suzuki Bokushi's six wives, only three managed to bear children.[80]

Relations between parents and children were presumably governed by Confucian precepts of filial piety, which emphasized the obligatory nature of human relations rather than the natural bonds of affection that exist between parent and child. A mother's love was criticized, in fact, because it led to indulged and spoiled children, and a son who allowed his affection for his mother to grow beyond the bounds of obligation risked putting himself in her power.[81] In *The Doctor's Wife*, a novel by Ariyoshi Sawako, Seishu's mother insists that she come before his wife, saying, "I am the mother who gave birth to you, so I, more than anyone else, understand what you want to accomplish."[82]

Genuine affection between mother and son is amply documented in our sources on wealthy households. The following three examples are typical. Maejima Zengorō, from the Ina valley, learned both poetry and nativism (*kokugaku*) from his mother, Mino, and for his nom de plume,

78. Yamana, "Nōkakun," 205. When Hirose Tansō (1782–1856) was still in his mother's womb, his grandmother made a pilgrimage through all the eighty-eight temples on the Shikoku circuit to pray for her son's bride's safe birth; see Tsukamoto Manabu, *Chihō bunjin* (Kyōikusha, 1977), 144. The Katō family from a village in Owari preserved two documents concerning childbirth: one described the methods for changing a child's sex to that of a boy; the other described how to have a safe birth; see Hayashi Hideo, "Katō-ke monjo mokuroku," *Shien* 18, no. 1 (June 1957): 92.

79. Mori, "Bakumatsu ishin-ki sonraku josei no life cycle (pt. 2)," 161–62. These figures closely correspond to the findings of Hayami, who has shown that one in three children did not reach adulthood; see "Myth of Primogeniture," 21. See also Miyashita, "Kinsei ie ni okeru boshinzō," 24; and Ann Bowman Jannetta, *Epidemics and Mortality in Early Modern Japan* (Princeton: Princeton University Press, 1987), 205.

80. *Suzuki Bokushi no shiryō shū*, 4, 42, 46, 54, 60, 62; Takahashi Minoru, *Hokuetsu seppu no shisō* (Niigata-shi: Etsu Shobō, 1981), 242. Bokushi divorced all three of his children's mothers.

81. Miyashita, "Kinsei ie ni okeru boshinzō," 25, 36–40.

82. Ariyoshi, *Doctor's Wife*, 105.

Seibi, he used the first character of her name. (Mi and Bi are both readings of the Chinese character for beauty.) Together they chose eight
views of Ōshika, modeled after the famous eight views of Ōmi, for him
to paint; after she wrote a poem on each picture, he capped it with his
own verse. In the second case, Sekiguchi Tōemon, from a village near
Yokohama, was so generous with allowances and travel expenses that
his mother, Rie, was able to start her own moneylending business
(charging even her son interest on his loans). His wife received considerably less attention.[83] The third example is Suzuki Heikurō, who
grieved deeply for his mother and eulogized her as follows: "Anyone
would make some claim about his good fortune to have had such a
mother, and nothing can be compared to the separation of parent and
child. At my sick mother's pillow, I pass the fullness of days, feeling how
inadequately I have repaid her."[84] Heikurō fancied himself a poet, and
the sorrow he expressed might be attributed to an excess of poetic hy-
perbole. Yet his eulogy, like our other examples, surely suggests that a
close relationship between mother and son was one of the central facts
of life for any family.

Once a mother of a wealthy peasant family became a mother-in-law,
she had the leisure to indulge in travel. For rural women, freedom and
responsibility were not compatible: only after they had surrendered
their authority to their daughters-in-law could they go where they
pleased. Suzuki Toyo chose to make a pilgrimage to the Chichibu
shrine, then continued on to see the beautiful beaches of Enoshima, the
medieval city of Kamakura, and the plays and spectacles of Edo. She
visited the shogunal shrine at Nikkō, and she went to see the sights of
Niigata with in-laws and friends. At age seventy-two, she completed her
seventh pilgrimage to the Zenkōji, a famous temple jointly run by the
Pure Land and Tendai Buddhist sects in Nagano city and a popular
destination for women pilgrims. Sekiguchi Rie went to temples, to hot
springs, and to Edo to visit her granddaughters for a total of 410 trips
before her death. Her daughter-in-law too, after becoming a mother-in-
law, began to travel, making 238 trips, including visits to her natal home,
a tradition that her son's wife continued.[85]

Even ordinary peasants encouraged their mothers to travel. Fuzō's
old mother from Sagamihara and four of her cronies made a pilgrimage

    83. *Ōshika sonshi* 3:115–16; Nagashima, "Bakumatsu nōson josei no kōdō," 154, 165.
    84. Kawano, "Kōshi nikki ni miru bakumatsu-ki nanushi no tsuma," 20.
    85. *Suzuki Bokushi no shiryō shū*, 14, 22, 29, 81; Nagashima, "Bakumatsu nōson josei no
kōdō," 157–61, 168. By the 1820s and 1830s, some women travelers wrote diaries of their
experiences. Kutsukake Naka from Shinano even managed to publish her record in 1817,
at the age of sixty-nine. See Maeda Yoshi, "Tabi nikki no josei," in *Jinbutsu Nihon no joseishi*,
vol. 6: *Nikki ni tsuzuru aikan*, ed. Enchi Fumiko (Shūeisha, 1977), 211–44.

to Chichibu in 1843, where they managed to visit twenty-one temples in two days, climbing up and down stairs and walking the whole way. They went to Zenkōji, then back to Nikkō, before returning home after a thirty-one-day trip. In the precincts of a shrine in Kamikarako, Saitama prefecture, is a stone monument commemorating a pilgrimage made by sixteen women up Mt. Fuji in 1860—despite the fact that Mt. Fuji was forbidden to women.[86] Sons allowed these ventures out of respect for their mothers' piety, but also perhaps because their absence eased strains within the family.

Rural women traveled for three reasons: to go on pilgrimage and see foreign sights, to visit relatives, and to take the waters at hot springs. These activities were also done by men, and they tied both sexes into the local network of interpersonal relations, entertainments, leisure pastimes, and the national culture. Since it was usually women who left their natal families at marriage, they were more likely to travel to see their parents and siblings, but they could expect reciprocal visits and inquiries after their health. Suzuki Bokushi, for example, maintained regular contact with his sisters, Kono and Fuji. Unlike China, where once a daughter left home she was gone for good, Japanese daughters preserved ties to their kin, celebrating their births and mourning their deaths.[87]

Whereas the key to old-age security for a man was his wife, women were dependent instead on their children,[88] largely because most husbands died first, leaving the women, if they were lucky, with a grown son to take over the family enterprise. In some areas of Japan, when a man with adult sons formally retired from the family headship at fifty to sixty years of age, his wife too relinquished her authority in the household—though in other areas (Dewa, for example) men continued in their position as family head until they died. In one village near Edo, succession took place at the death of the househead 53 percent of the time, and at his retirement 19 percent of the time. As Hayami Akira has pointed out, "Peasants arranged inheritance flexibly, without any particular principles in mind, and as the occasion demanded."[89] For the wife

86. Osada, "Kinsei nōson josei no ichidanmen," 32; *Higashi Matsuyama–shi no rekishi*, 457.

87. Ellen R. Judd suggests that, especially in modern times and in certain regions of China, women have been able to maintain close ties with their natal families; see *"Niangjia*: Chinese Women and Their Natal Families," *Journal of Asian Studies* 48, no. 3 (August 1989): 525–544.

88. Cornell, "Old Age Security." Mori's study of Taishidō shows that on the average women spent thirty-six years with their husbands and seventeen years as widows; see "Bakumatsu ishin-ki sonraku josei no life cycle (pt. 2)," 162–64, 170, 186–89. Henderson, *Village "Contracts,"* 137–40, has translated two documents that show agreements made to provide allowances to widows.

89. Laurel L. Cornell, "Retirement, Inheritance, and Intergenerational Conflict in Pre-industrial Japan," *Journal of Family History* 8, no. 1 (1983): 55–69; Ōguchi, "Kinsei kōki ni

and mother who had to adapt her "personal trajectory and tempo of biographical events" to the family's life course, the quality of her life after the death of her husband depended on her children's character.

Peasant and merchant families followed radically different strategies in trying to maintain themselves when a man died, disappeared, or was disinherited before his children were fully grown. William Hauser found that in Osaka, women seldom became household heads after 1730: the desire to restrict the scale of licensed households and their ability to set up branch shops may well have outweighed the imperative of family continuity.[90] Among peasant families, in contrast, the rate for female succession increased in the early nineteenth century, when difficult economic times required simply mature adult leadership, whether male or female.

Nevertheless rates of female succession varied according to class and region. Even if her children were infants, a mother was less likely to be registered as household head in a wealthy family than in a poor one. Ōguchi Yūjirō has found that the likelihood of women being entered on the registers as family heads was least in the area around Edo, somewhat greater in Northern Japan, and greatest in the region near Osaka.[91] In Higashideto, near Osaka, five women became heads of household even though their sons were over eighteen. In one village along the lower reaches of the Tama river, daughters occasionally took over the family even though an adult brother was still living at home. Most female househeads served only until their sons reached the age of seventeen or eighteen, but some continued to play a role in public affairs until their deaths.[92]

When women did become heads of household, their customary role varied from region to region. When one woman in Fuchinobe tried to attend an important meeting, she was turned back with the retort, "We need people with balls to handle this affair." In the Tama region, widows signed village documents along with the men, but they were exempted from the corvée duties assessed by the ruling authorities. In Ogatayama village (now part of Tsuru city), a recent search through farmhouse documents turned up the signed ballots used for voting for village officials. Among the signatures were those of six women, which

okeru nōson," 202; Mori, "Bakumatsu ishin-ki sonraku josei no life cycle (pt. 2)," 174–75; Hayami, "Myth of Primogeniture," 23.

90. William B. Hauser, "Why So Few?: Women Household Heads in Ōsaka Chōnin Families," *Journal of Family History* 11, no. 4 (1986): 349–50.

91. Ōguchi, "Kinsei kōki ni okeru nōson," 194–225.

92. Miyashita, "Kinsei ie ni okeru boshinzō," 26–28; Symposium, "Zenkindai no kazoku o megutte," *Rekishi hyōron*, no. 419 (March 1985): 11.

shows that they had the right to vote before the Meiji period.[93] The granting of this right was probably a pragmatic response to family exigencies, but it also demonstrates that women might play what was normally a man's role depending on their structural position within the family. Only in the Meiji period did gender definitions become so strict as to preclude flexibility in role adaptation.

The quality of a woman's declining years depended on her family's composition and economic status. According to Suzuki Bokushi, his mother, Toyo, became quite pious in her old age. When her son was not reading military tales to her, she concentrated her efforts on being reborn in the Pure Land of Amida. In her final preparations for death she had a white kimono sewn for her funeral, paid the priest at Chōonji two hundred *mon* to write sutras, and gave her son her last testament in a sealed bag to be opened after her death.[94] We can assume that Toyo had a good life. Her sole surviving son remained devoted to her, her family prospered, she had many relatives, friends, and neighbors with whom she could visit, she indulged in her hobbies, and she ordered her existence to its end. Other women were not so fortunate. Penniless and alone, Ken died at the age of seventy-six, and then it became the community's responsibility to erect a gravestone for her.[95]

To die without family and be buried alone was a terrible fate in Tokugawa Japan. For this reason it was important to have descendants who would guarantee that the funeral was performed properly and that memorial services were held on a regular basis. Suzuki Bokushi carefully recorded the death anniversaries and memorial services held for his sisters and his ancestors, and he made sure that his little sister Taka, who died without heirs, would not be forgotten after her death. After his third wife, Uta, died, he had a stone pagoda carved in her memory, and he set aside fields and paddies as an endowment for her memorial services, for she too died without direct descendants. "These fields are more important than words can express," he wrote. "They represent the family's prayers."[96] Memorial services were held for women as well as men, whether mothers, wives, or sisters. The requirements of the peasant family enterprise exploited all members of the household, but it also guaranteed them a secure future in the hereafter. Women who left their natal home for that of a stranger were indeed at a disadvantage, but

93. Osada, "Onna no kurashi," 129; Itō, "Shūmon ninbetsu-chō ni awareta kinsei Tama no josei," 8–9; Kawanabe Sadao, "Hakken sareta Edo jidai no tōhyō yōshi," *Tsuru shishi hensan tayori*, no. 3 (August 1984): 6.

94. *Suzuki Bokushi no shiryō shū*, 30.

95. Ozaki, "Shinshū Saku-gun Makibase-mura kenjo ikken," 65–66.

96. *Suzuki Bokushi no shiryō shū*, 50, 53, 54, 62, 83.

at least in wealthy families they were ultimately included in the rituals performed for the ancestors.

CONCLUSION

Given the diversity of local practices in Tokugawa Japan, it is difficult to draw firm conclusions about the typical role of women. The last half of the Tokugawa period brought changes into the preindustrial agricultural order that had a profound impact on women's lives. Their exposure to education and travel, their work experiences both before and during marriage, and their sexual history constitute social data that defy any narrowly focused assumptions. Although the survival of all family members depended on the cooperation and harmony of husband and wife, mother and son, the specific strategies followed by each family and, indeed, the constitution of the family itself depended on access to economic resources and the possibilities contained by each region.

Thus, two seemingly contradictory views of peasant women that currently exist in Japanese research may merely represent two ends of the broad spectrum of peasant family practices shaped by economic circumstance, historical processes, regional differences, and variations in household composition. In one view, Inoue Kiyoshi argues that women were oppressed by the patriarchal system and dominated by their mothers-in-law. In the other view, Ienaga Saburo claims that female labor played such a crucial role in household finances that women were more important than their husbands in maintaining the family over time.[97] To a certain extent, both views are correct. Women in wealthy families were more likely to experience the weight of family traditions epitomized by the mother-in-law's authority; while this was less true for women in poor families, they had to struggle for a livelihood.

As our data show, however, even these generalizations do not always hold true. If there is any one conclusion we can draw from our diverse research findings, therefore, it is this: survival in preindustrial society required that rural women's roles be flexible, and this flexibility led to much more variation in social relationships between the sexes than the leaders of the Meiji state in the late nineteenth century either expected or condoned.

97. Miyashita, "Nōson ni okeru kazoku," 31–32.

THREE

The Deaths of Old Women: Folklore and Differential Mortality in Nineteenth-Century Japan

Laurel L. Cornell

One of the most startling stories in Japanese literature is the folktale "Obasuteyama" (literally, "Old Woman–Abandoning Mountain").[1] In this legend, a peasant, adhering to local custom, carries his aged mother up the mountain to abandon her to die. As they go along the trail through the wilderness, he notices her breaking off twigs from the surrounding bushes. When he asks her why, she replies: "So you will not get lost on your way home." Overwhelmed by gratitude and shocked by the magnitude of the offense he was about to commit, the son defies custom, turns around, returns home, and vows to keep his mother until

I am indebted to Gail Lee Bernstein, John D. Campbell, Griffith Feeney, Sumiko Fujimi, Kanji Masaoka, Tatsuo Sakai, G. William Skinner, and Robert J. Smith for their very helpful comments on this paper. Of course, its preparation would have been impossible without the generous assistance of Akira Hayami, who not only provided the documents themselves but who, for more than a decade, has encouraged and supported me in my investigation of them. An earlier version was presented at the Second Workshop of the Nobi Regional Project, Sangyō-Bōeki-Kaikan, Nagoya, Japan, January 6–10, 1988, sponsored by the U.S.-Japan Cooperative Program in the Humanities and Social Sciences, jointly operated by the Japan Society for the Promotion of Science and the ACLS-SSRC Joint Committee on Japanese Studies, and published as "Yome, shutome, obasuteyama" in *Tokugawa shakai kara no tenbō*, ed. Hayami Akira, Saitō Osamu, and Sugiyama Shin'ya (Dōbunkan, 1989).

1. This tale is known variously as "Obasuteyama" and "Ubasuteyama"; see Richard Dorson, *Four Legends of Japan* (Rutland, Vt.: Charles E. Tuttle, 1962), 222–25; and *Kodansha Encyclopedia of Japan*, vol. 6 (1983), s.v. "*obasute*," "Obasuteyama." Following the standard Japanese-language dictionary *Kojien* (s.v. "*obasute*"), I will use "Obasuteyama."

her natural death. Her accumulated wisdom later turns out to be invaluable, for it saves the village from disaster.[2]

Is this folktale a true representation of elderly women in Japan in the
Tokugawa period? Scholars consistently deny that geronticide was ever
a regular feature of Japanese society.[3] The few societies in which geronticide is documented are commonly forager societies in hostile environments with climates much less benign than that of the Japanese
archipelago.[4] In addition, the stem-household (*ie*) family system characteristic of Japan in the preindustrial period would not seem to put
elderly women at special risk. When we examine evidence from the
Tokugawa and early Meiji periods, we find that geronticide engendered
far less concern than did abortion and infanticide, whether with the rulers of the country or with Western observers. Finally, a similar story is
reported from other East Asian sources.[5]

Nevertheless, the tale is widely distributed in Japan, with versions
arising throughout history—for instance, in the twelfth-century com-
pendium *Konjaku monogatari* and in a fifteenth-century Nō play by
Zeami.[6] It is represented in the name of a mountain in Nagano prefecture, Obasuteyama; Fukazawa based his prize-winning story "Na-
rayamabushiko" (1957) on the legend, and this in turn has been made
into two well-known and popular movies, one by Kinoshita (1958),
the second by Imamura (1983); and Western readers will have encountered it both in Sugimoto's classic *Daughter of the Samurai*[7] and
as a selection in one of the principal readers for foreigners learning Japanese.[8] The perpetrator in these tales is sometimes the son,
sometimes the daughter-in-law, and sometimes village custom generally. Finally, as one scholar points out, a society that definitely was not
benign toward its infants could have been equally cruel to its elderly as
well.[9]

Whether the tale of Obasuteyama reflects actual behavior or not, it
paints a clear picture of elderly women as useless and costly members of

2. *Kodansha Encyclopedia of Japan*, s.v. "*obasute*"; and Ito Sei, "On 'The Oak Mountain
Song,' " *Japan Quarterly* 4, no. 2 (1957): 235.

3. *Kodansha Encyclopedia of Japan*, s.v. "*obasute*."

4. Charlotte C. O'Kelley and Larry S. Carney, *Women and Men in Society*, 2d ed. (Bel-
mont, Calif.: Wadsworth, 1986).

5. Dorson, *Four Legends of Japan*, 223.

6. *Kodansha Encyclopedia of Japan*, s.v. "*obasute*."

7. Etsu Sugimoto, *A Daughter of the Samurai* (New York: Doubleday, Doran, 1934),
101–4.

8. Howard Hibbett and Gen Itasaka, *Modern Japanese: A Basic Reader*, 2nd ed., vol. 2
(Cambridge, Mass.: Harvard University Press, 1967), 80–82.

9. Conrad Totman, "Tokugawa Peasants: Win, Lose, or Draw?" *Monumenta Nipponica*
4 (1986): 457–76.

traditional Japanese society. Given the dearth of other pictures of such women, it thus provides a standpoint from which to begin.

In addition, asking whether gcronticide existed in Tokugawa Japan enables us to contribute a new perspective to the demographic literature on differential mortality. The current consensus is that, in the absence of discrimination, female mortality rates at every age except the reproductive years should be lower than male rates at the same age: that is, women are intrinsically more likely than men to survive from one year to the next.[10] Yet data from a number of areas of the world demonstrate that this is not always the case. Females, especially infants and children, die at a greater rate than do males, sometimes because of deliberate killing, as in female infanticide, but more often because of unconscious or culturally based resource deprivation. Most of this literature, however, deals with differential female mortality in infancy and childhood, and it is only recently that scholars have begun to examine how relationships within the family or household influence mortality rates.[11] Thus, an inquiry into the question of whether elderly women were deliberately killed and whether the likelihood of their death varied with the composition of the households in which they lived will shed new light on a long-standing demographic issue.

DATA AND METHODS

The ideal way to examine the issue of geronticide would be to assemble an amalgam of evidence from a variety of sources. One would like to have contemporary discussions of the ideology that motivates such behavior, a depiction of the overall demographic patterns that would result if such behavior were employed, and evidence from individuals who had actually engaged in it. Together these sources would demonstrate conclusively that the relatively disfavored behavior under consideration was actually carried out.

Unfortunately, such multifaceted evidence is not available; we have only behavioral data from one area. But fortunately, that information is of very high quality: its source is the population registers (shūmon aratamechō) that were compiled annually by headmen in villages throughout Japan from sometime in the mid-1600s through 1872. These record a considerable amount of detail, including the name, age, sex, relationship to household head, and change of residence for each resident of a

10. C. A. Nathanson, "Sex Differences in Mortality," *Annual Review of Sociology* 11 (1984): 191–213.

11. Monica Das Gupta, "Selective Discrimination Against Female Children in Rural Punjab, India," *Population and Development Review* 13 (1987): 77–100.

given village or city ward. Our strategy in using this information has two parts: (1) to model the demographic patterns we would expect to find if the practice of female geronticide were being carried out; and (2) to determine whether actual demographic patterns conform to these expectations.

The women whose lives are examined here are the fifty-six from the birth cohort of 1751–1775[12] who survived to age sixty in the rural village of Yokouchi, Shinano province, located in an intermountain valley in central Japan about a five-day walk from Edo to the southeast and Kyoto and Osaka to the southwest.[13] To circumvent the possibility that ages were reported incorrectly, I have assigned these women a year and month of birth based on their age at first entry, thus creating an age that remains consistent until they die.[14] For the purpose of analysis, women are assumed to enter old age when they reach age sixty (by Western reckoning). This figure is chosen principally for convenience, though men who are household heads do in fact retire almost precisely at this age.[15]

The methods used involve demographic measures of mortality that describe what proportion of the population survives from one year to the next—or from the beginning of the period, age sixty, to its end, age ninety, by which time all the women are dead. I thus include graphs of

12. These women reached old age between 1811 and 1835, so one may argue that their experience is too late to be representative of "traditional" Japan. However, although the definition of "traditional" Japan fluctuates widely from author to author, it is most commonly located in the Tokugawa period. Differential mortality is characteristic not only of less developed societies, but characterizes industrial ones as well. See Evelyn Kitagawa, "Socioeconomic Differences in the U.S. and Some Implications for Population Policy," in *Demographic and Social Aspects of Population Growth*, vol. 1 (Washington, D.C.: Commission on Population Growth and the American Future, 1972), 89–110; and R. T. Ravenholt, "Addiction Mortality in the United States, 1980: Tobacco, Alcohol, and Other Substances," *Population and Development Review* 10 (1984): 697–724.

13. Six women are omitted from the analysis at various times: four women who have a daughter rather than a daughter-in-law as the woman in the junior generation, and two anomalous nonlineal women described later. If these groups were included here, the contrasts would be even sharper.

14. For further discussion of these data, see Laurel Cornell and Akira Hayami, "The *Shūmon Aratame Chō*: Japan's Population Registers," *Journal of Family History* 11, no. 4 (1986): 311–28. Other analyses may be found in Hayami Akira, *Kinsei nōson no rekishi jinkōgakuteki kenkyū* (The historical demography of early-modern Japan) (Tōyō keizai shinpōsha, 1973); Thomas C. Smith, *Nakahara: Family Farming and Population in a Japanese Village, 1717–1830* (Stanford: Stanford University Press, 1977); Susan B. Hanley and Kozo Yamamura, *Economic and Demographic Change in Preindustrial Japan, 1600–1868* (Princeton: Princeton University Press, 1977); L. L. Cornell, "Why Are There No Spinsters in Japan?" *Journal of Family History* 9 (1984): 326–39; and L. L. Cornell, "Peasant Women and Divorce in Early Modern Japan," *Signs* 15, no. 4 (1990): 710–32.

15. L. L. Cornell, "Retirement, Inheritance, and Intergenerational Conflict in Preindustrial Japan," *Journal of Family History* 8 (1983): 55–69.

the proportion of women of various statuses who survive throughout the last three decades of life, as well as measures of the median number of years a woman at a given age could expect to continue living. I will also use a statistical method called "event history analysis" to describe how much a particular variable influences survival.[16]

In addition, since the population registers provide us with not only aggregate data but also the details of individual lives, I will illustrate my argument by looking at two more or less typical women, known to us only as "Kyūmon's wife" and Heinojō's wife."[17] Both were born in the same year (1768) and thus experienced the same historical events; each was married for almost fifty years and each bore three children, two boys and a girl.[18] Yet one, Heinojō's wife, lived to eighty-nine, while the other, Kyūmon's wife, died at sixty-eight. The details of their lives will therefore provide insight into the personal variability that accompanies the general patterns examined here.

This paper is not concerned with the specific question of whether elderly women were actually abandoned on mountainsides, an issue for which these data provide no evidence. Rather, the question is whether old women in certain positions in the family were more or less likely to die than those in others. The cause of death, as long as it is deliberate, is assumed to be irrelevant. Thus, although an elderly woman could die

16. Event history analysis is a regressionlike technique for time series data. Once the underlying risk of an event, such as death, is known, it gives three figures of use to those trying to determine the importance of a particular variable: (1) a measure of the direction of its influence (does it increase or decrease the likelihood of an event occurring?); (2) a measure of significance; and (3) a measure of the size of the influence. The test of significance is computed by dividing the coefficient by its standard error. The result is interpreted as a t-statistic with infinite degrees of freedom. Discussions of this method are provided in Paul D. Allison, *Event History Analysis: Regression for Longitudinal Event Data*, Quantitative Applications in the Social Sciences #07-046 (Beverly Hills, Calif.: Sage, 1984); and Jane Menken, James Trussel, Debra Stempel, and Ozer Babakol, "Proportional Hazards Life Table Models: An Illustrative Analysis of Sociodemographic Influences on Marriage Dissolution in the United States," *Demography* 18 (1981): 181–200. See also L. L. Cornell, "Analyzing the Consequences of Family Structure with Event History Methods," *Historical Methods* 23, no. 2 (1990): 53–61.

17. Married women are designated in the population registers by their husbands' names, and so their personal names are lost to us. Since the descendants of these individuals may still reside in the same locality, the two names used here are pseudonyms. In 1828, when Kyūmon's wife and Heinojō's wife reached sixty years of age, twenty-three other elderly women lived in the village (two died that year). Most were in their sixties, with a handful in their early seventies; the four oldest were seventy-six and seventy-seven. Elderly women were scattered throughout the village—one in about every fourth household—and made up about 5 percent of the total population.

18. These women undoubtedly bore other children whose existence is unknown to us because they did not survive the first year of life. Such children do not appear in the population registers because these documents were compiled only once a year; thus, a child born in the fourth month who died in the tenth month would not be listed.

by being tossed off a mountain, more likely she would die from being
systematically denied food, leisure, medicine, or love.

ANALYSIS

What might bring about geronticide? To determine whether geronticide
in fact occurred, we need a theory of household relations that will indicate which elderly women are more likely to die and why. In short,
which women are at greater risk?

The folktale gives us some help here. Ordinarily we would expect
that those who are outside the social group would be more likely to die.
In the traditional Japanese peasant context, this means both beggars
and vagrants of various sorts[19] and women outside the direct line of the
household, such as aunts, cousins, and unmarried sisters. Yet the range
apparently extends beyond these categories. The tale reports that a man
takes his mother to die at the behest of the community. This is a great
surprise, for it implies that even women who were successful, who had
attained permanent positions within the household, who had become
wives and mothers and grandmothers, would be exposed to a risk of
deliberate death once they got old.

We can develop a reasonable model of this relationship, first by asking what household circumstances might put elderly women at greater
risk, and then by examining patterns of conflict within the household.
The tale suggests that elderly women were perceived as burdens, that
they became costly to the household when their demands outstripped
their contributions. One category of women who would seem to be at
great risk, then, comprises those who are especially costly, perhaps by
being ill-tempered, sickly, or feeble, or by being unable to provide valuable labor to the household. Unfortunately, the data set used here does
not provide information on the health status or labor force contribution
of individuals, so we cannot use those variables in this analysis. Let us,
then, approach the problem from another direction: let us argue that
there is a standard amount of women's work, both productive and reproductive, to be done in a peasant household; that doing it well is crucial to a woman's social status and psychological well-being; and that the
adult women in a household compete to control that work. Thus, a sole
adult female in the household not only is essential to its existence but
will also have complete autonomy in her management of female tasks.
Once another woman enters, the first woman's contribution is no longer
so necessary, and her ability to control the allocation of work is challenged, particularly if the new woman is younger and hence more ro-

19. Cf. Robert J. Smith and Ella Lury Wiswell, *The Women of Suye Mura* (Chicago: University of Chicago Press, 1982).

bust. The older woman may therefore experience either greater stress or less access to resources, both of which would tend to increase her risk of mortality. Two adult women can come to share household responsibilities in many instances, as when a bride moves into a household that includes her husband's unmarried sisters. Most commonly, however, this situation will arise when a woman's son takes a bride. Thus we might expect that the presence of a daughter-in-law will increase an elderly woman's risk of dying, owing to conflict over the management of household roles.

Indeed, much of the literature on household conflict in Japan suggests that the two people most likely to have opposing interests are the mother-in-law and daughter-in-law. On the one hand, the new bride is systematically pressed by her strict mother-in-law to conform to the "ways of the household"; on the other, a middle-aged daughter-in-law may connive to seize the reins of power from her husband's aging mother. This node of conflict is structurally embedded in the stem-family household, and examples of it are legion.[20]

These facts suggest three hypotheses:

1. Women with daughters-in-law are likely to experience higher mortality than women without them;
2. Women with daughters-in-law who are close in age to themselves will experience higher mortality;
3. Women with daughters-in-law who have families of their own will experience higher mortality.

In short, because there can be only one domestic manager in a household, as a daughter-in-law comes closer and closer to being that manager she is increasingly able to deprive her mother-in-law of significant resources.

MORTALITY PATTERNS IN YOKOUCHI

Before examining these hypotheses specifically, we must outline the general pattern of old-age mortality in nineteenth-century Yokouchi. First, the expectation of life at age sixty for the women of this cohort was sixteen years.[21] Second, the likelihood of survival for elderly men

20. Richard K. Beardsley, John W. Hall, and Robert E. Ward, *Village Japan* (Chicago: University of Chicago Press, 1959); and Gail Lee Bernstein, *Haruko's World: A Japanese Farm Woman and Her Community* (Stanford: Stanford University Press, 1983).

21. While scholars might consider this figure too high to be accurate for a national population in the preindustrial period, it is reasonable for a local population protected from the force of mortality by living in settled rather than transient households and in a rural area rather than a city where infectious diseases were more pervasive. Kito Hiroshi, *Nihon 2000 nen no jinkōshi* (PHP Press, 1983), 148, gives figures of 13.6 and 13.0 for men

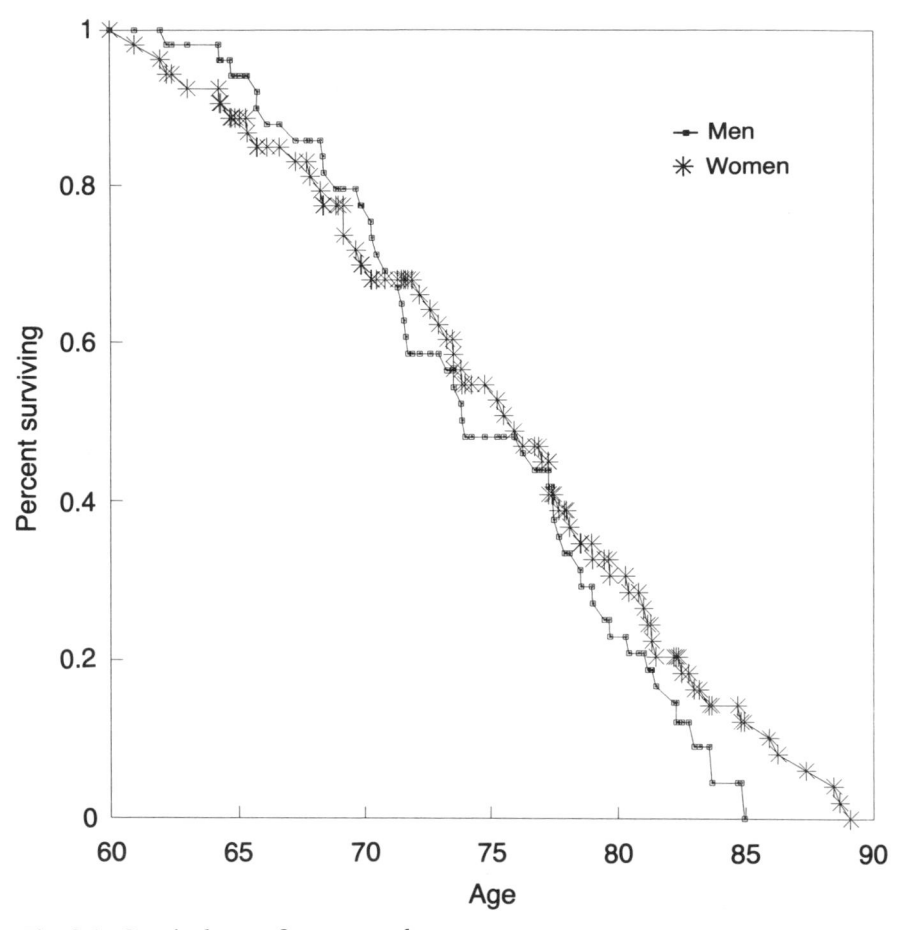

Fig. 3.1. Survival rates for men and women

and women was about the same. Figure 3.1 presents survival rates from age sixty on for two groups: the set of women described above and the fifty-two men in Yokouchi from the same birth cohort who survived to the age of sixty. In both cases, at age seventy about four-fifths of the cohort was still alive; at age seventy-four, about one-half; and at age eighty, about one-fifth. Since lower mortality rates for women are a common feature of modern societies, this lack of a differential might suggest that

---

and 13.5 for women in the village of Yubunezawa in the periods 1675–1740 and 1741–1796, respectively. A graph of the age structure of death in Shimomoriya from 1716 to 1872 in Narimatsu Saeko, *Kinsei tōhoku nōson no hitobito* (Kyoto: Mineruba Shobō, 1985), 76, reveals a similar pattern. The expectation of life at age sixty-five for white females in the United States in 1800 and 1900, respectively, is given by Susan Cotts Watkins, Jane A. Menken, and John Bongaarts, "Demographic Foundations of Family Change," *American Sociological Review* 52 (1987): 346–358, as 10.4 and 11.8; in the Yokouchi population, life expectancy at age sixty-five is 12.4 years.

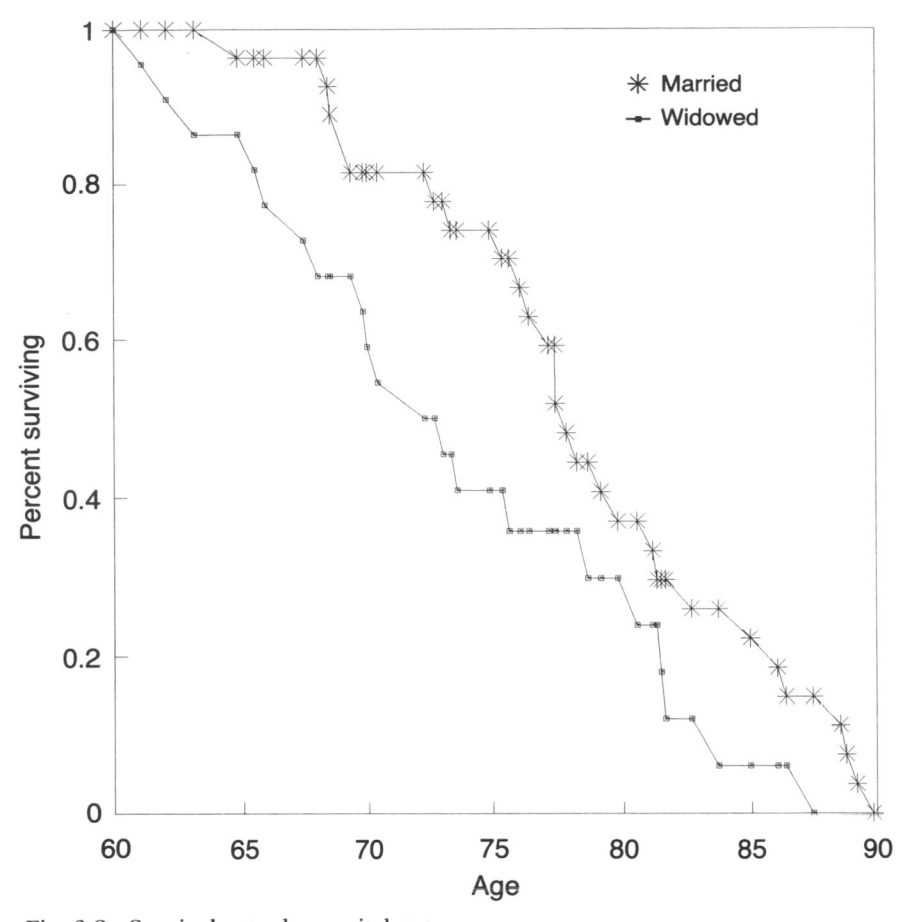

Fig. 3.2. Survival rates by marital status

elderly women were systematically discriminated against and that fe-male-specific geronticide was in fact being carried out. However, this hypothesis must be rejected, because a higher survival rate for women than for men is a pattern that typically appears with development, and is not characteristic of preindustrial societies.

We do observe differential mortality when we compare currently married women with widows. In figure 3.2, the line portraying the per-centage of surviving widows is lower at every age. Statistical analysis re-veals that their risk of death was about 80 percent higher (p = .04). Yet while a widow in nineteenth-century Japan was more likely to die than her married counterpart, the same is true of widows in contemporary Japan, widows in historical Europe, and, indeed, widowers. People who lose their usual social roles or social supports are, as Durkheim argued, almost inevitably more likely to die. One might argue that with her husband's death a Japanese wife lost her meaningful role in the household and became a troublesome burden for her daughter-in-law.[22] The higher mortality of Japanese widows, then, is not evidence that Japanese peasants were carrying out geronticide. It is merely a general human pattern.

HOUSEHOLD STRUCTURE AND MORTALITY

Let us now turn to the hypotheses proposed above. As you will recall, they suggest that the agent who creates the conditions for female geronticide is likely to be a woman's daughter-in-law, for her interests are least likely to coincide with those of the elderly woman herself. One can examine these issues in three ways: first, by analyzing the effect of the presence or absence of a daughter-in-law; second, by looking at whether an older daughter-in-law has more power in the household relative to her mother-in-law; and third, by determining whether the presence of grandchildren strengthens a daughter-in-law's hand.

It is here that the experiences of Kyūmon's wife and Heinojō's wife begin to diverge. Although both still had husbands at the age of sixty, the composition of their households was different in a significant way. Heinojō's wife (the one who lived to eighty-nine) had experienced a family tragedy, for her eldest son had died at age twenty-five when he was already head of household. Luckily, her second son stepped in, took his place, and married. Thus, at sixty Heinojō's wife shared the household with her husband, her son, and a daughter-in-law thirty-eight years her junior.

Kyūmon's wife (who lived to sixty-eight) also shared the household with her husband and her second son, the first having died in childhood. This son must have been something of a worry to her, for at thirty-five he was not married and never had been—an unusual situation, for most men, though they might later be divorced or widowed, had married by their late twenties. In any event, this son disappeared from our records of the household (probably an unrecorded death), leaving Kyūmon's wife with neither daughter-in-law nor grandchildren. Did such family circumstances affect the two women's likelihood of survival?

Daughters-In-Law

The majority of women in this cohort (about three-fifths) were living with a daughter-in-law when they reached old age; a few had a co-resi-

22. A wife was essential to a husband, especially an elderly husband. See L. L. Cornell, "Old Age Security and Fertility: A Microdemographic Analysis of the Difference Between Men's Motives and Women's," Working Paper Series WP #7 (Indiana University, Population Institute for Research and Training, 1987).

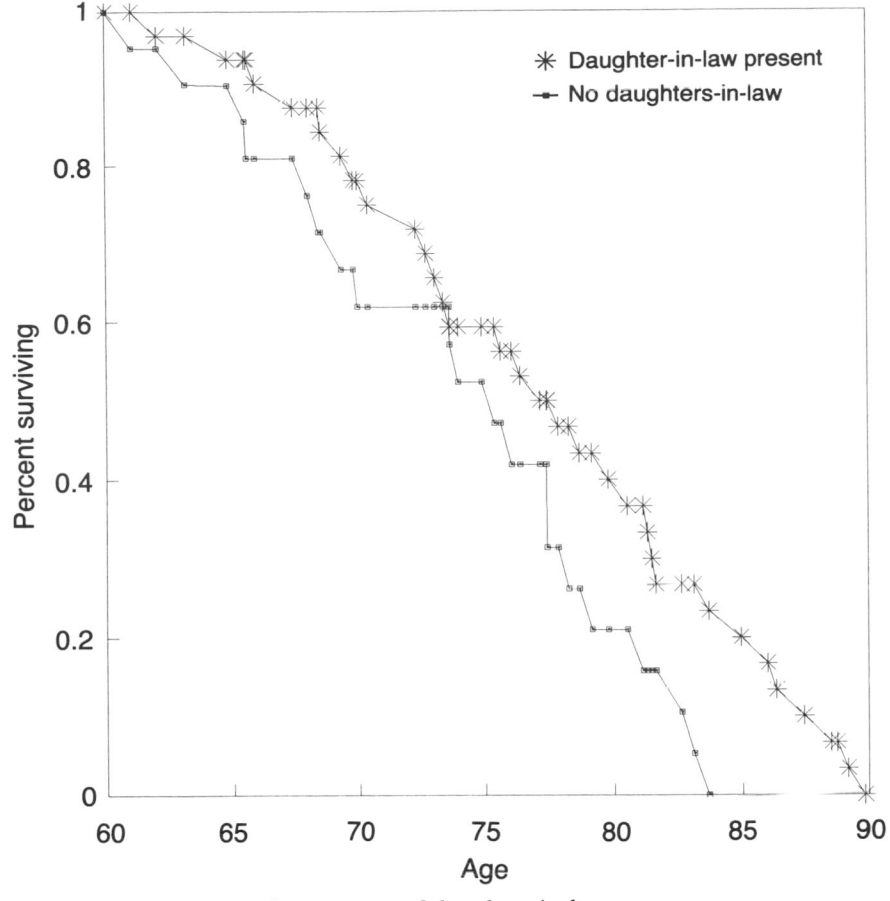

Fig. 3.3. Survival rates by presence of daughter-in-law

dent daughter who had taken a husband into the household; and about one-third lived with neither a daughter nor a daughter-in-law. In examining the effect of the presence of a daughter-in-law, we find the result to be the opposite of that anticipated. As figure 3.3 demonstrates, an elderly woman living with a daughter-in-law was somewhat more likely to be alive at every age than her counterpart without one. While this effect is not especially strong and does not reach statistical significance (p = .14), it suggests that women like Heinojō's wife were better rather than worse off.

Age Differences

The hypotheses presented above also suggest that if there is a struggle for control between women of adjacent generations, women who are close in age should experience it more strongly than others. Let us now look at how a daughter-in-law's age, both absolute and relative, affects the older woman's chances of survival.

Strikingly, there is a wide age gap between elderly women and their daughters-in-law. Heinojō's wife, for instance, was nearly forty years older than her son's wife. The range for the entire cohort was twenty to more than forty years' difference, with most daughters-in-law thirty to thirty-five years younger. Thus, a woman of sixty was likely to have a daughter-in-law between twenty-five and thirty years of age. This wide gap undoubtedly contributed to household harmony, for the two women were in such different stages of life that their interests would conflict relatively seldom.[23]

Statistical measures show that this is true: for every year that a daughter-in-law was closer in age to her mother-in-law, the older woman's mortality increased by about 9 percent (p = .03). Although the difference from year to year is not very large, it is cumulative. Thus, given two sixty-year-old women, one with a daughter-in-law of twenty-five, the other with a daughter-in-law of thirty, we find mortality levels of 100 and 154, respectively; that is, the second woman's level is about half again as high as the first woman's. In addition, while life expectancy at age sixty for women with older daughters-in-law was sixteen or seventeen years, it was much longer, twenty-five years, for women whose daughters-in-law were significantly younger than themselves (aged nineteen to twenty-five). Thus it appears that an older daughter-in-law may have had some power to harm the elderly woman with whom she shared her household, and that choosing a younger daughter-in-law may have been advantageous.

Grandchildren

A third argument that emerges from the literature is that although a bride entered the household with few economic and psychological resources, she acquired them as she produced children and proved her value. Thus the presence of grandchildren should have enhanced the daughter-in-law's power and undermined the hegemony of the mother-

23. The age difference between spouses in Japan has decreased considerably over the last three centuries. The mean age at first marriage for men has remained about the same, but that for women has risen from under twenty to about twenty-five. As women become more comparable in age to their husbands, the age gap between them and their mothers-in-law also narrows. This leads one to wonder whether the intergenerational conflict so widely reported in the ethnographies is a relatively new phenomenon, one resulting not only from the dilution of traditional household ideology, but from demographic changes as well.

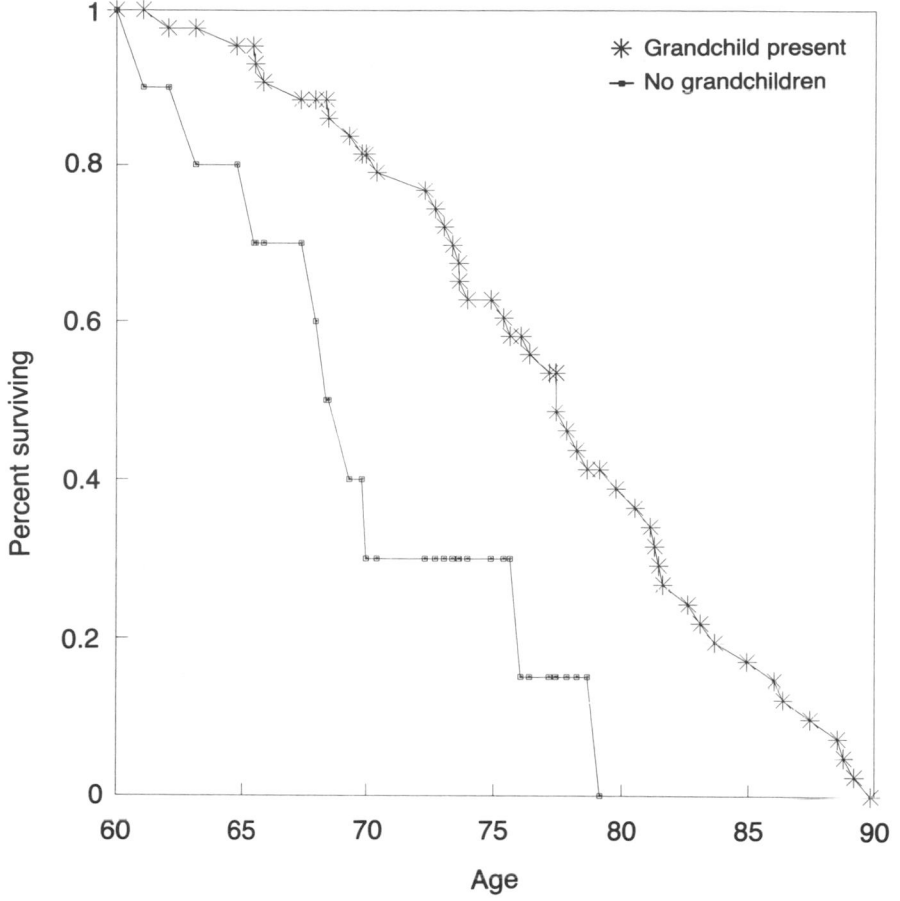

Fig. 3.4. Survival rates by presence of grandchild

in-law, thereby increasing her likelihood of dying. Do the statistics bear out this assumption?

In fact, the presence of grandchildren produced the opposite effect, increasing a woman's chances of survival strongly and significantly.[24] The evidence is presented in figure 3.4, which contrasts those with grandchildren and those without; the mortality of the latter group is three times as high as that of the former (p = .001).

24. Note that only co-resident grandchildren are included here. Grandchildren produced by sons and daughters who have left the household are both conceptually different and difficult to trace in the population registers. They are referred to as grandchildren "outside the boundaries of the household" (*soto no mago*), who are thereby extraneous to an individual's economic and ritual welfare.

Why was the presence of grandchildren so powerful a predictor of a woman's prospect of survival? Perhaps simply having a job that was essential to the household—namely, caring for her grandchildren—was enough to increase her life expectancy; this factor may also help to explain the correlation between greater survival prospects and a younger daughter-in-law, for she would also be more likely to have young children. Most importantly, though, the presence of grandchildren is an indicator that the woman has successfully negotiated a whole panoply of difficult life passages: she has married, produced children, enabled them to survive to adulthood, helped them to marry and made it possible for one of them to remain with her, and seen them successfully bear her grandchildren and keep them alive through infancy. Failure was possible at each of these points.

Both Heinojō's wife and Kyūmon's wife had long-lasting marriages, but both also bore only three children and saw at least one of them die young. Though Heinojō's wife's son married at an appropriate age, it was not until six years after that marriage that a grandchild survived, and fourteen years until a grandson arrived. Kyūmon's wife had an even more difficult time. After her son's disappearance, she and her husband attempted to repair the damage by adopting a married couple from the household into which their daughter had married (the thirty-eight-year-old man was the fifth son of that household; his wife was thirty-six). Unfortunately, that couple brought no children with them, and produced no grandchildren by the time Kyūmon's wife died. Thus, although the means—divorce, remarriage, adoption—existed for overcoming many of these problems, they were not always successful. The fact that forty-four of the fifty-six women both reached age sixty and acquired grandchildren to sustain them in old age is a testament not only to luck and a woman's own longevity, but also to her own and her family's skill at fending off hazards time and time again.

Nevertheless, the discovery that having grandchildren enhances rather than detracts from a woman's survival chances deals a sharp blow to the theory proposed earlier. One hypothesis—that the relative age of a daughter-in-law affects a woman's survival—is strongly supported, but widowhood has a weak effect in the opposite direction, and the hypothesis about grandchildren is strongly rejected. Female geronticide does not seem to have existed.

DIFFERENTIAL MORTALITY

Was there then no differential mortality in old age? Were women of a given age equally likely to die irrespective of the kind of household in which they lived? By no means. The variables described above were not

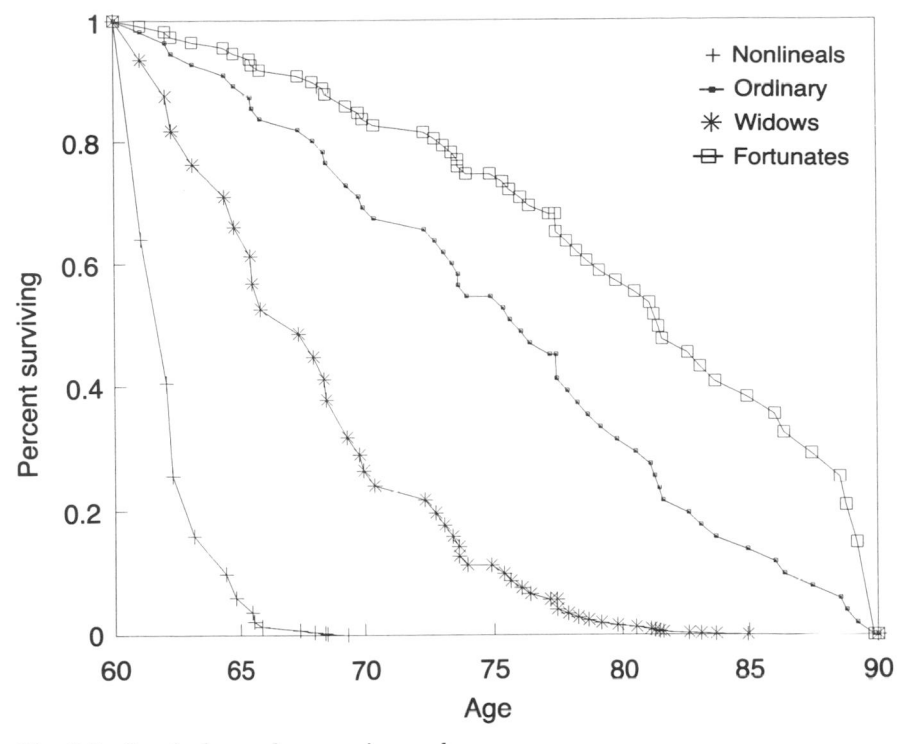

Fig. 3.5. Survival rates by experience class

distributed randomly among this set of women, and a woman's chances were highly dependent on the household she—and fate—had worked to create for her. Although they were born in the same year, Kyūmon's wife and Heinojō's wife had very different experiences of old age. One lived only to sixty-eight, leaving a household that, because of dwindling membership, was shortly to go out of existence. The other lived twenty-one years longer, to eighty-nine, and saw not only the marriages of her children but those of her grandchildren as well. Nor are those results a consequence of idiosyncratic differences alone, for as figure 3.5 indicates, social environment was highly influential in determining a woman's prospects.

Consider first the women who at sixty were not lineal members of their households of residence: one was an elder sister who had returned to her household of origin after two divorces, the other a distant cousin of the household head who apparently moved in after the other members of her own household emigrated elsewhere. Both lived for a very

short time past sixty—one slightly over two years, the other four and a
half years. By contrast, women who entered the household as brides
could expect to live to the age of seventy-seven—an additional seventeen years.

Next consider those who did marry and became the principal women
in their households but who, for some reason, entered old age as widows
with neither daughter-in-law nor grandchild. (Had her husband died,
Kyūmon's wife would have fallen into this group.) Fate dealt hard blows
to the six women in this category. Two bore no children during thirty-
odd years of married life. The other four did, but suffered misfortunes
nonetheless: a daughter died in early childhood; a son left for a merchant's household in Edo; a divorced daughter died, leaving her twelve-
year-old son with his elderly grandmother; a stepson most strangely
married only when he reached his late fifties. These difficulties were
compounded in one household by losing a husband early. Thus, while
the life expectancy at sixty of these women's still-married peers was seventeen years, for them it was only five and one-half years.

Those women who lived the longest almost all fall into yet another
group, which included Heinojō's wife. They died at ages that even in
the late twentieth century are old: at eighty-five, eighty-six, eighty-nine,
and even ninety. Thus at sixty, these women could look forward to a
full quarter-century of life yet. This group comprised women who were
still married at sixty and who had daughters-in-law who were young and
who produced grandchildren. But these women were lucky, not extraordinary—lucky that their husbands survived well into old age (most
lived into their seventies and eighties), even though the age difference
between husband and wife was not especially small. In other respects
they were fairly typical: they lost their share of infants and children, and
some of their sons were feckless and their daughters unhappy in marriage. In addition (though admittedly these population registers are a
poor source of economic information), they were not obviously well
off—if large size, complex structure, or many branches of a household
indicate wealth. Good sense and good luck seem to have been the cards
they drew.

But most women—two-thirds of them—were perfectly ordinary, neither prosperous nor penurious in their allotted years. Among them it is
difficult to disentangle the sources of mortality: none of the variables
that divide the population as a whole into such neat groups has power
or reaches significance in this particular category of women. Perhaps it
is here that health, or strength, or personality makes the difference.
Certainly, though, these women did live long: even if we discount both
the fortunates and the unfortunates, at age sixty they could expect to
live into their late seventies.

CONCLUSION

The results of this study suggest that geronticide did not exist, or if it did, it did not leave the behavioral traces one would expect to find. The peasant of legend who carries his mother up the mountain was apparently not motivated by the imprecations of his wife. Indeed, if we are to believe the notations in one peasant's diary, he held his aged mother in great esteem.[25]

Yet this is not to deny the existence of differential mortality. Variations in the likelihood of survival from one age to the next did exist—but among exactly those classes of people where one would expect to find them in any society: the widowed, the outsiders, and the familyless. If there was neglect of the elderly in Japan, then, it likely followed patterns common to any society; there was no culture of geronticide specific to this one.

Why, then, does the tale of Obasuteyama appear so prominently in the portrayal of the Japanese elderly in traditional times? The reason, I suspect, is that while geronticide may not have existed in people's behavior, it did exist in their hearts and minds. Over 90 percent of the women in this sample became widows at some point in their lives, and given a high life expectancy in old age and a considerable age difference between husband and wife, it was likely that widowhood would be long. A few of these grandmothers—10 percent—died promptly, within two, three, or four years of their husbands' deaths. More than half, however, remained alone as elderly women for a decade or more, and about one in five was, like Heinojō's wife, an elderly widow for over twenty years. Given what ethnographers report about tension between mother-in-law and daughter-in-law, the peasant husband and his wife must have wished, often, that they could abandon grandmother on the mountain.

25. See Walthall's essay in this volume (chap. 2).

FOUR

The Shingaku Woman:
Straight from the Heart

Jennifer Robertson

One of the most distinctive features of the Shingaku (Heart Learning)[1] movement was its timeliness. Founded in Kyoto in 1729 by Ishida Baigan (1685–1744), a farmer-turned-merchant, this movement had as its overall objective the rectification of a social system destabilized by rapid expansion of the market economy. Although merchants were officially at the bottom of the four-class hierarchy, Baigan argued that they, as the de facto managerial class, performed a function in society homologous to that of the samurai; that is, it was incumbent on both groups to conduct their businesses with honesty and in a spirit of selfless service. Thus, by giving moral and spiritual justification to commercial activity, Shingaku sought to rationalize the expedient pursuit of profit.[2] Baigan translated the "bourgeois tenor of the age"[3] into a "national" canon of social morality that amounted to a synthesis of the Way of the samurai and of the merchant.

Research for this paper was made possible by a Social Science Research Council research grant (1987), a Northeast Asia Council of the Association for Asian Studies grant (1987), and a Japan Foundation Professional Fellowship (1987). Heartfelt thanks to the late N. Serena Tennekoon.

1. An alternate reading for *shin* is *kokoro*, one of the most compelling and ubiquitous terms in the Japanese language. This is the "heart-mind," which I have abbreviated for convenience: the locus of feelings, consciousness, and authenticity.

2. See Robert Bellah, *Tokugawa Religion: The Values of Pre-Industrial Japan* (Glencoe, Ill.: Free Press, 1957); and Jennifer Robertson, "Rooting the Pine: Shingaku Methods of Organization," *Monumenta Nipponica* 34, no. 3 (1979): 311–32.

3. Ivan Morris, "Introduction," in Ihara Saikaku, *The Life of an Amorous Woman*, ed. and trans. I. Morris (New York: New Directions, 1969), 32.

Throughout the seventeenth century, merchants and artisans (collectively, *chōnin*, or townspeople) in general, and females in particular, had been marginalized within a social system that embodied the androcentric values of the samurai minority. Baigan and his chief disciple, the wealthy merchant Tejima Toan (1718–86), now undertook to convince townspeople that they were actually the social vanguard. At the crux of Shingaku teachings was the discovery and cultivation of "original heart" (*honshin*), which, though good in itself, was subject to corruption because of the deterioration of people's material circumstances.[4] Whereas male merchants and artisans were encouraged to cultivate a moral, rational approach to commerce, advice to females was not similarly bound by status or occupation. Owing to their anatomy and attendant vices, females of all classes were regarded by Shingaku theorists and their contemporaries as a problematic constituency in need of moral rehabilitation. Toan, in particular, constructed a canon of "female-likeness" (*onnarashisa*) premised on the strict alignment of sex and gender roles.[5]

TOKUGAWA-PERIOD DISCOURSE ON WOMEN

In Tokugawa times as now, the suffix *-rashii* indicated approximation to an ideal mode or model of existence (*kata*)—for example, the "farmer model" or the "samurai model." Detailed edicts and decrees were issued at regular intervals by the *bakufu* (the shogunal military administration) to define and further refine the parameters of each existential model. The authors of agricultural manuals, for instance, presented their readers with "farmer-like" vocabulary lists, descriptions of "farmer-like" clothing, and recipes for "farmer-like" meals. This hierarchy of ideal social and occupational statuses was further complicated by the coexistent operations of a separate sex-gender system, which effectively bisected each of the four social classes into female and male divisions. Age grades provided additional denominators.

Only the female divisions, according to the male intelligentsia, required specific attention. Consequently, in the writings of men like Kaibara Ekken, Kumazawa Banzan, Uesugi Yozan, Sakuma Shōzan, and

4. Baigan derived this perspective from Mencius; see Chan Wing-tsit, *A Source Book in Chinese Philosophy* (Princeton: Princeton University Press, 1963), 55, 294. Shingaku teachings were culled from Confucian, Shintō, and Buddhist vocabularies.

5. Sex, gender, and sexuality may be related, but they are not the same thing. The degree of their relationship—or the lack thereof—is sociohistorically negotiated and negotiable. Sexuality can thus overlap with gender and sex but remains a separate domain of desire and erotic pleasure. See Carol Vance, "Pleasure and Danger: Toward a Politics of Sexuality," in *Pleasure and Danger: Exploring Female Sexuality*, ed. Carol Vance (Boston: Routledge & Kegan Paul, 1985), 9.

Yoshida Shōin one finds both generic models of and for female-likeness, and more specific models of and for particular types of females, such as farmers, brides, or courtesans.[6] Much of the fiction of the seventeenth-century short story writer and satirist Ihara Saikaku similarly dwelled on female dramatis personae, ranging from "high-ranking courtesans" to "streetwalkers" and other "amorous women." Shingaku theorists likewise devoted a large portion of their lectures and essays to the construction of the "Shingaku Woman"; but whereas Saikaku's interest lay in the formal details of women's dress and hairstyles, the Shingaku literature focused on instructions in social etiquette and deportment. Every amorous woman was a potential Shingaku Woman.

The Japanese had long recognized two sexes and two genders, but female-likeness (*onnarashisa*) and male-likeness (*otokorashisa*) were not necessarily viewed as exclusive provinces. During the Tokugawa period (and beyond), the paragons of female-likeness were *onnagata*: male Kabuki actors who performed "female" roles, sometimes offstage as well as on. Shingaku rhetoricians, however, sought to fuse sex and gender, based on a rationale expressed by Baigan as "the heart that conforms to the model" (*kata ni yoru kokoro*). Sex was perceived as subordinate to gender; females were to approximate—or bring their innermost temperaments in accord with—female-likeness, as defined by Baigan and Tōan. According to Shingaku tenets, female sexual being and sexuality were contingent on the prior existence of "female" gender.

That the male intelligentsia's preoccupation with the "woman problem" paralleled the rise of merchants was not fortuitous. The growing market economy, together with the proliferation of performing and fine

6. "Model of" refers to the *definition* of "female" gender, whereas "model for" refers to its *emulation*; see Kakehi Kumiko, "Edo shoki san jūsha no jokun shisō ni miru haha to onna," in *Bosei o tou*, ed. Wakita Haruko, vol. 2 (Jinbun Shoin, 1986), 41–70; Kurokawa Masamichi, *Nihon kyōiku bunko: jokun hen* (Nihon Zusho Sentā, 1977); Shiba Keiko, *Edo jidai no onnatachi* (Hyōron Shinsha, 1969), 30–49.

Female intellectuals also participated in the discourse on "female" gender, although their writings have yet to be acknowledged and reclaimed by Japanologists. The "daughter of Tamura Yoshio," as she is identified, toed a Confucian patriarchal line. In her admonitory text *Onna imagawa nishiki no kadakara*, for example, she proclaims that "husbands, like heaven itself, must be venerated." See Koyama Shizuko, "Ryōsai kenbo shugi no reimei," *Joseigaku nenpō* 7 (1986): 13.

Others, such as Tadano Makuzu, joined her male *kokugaku* (nativism) colleagues in positing a morphological basis for "sexual antinomy" (*danjo no shobu no arasoi*). She derived her argument from the dialogue in the *Kojiki* between Izanami and Izanagi, when the former said that she was incomplete in one part, and the latter that he was overdetermined. Whereas Makuzu proposed the existence of two essentially incommensurate hearts (*kokoro*) based on sex, her Shingaku contemporaries stressed the singularity of original heart (*honshin*). See Miyazawa Tamiko, "Bakuhansei kaitaiki ni okeru hitori josei no shakai hihan," *Rekishigaku kenkyū* 423 (1975): 17–30.

arts, occasioned the possibility of independently employed women. The all-male Kabuki theater in particular stimulated a number of employment opportunities for women, including *shamisen* and song instruction, hairdressing, and *joruri* (ballad drama) performances staged by female troupes at a patron's house.[7] The *bakufu*, however, prohibited females from theater-related and "nonprescribed" labor—that is, work other than domestic sewing and weaving. Significantly, the government referred to such prohibitions as *fūzoku torishimari*: literally, the "supervision and control of traditional manners and customs."[8] Women working in nontraditional fields were singled out for resocialization into *bakufu*-defined gender roles. Under Toan's leadership, the Shingaku movement became an integral part of this process.

Discourses on female-likeness reflect *bakufu* and private interests in the education (or rather, indoctrination) of girls and women. The entrenchment of a Confucian patriarchy, together with the bureaucratization of the samurai class, effectively indurated the concept of females as "inferior to males." Kaibara Ekken's widely circulated, consulted, and cited *Onna daigaku* (Greater learning for women, 1672) epitomized the misogyny of the Tokugawa social system and its spokespersons.[9] A leading representative of the "practical school" (*jitsugaku*) of Confucianism and a self-appointed critic of females, Ekken proclaimed that female genitalia, while necessary for the reproduction of male heirs, were linked to dull-wittedness, laziness, lasciviousness, a hot temper, and a tremendous capacity to bear grudges.[10] Ironically, none of these were female-like (*onnarashii*) traits; Ekken was not alone in suggesting that female sex was contrary to and even precluded "female" gender.

The male critics in the *bakufu* were no less misogynous. Yoshida Shōin, known for his advocacy of the restoration of the emperor, wrote a Confucian-inspired *jokun* (instructions for females) in which he insisted that female subordination was essential to social, and ultimately national, stability.[11] Even male intellectuals whose political views clashed shared with Ekken the conviction that for females, anatomy is destiny;

7. Seki Tamiko, *Edo kōki no joseitachi* (Aki Shobō, 1980), 23, 38.

8. Ibid., 84.

9. *Onna daigaku*, conventionally translated as *Greater Learning for Women*, was intended for both girls and women, that is, for members of the female sex, and is more precisely translated as *Greater Learning for Females*. It was a virtual copy of the "Oshie joshi hō" (Female education) section in Ekken's earlier work, *Yamato zoku dōjikun* (Customary precepts for Japanese children, 1710). Some scholars have also entertained the possibility that Ekken's wife wrote *Onna daigaku*; see Ōkura Seishin Bunka Kenkyūjo, ed., *Nihon shisōshi bunken kaidai* (Kadokawa Shoten, 1965), 287.

10. Kaibara Ekken, *Onna daigaku* (1672), in *Women and Wisdom of Japan*, ed. Takaishi Shingoro (London: John Murray, 1905), 33–46.

11. Kurokowa, *Nihon kyōiku bunko*; Shiba, *Edo jidai no onnatachi*, 40–42.

that the "great lifelong duty of a woman is obedience"; and that the "five infirmities" (indocility, discontent, slander, jealousy, and silliness) found in "seven or eight out of every ten women" arise from and exacerbate "the inferiority of women to men."[12]

The importance attached to proper performance of one's gender role is poignantly illustrated by the case of a woman named Take who, in the 1830s, openly defied both the social status and the sex-gender hierarchies. She was arrested, punished, imprisoned, fined, and eventually exiled for, essentially, appropriating "male" gender.

As a girl, Take had played with boys and later found "male work and activities" more exciting than "female work." Cutting off her hair, she created a dramatis persona for herself and, in the guise of a young man, renamed herself Takejirō. This act so provoked the indignation of the male innkeeper who employed her that he raped her, ostensibly to make Take/Takejirō aware of her female sex. She became pregnant and ran away from the inn, but not before stealing an obi and a straw raincoat to hide her pregnancy and to protect her male-like appearance. When the child was born, she suffocated it.[13]

Thievery and infanticide notwithstanding, Take/Takejirō was charged with having committed the newly coined crime of "corrupting public morals" (jinrin o midashimasu mono) by dissociating sex from gender. Her second arrest came in 1837 when it was discovered that she was both appropriating "male" gender and impersonating a deputy magistrate, a flagrant violation of both the reigning social hierarchies. She was exposed when she attracted attention by tackling a robber she had caught red-handed.[14] If Take/Takejirō's actions indicated that she was aware of the arbitrary nature of gender attribution and of the sexual and gendered division of labor, her punishment, recorded in the "female section" of the bakufu publication Oshioki Reiruishū (Representative examples of punishments and executions, 1771–1852), illustrates the tenacity of the official emphasis on the fusion of female sex with "female" gender.

The idea that females, by dint of their anatomy, were inferior and, if not controlled, dangerous not only served to enshrine misogynist discrimination, but also inspired a prolific genre of male-authored jokun. At least three of Toan's twenty-three or so major works were conceived as jokun, and nearly all of his other treatises contain sections devoted

---

12. Kaibara, Onna daigaku, 38, 44–45.

13. Ishii Rosuke, ed., Oshioki reiruishū: Onna no bu, 16 vol. (Meicho Shuppan, 1974), 12–13, 142–43. As the Japanese title suggests, this is a collection devoted to the crimes and punishments of females. Seki, Edo kōki no joseitachi, 76–79.

14. Seki, Edo kōki no joseitachi, 76–79.

exclusively to the "woman problem."[15] Although Shingaku spokespersons challenged the view that any one class was superior to any other, they continued to view sex and gender differences in terms of superiority/domination and inferiority/subordination.

THE MAKING OF THE SHINGAKU WOMAN

Tejima Toan was particularly active in establishing seminars and public lectures for girls and women. Under his leadership, these educational fora were standardized by the middle of the 1770s, beginning with *Zenkun*, a "preparatory lecture" series inaugurated in 1773. The lectures were designed to socialize girls (and boys) before they fell into delinquent ways, and to resocialize women who had already fallen. Recorded verbatim and published, *Zenkun* became one of the most widely distributed Shingaku textbooks. It consists of four lectures for boys, one for girls, and one for women, but none for men, who evidently did not require resocialization.

The *Zenkun* lectures drew from such Japanese classics as *Tsurezuregusa*, *Ise monogatari*, the *Yamato monogatari*, and the *Nihon shoki*, and from such Chinese classics as the *Four Books*, the *Small Learning*, the *Book of Filial Piety*, the Han-dynasty *Precepts for Women*, and the Sung-dynasty *Explanation of the Six Womanly Virtues*. For some reason Toan chose to cite directly from the classics, interpreting them in light of the movement's aims, rather than make use of the large number of "instructions for females" published throughout the Tokugawa period by male intellectuals who were either familiar or in some way affiliated with the Shingaku movement.[16]

The women's lecture in *Zenkun* begins with a promotion of "likeness" (*rashisa*). Most important, intones Toan, is an awareness of the "natural" distinction of females and males. Females must be female-like, and males male-like; any mixup should be quickly corrected. Toan espoused the strict alignment of sex and gender—unlike Sadaijin, a character in the eleventh-century tale "Torikaebaya Monogatari" who attributed the female-likeness of his male child and the male-likeness of his female child to their respective karmas and simply called the former "daugh-

15. These three works, *Joji nemurisamashi* (1771), *Zenkun* (1773), and *Onna myōga kai* (1776), are included in *Zōho Tejima Toan zenshū* enl. ed., ed. Shibata Minoru (Osaka: Seibundō, 1973).

16. Kurokawa, *Nihon kyōiku bunko*, 7–8; Shiga Tadashi, *Josei kyōikushi* (Fukumura Shuppan, 1968), 253. For example, Yoshida Shōin noted in his *jokun* that Shingaku teachings for females were most appropriate, and he urged his younger sister to read Shingaku texts on a regular basis.

ter" and the latter "son," raising them accordingly.[17] In Toan's view, by contrast, females who strayed from *onnarashii* deportment were monsters disguised as humans. Because of her negatively valued sex, a female who did not discover her original heart (*honshin*) merely accelerated her descent to the level of beasts.[18]

The "discovery of original heart" (*honshin hatsumei*) not only distinguished humans from nonhumans, but also differentiated females from males. Despite Toan's insistence that *honshin* was constant across both sex and gender, a woman's discovery of original heart was tantamount to her achievement of the Confucian "six virtues for women": obedience, purity, goodwill, frugality, modesty, and diligence. Female-likeness was thus best achieved, according to Baigan and his successors, in the context of marriage, for in order to become an effective household manager a woman had to learn how to shrink the "ego" (*ware*) that obscures and pollutes her pristine original heart. Each degree of shrinkage signified an expansion of *honshin*. Marriage, in other words, made more possible a woman's achievement of "female" gender.

On the surface, the Shingaku construction of "female" gender matched that of the Confucian-oriented *bakufu* and the male intelligentsia in general. Echoes of Ekken's *Onna daigaku*, for example, are evident in Toan's assertion in *Zenkun* that the proper conduct for females is to obey their parents, parents-in-law, husband, and, in the case of widows, their children.[19] Unmarried women were considered anomalous and dangerous mavericks, since they were not locked into a sociopsychological framework of overlapping obediences.

The women's lecture in *Zenkun* dwells heavily on the gender role of "wife," with only cursory attention paid to mothering. The virtually exclusive emphasis on wifehood is typical of Tokugawa-period tracts on female-likeness, for the twofold gender role of "good wife, wise mother" was not refined until the Meiji period, when pronatalism was trumpeted by the state in a context of industrialization.[20] Rakuhoku Shōko did make brief mention of a kind of prenatal care in her primer *Shinsen onna Yamato daigaku* (The new greater learning for Japanese women, 1785), warning that the mind and character of an unborn child—whether or not it was smart or stupid, good or bad—was determined by the pregnant mother's attitude and behavior. (She did not dwell at all,

17. R. F. Wittig, trans., *The Changelings: A Classical Japanese Court Tale* (Stanford: Stanford University Press, 1983), 16–20.

18. Tejima Toan, *Zenkun*, in *Sekimon shingaku: Nihon shisō taikei*, ed. Shibata Minoru, vol. 42 (Iwanami Shoten, 1976), 172.

19. Ibid., 173.

20. Mitsuda Kyōko, "Kindaiteki boseikan no juyō to henkei," in Wakita (ed.), *Bosei o tou* 2:124–27.

however, on postnatal care.)[21] Kaibara Ekken, in *Wazoku tojikun* (Traditional Japanese precepts for children, 1710), averred that because females were foolish by nature, and also because a mother's love was detrimental to the development of her child, the task of educating and disciplining children should be the father's responsibility.[22] The belief that a mother's love interfered with a father's discipline was not altogether new; indeed, it had been voiced years earlier by the unorthodox Confucianist Yamaga Soko.[23]

Shingaku rhetoricians did anticipate the Meiji-period discourse on the "good wife, wise mother" when they treated "reliable mothering" (*tanomoshiki mono*)[24]—particularly among poor (*shitashita*) urban women—as part of "female work" (*onna no waza*). Nevertheless, that the roles of "wife" and "daughter-in-law" took precedence over mothering was emphasized in *Zenkun* by Toan's inclusion, in the women's lectures, of a story about a Chinese woman who, ignoring the cries of her newborn child, instead offered her breast to her ailing and (fortunately for her) toothless mother-in-law.[25] It is likely that poor urban women were singled out for "reliable mothering" because, as mothers, they alone, and not wet/dry nurses or foster mothers, were responsible for child care; not having access to the expertise of such female child-care specialists, they were therefore an ideal target (or test) audience.[26]

The "female work" central to "reliable mothering" was described in *Zenkun* as splitting hemp for spinning thread, weaving and sewing, and cooking. It was most shameful for a woman to be unskilled in any of these activities—though significantly, she was not encouraged to parlay this sartorial and culinary expertise into an extradomestic career. By the same token, a poor urban woman would be a more "reliable mother" if

21. Koyama, "Ryōsai kenbo shugi no reimei," 12–13.

22. Miyashita Michiko, "Kinsei ie ni okeru hahaoya zō," in Wakita (ed.), *Bosei o tou* 2:32–33.

23. Shiga, *Josei kyōikushi*, 224.

24. Shingaku rhetoricians posed analogies between the principles of financial management and methods of raising children in terms of the intensity and intimacy required; see Robertson, "Rooting the Pine," 320–21; and Wakizaka Gidō, *Yashinaigusa*, in *Shingaku dōwa zenshū*, ed. Shingaku Dōwa Kankōkai (n.p., n.d.), 2034–35. Thus, a savings and loan association based at Keishinsha in Hiroshima was named *tanomoshikō*; see Ishikawa Ken, *Sekimon Shingakushi no kenkyū* (Iwanami Shoten, 1975), 950.

25. Tejima, *Zenkun*, 178.

26. The "samuraization" of family law under the auspices of the 1898 Civil Code, together with the Meiji state's advocacy of the "good wife, wise mother" gender role for all classes of women, occasioned the eventual hegemony of male "experts" on motherhood; see Koyama Shizuko, "Kindaiteki joseikan to shite no ryōsai kenbo shisō," *Joseigaku nenpō* 3 (1982): 1–7.

she engaged in no other occupations than these[27]—a highly unlikely event given her necessary role in the family's livelihood. The Shingaku rhetoric of women, in this case, dwelled on select crafts over childraising and shopkeeping, and was removed from mundane reality, focused as it was on an ideal-type female-likeness and not on individual women.

The space within which "female work" was to be undertaken was similarly categorized by gender. From the age of ten, Toan admonished in his *Zenkun* lectures, females must not venture past the door (*nakado*) dividing the inner living quarters (*oku*) from the outer store (*omote*). Likewise, married women must not become involved in "outward facing" (*omotemuki*), or public, matters; these were their husbands' affair.[28] Toan was here addressing girls and women of the merchant and artisan sectors, although the gist of his teachings, like the Shingaku corpus as a whole, was intended for females from every class and status group. Since urban women were actively involved in the running of shops and trading concerns, "outward facing" very likely referred to sales and business trips away from the premises. Gender was thus used as a rationale for setting the spatial parameters of those activities; it was not intended to prohibit women (especially *chōnin*) from shopkeeping altogether.

The architecture of the Shingaku colleges (*kōsha*) symbolically extended the sexism and gender ideals that informed the movement. Virtually all of the 180 colleges founded in forty-four provinces throughout Japan were modeled after Meirinsha (1782), the head college in Kyoto. Meirinsha was divided into eight rooms, including one reserved for women labeled *fujin*. When public lectures were held at a college, the sliding doors separating the rooms were removed to create maximum space and bamboo blinds were installed to separate female from male listeners. This temporary, gendered space was labeled *nyoshi seki*, or "females' place."[29]

The inspiration for the gendered division of space may have derived from the interior design of both the imperial palace in Kyoto and the castles of the shōgun and his vassals. Just as the strict separation of "female" and "male" work was more typical of samurai than of *chōnin* households, so the architectural representation of gender bore little resemblance to the exigencies of urban life. The innermost quarters (*ōoku*) were both the home and workplace of female members of the court and military elite. These castles, with a female staff numbering in the thousands, were targeted by Shingaku leaders in their campaign to recruit female members and disciples. Since females were prohibited from

27. Tejima, *Zenkun*, 173–74.
28. Ibid., 173.
29. For illustrations, see Robertson, "Rooting the Pine."

exiting and males from entering the innermost quarters, the task of educating the wives of male courtiers and daimyō and their attendants fell to the movement's female instructors.

It was in the *fujin* room of a Shingaku college that the women among the disciples and interested listeners received instruction on *onnarashisa*. This room was a laboratory for the creation of the Shingaku Woman. Here women were introduced to the Shingaku texts for female disciples, including Toan's *Zenkun* and *Onna myōga kai* (A treatise on female fate, 1776). They were urged to follow the "four virtues," which were promoted as the basis of household health: wifely words (*fugen*), wifely morality (*futoku*), wifely merit (*fukō*), and wifely etiquette (*fuyō*). The implication was that women must self-consciously strive for these virtues and that the first step toward reaching their goal was marriage; this in turn evoked a special nomenclature in acknowledgment of their success: "wifely morality," as opposed to morality per se. The interface between social morality and the sex-gender hierarchy is evident here.

Whereas in *Zenkun* married women were the linchpins of the household as a body politic, females in general were castigated as having "constricted hearts, making them easily prone to stinginess and vain pride."[30] It was an impossible situation: virtuous females were crucial in every sense for household posterity, yet female anatomy precluded virtuous behavior. Toan's solution was the arbitrary separation of sex roles (specifically childbirth) from sexuality (desire) in married women. Sexuality proper was limited to concubines and courtesans.

Marriage effectively was the rite of passage that not only severed a woman from her sexuality but also "killed" her. As Toan expounded in *Zenkun*, "a bride must become like a dead person; she cannot return to her natal household" where as a daughter she had been whole. "To signify her death, she must build a [funeral] bonfire to break her attachment [*en*] to her parents." The married and consequently dis-membered and "dead" woman could be reconstructed and rejuvenated only "by becoming one with the heart of her husband."[31] In *Onna myōga kai*, Toan warned that for married women to postpone discovering original heart was tantamount not merely to beastiality, but to "privatizing [their] entire being" (*watakushi suru mi*); moreover, the woman who happened to "regard her privatized being as splendid and wonderful" was warned that she would automatically "break out in filthy, smelly, blood-and-pus-filled sores."[32]

A woman who had successfully identified herself with her husband would have "a loving and endearing attitude toward his concubine." Ad-

---

30. Tejima, *Zenkun*, 173–74.
31. Ibid., 175.
32. Tejima Toan, *Onna myōga kai*, in Shibata (ed.), *Zōho Tejima Toan zenshū*, 194.

monished Toan, himself married and a father: "Because a woman's heart is constricted, she is more prone to jealousy, and therefore perceives many shortcomings in her husband. Do not be jealous of your husband's concubine [*mekake*]; rather, respect the depth of his attachment to her. This way you will not be seen as a wife ashamed of her husband's behavior. Nor will the concubine dislike or scorn you."[33]

Although a male could traverse both of the arbitrarily separated wifely and erotic spheres of female being, a female was limited to one or the other. A wife should refrain from having extramarital affairs of her own and from criticizing those of her husband. She was also instructed to indulge the concubine and, in effect, to perceive the latter's sexuality as her own. The wholeness of males, the posterity of the patriarchal household, and the stability of society, in short, were contingent on the dis-memberment of females: the separation of sex from sexuality, and the separation and isolation of females from each other by intervening males.

Toan's "Lectures for Women" reflect his conviction that females generically were creatures in need of civilizing, and that Japanese women in particular were retrograde. The latter bias is evident in his reference in *Zenkun* to historical Chinese women exclusively as exemplars of female-likeness.[34] Toan set about constructing the Shingaku Woman in part by assembling a vocabulary of images of non-Japanese women to meet the ideological needs of Shingaku and, by extension, of the patriarchal and misogynist society in which the movement was embedded. From his androcentric perspective, all females were Others, but Chinese women were "good" Others and Japanese women "bad" Others; among the latter, only the Shingaku Woman was "good." These images acquired the significance of symbols that were used to conceptualize the contrast between females and males, and between females and female-likeness. As in any society, these constructed Others were "perpetuated, resurrected, and shaped through texts containing the fantasy life of the culture, quite independent of the existence or absence of the group in . . . society. . . . Qualities assigned to the Other readily form patterns with little or no relationship to any external reality."[35]

It was in the space between the "fantasy life" spun around the Shin-

33. Tejima, *Zenkun*, 179.

34. The prevalence of historical Chinese women is due to the fact that Toan based much of his "Lectures for Women" on the Northern Sung statesman-scholar Sima Guang's (1019–86) *Jiafan* (Exemplary household), in addition to other Chinese classics and dynastic histories.

35. Sander Gilman, *Difference and Pathology: Stereotypes of Sexuality, Race, and Madness* (Ithaca, N.Y.: Cornell University Press, 1985), 20–21.

gaku Woman and the "external reality" impacting on Tokugawa-period girls and women that female disciples and teachers operated. Jion-ni Kenka was one woman who actually appropriated that space in her search for a significant life.

FEMALE DISCIPLES: THE EXAMPLE OF JION-NI KENKA

From the outset, girls and women were not only the subjects but also the disseminators of Shingaku teachings. Among Baigan's earliest disciples was Jion-ni Kenka (1716–78), a former Buddhist nun who paved the way for the expansion of Shingaku into the Kantō region.

Kenka was born in the village of Tokiwa, Kurita county, Omi province, the daughter of Shirai Hanbei, a wealthy sake brewer. Her given name is unknown. What little is known about her life and work comes from her partly autobiographical book, which, originally titled *Kenka hogushū* (Kenka's scribblings, 1756), was reprinted in 1774 under the more sober heading *Dōtoku mondō* (Moral dialogues).[36]

Kenka's book opens with a section headed, "[I] decided to seek buddhahood upon my mother's death when I was eight years old." Given the invisibility of the "mother" in Tokugawa-period discourses, it is significant that Kenka, who never mentions by name or describes her mother in the book, should have linked the death of her mother with the start of her unorthodox life. Her mother's absence apparently was more important than her presence.

At her mother's funeral, Kenka had been scolded by the Tendai Buddhist priest officiating for misbehaving during the otherwise solemn ritual. He advised the feisty girl to ensure her mother's well-being in the afterworld by chanting the Lotus Sutra. She did, and quickly decided she wanted to become a Buddhist priest (*bōzu*)[37] and to spend her life reciting sutras for her dead mother. This episode at the beginning of her book suggests not only the bond between mother and daughter, but also the emotional centrality of a mother—even if deceased—in her daughter's life, despite the fact that a mother's love was not emphasized by the Shingaku rhetoricians and their contemporaries.

Kenka's desire to become a priest foreshadowed her rejection of

36. In Akabori Matajirō, ed., *Shingaku sōsho* (Hakabunkan, 1905), 165–235.

37. The term *bōzu* (shaved head) applied to both females and males, though it is most tenaciously associated with priests. Since females who shaved their heads were those who had renounced their prescribed gender, it is interesting to note the existence of *obōzu* among the female employees of the various castles. These were women who assumed or were assigned "male" gender in order to mediate between the innermost (female) and outermost (male) courts; they shaved their heads and dressed in *haori* and *hakama*, formal attire for males. See Takayanagi Kaneyoshi, *Edojō ōoku no seikatsu* (Yūzankaku, 1965), 17.

the conventional gender role(s) allotted females. Yet Kenka's father refused her permission to take holy orders, whereupon she ran away. In between her mother's death and her departure from her father's house at age fourteen, the strong-minded girl pursued a self-styled course of prayer and continued to rebuff her father's attempts to arrange a marriage for her. She even cut off her hair, a symbolic act of defiance marking her withdrawal from the world of mundane, secular affairs.[38] "She's not the least bit female-like" (*hitotsu to shite onnarashiki wa nashi*), Kenka's father despaired. "All she does, day and night, is pray to the buddhas and *kami* [Shintō deities], and she roughhouses with the boys. What a terrific monkey she'll become!"[39] In preparation for her flight from home, the teen-ager made secret inquiries about accessible nunneries (*amadera*) before stealing off to Ichiyō-an, an Ōbaku temple in Kyoto's western Kamo area. Her father, discovering her absence, set out after her, but she refused to turn back.

Becoming a nun in the Tokugawa period did not necessarily imply that a girl or woman was religiously inclined. Taking holy orders marked a female's rite of passage from an active secular life as a wife, widow, or concubine to an inactive secular life; a married to a divorced state; a fertile period to an infertile one; or a (hetero)sexually active period to an inactive one. Girls and women also looked to religious institutions as refuges from marital oppression and male violence, as in the case of the Tokugawa-period "divorce temples" for nonsamurai women.[40] For Kenka, then, religion offered an alternative to prescribed female gender roles.

The Tokugawa period saw an unprecedented increase in the number and diversity of nuns.[41] This trend has been linked to the entrenchment of a Confucian patriarchy and the concomitant reification of repressive gender roles.[42] Women from all walks of life—court aristocrats, samurai, merchants, farmers, maidservants, litterateurs, poets, artists, Buddhist scholars, publishers—chose to become nuns; many took holy

38. Conventionally, at least since the Heian period (794–1185), women cut their hair to signal their disengagement from the secular world.

39. Jion-ni Kenka, *Dōtoku Mondō*, in Akabori (ed.), *Shingaku sōsho*, 170.

40. Kaneko Sachiko and Robert E. Morrell, "Sanctuary: Kamakura's Tōkeiji Convent," *Japanese Journal of Religious Studies* 10, nos. 2–3 (1983): 195–228.

41. Many pertinent documents were destroyed by fire. It is estimated that more than two thousand women were granted divorces through the Tōkeiji offices from about 1700 to 1870. This figure represents but a minuscule fraction of (unhappily married) women, much less nuns, in the Tokugawa period. See ibid., 214–15.

42. Araki Ryōsen, *Bikunishi* (Shōdō Shoten, 1929; reprint Tōyō Shoin, 1977); Jōdoshū Nisōshi Hensan Iinkai, ed., *Jōdoshū nisōshi* (Kyoto: Yoshimizu Gakuen Kōtō Gakkō, 1961), 24–29; Sōtōshū Nisōshi Hensankai, ed., *Sōtōshū nisōshi* (Sōtōshū Honbu, 1955), 226–34.

orders as an alternative to marriage, often, as they noted in their (auto)biographies, in defiance of their fathers.[43] Thus Kenka was not entirely unusual in choosing convent over convention.

During her stay at Ichiyō-an Kenka learned to read the Buddhist sutras, but she felt that this alone was insufficient for enlightenment and sought out other teachers. Eventually she became the disciple of a Sōtō nun, Tōkoku-ni, based at Nansen-an in Hikone, under whom she studied Zen koan. Still dissatisfied with her progress, however, she soon turned to ritual austerities as a means of facilitating enlightenment. She began with all-day fasts and temporarily retired to Ishiyama Temple in Kyoto to conduct a week-long fast. She gave up drinking tea, engrossed herself in prayers of several days' duration, and added cold water ablutions to her spartan regimen. Yet none of the available techniques designed to bring about enlightenment worked for her.

Kenka did succeed, by the age of twenty-four, in destroying her health. Pending consultations with her family, she rented a house in Kyoto for her convalescence. Her father's death shortly before her move exacerbated her ill health, and she became plagued by feelings of remorse for having caused him so much suffering. It was during her convalescence in Kyoto that she met Baigan, who lived and lectured in the area, and became his disciple.[44]

Regardless of the veracity of Kenka's trials and tribulations, the teleology of the account—leading as it does to her eventual discovery of original heart—served well as Shingaku propaganda. Toan likely interpreted Kenka's account of her youthful rebelliousness as the compelling story of a young woman in search of what Shingaku had to offer. Kenka herself praised Baigan profusely, for it was through his eclectic teachings, she insisted, that she regained her mental composure and physical health, and finally experienced enlightenment.[45] Nevertheless, her book is also a chronicle of an unmarried woman's quest for knowledge and self-sufficiency in late-eighteenth-century Japan. It is two texts in one: a memoir of her unorthodox life and livelihood, and a Shingaku primer. This ambiguity allowed her readers to extract whatever they wished from her words. Jion-ni Kenka was hardly a model Shingaku Woman,

43. See, for example, *Sōtōshū nisōshi*, 235–311.

44. Before Kenka there was another female disciple, twenty-nine-year-old Yamakawa Yuri, about whom virtually nothing is known; see Ishikawa, *Sekimon Shingakushi no kenkyū*, 215.

45. Kenka's enlightenment probably was along the lines of Toan's experience. One evening, as Toan was slipping into his *yukata* (robe) after bathing, he suddenly cried out, "Am I wearing my *yukata* or is my *yukata* wearing me?" Bursting with profound joy, he ran to tell a senior disciple about his experience. Without warning, the disciple slapped Toan's cheeks—a shock tactic intended as a final touch to enlightenment. See Iwauchi Seiichi, *Kyōikuka to shite no Ishida Baigan* (Ritsumeikan Shuppanbu, 1934), 257–58.

for she had rebelled against female-likeness, patriarchal authority, marriage, and orthodox Buddhism. She was, to borrow the language of the 1960s, a woman against the Establishment. Yet Kenka found a niche for herself within an essentially misogynist organization.

During her convalescence in Kyoto, Kenka developed a strong interest in Baigan's lecture series and eclectic mode of argumentation. His morning discourses were devoted to an exegesis of the Chinese and Japanese classics, and his evening ones to an interpretation of the Nō play *Yamauba* (Mountain witch). Kenka made a point of noting that Baigan encouraged women as well as men to attend his free lectures, although the sexes were separated by bamboo blinds: thus, until Toan's curriculum designed for females exclusively, women and men apparently listened and responded to the same lecture material. Significantly, part of Kenka's text consists of a running dialogue between herself and Baigan. Among various reasons for her becoming a Shingaku disciple was perhaps the opportunity to debate and lecture publicly, which the *bakufu* discouraged nuns from doing.[46]

Kenka arrived in Edo sometime during 1750, her nun's habit, which she retained, doubtless facilitating her freedom of movement through the many border stations en route.[47] Following Baigan's precedent, she then hung out a shingle advertising her free lectures for the women and men of Edo. Her talks incorporated the sutras, *Tsurezuregusa*, Nō songs, and Baigan's works. While it is not clear where she lived or how she went about her proselytizing activities, we do know that she wrote *Kenka hogoshū* during the first part of her ten-year residence in Edo. She noted that her morning lectures drew a peak audience of 700–900 women and men, and her afternoon and evening sessions some 1,200 persons. Kenka estimated that over a six-month period she addressed more than 102,500 women and men, many of whom were undoubtedly repeat visitors. The authorities must have been suspicious of the crowds around her, for as another disciple noted thirty years later in a letter to Toan, the potentially antagonistic *bakufu* posed a constant worry to the movement.[48]

Kenka returned to Kyoto in 1760 to participate in the ceremonies for the seventh anniversary of Baigan's death. There she spoke on the sutras, *Tsurezuregusa*, and Baigan's *Tohimondō* (City-country dialogues, 1739). At first, the disciples who had joined the movement in her absence "mistook her for a mountain ascetic or sermonizer before recog-

---

46. *Sōtōshū nisōshi*, 317.

47. Kogure Kikuko, "Kinsei ni okeru josei no sekisho tsūkō ni tsuite," in *Kinsei joseishi*, ed. Kinsei Joseishi Kenkyūkai (Yoshikawa Kōbunkan, 1986), 44–99.

48. Shiba Keiko, "Jion-ni," in *Shinkō to ai to shi to*, vol. 7 of *Jinbutsu Nihon no joseishi*, ed. Enchi Fumiko (Shūeisha, 1977), 161.

nizing the profundity of her knowledge." It is on this self-affirming note that Kenka ends the autobiographical portion of her book. She remained in Kyoto, never to return to Edo owing to her frail health; her last years were spent in her native village. After sixty-three years, she had come full circle.

The majority of *Kenka hogoshū* is a reiteration of Baigan's teachings; seven of the nineteen chapters were copied directly from *Ishida sensei goroku* (The analects of Teacher Ishida, 1740s). The title of the single chapter aimed explicitly at women, "For Women There Is the Path of the Three Obediences," captures the conventional tenor and content of the nonautobiographical sections of her book. It is ironic that Kenka should have contributed to the construction of the Shingaku Woman when she herself had rejected the Path of Three Obediences. Perhaps the fact that she had, by taking the tonsure, withdrawn from secular and sexual affairs helped disqualify her as a "real" female in need of reform. Also, the movement in its initial stages was still unsystematized and therefore flexible enough both to attract and to accommodate mavericks like herself.

OTHER FEMALE DISCIPLES

Kenka's work to introduce Baigan's teachings to Edo paved the way for Nakazawa Dōni (1725–1803), a male disciple who established in that city one of the most influential Shingaku colleges, Sanzensha (1781). Dōni made friends with the many daimyō temporarily residing in Edo as part of their obligatory attendance upon the shōgun, and, impressed by their initial exposure to Shingaku, many sponsored the establishment of colleges in their domains as well. Thus, as a result of Dōni's efforts, Shingaku permeated a good part of the samurai class; yet his success was contingent on Kenka's pioneering efforts.[49]

Among Dōni's disciples was Asai Kio and her low-ranking samurai husband. In the spring of 1794, Kio was invited to develop a Shingaku curriculum for maidservants at Edo (Chiyoda) Castle, and she lectured there and at other daimyō residences for several years.[50] "She can go where I cannot tread," Dōni wrote in a letter in 1796. "We are fortunate to have her among us."[51] In an age of censorship and prohibitions, Shingaku lecturers had to take great care that the movement was not mis-

---

49. Ishikawa, *Sekimon Shingakushi no kenkyū*, 304; Takenaka Yasukazu, *Sekimon Shingakushi no keizai shisō* (Kyoto: Mineruba Shobō, 1972), 541.

50. Ishikawa Ken, *Shingaku kyōka no honshitsu narabi ni hattatsu* (Shōkasha, 1931), 290; Ishikawa, *Sekimon Shingaku no kenkyū*, 463.

51. Ishikawa, *Sekimon Shingaku no kenkyū*, 463.

taken for a subversive or heterodox outfit, and here too Dōni praised his disciple for doing a "most difficult, delicate task."[52]

The three other female lecturers acknowledged in the literature were all based in Hiroshima, where the movement was noted for the large number of women disciples[53]—though apart from Kenka, none of these is described as coming to Shingaku on her own accord. Yaguchi Nakako (1790–1846) was a particularly active member, evidently owing to the influence of her husband, the lord of Hiroshima, who had become a disciple in 1811. He founded and served as the nominal head of Keishinsha (1819), the first of several Hiroshima colleges;[54] yet Nakako took over in his absence, conducting on her own the small study groups and meditation seminars convened for the benefit of disciples.[55] These sessions did not seem to be segregated by sex, though female disciples received additional lectures in the women's room. Nakako often held round-the-clock study sessions with disciples of both sexes at her home or theirs, sometimes for two weeks at a stretch.

Nakako's official role was as a guidance counselor for the female staff in Hiroshima, among whom were two others who achieved renown as Shingaku lecturers as well: Bandai Kumiko (1783–1837) and Tagami Tatsuko (1802–67). Both women—whose husbands were likewise disciples and served as key administrators of Keishinsha—earned teaching permits known as *zendō inkan*, enabling them to give public lectures. Tatsuko also served as a lecturer at Kanshinsha (founded in 1827) in Hiroshima—the only female of eight lecturers. (Her husband was a key administrator there as well.) Toan had established the policy of issuing permits to lecturers, called *kōshi*, both to ensure the quality of the Shingaku staff and to identify *kōshi* as bona fide Shingaku representatives, since they made regular lecture tours to outlying provinces. Female and male disciples were appointed to lectureships on the basis of their exemplary character, oratorical skills, working knowledge of the Chinese and Japanese classics, and enlightenment experience. Toan also set a precedent of awarding certificates (*dansho*) thrice yearly to disciples, such as Kumiko and Tatsuko, who had achieved enlightenment.[56]

Public lectures were held not only at the colleges, but also on a circuit basis, with *kōshi* spending a month or so on the road, lecturing at post

52. Kio continued to supervise new recruits long after Dōni died. Philanthropy was one of the tangible results of her efforts: the contributions of cloth made by seven maidservants and ladies-in-waiting at Tokugawa Castle amounted to seven hundred bolts between the 1790s and the first two decades of the 1800s. See ibid., 846, 866–67.

53. Oikawa Giuemon, "Hiroshima Shingaku no hattatsu," in *Shingaku*, ed. Nagasaka Kaneo, vol. 1 (Yūzankaku, 1941), 8.

54. Ibid., 4; Ishikawa, *Sekimon Shingaku no kenkyū*, 945–46.

55. For details, see Robertson, "Rooting the Pine."

56. Ibid.; Shibata Minoru, *Shingaku* (Shinbundō, 1967), 163.

stations, towns, and villages. Letters from the peripatetic lecturers to their Shingaku colleagues provide some indication of audience attendance. One from 1797 notes that a *Zenkun* class taught by Dōni at Kyōkansha (founded in 1787) in Osaka during the third month was attended by nearly 1,500 women and men, about 70 of whom sought to become members of the movement. Another report dated 1794 notes that a week-long lecture series in a Tanba-province village drew an average of 513 women and men each day, for a total of 6,672 persons.[57] As for the female disciples discussed above, although they were recognized lecturers,[58] it is not clear whether—or how often and how far—they conducted lecture tours. Kenka's pioneering efforts in Edo may not have set a precedent for female disciples.

Much of the lecture rhetoric was phrased in the form of parables (*dōwa*), a composite of proverbs, commonsense precepts, Shingaku principles, and local historical incidents. The basic strategy of the parables was to "direct by appearing to clarify," as they enunciated social problems and simultaneously proposed solutions for them.[59]

Females were the featured subject of many Shingaku parables. Unlike the women's lecturers in *Zenkun*, in *dōwa* both the good and bad Others were Japanese commoners inhabiting the here and now. This change reflected the informal nature of both the parables and the context of their recitation, and rendered their didactic content more accessible to untutored listeners. Like Tokugawa-period fiction in general, the narrative structure of *dōwa* was based on the juxtaposition of stock characters: among the stereotypic bad Others were the "evil woman" (*akujo*),[60] the "jealous wife" (*tofu*), and the "ogre woman" (*kijo*); and among the good Others, the "virtuous woman" (*reppu, teijo*) and the "filial woman" (*kōjo*).[61] Maidservants (*jochū*) were almost always depicted unfavorably in Shingaku parables and other texts—as delinquent, but not evil, women with an incorrigible penchant for expensive clothing and cosmetics, gossip, snickering, and other bad habits. Rare was the portrayal of a loyal, hardworking, practical-minded maidservant.

Good and bad Others came from urban as well as rural areas (though in one parable, Dōni stereotyped Kyoto and Osaka women as smallminded and extravagant in their sartorial and gustatory habits—"they

57. Ishikawa, *Sekimon Shingaku no kenkyū*, 169.

58. Kaneko Genjirō, "Dōwa ni mietaru josei," in Nagasaka (ed.), *Shingaku*, vol. 3 (Yūzankaku, 1932), 4–5.

59. Roger Abrahams, "Introductory Remarks to a Rhetorical Theory of Folklore," *Journal of American Folklore* 81, no. 3 (1968): 150.

60. The "evil woman" was a particularly prevalent image of women in literature and Kabuki alike during the early nineteenth century, her "evilness" stemming from her self-sufficiency and "privatized being"; see Shiba, *Edo jidai no joseitachi*, 55–58, 75.

61. Kaneko, "Dōwa ni mietaru josei," 35–37.

wear expensive clothing, eat [white] rice three times a day, and complain about trivial matters"—while a certain farm woman of Shinano province was cast as the epitome of frugality and diligence).[62] The urban-rural contrast here paralleled the official four-class hierarchy in which farmers were eulogized and urbanites (merchants) disparaged. Their differences notwithstanding, the *Zenkun* lectures and parables were similar in that the qualities assigned women were gender constructs, and not necessarily behaviors manifested by real women. In keeping with the Tokugawa-period rhetoric of women, "brides," "wives," "daughters," and "daughters-in-law" were the types of females depicted in the Shingaku parables.

CONCLUSION

Female disciples and teachers of Shingaku did not epitomize the Shingaku Woman, even though they participated in her construction. The paradox, however, is only an apparent one. For Kenka, Kio, Nakako, and all female disciples, their sex actually prevented them from representing the Shingaku Woman: female anatomy, after all, precluded female-likeness. The logic of anatomical reductionism virtually assured that females could participate only in the *deconstruction* of female-likeness as it was defined by the patriarchical intelligentsia.

Shingaku disciplehood did neutralize some of the negative value imposed on female sex, however. Likewise, by participating in the construction of the Shingaku Woman, female disciples compensated for their "natural" misrepresentation of her. Kio, Nakako, Kumiko, and Tatsuko, because they were married, were less maverick than Kenka; moreover, the records (which may be incomplete or partial) indicate that they did not travel widely. Their lives as Shingaku disciples and teachers more or less conformed to the spatial parameters of female-like activities set by Toan. Yet like Kenka, they lectured publicly and enjoyed a legacy beyond their conjugal households.

The paragon of female-likeness in Tokugawa society remained the Kabuki *onnagata*: male actors who modeled gender constructs developed by male intellectuals. In effect, women's hypothetical achievement of "female" gender was tantamount to their impersonation of female-like males, who, in turn, were not impersonating particular females but rather enacting an idealized version (and vision) of female-likeness. *Bakufu* ideology did not and could not accommodate women's control over the construction and representation of "female" gender.

Tokugawa-period discourses on women, and specifically on female-

62. Ibid., 9.

likeness, were articulated in a number of guises, including *jokun*, the coining of crimes, architectural conventions, and Kabuki performances. They were also played out in the conventional and unconventional ways in which females lived their lives. This suggests that the significance of the life and work of individual Japanese girls and women at any particular time and place needs to be reclaimed from the space between the ideal and the real—between discourses on female-likeness and the actual experiences of real females.

FIVE

Female *Bunjin*: The Life of Poet-Painter Ema Saikō

Patricia Fister

Ema Saikō (1787–1861) was one of the finest Chinese-style poets and painters active in nineteenth-century Japan. Many Edo-period Japanese were drawn to Chinese culture as a result of the Tokugawa shogunate's promotion of Chinese Neo-Confucianism, a philosophy of ethics and government that introduced the Japanese to other facets of Chinese culture, including artistic traditions. Men and women aspiring to become *bunjin* (scholars of Chinese arts and letters) established local Chinese language study groups, practiced composing Chinese-style verse (*kanshi*), and occasionally held exhibitions of Chinese art. By the latter part of the eighteenth century and throughout the nineteenth, literati painting (termed *bunjinga* or *nanga*) enjoyed widespread popularity among men and women of the samurai and educated urban classes.

The earliest female *bunjin*, active in the second half of the eighteenth century, were primarily the wives, sisters, or daughters of well-known *bunjin* artists.[1] The nineteenth century saw a dramatic increase in the number of women literati, for many scholars, inspired by the actions of contemporary masters in China, now encouraged women to join their ranks.[2] As opportunities for education blossomed for both men and

I would like to express my deep appreciation to Ema Shōjirō and his wife, Sumiko: they have welcomed my interest in Saikō and have generously provided me with source material and made their collection available to me for study. I am also indebted to Kado Reiko and Miyake Riko for information on Saikō's life and poetry.

1. For further information, see my *Japanese Women Artists, 1600–1900* (Lawrence, Kans.: Spencer Museum of Art, 1988).

2. In particular, the Ch'ing-dynasty poet Yüan Mei (Sui-yüan) was known to have had many female pupils; in 1796 he published their poetry in a volume entitled *Sui-yüan nü-*

women in Japan, more women became versed in poetry and calligraphy as well as painting. In keeping with the traditional Chinese models favored by literati artists, the subject matter of women *bunjin* was predominantly landscapes and nature studies of the "four gentlemen": bamboo, plum, orchid, and chrysanthemum.

Ema Saikō was one of the first female *bunjin* to gain general recognition and was celebrated for her Chinese-style verse, calligraphy, and austere ink paintings. Her life story, important in its own right as part of the art history of Tokugawa Japan, is also instructive for what it can tell us about the factors that helped produce acknowledged women artists in a male-dominated society. How did a woman artist, especially one from a rural society, come to receive the training, financial support, and encouragement needed to master her craft and to win acclaim from other artists and patrons?

Throughout her life, Ema Saikō's career as an artist was promoted by male mentors. She was born in the village of Ōgaki in Mino province (present-day Gifu prefecture), a region known for its large number of scholars, poets, and artists.[3] From the time Saikō was very young, her father, Ema Ransai (1747–1838), a doctor of medicine and an avid scholar of both Confucianism and *rangaku* (Dutch studies),[4] encouraged her to develop her literary and artistic talents. Her ties with her father were unusually strong, perhaps in part because both her mother and her older brother died when she was only three. Ransai seems to have doted on Saikō, his second child and first daughter, teaching her Chinese literature and the basic skills of calligraphy and painting. Her youthful talents are apparent in a painting of bamboo and sparrows (fig. 5.1) done at age five, and in the calligraphy of a Chinese poem (fig. 5.2) that she wrote at age nine.[5] From the following verse, written many years later, it is clear that Saikō's father served as a strong role model:

A Winter Night

My father deciphers and studies Dutch books;
His daughter reads Chinese poetry.
Divided by a single lamp,
We each follow our own course.
I read on without stopping,

---

ti-tzu hsüan (Selections from Sui-yüan's women pupils). This book was subsequently republished by the poet Ōkubo Shibutsu (1766–1837) in Japan, where it had a catalytic effect on Japanese scholars of Chinese studies, who soon began to cultivate women pupils.

3. The daimyō of this region were ardent supporters of Sinophile scholarship and arts.

4. The most accurate source of information on Saikō is Itō Shin's *Saikō to Kōran* (Gifu: Yabase Ryūkichi, 1969); unless otherwise noted, the biographical information in this chapter comes from this volume.

5. Both scrolls are in the present-day Ema family collection.

Fig. 5.1. Ema Saikō. *Bamboo and Sparrows*. Hanging scroll, ink on paper, 28 × 39 cm. (Ema Shōjirō Collection)

> But become tired, letting my mind wander to chestnuts and
>   sweet potatoes.
> Ashamed that I cannot attain the spirit
> Of my eighty-year-old father, whose eyes are not yet cloudy.[6]

When Saikō was thirteen, her father, recognizing her talents, arranged for her to become a painting student of the Kyoto monk Gyokurin (1751–1814), who specialized in bamboo. This became her favored subject, and Saikō was known throughout her life for her depictions of bamboo. At this early age she did not travel to Kyoto to study with her painting teacher; instead she learned in a manner similar to today's correspondence courses: Gyokurin would send her model-books to copy, and she would respond by sending him examples of her practice work. An early bamboo painting by Saikō in the collection of the Gifu City Museum (fig. 5.3) bears an inscription saying that she modeled it on a Ming painting; however, the thick brushwork forming the culms resembles the style of her teacher, Gyokurin.

Saikō's early exposure to both Chinese literature and art was exceptional for women in Edo-period Japan. Although an increasing number

6. This poem is included in volume 2 of Saikō's poetry collection *Shōmu ikō* (see below, note 15).

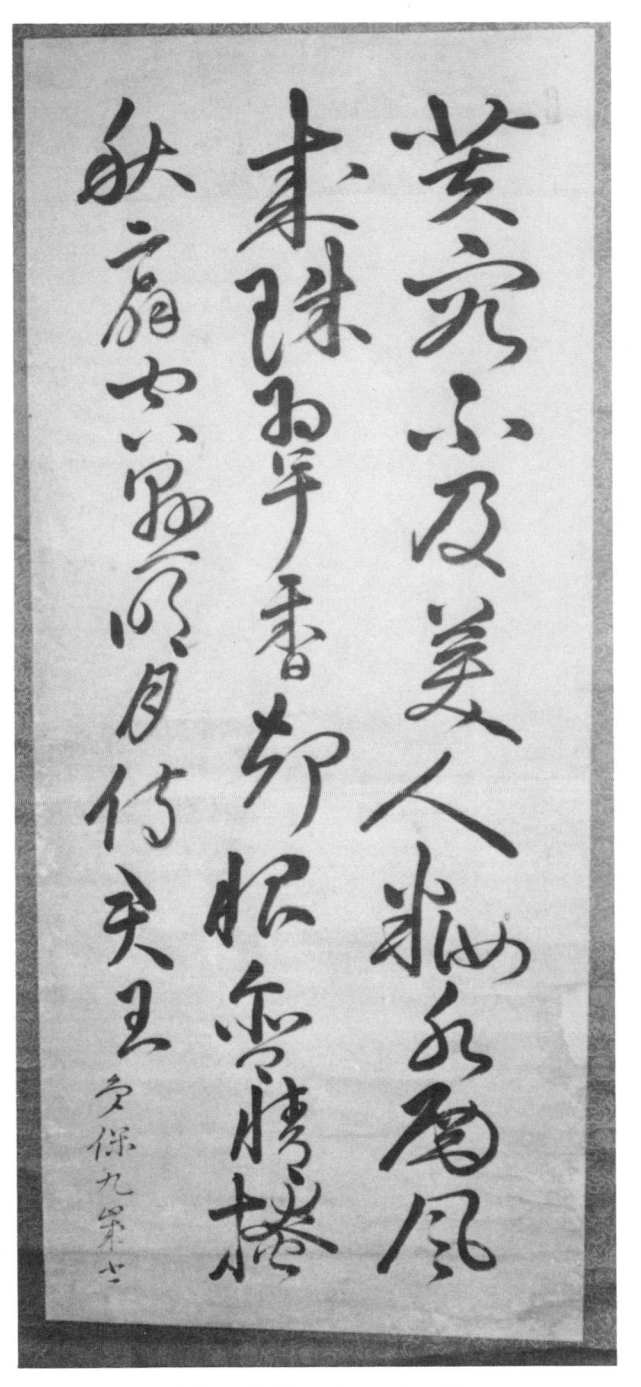

Fig. 5.2. Ema Saikō. *Calligraphy at Age Nine.*
Hanging scroll, ink on paper, 129 × 55 cm.
(Ema Shōjirō Collection)

Fig. 5.3. Ema Saikō. *Bamboo*.
Hanging scroll, ink on paper.
(Gifu City Museum)

of women were receiving some training in Chinese, the kind of long-term commitment that Saikō made was unusual. Quiet and withdrawn as a child, she was permitted to indulge herself thoroughly in her literary and artistic pursuits, perhaps because her father, after losing his only son, lavished his attention on her and saw that she received a full Confucian education more befitting a male member of the samurai class. Ransai's open-minded attitude and encouragement during her formative years were crucial to her adopting an independent life-style later on.

Ransai's deference to his daughter's wishes even extended to the question of her marriage. When she was eighteen, he tried to arrange a marriage between her and a young man named Shōsai, for he hoped to adopt a son-in-law as heir. When Saikō refused on the grounds that she was too deeply involved in her studies of painting, Ransai obligingly arranged for Shōsai to marry Saikō's coquettish and outgoing younger sister. When Ransai retired three years later, Shōsai inherited his father-in-law's position as physician to the daimyō of Ōgaki, with its stipend of one hundred *koku*. Ransai must have made special arrangements for Saikō, because her family continued to support her throughout her life, financing her lessons as well as her trips.

In 1813, Saikō met another man who would wield great influence on her life as an artist. This was Rai San'yō (1780–1832), a distinguished poet and scholar, and the only man Saikō ever wanted to marry. Born into a family of prominent Confucian officials in Hiroshima, in his youth San'yō was known for his brilliant scholarship and rambunctious personality. The latter part of his life was spent in Kyoto, where he opened a private school. He became a major figure in the literati world, renowned for his Chinese-style verse and an innovative history of Japan entitled *Nihon gaishi* (An unofficial history of Japan), as well as for his calligraphy and painting.

San'yō had been urged by a friend to visit the Ema household in order to meet her well-known father, but during his visit he was charmed by Saikō's beauty and talent. He agreed to become her poetry teacher, and the following year he asked Ransai for her hand in marriage. Ransai refused for reasons that are not clear. It is generally believed that Ransai was oblivious to Saikō's warm feelings for San'yō and rejected the proposal out of respect for her previously stated desire to devote her life to artistic pursuits. (Saikō was supposedly absent at this time.) Ransai was also probably aware of San'yō's history of dissipation and may not have wanted his daughter to marry a man of such character. When he found out that she favored the marriage, however, he sent someone to Kyoto to negotiate with San'yō, but by then San'yō had already arranged to marry a woman named Rie.

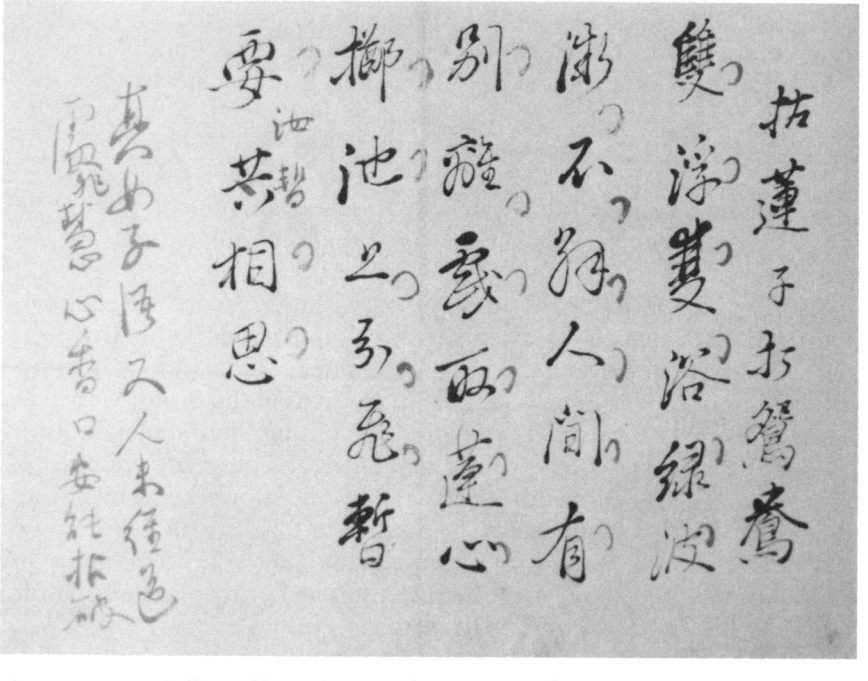

Fig. 5.4. Ema Saikō. *Chinese Poem with Corrections by Rai San'yō*. Ink on paper. (Ema Shōjirō Collection)

Heartbroken, Saikō never married, but she remained a close student and friend of both San'yō and his wife.[7] The letters and poetry that San'yō and Saikō wrote to each other tell us that Saikō remained one of his favorite pupils until his death. They carried on a spirited correspondence, with Saikō sending San'yō poems she had written, and him sending her his corrections. Many examples of Saikō's poems with San'yō's criticisms in red ink are preserved in the Ema family collection, including the page shown in figure 5.4.

Beginning in 1814 Saikō traveled to Kyoto once every two or three years, usually in the spring or autumn and generally accompanied by a servant or relative.[8] The length of her stays ranged from two weeks to

7. Many exaggerated stories have been passed down over the years regarding the relationship between Saikō and San'yō, primarily written in the Meiji and Taishō periods. Certain authors felt free to fictionalize and obviously had not read their letters. Accounts of Saikō written in her own time are all favorable.

8. Saikō made seven trips to Kyoto before San'yō's death: in 1814, 1817, 1819, 1822, 1824, 1827, and 1830.

one month. The main purpose of these visits was to meet and study with San'yō, as well as to view the celebrated Kyoto scenery. She went often to San'yō's home, where she formed a sisterly relationship with Rie. From the diary of San'yō's mother, Baishi, we know that Saikō accompanied San'yō and members of his family on many journeys, and that on several occasions she stayed overnight at his home. It is clear that they remained devoted to each other, and that their relationship went beyond that of teacher and pupil. They had a special friendship that blossomed over the years, and one could even surmise that a form of love existed between the two.

Nevertheless, rumors that San'yō and Saikō carried on a romantic affair after his marriage would seem to be unfounded. Saikō had been raised in a very strict and proper family, and it is unlikely that she would act in such a way as to offend the moral standards of the day. The fact that she was welcomed by San'yō's family and colleagues, who praised her for her quiet, gentle, and virtuous nature, suggests that she and San'yō were not lusting after each other in secluded inns, as some writers would have us believe![9]

San'yō introduced Saikō to many Kyoto artists and poets, including Uragami Shunkin (1779–1846), Nakabayashi Chikutō (1776–1853), Ōkura Ryūzan (1785–1850) and his wife Yoshida Shūran (1797–1866), Koishi Teien (pen name Genzui, 1784–1849), the monk Unge (1783–1850), and Yamamoto Baiitsu (1783–1856). These people formed a kind of salon, providing an appreciative audience for Saikō's work and stimulating her creative output. Over the years Saikō became especially close friends with Shūran, another of San'yō's female students. She also collaborated with Shunkin and his father Gyokudō (1745–1820): in a painting that the three *bunjin* produced in 1814 during Saikō's first visit to Kyoto, Saikō painted the rock and bamboo jutting inward from the lower right corner; Shunkin did the chrysanthemums; and Gyokudō contributed the landscape partially enclosed in a circle (fig. 5.5). Such joint endeavors were common in *bunjin* circles among individuals who shared similar sentiments about art and poetry. That same year, Saikō also contributed a painting to an album that was compiled and presented to Gyokudō on his seventieth birthday, and a woodblock illustration of one of her bamboo paintings was included in the 1814 *Meika gafu* (A book of paintings by famous masters).

Saikō's first visit to Kyoto was further commemorated by a poem written by Unge:

9. See, for example, Sakamoto Tatsunosuke (Kizan), *Rai San'yō* (Keibunkan, 1913) and Ichijima Kenkichi (Shunjō), *Zuihitsu Rai San'yō* (Waseda Daigaku Shuppanbu, 1925); also Itō, *Saikō to Kōran*, 174.

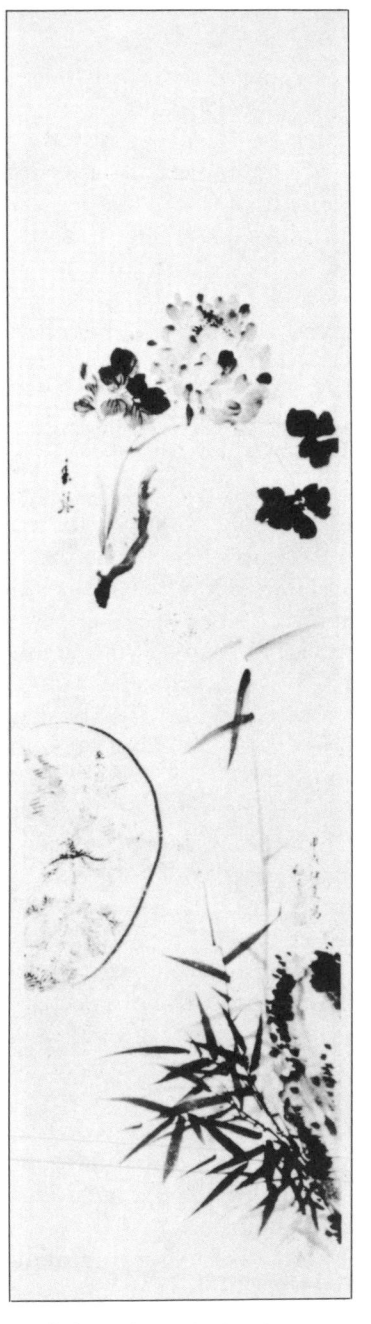

Fig. 5.5. Collaborative painting by Ema Saikō,
Uragami Gyokudō, and Uragami Shunkin, 1814.
Hanging scroll, ink and light color on paper,
118.4 × 28.5 cm. (Private collection, Japan)

Presented to Saikō Joshi from Mino while at a teahouse

This elegant, refined lady's brush has the spirit of the wind;
A delicately scented fragrance is emitted from her green sleeves.
One flourish of ink results in bamboo on a round fan;
Untainted by cosmetics, she is unsurpassed.

Over the years Unge, who was clearly a great admirer of hers, dedicated several other poems to Saikō.[10] The following, written ten years later, is indicative of the high esteem in which he and other *bunjin* held their colleague; it was presented to Saikō when she was about to return to Mino. Unge alludes to the fact that while in Kyoto she plunged whole-heartedly into the life of a *bunjin*, but when she returned home, she had to adopt a more traditional feminine role:

You entered Kyoto carrying a curved bamboo brush,
Not interested in fashionable matters like applying makeup.
You nonchalantly brushed a few bamboo and pale plum
      blossoms on paper
And inscribed your superb landscapes with poems.

Before you depart, in this lingering candlelight,
Don't refuse the farewell wine—let me fill your cup once more.
Tomorrow you will leave with your cosmetic box—
May the hazy moon in Mino call forth memories of our
      camaraderie.

San'yō made sure that Saikō was included in any *bunjin* gatherings that occurred while she was visiting, and over the years she made many group excursions with other artists and poets to scenic places all over Kyoto and Nara, such as Arashiyama and Yoshino. Traces of the friendship Saikō shared with her colleagues are visible in such objects as a purse that she once owned, with inscribed poems by San'yō and Shunkin (fig. 5.6). San'yō urged her to consider moving to Kyoto, but any such hopes she might have entertained were dashed when her brother-in-law died in 1820; henceforth she was expected to remain home and help with the family. A poem composed by San'yō when Saikō was about to return to Ōgaki after one of her Kyoto visits captures the spirit of their close friendship:

A parting meal, low lamp—stay and enjoy it a bit longer;
New mud on the road home—better wait till it dries.
On peaks across the river, clouds only now dispersing;
Strings and songs in the house next door beginning to fade in
      the night.

10. For Unge's poems, see Akamatsu Bunjirō, ed., *Unge Shōnin ikō* (Nakatsu: Gochō-kaku, 1933).

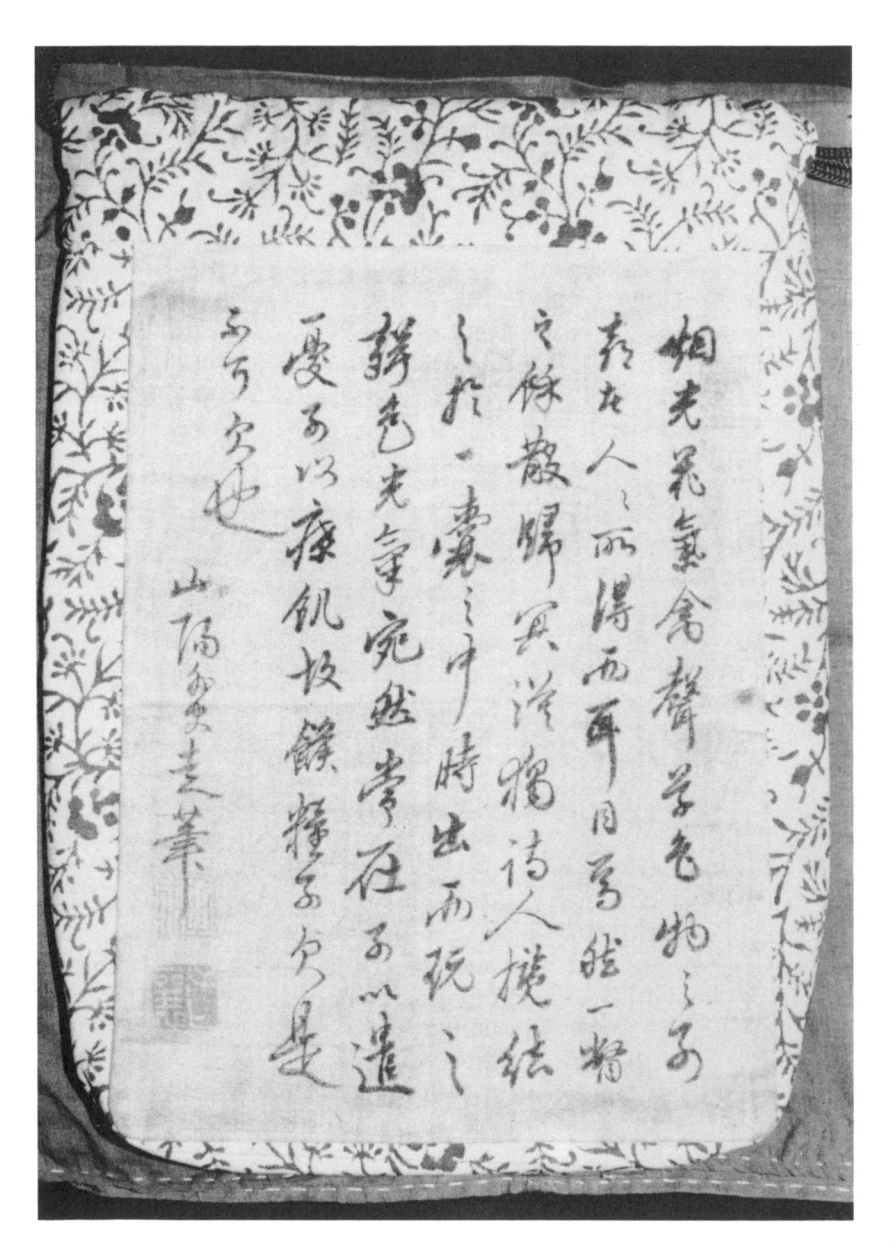

Fig. 5.6. Purse owned by Ema Saikō with inscriptions by Rai San'yō (above) and Uragami Shunkin (right). (Kyoto National Museum)

Intercalary month this spring—my guest lingers on,
Though last night's rain heartlessly scattered the cherry flowers.
From here you go to Mino—not a long way away.
Though, growing old, I know how hard it is to meet now and
    then.[11]

In this small world of unconventional intellectuals, women artists like
Saikō were able to develop their skills in an atmosphere of equal relations with men. In addition to studying Chinese poetry with San'yō,
Saikō continued to refine her skills in calligraphy. From 1814 on, San'yō
sent her modelbooks filled with characters he had brushed for her to
copy. As a result of this practice, Saikō's mature calligraphy shows her
teacher's distinctive influence, featuring smooth and rounded characters brushed with a strong stately rhythm.

Although Saikō had initially studied painting with Gyokurin, on
San'yō's urging she became a pupil of Uragami Shunkin around 1817.
When in Kyoto she would meet and study directly with Shunkin,
but otherwise she learned through the correspondence method, with
Shunkin brushing his criticisms on her exercise scrolls in red ink (fig.
5.7). Saikō would repeat the same motif over and over again, following
the Oriental training practice in which pupils copy the work of their
teacher until they have mastered his technique. Saikō continued to focus
on bamboo, but expanded her repertoire to include other bird-and-
flower subjects. Her second favorite "gentleman" was the chrysanthemum, a symbol both of fortitude and of the poet recluse T'ao Yüan-
ming. In figure 5.8 we see the blossoms growing up behind an eroded
Chinese rock; her brisk and confident handling of the brush and her
use primarily of ink and pale washes of yellow, green, and blue result
in an image that embodies the lofty and austere qualities praised by
bunjin.

San'yō was proud of his pupil's progress and to promote her talents
took examples of her painting with him when he traveled. The following letter, written by San'yō to his friend and patron Chikka, demonstrates his support for Saikō (as well as his somewhat immodest evaluation of his own contributions to her artistic development):

I am sending you an ink bamboo painting by my female student, Saikō.
Recently, you have been careful not to spend money, and have not bought

---

11. Translation by Burton Watson, from *Japanese Literature in Chinese*, vol. 2 (New
York: Columbia University Press, 1976), 152. For more information on Chinese-style verse
in Japan, see Watson's *Kanshi: The Poetry of Ishikawa Jōzan and Other Edo-Period Poets* (San
Francisco: North Point Press, 1990). Unless otherwise indicated, all translations are by
author.

Fig. 5.7. Ema Saikō. *Section from a Practice Scroll with Corrections by Uragami Shun-kin*. Ink on paper. (Ema Shōjirō Collection)

Ming paintings. Luckily this bamboo painting has been mounted and I send it to you because I thought you might find pleasure in this sort of painting as well.... P.S.: I would like to add that, although this lady's painting is famous, it used to be of a vulgar kind, similar to the paintings by Gyokurin and that after becoming my student she corrected these vulgar aspects, so that now this painting looks like a genuine Chinese painting by a Ming painter, with many of the Southern School characteristics: notice, for example, the texture strokes in the rocks around the lower part of the painting.[12]

Saikō's mature bamboo paintings, as represented by figure 5.9, a scroll done when she was sixty-five years old, are characterized by crisp and deliberate brushwork imbued with the strength that connoisseurs refer to as "bone." Tall, thin culms, from which spring slender, sharply tapering leaves, were also typical of her style; although many leaves overlap, Saikō preserved their clarity of structure. She varied the tone of her ink, presenting the bamboo closest to the viewer in rich black and gradually lightening the tones to create the illusion of receding planes. Saikō described the painting process in her quatrain in the upper right

12. Translation by Yoko Woodson, from "Traveling *Bunjin* Painters and Their Patrons: Economic Life Style and Art of Rai San'yō and Tanomura Chikuden" (Ph.D. diss., University of California, Berkeley, 1983), 42.

Fig. 5.8. Ema Saikō. *Chrysanthemums*.
Hanging scroll, ink and light color on paper,
122 × 27.3 cm. (Ema Shōjirō Collection)

Fig. 5.9. Ema Saikō. *Bamboo and Rock*, 1852.
Hanging scroll, ink on satin, 132 × 58 cm.
(Ema Shōjirō Collection)

of figure 5.9, comparing her bamboo to "azure dragons" emerging from misty clouds:

> I have filled this scroll with misty clouds of ink:
> Azure dragons, halted by a wall of rocks,
> Snake forth their claws in the lower foreground,
> Seeming to drink the inkstone until it is dry.

In such paintings, Saikō was not striving to capture the outward likeness of her subject; instead she was more concerned with expressing her inner nature, through the medium of brushwork, while depicting subjects laden with symbolic meanings. Chinese and Japanese literati often discounted the representational aspect of painting, since it was felt to limit the imagination of both the artist and the viewer. In the circles of scholars and artists with whom Saikō associated, personal expression in art was more highly valued than fidelity to outward appearances. Saikō avidly collected Chinese books and was familiar with the major scholarly treatises on painting.[13] The following poem by her, titled "Painting," contains passages taken from the writings of two great Chinese literati masters, Su Tung-p'o (1036–1101) and Ni Tsan (1301–74):

> Discussing painting in terms of formal likeness
> Is the point of view of a child.
> Who is it that speaks these words?
> It is the scholar Su Tung-p'o.

> I take his words as inspiration;
> Without forethought, I spill ink out upon the paper,
> Creating a scroll of Chinese bamboo,
> All of which has sprung forth from the tip of the brush.

> If I am able to capture what is in my breast,
> Why should I care about the criticisms of others?
> It may look like hemp or rushes—
> I just leave it up to the viewer.[14]

In addition to making a name for herself in Kyoto, Saikō also became a major cultural figure in her home village of Ōgaki. Around 1820, Yanagawa Seigan (1789–1858) formed the Hakuōsha poetry society there, and Saikō was one of the ten original members. A portrait of this society painted in 1822 shows Saikō in the lower right, with Seigan's wife, Kōran (also a member), seated just behind her (fig. 5.10). The following

---

13. Among the many books once in her possession were the *Hasshū gafu*; *Kashien gaden*; *Jūchikusai gafu*; *Chikubu shōroku*, compiled by Li K'an; *Bai Dōjin boku chikubu*, edited by Nakayama Kōyō; *Genmeishinjin meiroku*; *Honchō gashi*, edited by Kano Einō; and *Rongashi*, by Uragami Shunkin.

14. From volume 2 of the *Shōmu ikō*. These volumes are unpaginated, and the poems are unnumbered.

Fig. 5.10. *Portrait of Hakuōsha*, 1822.

year several of Saikō's poems were published in the *Mino fūga*, a compilation of verse by *bunjin* living in the Mino area. San'yō, who was actively involved in the publishing world, later tried to persuade Saikō to allow a collection of her verses to be published. She refused out of modesty.[15] Nevertheless, some of her work did appear in poetry compilations, and Saikō became so famous that traveling *bunjin* made a special point of stopping in Ōgaki to meet her.

The years 1831–32 were unlucky ones for Saikō, for both her stepmother and Rai San'yō died, and her father became quite ill. (He died in 1838.) Yet although San'yō's untimely death must have been a particular blow, it did not dampen her enthusiasm for composing verse and painting. She turned to San'yō's pupil Gotō Shōin (1797–1864) for instruction in poetry, periodically visiting him in Osaka and maintaining an active correspondence. Saikō also continued to journey to Kyoto with more or less the same frequency as before, visiting with San'yō's family and other Kyoto *bunjin* and participating in banquets and excursions like those in the days when San'yō was still alive.

Thanks to the energies of Saikō and other *bunjin*, Ōgaki continued to flourish as a cultural center. In the 1840s and 1850s she was a member of two poetry societies there, the Reikiginsha and Kōsaisha (she eventually became the leader of the latter group). She was such a distinguished figure that in 1852 her name was listed in the *Heian jinbutsu shi* (Who's who in Kyoto) in the section on well-known people from other provinces, and four years later, at the age of seventy, she began to receive the patronage of the wife of the Toda daimyō.[16]

Also in her seventieth year, Saikō suffered a cerebral hemorrhage from which she never fully recovered. Nevertheless, she continued to paint and was even invited to Ōgaki Castle, where she received gifts in return for her paintings. At the age of seventy-three, she produced a landscape painting (fig. 5.11)—a departure of sorts for her, for she apparently turned to this subject late in life, and landscape scrolls by her are rare. Although she probably received her initial training in this genre from Shunkin, in this painting—a mountainscape on satin—Saikō demonstrated an individualistic manner of applying brushstrokes that distinguishes her landscape from those by her colleagues.

In this landscape, Saikō evoked the tranquil, mysterious forces of nature through a combination of soft, gray washes and fibrous texture

15. Ten years after her death, a two-volume collection of three hundred of Saikō's verses, entitled the *Shōmu ikō*, was published by her nephew and niece. Later, twenty-six poems were included in volume 40 of the *Tung-yang shih hsüan* (*Tōei shisen*), an anthology of Edo-period *kanshi* compiled by the Chinese scholar Yü Ch'ü-yüan and published in China in 1882. See Sano Masami, annot., *Tōei shisen* (Fukko Shoin, 1981).

16. She was also patronized by a branch family of the Toda daimyō.

Fig. 5.11. Ema Saikō. *Landscape at Age Seventy-three.*
Hanging scroll, ink on satin. (Private collection, Japan)

strokes. The foreground is dominated by two majestic pine trees that curve upward toward the distant waterfall, while in the lower right a scholar, followed by a boy servant carrying his *ch'in* (zither), crosses a stone bridge. Black accents in the form of clusters of dots are sparsely scattered throughout, animating the mountain forms. The complex interplay between her dry brushstrokes and moist washes enriches the surface texture of Saikō's painting, providing the subtle excitement that literati looked for in one another's works. The sublime mood is further conveyed in Saikō's quatrain in the upper left, which reads:

> Who is this traveler in the mountains,
> With a young boy carrying his precious *ch'in?*
> As he walks toward the castle gate,
> White clouds obscure the deep paths.

In 1861, two years after completing this poem, Ema Saikō died at the age of seventy-five. She was buried alongside her father at the temple Zenkeiji in Ōgaki.

By making imaginative, individual contributions to the Sinophile *bunjinga* tradition, Ema Saikō established her position in Japanese art history as one of the fine literati painters of her day. Hallmarks of her personal style include an austere sense of design; keen, spirited brushwork; and restrained yet infinitely varied use of ink. During her lifetime, her landscapes and "four gentlemen" paintings were praised and sought after by contemporaries in Ōgaki and Kyoto.

Although by her time more women were becoming recognized as artists, Ema Saikō's life was unconventional, and this, in part, accounted for her success. Her career was nurtured by a number of special circumstances. For one thing, she was given an exceptional education in Chinese studies and in painting, with encouragement and financial support from her family. Her father's scholarly pursuits and cultural attainments, coupled with the fertile literary environment of the Mino region, further sustained Saikō, as did her several male teachers and her numerous trips to Kyoto and contact with important *bunjin* there. In addition, by remaining single Ema Saikō enjoyed an unusual degree of autonomy. Freedom from childbearing, conjugal domestic responsibilities, and manual labor allowed her to mature fully as an artist. The livelihood of women less well born and provided for would have seriously circumscribed her artistic pursuits—unless, of course, she had married a fellow *bunjin* like Rai San'yō. Most important, of course, were her innate talent and determination, which spurred her to extraordinary achievements.

Fame did not fully satisfy her, however. Throughout her career she wrote poetry suggesting that she occasionally mused over whether a "normal" married life would have been preferable to that of a spinster. In one poem, written in 1815, she alludes to loneliness:

> The peaceful night gets quieter and I am slow to go to bed.
> Trimming the wick of the lamp, I leisurely read books written
>   by women.
> Why should it be the lot of talented women to end up like this,
> Most of them in empty boudoirs, writing poems of sorrow.

In another she refers to the "one mistake" that led to a life of chastity and barrenness—the "mistake" probably being the misunderstanding that led Rai San'yō to marry someone else:

> *To inscribe on my portrait, written in 1831*
>
> Lonely room, fiddling with a brush as the years go by;
> One mistake in a lifetime; not the kind to be mended.
> This chaste purity to rejoice in—what do I resemble?
> A hidden orchid, a rare bamboo—sketch me in some cold form.[17]

A few years later, in her fiftieth year, Saikō again expressed sorrow over this unfortunate event in her early life:

> As I reach fifty, I begin to understand the mistakes of the past;
> As the years slowly pass, they have gone against my ambition.
> Cranes are tall, ducks short—it is not men who made them thus;
> Fish leap, hawks soar—all follow the course of nature.
> My intentions have melted like snow in springtime;
> Old friends have vanished like stars in the morning brightness.
> In the end there is no use for Taoist practices for longevity—
> I only love to paint bamboo, its greenness reflected on my
>   garment.

And again in 1852:

> Because of one mistake, I have no family to serve;
> Aimlessly, I have indulged in writing amidst rivers and lakes.[18]
> But I am shamed by your verse coming from far away
> In which I am praised as the outstanding woman of the
>   literary world.

Perhaps because she had felt so strongly the conflict between being a "talented woman" and having a "family to serve," Saikō purportedly tried to discourage the young women who idolized her from imitating

17. Translation by Burton Watson, from *Japanese Literature in Chinese* 2:58.
18. By referring to rivers and lakes, Saikō alludes to the fact that she has not mingled with society.

her life-style. Nevertheless, Saikō was obviously proud of the accomplishments of her female colleagues, for she collected examples of the paintings and calligraphy of twenty-two women artists whom she had met over the years and had their works mounted together. This remarkable handscroll stands as a rare testament to the women active in nineteenth-century artistic circles in Japan.[19]

19. The women included in this handscroll are Hirata Gyokuon, Kobayashi Haihō, Chō Kōran, Shōkō, Teitei, Baien, Renzan Joshi, Sennanseihō, Gyokuei-jo, Toshi (wife of Uragami Shunkin), Yoshida Shūran, Rie (wife of Rai San'yō), Shidō (wife of Okada Hankō), Fusen-jo (wife of Yokoi Kinkoku), Sennanhōmei, Kan-shime Yao, Hara Saihin, Ryūtai Joshi, Shinoda Bunpō, Mankō-jo, Oda Shitsushitsu, and Ran-jo. The handscroll is presently in the Ema Shōjirō collection.

SIX

Women in an All-Male Industry: The Case of Sake Brewer Tatsu'uma Kiyo

Joyce Chapman Lebra

WOMEN IN THE SAKE INDUSTRY

The brewing of sake (rice wine), Japan's oldest industry, has traditionally been an all-male occupation. Both the brewmasters and the brewers who prepared the mold, mixed the yeast and rice, and tested the mash were always male, because women were thought to endanger the fermentation, a process that could not begin without invoking the appropriate Shintō deities. "Let a woman enter the brewery," the proverb goes, "and the sake will sour." This warning against the polluting nature of females prevailed in all sake breweries during the Tokugawa and Meiji periods, and in prior centuries as well.

Closer examination, however, reveals several exceptions. One of the most interesting was Tatsu'uma Kiyo, the daughter of a Nishinomiya brewing family, who in the nineteenth century built the largest sake empire in Japan. Yet her achievement, remarkable in itself, had historic and even prehistoric precedents.

Sake has been brewed since earliest times in Japan. According to the first historical chronicles, the *Kojiki* and *Nihongi*, it was a goddess, Konohana Sakuya Hime, who originated the process by chewing mouthfuls of rice to achieve natural fermentation. One theory of the beginnings of brewing in Japan, therefore, is that virginal girls would chew rice, thus stimulating the release of enzymes in their mouths that activated the fermentation process. The girls would then spit the mixture into large bowls, which were sealed and allowed to sit for three days, whereupon the brew was drunk with proper ceremonial at the harvest festival.[1] The fact that young girls, not boys, chewed the rice calls into question the assumption that brewing was from its inception a male enterprise.

Further evidence to support this theory of sake's origin comes from Okinawa, where one octogenarian reports that as a child she participated in just such a method of production: girls some fourteen years old sat in a circle around a large ceramic pot, chewing each mouthful of rice until their jaws ached. In this apparent survival of a prehistoric process, there was no hint of pollution by women; instead young females were specified as the natural brewers.[2] Indeed, the ancient brewers may have been exclusively female, as evidenced by the term for brewer, *toji*, which was originally written with Chinese characters that mean lady or madame. The word is used to this day to mean brewmaster, though now it is written with different characters.

A combination of Shintō, Buddhist, and folk beliefs about the polluting nature of women eventually made the brewery strictly a male space: according to one folk belief, for example, the spirit of sake is female, and the entry of females into the brewery would arouse the jealousy of this sake spirit.[3] Precautions against pollution by women were thus observed for centuries. One intriguing exception to this discrimination, however, is found in Aizu-Wakamatsu, a region that for generations has been a center of production of fine sake. By wearing in their obi a small ticket bearing a drawing of a stylized skeleton (fig. 6.1), women could cancel their polluting effect and safely enter the brewery without risk to the year's cellar. Unfortunately, we do not know how many women took advantage of this waiver or under what conditions.

The general ban on women in the brewery was lifted only in recent years. Reasons for hiring women are not hard to find. As one manager admitted, women workers cost less, and at a time when breweries are struggling to survive, hiring women workers makes sense as a management strategy to cut production costs. Moreover, in most areas housewives are available as part-time workers, in a latter-day variant of the *dekasegi* (migrant work) pattern that once led men from poor farming

1. Sake museum plaque at Miyaizumi Brewery Museum, Aizu-Wakamatsu. Sakurai Hirotoshi, *Seishugyō no keiei to keizai: Seishugyō no rekishi to sangyō soshiki no kenkyū* (Koyo Shoin, 1982), 525, confirms the role of Konohana Sakuya Hime in brewing sake from rice. Professor Sakurai is a leading authority on the technology and history of the sake industry; I am indebted to him for guidance.

2. Miyagi Fumi, "Mishi omiki," *Nihon jōzō kyōkai zasshi* 71, no. 1 (1982–83): 29–31. Eyewitnesses to this method are also reported in Sakaguchi Kin'ichirō, *Koshū shinshū* (Kodansha, 1974), 13–14; Akiyama Hirochi, *Sakezukuri no hanashi* (Hokosha, 1983), 88; and William P. Lebra, *Okinawan Religion* (Honolulu: University of Hawaii Press, 1966), 66, who reports that ritual sake in recent times has been made by priestesses.

3. Conversation with Sakakura Takeko, Boulder, Colo., August 3, 1987.

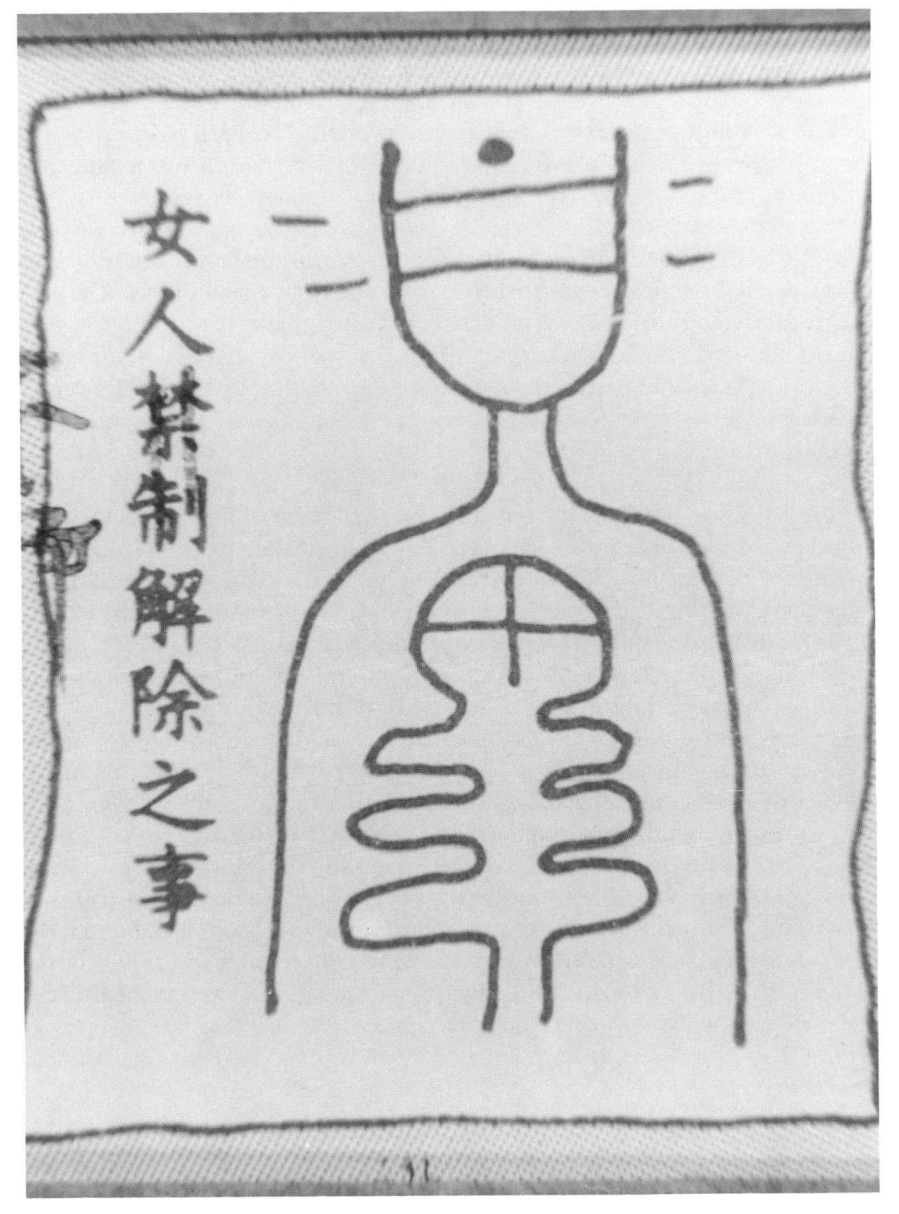

Fig. 6.1. Pollution cancellation ticket, Aizu-Wakamatsu region, Tokugawa era.

areas to find wage-paying labor in the cities and towns during the slack season. Today men are extremely scarce as migrant workers, but housewives are in ready supply as part-time or temporary workers in breweries close to their homes—although some female brewers still hesitate to enter buildings where sake is brewed. Hiring women brewery workers has thus become one survival strategy for brewers (if not a prevalent one).

Examples of successful female entrepreneurs in sake brewing are also not hard to find in present-day Japan. Although most middle-scale women entrepreneurs work in the food, fashion, or children's clothing industries, women brewers, particularly in small- and medium-scale plants, are not altogether uncommon. Some of the dozen or more women sake brewers are the widows of brewers. The largest female-headed enterprise in Kobe is Sakura Masamune, numbered among the ten largest breweries. The director, the widow of the former owner, retains the manager who worked for her husband as well as the traditions of the brewing house, which for generations researched and produced mold for other brewers in the Nada area. Another example of a sake brewery successfully run by an enterprising widow is Sanwa Shuzo in Shizuoka prefecture. When faced with stiff competition, rising costs, and the preference of many customers for beer and potato whiskey (shō-chū), this woman developed an innovative strategy to cope with the situation: she combined with two other local small breweries.

Less common, but no less significant, female entrepreneurs in the sake industry are brewery house daughters. Dr. Kono Mitsuko, the owner of Konohana in Aizu-Wakamatsu, is the daughter of a brewing house that not only has been in business for fourteen generations but was also purveyor to the daimyō during the Tokugawa period. Kono (who was trained as an entomologist) personifies the pride and ability of a merchant house with a long and proud family reputation. She personally supervises both the brewery and the museum she had built to house her family's documents and memorabilia and to honor several individuals, women as well as men, who figured prominently in the civil war of the mid–nineteenth century. Her entrepreneurial and marketing skills are reflected in the attractive bottles, decorated with paintings by famous artists, in which the sake is packaged. Her son, who graduated in business administration from Keiō University, will succeed her and continue the family business into the fifteenth generation.

Despite the modernization of the sake industry, brewing retains much of its traditional character as a family business. Companies producing less than one thousand koku annually are all either individual enterprises or family enterprises.[4] This is true of some of the largest

4. Imori Rikuhei, *Sake no shakaigaku-teki kenkyū* (Kyoto: Mineruba Shobō, 1972), 8.

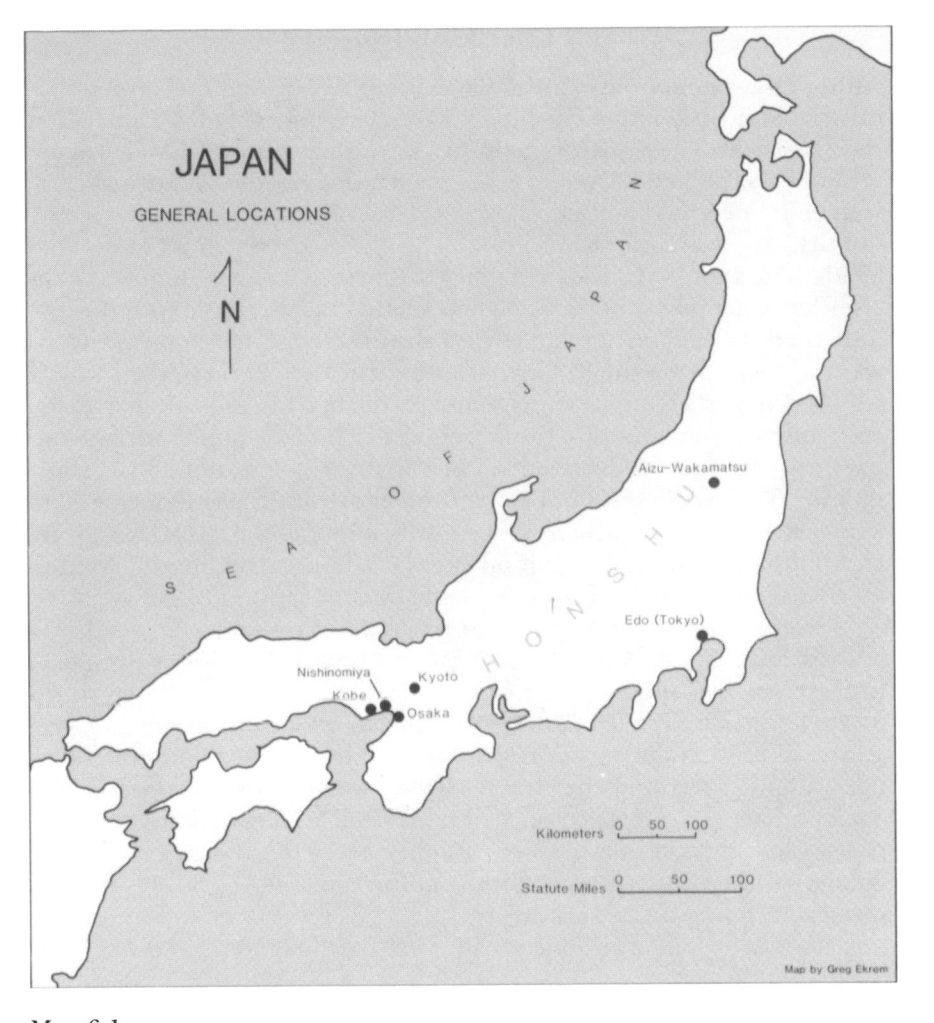

Map 6.1.

breweries as well, in which the owner, like Kono, is often a direct descendant of the founder. The family character of brewing may explain the presence of women in the industry: family businesses, as we shall see in the case both of Tatsu'uma Kiyo and of women in other industries, have at times given scope for women to become involved in manufacturing and commerce.[5]

5. It is difficult to say why the industry retains this family-based character. The answer may lie in part in the ancient mystique of rice. As one woman brewer said, "We were taught at the table that rice is sacred." During much of Japan's history, sake functioned as a mediator between gods and men in numerous rituals. Nakane Chie, "Sake to shakai," in

WOMEN IN OTHER INDUSTRIES

Although women were banned from breweries during much of preindustrial and early industrial Japan, they were not excluded from other
mercantile activities, particularly in the Kamigata, or Kansai, region
around Osaka and Kyoto. In Kamigata during the Tokugawa era,
women in merchant houses enjoyed several prerogatives not enjoyed by
samurai women in the city of Edo or elsewhere. Even though household
heads were required to be male, and this rule was observed in Osaka as
elsewhere, the power of the male household in family businesses was not
unlimited. So long as the house and the enterprise were one entity, as
was the case during the Tokugawa and early Meiji periods, the owner's
wife could participate in management with her husband. It was often
she who carried the keys to the warehouse and made important personnel decisions, such as the selection of apprentices and adoption of sons-
in-law. She was also responsible for the welfare of the live-in workers, to
whom she often gave lessons while also tending to their food, clothing,
and housing needs. If in addition she was a house daughter married to
an adopted son-in-law (*mukoyōshi*), her position was doubly powerful.

A woman who married into an Osaka merchant family enjoyed several advantages: she kept her own family crest (*mon*), and, like samurai
women, she often blackened her teeth and shaved her eyebrows to indicate her married status. Moreover, she took with her a dowry (*shikigin*)
as a kind of guarantee against divorce: her husband could not divorce
her without returning the dowry, which was her own property. She
could in fact own property in her name, unlike her samurai counterparts. Clothing and utensils were also her property. If a successor died
young, all the property went to his mother, another right not allowed
women in Edo. In cases of divorce, the children did not all go to her
husband, as in samurai houses: she took the daughters, and her husband kept the sons.[6]

What is more, in Osaka during the Tokugawa era a townsmen's rule
prescribed that under special circumstances a woman could serve as
househead for up to three years, or until another male successor was

---

Sake, ed. Hayashi Kentarō (Daigaku Shuppanbu, 1976), 239. Resulting anachronisms and
anomalies survive: government controls and rationing, a tax bureaucracy that has no relation to revenue derived from sake, and the persistence of merchant houses in brewing
when such a system has long since ceased to be profitable.

Apart from the religious significance of rice, there is also the matter of status. Large,
wealthy farming houses traditionally went into brewing because a substantial rice surplus
was necessary in order to brew. Brewing houses were thus ipso facto wealthy houses, and
this proof of earlier status is something a family is reluctant to relinquish, even though
brewing may no longer be profitable in the wake of postwar land reforms.

6. Miyamoto Mataji, *Ōsaka bunka shiron* (Bunken Shuppan, 1979), 306.

chosen (though she had to use a man's name). Her position as temporary househead required authorization from the five-household association (*gonin gumi*), from town officials, and from the shogunal commissioner (*bugyō*). Despite these limitations, the empowered women in Osaka merchant families had few counterparts in Edo, where no woman, samurai or otherwise, could succeed to the family headship.[7]

After the Meiji Restoration, the power of Osaka's women entrepreneurs waned. In the process of modernization, the house and the enterprise were separated both physically and financially; thus the wife of the company head moved to the outskirts and lost her hold on the family business, which began to assume the character of a modern enterprise. The abolition of official class distinctions, moreover, undermined the hereditary nature of merchant house businesses, also weakening the woman's position in family enterprises.

Although female entrepreneurs declined in number during the Meiji era, they did not disappear altogether. One representative Osaka female entrepreneur whose life spanned the Meiji and Taishō periods was Yoshimoto Osei, the prototype for the heroine of Yamasaki Toyoko's novel *Hana noren*. Osei married a hardware dealer with a penchant for the entertainment world: he trained dancers and other performers. When he died in 1920, she took over all phases of his entertainment business. She combined twenty-eight separate groups of entertainers, many of them in Yose, and brought them all under her control. Any actor who did not measure up was ousted. Osei scouted talent, provided for her employees' welfare, presided at the ticket doors, and watched all the performances.[8]

In another Yamasaki novel, *Bonchi*, also set in an Osaka merchant house (this one in the *tabi* [Japanese socks] business), the mother and grandmother dictate not only when and whom the young male househead will marry and divorce, but even which mistress he should support, with the view to producing a daughter whose husband they could then select and control.

These examples of female entrepreneurs in the Osaka merchant house tradition provide the necessary background for understanding the success of Tatsu'uma Kiyo, who drew on the strategies and precedents set by her female predecessors in the business world. The practice of relying on wives and daughters to run the venerable family business was already well established by the time Kiyo was born. Rather than automatically entrusting the business to a son with questionable ability, merchant houses could select the most talented apprentice-clerk as an

7. Ibid., 307–8.
8. Ibid., 317–20.

adopted husband for their daughter, thus ensuring the success and continuity of the family business. This practice was in fact common among merchant families as a way of circumventing the hereditary class system, the custom of primogeniture, and the rules governing householders. In one present-day Nishijin wholesale house, for example, the family over the past eight generations has successively adopted sons-in-law as a matter of policy, overlooking their own sons as potential successors.[9] The Tatsu'uma family of sake brewers followed some of these same customs in the years that the daughter of the family managed the business.

THE CASE OF TATSU'UMA KIYO

The Tatsu'uma house had for many generations since its founding in 1662 produced sake and barrels in Nishinomiya (see map 6.2). One of the earliest and subsequently largest brewers, the pattern of its growth matched that of the industry as a whole in the late Tokugawa and early Meiji eras, when it was a major supplier of government revenues and expanded in ways that bespoke great vigor.

The dramatic expansion of brewing in Nishinomiya and in the port areas around Nada and the surrounding hinterland in the Tokugawa era was predicated on several factors. The first refined sake was brewed at the end of the sixteenth century in Nara, and the process was commercialized and perfected in Ikeda and Itami north of Nishinomiya and Osaka in the following century. The rationalization of this process marked a signal advance in technique compared with the centuries-old brewing of unrefined sake.

Traditionally the polishing of rice had been done by means of the foot treadle (*ashibumi*). In the eighteenth century, however, use of the water wheel for polishing rice was perfected—another advance that amounted to a technical revolution in production, with a rate of efficiency some forty times that of the foot treadle.[10]

Another fortuitous development hinged on the discovery in 1840 of a spring in Nishinomiya, whose water, called *miyamizu*, was uniquely suited to the brewing of sake. A brewmaster at the Sakura Masamune brewery, which owned factories in both Nada and Nishinomiya, observed that the sake from the Nishinomiya cellar was consistently superior in quality to that from the Nada plant. After painstaking analysis, he discovered that in fact the water from the Nishinomiya spring ac-

9. Interview with Kimura Uhei, Kyoto, December 2, 1981.
10. Yunoki Manabu, *Nihonshu no rekishi* (Yuzankaku, 1975), 160–62. Professor Yunoki is a leading authority on the history of the sake industry in Nada and Nishinomiya; I am indebted to him for his assistance. I am also grateful to Maekawa Kazuko, former librarian at Tokyo University, for her efficient help and encouragement.

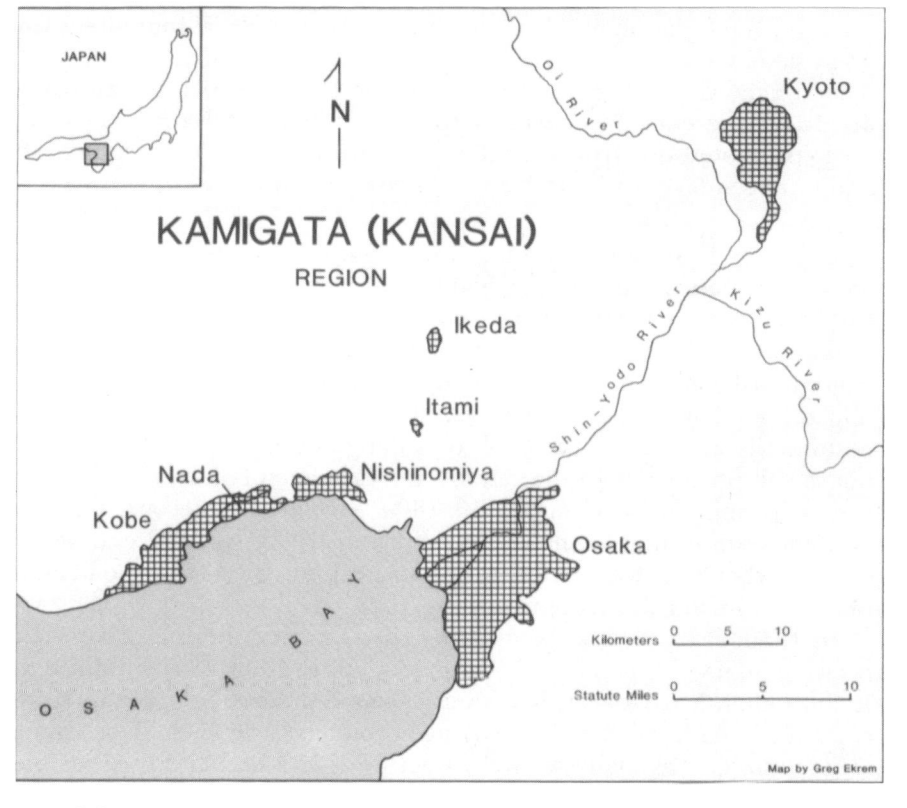

Map 6.2.

counted for this excellence. From that time on, Nishinomiya spring water was sold to other brewers who recognized its unique mineral properties: high in calcium, phosphorous, and magnesium, and low in iron.[11]

Expansion of the Edo market for refined sake was yet another factor behind the industry's spurt of growth. Whereas earlier in the Tokugawa period brewers in Itami and Ikeda shipped their product overland by horse or by ox cart as far as Edo, the evolution of the sail-powered cask ship (*taru-kaisen*) made it possible in the last half of the seventeenth century to ship sake in larger quantities to the Edo market, where wholesalers then acted as distribution agents to retailers.

Climatic factors, such as penetrating winter temperatures and winds that blasted down from the Rokko mountains toward the sea, also favored sake brewing in the Nada and Nishinomiya areas. In addition, rice grown in the hinterland north of the coast (the Yamada Nishiki is

11. This story was told by several respondents in Nada and Nishinomiya, including the manager at Sakura Masamune.

famous even today among brewers) was another essential ingredient for good sake. Given all these advantages, the nearby Tamba brewmasters gained renown for their technical skills in the breweries of the Nada area, and the entrepreneurial skills of merchants of Kamigata vigorously promoted the growth of the sake industry during the eighteenth and nineteenth centuries in Nada and Nishinomiya.

By the beginning of the nineteenth century, Tatsu'uma, benefiting from these natural advantages, had become a medium-large brewer. Yet the house's good fortune in geography and business was not matched in the production of children: Tatsu'uma Kichizaemon IX had only one child, a girl. As we have seen, though, daughters were welcome in Kamigata merchant houses: midwives emerging from confinement rooms customarily announced the birth of a daughter with "It's a girl, so the house will prosper."[12] In the case of the Tatsu'uma family, this proverb proved prophetic. Born on July 16, 1809, Kiyo grew to become a bright and energetic young woman who lived until 1900. Her life spanned a century when sake was one of Japan's major industries—and she herself played no small role in its growth (fig. 6.2).

In 1830, at the age of twenty-one, Kiyo married the son of another brewing house, who in 1842 assumed the headship of her family as Kichizaemon X (that year, his family received a thousand *ryō* loan from the Tatsu'uma family).[13] The marriage produced several children (some sources suggest as many as twelve) before Kiyo's husband died, at the age of forty-eight, in 1855.

For the next fifty years the Tatsu'uma brewery, called Hakushika, prospered as no other brewery had: Kiyo developed the family enterprise into a sake empire without peer. By 1894, at an output of twenty-two thousand *koku* annually, Hakushika was three times larger than its nearest competitor.[14] Although Kiyo's management strategies made her a pioneer in the industry during its period of most rapid growth and prosperity, she did not assume the nominal family headship herself, not

12. This proverb, and the prevalence of the custom of adopting sons-in-law in merchant houses, give credence to the view of the *ie* as a corporate unit. The latter interpretation has been developed by several scholars, notably Nakano Tadashi, *Shoya dōzokudan no kenkyū*, 2 vols. (Miraisha, 1978).

13. Yano Konosuke, *Daijūsandai Tatsu'uma Kichizaemon o kaerimite* (Osaka: Toppan Insatsu, 1975), 19. The following information on Tatsu'uma and on Kiyo is derived from this privately published volume. I am indebted to the staff of the Hakushika Museum and to the son of the author, Yano Mitsuo, for making the work available to me.

14. Tatsu'uma's production of sake grew from 1,400 *koku* in 1804, to 4,000 in 1867, 7,000 in 1877, 9,000 in 1882, and 17,000 in 1889. In 1894, at a production volume of 22,000 *koku*, Tatsu'uma was three times larger than its nearest competitor. This spurt occurred while Kiyo's son and daughter-in-law were householdheads.

Fig. 6.2. Tatsu'uma Kiyo (1808–1900).

even for the three years allowed in Kamigata. Rather, she was the power behind the successor from 1842 through 1897, first under her husband, then under her eldest son, and finally under her daughter-in-law (the last two of whom she trained herself). In this regard she followed a pattern well established in Kamigata merchant houses.

Kiyo's familiarity with the family business grew naturally from a childhood spent in an important brewing house. Although in her day women were still restricted from entering the brewery itself, Kiyo learned to supervise the workers closely and to wash the barrels between batches. By the time of her marriage, she was as knowledgeable about the sake industry as anyone in Nada or Nishinomiya.

Yet as a woman there were limits to the functions Kiyo could perform. The brewing process itself depended on a brewmaster. At Haku-

shika, and at the Nada breweries generally, the brewmaster came from
Tamba, where he annually recruited other brewery workers. This migrant labor during the winter months (called one-hundred-day labor)
complemented the summer agricultural cycle and thus provided employment year-round for farm families from poorer districts.

Resolution of management problems also required a male assistant.
Even among the merchant population of the Osaka area, women remained in the back room (*oku*) behind the front office, separated from
the office or shop area. What they did there, however, was often more
important than what went on in the front office, for the back room was
where many critical policy decisions were made. Nevertheless, women
were excluded from a number of functions, such as open negotiations
with other business houses. There were rules of protocol and customs
that even Kiyo had to observe. For these reasons, Kiyo required a *bantō*,
a head clerk trained to work as her deputy.

Significantly, it was Kiyo, rather than her husband, who selected
the *bantō*, a bright young boy of thirteen originally hired to work in the
kitchen, where he cooked for the brewery workers who slept in the
brewery in the usual live-in worker pattern. The exceptional ability of
this teen-ager caught Kiyo's attention, and she promoted him to the office, where he served first as an apprentice and ultimately rose to the
status of head clerk. Renamed Tatsuenosuke, a name Kiyo chose using
the first character of her family name, he became indispensable to Kiyo's management of the family's expanding endeavors for the next five
decades.

Kiyo taught her *bantō* all phases of the family business, paying particular attention to questions of timing—when to expand and when to wait
or retrench—elements essential to management policy. Kiyo was some
twenty years her *bantō*'s senior and the most powerful member of the
family, and we must assume that Tatsuenosuke was at first completely
under her direction, though eventually he probably began to make policy recommendations on his own. At any rate, his loyalty to Kiyo and,
by extension, the Tatsu'uma house was absolute.

An essential aspect of Kiyo's entrepreneurial style was revealed in the
marriages she arranged for her several children (fig. 6.3). Kiyo's marriage management embodied a four-part strategy: marrying daughters
into other brewing houses; marrying sons out as *mukoyōshi* to brewing
houses; sending out sons, daughters, and grandchildren to establish
branch houses (*bunke*); and adopting a *mukoyōshi* for one of her daughters, whose child was later designated heir to the main house (*honke atotori*). We may surmise that the distinction she made between the son she
retained as heir, the children she sent out as heirs to other families, and
those she sent out to establish branch houses was significant. Similarly,

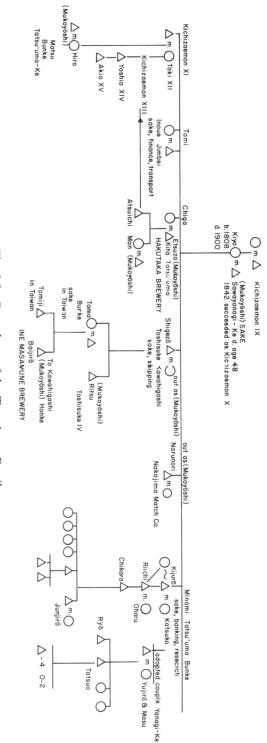

Fig. 6.3. Genealogy of the Tatsu'uma Family.

she must have recognized the daughter for whom she chose an adopted husband as one requiring a special strategy, no doubt in part because Kiyo's first-born son had not fathered a son.

Of her six children who appear in the available family records, all were married to sons and daughters of other brewers.[15] Kiyo's eldest son, whom she trained, became Kichizaemon XI. He predeceased his wife, Taki, who, also trained by Kiyo, then became the twelfth house-head for seven years, overriding the prevailing three-year rule. One of Kiyo's daughters, Tami, married Inoue Nihei, a man from a family prominent in brewing as well as in finance and shipping. Kiyo sent out two other sons as *mukoyōshi* to other brewers. Hanzo, one of these sons, married into the Kawahigashi brewing and shipping house, becoming Risuke III. His daughter, Tama, Kiyo's granddaughter, in turn took a *mukoyōshi* and in 1895 became the first brewer to market sake in Taiwan, immediately following Japan's establishment of control there after the Sino-Japanese War. Tama's son Baijirō later inherited the Kawahigashi headship and resumed brewing in Nada. Kiyo's son Kijurō established a junior branch of the family, the Minami Tatsu'uma, and also brewed. One of his daughters took a *mukoyōshi* who succeeded to the house; the other, an adopted daughter, Jun, together with a *mukoyōshi*, established the branch family of Yanagi Tatsu'uma.[16]

There were several cogent reasons for a main house (*honke*) to establish branch or junior houses (*bunke*). For one thing, younger sons who did not succeed needed to be provided for, and a large, prosperous family could afford to set up younger sons in business rather than simply sending them off to fend for themselves or to serve as apprentices to other houses. Moreover, if the branch family's occupation was the same as or ancillary to that of the main house, then the status and wealth of the main house was enhanced. Thus, a main house that was able to found several branch families in effect became a kind of family empire. In some parts of the country, for example, nearly every family in a geographic area had marriage connections with the most powerful house in a given business. This is still true of the brewing houses in Aizu-Waka-matsu. Kiyo, then, through her strategy of founding branch families, sending out sons as adopted sons-in-law, and marrying daughters to other brewing houses, created her own family empire.

The most complex maneuver of all was the marriage Kiyo arranged for her daughter Chiga (or Chika). Although Kiyo had at least four sons, she adopted a *mukoyōshi*, Etsuzō, for Chiga, trained him for several

---

15. Yano, *Daijūsandai Tatsu'uma Kichizaemon*, 4.

16. Ibid., 12–18. If Kichizaemon X had six additional children, they must have been by other women, as they do not appear in this family account. The author, Yano, himself followed Tatsuenosuke as *bantō* for over fifty years.

years beyond the apprenticeship he had already served in another house, and then sent him out as a *bunke* founder. He established the Kita Tatsu'uma house, which today operates the Hakutaka brewery in Nishinomiya. A second anomalous feature of this adoption was that Etsuzō was the only child of his brewing house. One can only imagine how she engineered this coup!

Although Kiyo's daughter bore a son, Atsuichi (or Tokuichi), he was not slated to become heir to his father's house; rather a daughter, Mon, took a *mukoyōshi* to succeed to the Kita Tatsu'uma house. Kiyo and her *bantō* had other, more elaborate plans for this grandson. Atsuichi was scheduled to marry his cousin Hiro, the only child of Kichizaemon XI and his wife, Taki (the woman who was twelfth successor for seven years). Hiro was groomed by Kiyo, and especially by the old *bantō*, for the express purpose of succeeding her parents as head of the main house of Tatsu'uma, with Atsuichi chosen to be the *mukoyōshi*. Atsuichi, however, refused, causing a great stir among the brewers of Nishinomiya and Nada: not even Kiyo, it appeared, could always get her way. Hiro took another *mukoyōshi* instead and founded the Matsu Tatsu'uma branch family, which also brewed for a number of years. Atsuichi married the daughter of the aristocratic Matsudaira house, became a renowned Diet member, and himself took over the headship of the main house of Tatsu'uma, continuing its success.

Bitterly disappointed that his protégée, Hiro, had been overlooked in the succession, Tatsuenosuke, now over sixty years old, retired in 1898 from all the family's enterprises, which by this time were extremely diversified. Kiyo, nearly ninety when the new successor took over, died three years later, in 1900, and her faithful *bantō* followed her in another two years. A few months before his death his family received the astonishing pension of four hundred thousand yen (about four hundred million yen in today's equivalent), together with letters of commendation for his years of exceptional service to the far-flung Tatsu'uma family enterprises.

Kiyo's entrepreneurial style can be seen as well in the extraordinary diversification and technological innovation she fostered throughout the Tatsu'uma empire—part of which was a response to the numerous hazards faced by brewers of her time. Despite the prosperity achieved by the sake industry in the first half of the nineteenth century, sake brewing was attended by great risks, and the Tatsu'uma house did not escape their effects. One ever-present threat was bacteriological contamination, which could ruin a brewer's entire cellar of a single year. This happened at the Tatsu'uma brewery in 1841—the year before Kiyo's husband succeeded to the headship—and the family lost 980 *ryō*. No doubt this calamity affected her resolve to wash all the barrels herself.

Another peril was fire. Fire struck the Tatsu'uma brewery in 1847, destroying virtually all earlier records of the family's operation.

Yet another problem that afflicted the industry was the rapid and continual fluctuation in the price of rice owing to three factors: the size of the harvest, government tax policy, and speculation. In order to alleviate the effects of this price instability, the Tatsu'uma house began to operate an exchange and financial facility, a not uncommon safety hedge among brewers. Tatsu'uma expanded in these areas in the 1840s, exchanging the gold used in Edo transactions for the silver used in Osaka. Moreover, as an exchange broker and moneylender Tatsu'uma could ensure short-term profit, whereas the return on capital invested in brewing required two years; in other words, not only was brewing a long-term investment, but it was far riskier than moneylending as well. Tatsu'uma loaned to other brewers and in the early Meiji years to the new government, from which the house also borrowed.

In 1879, in another shift of policy, Kiyo and Tatsuenosuke began lending money to the family temple in Kyoto at the going rate of interest (for generations the family had simply donated funds). When the principal and interest reached fifteen thousand yen and the temple was unable to make payments, Tatsu'uma assumed some temple properties in Osaka to settle the debt. A similar practice was followed with loans to other brewers; some of the properties thus acquired became the foundation for later Tatsu'uma real estate ventures.

Tatsu'uma also became one of the earliest brewers to ship sake to Edo on a large scale. By 1834, 95 percent of the Hakushika output was being shipped to Edo, at an average profit rate of 19 percent.[17] Yet this endeavor was not without risk, for a continual threat to the *taru-kaisen* sailing ships en route to Edo and back was shipwreck. In 1834, Tatsu'uma lost one hundred barrels in such a disaster. Thus, to reduce this risk, Tatsu'uma in 1846 began to purchase their own ships rather than relying on charters, and expanded steadily in the next two decades. To finance this pioneering activity, the brewery borrowed primarily from two exchange houses in Osaka, to which they also loaned on occasion.

Tatsu'uma adopted several other strategies as well to cope with the risks in shipping. During the 1830s Tatsu'uma began to sell Hakushika sake in bulk (*okeuri*) to colleagues when the price of barrels rose. In 1839, too, the house bought sake in bulk from colleagues' cellars (*okegai*) when Hakushika ran short;[18] the sake was then sold under the Tatsu'uma label, generally blended with some Hakushika brew. Tatsu'uma thus pioneered two strategies that today are critical to the survival of

---

17. Ibid., 3.

18. *Hakushika no eigyō no kabushiki kaisha ni soshiki henkō-go no gyōrekisho* (Hakushika, privately printed), 1:25.

both large-name brewers with famous labels that ensure sale and small brewers without the name to survive in a competitive market.

With the collapse of the Tokugawa shogunate and the Meiji Restoration of 1868, significant changes in the production and marketing of sake were inevitable. The shogunal system of *kabu* licensing was abolished in favor of free production for a few years in the early Meiji period. In addition, it became possible to develop new routes and markets apart from the Edo route as markets were effectively nationalized.

Accordingly, during the first two decades of the Meiji era, Tatsu'uma increased the size of their fleet by ten ships and made a corresponding expansion in their routes and markets. Tatsu'uma ships sailed beyond the Edo route—to Shikoku, Kyūshū, Okayama, and the Kishu peninsula—helping to spur the development of regional marketing structures. The firm established a branch in Yokohama and agents in both Tōhoku and the Kantō area. In 1884, when Nihon Yūsen Kaisha introduced steamship transportation, Kiyo was quick to see the advantages in safety and speed and contracted with them. By the following year Tatsu'uma had founded its own shipping company, which was followed soon after by a marine and fire insurance venture. Ten years later Tatsu'uma purchased its first steamships from England. These two ships were chartered to the government during the Sino-Japanese War and sold soon after at a profit.[19] By this time Tatsu'uma was shipping not only sake but a variety of other products, including rice from Niigata and salt and coal from Kyūshū.

Another of Kiyo's innovations was the sale of the special spring water, *miyamizu*, to ten other brewers soon after its discovery in 1840; she continued this practice until 1877, after which Hakushika sold only to water dealers. A variety of other enterprises were initiated under Kiyo and Tatsuenosuke during the 1870s: rice wholesaling, wood and coal sales, real estate, and a match factory.

Kiyo's son Kijurō, founder of the Minami Tatsu'uma house, was another notable pioneer in technological innovation in brewing. He was one of the first to use coal for fuel, and he installed the first steam-powered rice polisher, rapidly incorporating five hundred of these machines into his brewery. He also built brick rather than wooden breweries and used tile roofs for the first time in the industry. Tatsuenosuke, in a manner typical of his aggressive style, studied Kijurō's innovations and followed his example at the main house.

Untouched by Western or modern ideas of the role of women, Tatsu'uma Kiyo, following in the footsteps of merchant families of Nishi-

19. Ibid., 34–35. A contemporary example of innovative entrepreneurial strategies is the plant that Hakushika is presently building in Golden, Colorado.

nomiya, wielded great power in the sake-brewing industry. Through a combination of shrewd family engineering, innovative entrepreneurship, and an extraordinary sense of timing, Kiyo and her *bantō* expanded the Tatsu'uma family enterprises until Hakushika stood as the largest brewer and shipper of sake, in an era when sake was one of Japan's major industries. She was the Kamigata merchant-house daughter at her most potent. Kiyo's entrepreneurial brilliance foreshadowed a powerful style of management in an industry that even today retains much of its traditional familial heritage, while demonstrating technological innovation and resilience. In Kiyo we find haunting echoes of Japan's mythic ancient women brewers.

Yet to the contemporary historian, a certain mystery surrounds this almost legendary woman. Although both the family history and general legend in Nishinomiya credit her personally with the achievements of her brewery during her lifetime, members of present generations (the fourteenth and fifteenth) of her family whom I interviewed seemed reluctant to talk about her. Her grave in the family plot is nearly hidden in a corner, while the most prominent gravestone is the one commemorating her grandson, the thirteenth-generation househead, who was the son of Kiyo's daughter Chiga and her adopted husband and who was also trained by Kiyo and her *bantō*. Family members were unable to produce the family genealogy or death records usually kept in the family temple, saying that both were lost. Because it is extremely unlikely that these crucial documents in so large and important a family would be lost or, if indeed lost, not redone, one can only wonder why Kiyo is so little recognized by her own family.

Perhaps, as several interviewees in Kobe and Nishinomiya suggested, the reason lies in tradition: by custom, if a woman was too successful in business, she might become an embarrassment to her family because she humiliated her competitors. Her successors might then keep her out of the family grave or delete her name from the family register. It is possible that Kiyo was just such a woman, for by the time of her death her family's business was three times larger than its nearest competitors. Kiyo's behind-the-scenes management of brilliant triumphs over business rivals, in other words, may have proven awkward not only to the Tatsu'uma family during her own lifetime, but to subsequent generations as well. Family deference to codes of modesty and humility may well have lost for Kiyo the central place she surely deserves in the history of modern Japan's most prosperous sake brewery.

PART TWO

The Modern Discourse on Family, Gender, and Work: 1868-1945

SEVEN

The Meiji State's Policy Toward Women, 1890-1910

Sharon H. Nolte and Sally Ann Hastings

The exclusion of women from politics has been normative for so much of history that explanation of this phenomenon in any society might well seem superfluous. In an East Asian society such as Japan, Confucianism and the "traditional" submissiveness of women make their political suppression in the early years of Japan's industrialization seem an obvious continuation of the practices of the previous era. The "naturalness" of women's political oppression in Japanese society has been so much a part of the folk wisdom on both sides of the Pacific that little attention has been given to the comprehensive policy of the Meiji state toward women. While there has been some interest in the negative aspect of state policy—that is, the exclusion of women from politics—no account of women's political exclusion to date has analyzed the reasons for this policy. The Japanese feminists who wrote the first histories of their movement believed that their task was not to understand their exclusion from politics, but to change it. For those whose fathers had been samurai, feudal patriarchy was explanation enough for their plight. Later historians close to the women's movement have likewise assumed that women's exclusion from politics was merely a perpetuation of the outmoded customs and attitudes of the former government.[1]

State attention to women's roles was a product of the sweeping political and social reforms of the Meiji Restoration of 1868. Inaugurating a thirty-year period of institutional reconstruction in the interest of industrialization and national power, the so-called Restoration initiated developmental processes that, by the time of World War I, made Japan

1. See, for example, Kodama Katsuko, *Fujin sanseiken undō shoshi: Kanshū Ichikawa Fusae* (Domesu, 1981), 21–22.

the only non-Western nation in the ranks of the advanced industrial empire-builders. Japan's modern history thus raises profound issues about the relationship of state policies to society and culture. We have a body of theory dealing with state-sponsored industrialization, but little of it refers to gender construction. An examination of governmental definition of and policy toward gender during Japan's early industrialization can thus contribute to more integrative comparisons of state power, industrialization, and changing gender systems.

The two decades from 1890 to 1910 were particularly important ones in the development of Japanese state policy regarding women. By 1890, the Japanese leaders behind the Meiji Restoration had consolidated their power, and their political reforms had been institutionalized in the Meiji Constitution of 1889. An era of experimentation—in which the government had even sent five young women to study in America—was over.[2] In the same year that propertied males participated for the first time in the national Diet, the state issued the initial ban on women's political participation. By 1911, feminists would begin to challenge that ban. It was in the two decades between 1890 and 1911, however, that the state articulated piecemeal its official definition of women's role in industrialization.[3]

The policies of the Japanese state toward women in these two decades, while sometimes cloaked in traditional rhetoric, summoned women to contribute positively to the state, not simply to refrain from detrimental activities. Various ministries articulated goals for women that included, but were not limited to, the twin ideals of "Good Wife, Wise Mother" (*ryōsai kenbo*), popularized by the Education Ministry. State propaganda exhorted women to contribute to the nation through their hard work, their frugality, their efficient management, their care of the old, young, and ill, and their responsible upbringing of children. The significance of these functions did not entitle them to political rights, however. In the simplest terms, the state pursued a classic carrot-and-stick policy, eulogizing women who were models of self-abnegation, thrift, and productivity while arresting activists and banning their publications.

The Meiji state had much more power than its predecessor, the Tokugawa shogunate, to impose the gender asymmetry that characterized

2. Sharon L. Sievers, *Flowers in Salt: The Beginnings of Feminist Consciousness in Modern Japan* (Stanford: Stanford University Press, 1983), 12.

3. Industrialization should be understood here in its widest sense. The architects of the Meiji state were well aware that the development of modern industry depended on the continued health of the agricultural economy and its attendant handicrafts; the state therefore required increased productivity from all aspects of the economy and increased savings from everyone.

the new comprehensive vision of national development in Japan. For two and a half centuries prior to 1868, real political power in Japan was shared among the shōgun and his vassal daimyō. Certainly no political theory of the Tokugawa era, whether orthodox Neo-Confucianism, *bushidō*, or some amalgam of these, advocated a public role for women. On the contrary, the bureaucratic state, which made broad claims of authority over morals, discouraged women's public activities.

The state, however, imposed its will on the women of Tokugawa Japan quite unevenly. Although the sequestration of women was most pronounced among the upper classes,[4] ruling-class definitions of gender roles also conditioned peasant women's political behavior, if to a lesser extent. Thus, Japanese farm women did not participate in the more formal peasant protests to the authorities, though they did initiate food riots. For the most part, however, local society was beyond the reach of ordinary state controls. For example, in some villages a well-off widow who headed her household was permitted to serve in her late husband's place on the village council.[5] Therefore, premodern customs militated against women's political participation but were not uniform across class or village boundaries.

Japanese state articulation of women's role, while more pronounced after 1890, began much earlier. Both Western observers of Japan and Japanese reformers concluded early on that the treatment accorded women was a measure of the level of civilization of a given society. Many believed that the social mores of Japan would have to change. In the years between 1868 and 1890, however, the nature and the degree of that change had not yet been determined.

Nevertheless, state policymakers in 1890 began with certain institutions in place. First, and perhaps most important for the definition of gender roles, when the leaders mandated primary school education in 1873, they required both male and female children to attend. Second, by 1890 women had become the backbone of the developing Japanese industrial economy. Female workers outnumbered males in light industry, especially in textiles, where a work force that was 60 to 90 percent female produced 40 percent of the gross national product and 60 percent of the foreign exchange during the late nineteenth century.[6] Fi-

4. For information on the exclusion of women from politics in the Tokugawa period (1600–1868), see Wakita Osamu, "Bakuhan taisei to josei," in *Nihon joseishi*, ed. Joseishi Sōgō Kenkyūkai, vol. 3: *Kinsei* (Tōkyō Daigaku Shuppankai, 1982), 11; and Seki Tamiko, *Edo kōki no joseitachi* (Aki Shobō, 1980), esp. 236–37.

5. "Hakken sareta Edo jidai no tohyō yōshi: Edo jidai no mura yakunin senshutsu ni tsuite," *Shishi hensan tayori*, no. 3 (August 1986): 5–6.

6. Nakamura Masanori, *Nihon no rekishi*, vol. 29: *Rōdōsha to nōmin* (Shogakkan, 1982), 101. On the economic importance of textile workers, see Gary Saxonhouse, "Country Girls

nally, a small number of high-ranking women were thrust into a more public role in order to impress the Western powers with the Japanese appreciation of the niceties of civilized behavior. The empress was deputed, in Western dress, to greet the diplomatic corps, and the wives of Japanese government leaders attended dinner parties, charity bazaars, and Western-style balls.

Despite these Western influences, the state policy that emerged in Japan between 1890 and 1910 differed not only from the Japanese past but also from policies of the day in Europe and America. The Japanese "cult of productivity" was not quite the same as the "cult of domesticity" that historians have described for the Western middle classes of the nineteenth century.

STATE PROHIBITION OF WOMEN'S POLITICAL ACTIVITY

The Meiji era was one of political flux. The Restoration, which launched Japan's development as a modern industrial nation, required considerable political restructuring. The Meiji leaders abolished hereditary restrictions on occupation and residence in 1868. During the 1870s they abolished the hereditary military class and instituted a system of prefectures staffed by imperial appointees. In the Meiji Constitution of 1889 they bestowed on the country, in the name of the emperor, a parliamentary system in which the lower house of the legislature had limited budgetary authority. The privilege of electing members to the lower house was determined by the property tax, not by hereditary privilege.

If, during these years of dramatic change, Japan had also extended suffrage to women in 1889, it would have been well in advance of Great Britain, the United States, France, and Germany. Far from enfranchising women, however, the Japanese government explicitly denied them the right to participate in politics at any level. In 1890, the cabinet enacted a Law on Associations and Meetings (Shūkai Oyobi Kessha Hō) that barred women from attending political meetings or joining political

and Communication Among Competitors in the Japanese Cotton-Spinning Industry," in *Japanese Industrialization and Its Social Consequences*, ed. Hugh T. Patrick (Berkeley and Los Angeles: University of California Press, 1976), 98–99, and William V. Rapp, "Firm Size and Japan's Export Structure," in ibid., 208. On the lives of the textile girls, see Mikiso Hane, *Peasants, Rebels, and Outcastes: The Underside of Modern Japan* (New York: Pantheon Books, 1982), 3–31, and Gail Lee Bernstein, "Women in the Silk-Reeling Industry in Nineteenth-Century Japan," in *Japan and the World: Essays on Japanese History and Politics in Honour of Ishida Takeshi*, ed. Gail Lee Bernstein and Haruhiro Fukui (New York: St. Martin's Press, 1988), 54–77. On textile girls' protests, see Sievers, *Flowers in Salt*, 78–83; and E. Patricia Tsurumi, "Female Textile Workers and the Failure of Early Trade Unionism in Japan," *History Workshop* 17 (Fall 1984): 3–27.

organizations.[7] These bans were redrafted by the Home Ministry as the Security Police Law (Chian Keisatsu Hō) of 1900. The provision against women's attendance at political meetings remained in effect until feminists won its abolition in 1922; the provision forbidding their membership in political organizations was the principal legal instrument of women's political exclusion until 1945. In a context of change so great that historians have called it "revolution from the top down," the government's decision to bar from politics all women regardless of class, even while providing them with basic literacy, deserves a better explanation than simply "tradition."

One reason for the exclusion of Japanese women from politics was the provocative role of the People's Rights movement, which included several elite women.[8] Inspired by works of Western liberalism, including John Stuart Mill's *The Subjection of Women*, the People's Rights movement politicized many rural women, who at local assemblies heard women speakers decry the patriarchal family as well as the authoritarian state. Before 1888 these women were constrained by restrictions on organizations, meetings, and the press that applied to men as well as women. The first restrictions applying to all women, and only women, were clearly directed against hotbeds of popular rights agitation. In January 1888, for instance, girl students at Kōfu Middle Normal School were forbidden to attend the meetings of three moral reform organizations, all of which were deeply influenced by the movement.[9] In the same year, the prefectural government in Kōchi ordered two villages to revise the local assembly laws (enacted in 1880) by terminating the rights of women to vote and to stand for election.[10] In February 1890, the police of Saruya village notified one Oi Yukiko that she could not join the Liberal party because she was a woman.[11]

Other interpretations subsume the exclusion of women from politics under the more general governmental assault on the burgeoning labor movement. The state's very obvious interest in the textile industry does not explain legislation that referred to all women and only women

7. *Nihon fujin mondai shiryō shūsei*, vol. 2: *Seiji*, ed. Ichikawa Fusae (Domesu, 1983), 131–34.

8. Sievers, *Flowers in Salt*, 52, 206n.63; Kano Masanao, "Fusen Kakutoku dōmei no seiritsu to tenkai: Manshū jihen boppatsu made," *Rekishi hyōron*, no. 319 (1974): 68. The efforts of these pioneers were little known to their twentieth-century successors; see Sievers, *Flowers in Salt*, 163–64.

9. The three were Joshi Kōfūkai, Fujin Kyōfūkai, and Jofū Kairyōkai; see Chino Yōichi, *Kindai Nihon fujin kyōikushi* (Domesu, 1979), 22–23, 71.

10. Sotozaki Mitsuhiro, *Kōchi-ken fujin kaihō undōshi* (Domesu, 1975), 28; Shiraishi Reiko, "1920 nendai Nihon ni okeru fujin kankei hōritsu ni tsuite ichi kōsatsu," *Ōsaka hōgaku*, no. 110 (1979): 36–72.

11. *Nihon fujin mondai shiryō shūsei* 2:131.

rather than to a minority of protesters or workers. Neither does it explain why male workers were allowed to attend political meetings (albeit under police scrutiny and regulation) while propertied women were not. The total ban on women's political activity makes sense only as part of a program in which the government allocated certain duties, characteristics, and behaviors to women whether or not they were also workers or activists.

The Japanese state denied political rights to women because the state's claims on the home preempted women's claims on the state. An 1887 work sponsored by the Ministry of Education, *The Meiji Greater Learning for Women* (*Meiji onna daigaku*), chillingly pronounced that "the home is a public place where private feelings should be forgotten."[12] The laws forbidding women's political participation reinforced and legitimized the family duties, social values, and poverty that kept most women out of the political arena, and also absorbed much of the energy of the activist minority. Most important, the laws were part of a systematic state interest in how women and the family system could serve the developing nation. Thus, when Kiyoura Keigo, the head of the Home Ministry's police bureau, appeared in the Diet to defend the exclusion of women from politics, he argued that women's political participation would undercut home management and education.[13]

The law of 1890 suggested conflicting images of women. The prohibition of attendance at political meetings coupled women with minors, implying that women were weak and vulnerable. Arimatsu Hideyori, the Home Ministry's principal architect of the 1900 Security Police Law, commented in an early draft that political meetings were disreputable affairs that might compromise women's virtue or entice youth to take a wrong turn.[14] In explaining the ban on women's membership in associations, however, Arimatsu suggested that women were not so much weak as dangerous, for he linked women's organizations with armed secret societies, citing French and German precedents for banning both types of groups.[15] Woman the innocent could readily become woman

12. Tanaka Sumiko, *Josei kaihō no shisō to kōdō*, vol. 1: *Senzenhen* (Jiji Tsūshin, 1979), 12.

13. Sotozaki Mitsuhiro, *Ueki Emori to onnatachi* (Domesu, 1980), 125.

14. Tōkyō Daigaku Hōgakubu Kindai Rippō Kenkyūkai, "Kindai rippō katei kenkyūkai shūchū shiryō shōkai: Arimatsu Hideyori kankei bunshō," *Kokka gakkai zasshi* 87 (1974): 625.

15. Tōkyō Daigaku Hōgakubu Kindai Rippō Kenkyūkai, "Kindai rippō katei kenkyūkai shūchū shiryō shōkai: Arimatsu Hideyori kankei bunshō," *Kokka gakkai zasshi* 86 (1973): 772. For information on German precedents such as the Prussian law of association of 1851, which prohibited women from attending political meetings or joining political organizations, see Richard J. Evans, *The Feminist Movement in Germany, 1894–1933* (Beverly Hills, Calif.: Sage, 1975), 10–11. French precedents are discussed in Stephen R. Hause and Anne R. Kenney, *Women's Suffrage and Social Politics in the French*

the animal. The image of riotous mobs of violent women was common enough in European conservative thought after the French Revolution; as Claire Moses has shown, French governments that could not control inflation greatly feared women's sensitivity to food prices.[16] Japanese bureaucrats in the late nineteenth century were unquestionably familiar with both Western conservatism and women's role in indigenous food riots.

Yet the ban on joining political organizations actually suggests a third image of woman, one neither innocent nor rebellious but responsible and authoritative. The ban placed women in the same category as public figures, including military men, public and private school teachers and students, and shrine and temple officers. The grouping implied that women were like civil servants whose political activity would be inappropriate or whose responsibilities so weighty as to preclude their participation. Gradually conservatives inside and outside the government would elaborate on the idea that wives were public figures, veritable officers of the state in its microcosm, the home. Their mission was a noble one that transcended petty partisan politics. Thus, the justification of women's political exclusion was primarily in terms of their home and family duties, and not of their physical, mental, or moral incapacity.

WOMEN AND WAR

The prohibition of women from political meetings affected all women and only women. In the Meiji era, however, most government policies addressed just women of a particular class. This was true of the educational system, which was one of the most important instruments of the bureaucracy in its reshaping of Japanese society. The two decades from 1890 to 1910 were crucial ones in terms of the establishment of government control over the education of women. Four years of compulsory education for both male and female children had been mandated earlier, but by 1890 only slightly more than 30 percent of the eligible girls were actually in school. By 1910, however, the compliance rate for girls had risen to 97.4 percent, and the years of compulsory education had been extended to six years.[17]

Third Republic (Princeton: Princeton University Press, 1984), 5, 8. However, both the Prussian and the French exclusionary laws had been abrogated by the time the Japanese law passed.

16. Claire Goldberg Moses, *French Feminism in the Nineteenth Century* (Albany: State University of New York Press, 1984), 6, 12--14, 20, 146.

17. Based on figures given in Elizabeth Knipe Mouer, "Women in Teaching," in *Women in Changing Japan*, ed. Joyce Lebra, Joy Paulson, and Elizabeth Powers (Stanford: Stanford University Press, 1976), 161.

More important to the state definition of women's proper role was passage in 1899 of a law mandating the establishment of at least one higher school for girls in each prefecture. This law had the simultaneous effect of increasing the number of public schools providing post-elementary education for women and narrowing the scope of the education offered to the women. Kabayama Sukenori, the education minister, argued on behalf of extending education to middle-class females as well as males precisely because households, which were the foundation of the nation, required good wives and wise mothers.[18] The role of the girls' higher schools should be to develop in young women refined taste and gentle and modest character. Women of leisure, then, should receive enough education—but no more than necessary—to fulfill their duties within the home. The curriculum of the girls' higher schools accordingly was not the academic equal of that provided to young men in middle schools, and it in no way prepared female students for entrance to the higher schools or universities, which remained male preserves for a number of years to come.

"Good Wife, Wise Mother" became the guiding aphorism for government policy on women, and the phrase resonates in Japanese society still today. The term evokes visions of women hovering over their children, providing tutoring and snacks with equal zeal. For precisely this reason, we need to note that in 1899 the term defined government policy in only one area, education, and for only one class, the middle. It was therefore not a call for women to return to the home from the workplace, for Japanese women of this social and economic class had by custom remained within the home. After 1911, when preparation to become "good wives and wise mothers" became a guiding principle in required elementary education as well, conscientious graduates may have felt torn between hearth and factory or crib and rice paddy. At the turn of the century, however, women below the ranks of the middle class could scarcely afford the luxury of focusing only on the care of their husbands and children, and official rhetoric did not ask them to do so. In 1900, in response to the increased number of girls attending elementary schools, the Education Ministry issued guidelines on training appropriate to each gender, which included admonitions that girls be educated in feminine modesty (*teishuku*), but there was no special emphasis on motherhood.[19] As we shall see, feminine modesty was quite consistent with economic productivity.

In the mobilization of women for the Russo-Japanese War of 1904–5, class distinctions, though operative, were deemphasized. This policy

18. Tanaka, *Josei kaihō* 1:135–36.   19. Ibid., 139.

reflected Japan's dependence on a conscript army. As the wife of a Foreign Ministry official wrote, "Even as all class distinction is put aside by the men in the army, which is composed of noblemen, merchants, students, and common laborers, so it is with women who do their part at home."[20] The Japanese state called on all subjects of the empire, women as well as men, to support the war effort. Through numerous women's organizations, many of them state-sponsored, women cared for wounded soldiers and the families of those killed. At the opposite end of the social spectrum, widows of enlisted men worked to support themselves and their children. A few women worked in hospitals as nurses; many raised funds or contributed their own savings or valuable possessions. Finally, within carefully delimited parameters, women joined men in the celebration of victory. All of these activities reinforced the image of women, not as weak and fragile beings in need of protection, but as national assets with particular nurturing skills.

At a time when the eyes of the nation were on its fighting men, representatives of the military did not hesitate to praise feminine responsibilities. Speaking to the students of the Tokyo Girls' Higher School in Mita, Vice-Admiral Kamimura said that their studying to become wise mothers or good wives was equally as valuable to the nation as was his fighting on the sea.[21] These were strong words indeed in the midst of celebrations for the taking of Port Arthur. It should be noted, however, that they were addressed not to all women, but to young women enrolled in a higher school. In 1905, the girls attending such schools were still a privileged few.

Their weighty educational responsibilities did not prevent young women of this class from contributing immediately and directly to the war effort. Early on, students and faculty at the Peeresses' School began devoting one and a half hours a day to making bandages, and later they prepared bags containing various articles for the use of men at the front (*imonbukuro*); at the Miwada Girls' Schools, meanwhile, the students knitted stockings and sewed clothes for the soldiers and sailors. Other girls' schools at which similar activities were carried out were Aoyama, Toyo Eiwa, and St. Hilda's,[22] the pattern for these feminine endeavors having been set for the students by their elders.

Charity had been accepted as a legitimate arena for upper-class women since early in the Meiji era; in wartime, this meant contributing to the care of the sick and wounded and providing for the survivors of

20. Mrs. Sadazuchi Uchida, "What the Women of Japan Are Doing," *Harper's Weekly*, March 12, 1904, 403.

21. *Japan Times*, January 22, 1905.

22. Ibid., March 8, July 15, December 11 and 23, 1904. Even some elementary school students contributed bandages; ibid., March 9, 1904.

those killed in battle. The empress herself provided a model for emulation: she visited military hospitals, rolled bandages, made donations to the Japan Red Cross, and bestowed presents on wounded soldiers and sailors.[23] One particularly poignant symbol of her motherly concern was her provision of artificial eyes and limbs to those injured in the service of the nation.[24]

Other women of the imperial family and women of the peerage engaged in similar activities. The empress herself dispatched women from her household to visit the sick and the wounded in hospitals throughout Japan.[25] Imperial princesses and members of the peerage, such as the Marchionesses Nabeshima and Ōyama, often acting as representatives of the Ladies' Volunteer Nursing Association of the Japan Red Cross,[26] visited hospitals and temporary shelters for wounded soldiers arriving in Tokyo for treatment. The crown princess and Princess Arisugawa sent to the military authorities boxes of bandages that they had rolled themselves, and the Ladies' Volunteer Nursing Association met regularly to roll bandages and hear lectures given by authorities on military medicine.[27] The association also provided head covers for hospitalized soldiers.[28]

Many more women—the wives of officials, businessmen, and military officers—were drawn into relief projects through the Ladies' Patriotic Association. This organization, which was founded in 1901, grew tremendously during the war. In 1904, the membership increased sixfold to 278,000; in 1905, it increased again to 465,000.[29] Although ostensibly a private organization, the Ladies' Patriotic Association enjoyed such extensive official support that the wartime activities it sponsored can be construed as state policy. This official support came in part as imperial patronage, with the emperor, the empress, and several princes of the blood making well-publicized donations.[30] The empress honored the society by her presence at their general meeting, and at the 1905 meeting she formally received Okumura Ioko, the association's founder.[31] Probably more important in terms of the growth of the organization, how-

23. Her visits to hospitals are reported in *Japan Times*, May 24 and November 16, 1904; her gifts of bandages, July 7 and September 30, 1904; her donation to the Red Cross, January 28, 1904; and her gifts to the wounded, October 13, 1904, and April 9 and May 24, 1905.

24. Ibid., March 31 and April 8, 1904, and January 22, 1905.

25. In December 1904 she dispatched Madame Kitajima to hospitals in Tōhoku, Maizuru, and Kanazawa; see ibid., December 2, 20, and 22, 1904.

26. Ibid., October 4, 8, and 15, 1904.

27. Ibid., June 12, August 31, and September 27, 1904, and May 26 and August 19, 1905. Descriptions of lecture meetings are given in ibid., January 17, February 7, March 6, May 8, June 17, July 3, July 30, August 20, and September 17, 1904.

28. Ibid., April 22, June 5, and July 3, 1904.   29. Chino, *Kindai Nihon*, 135.

30. *Japan Times*, March 1, 2, and 16, 1904.   31. Ibid., April 5 and 6, 1905.

ever, was the enlistment of the prefectural governors. Princess Kan-in, honorary president of the association, gave a dinner for the prefectural governors in Tokyo in October 1904 at which Princess Mori asked the governors to assist the work of the association's prefectural branches.[32] In January 1905, the officers of the association used a New Year's party to congratulate Admiral Tōgō and Vice-Admiral Kamimura on their recent victories and to request their support.[33]

The activities of the Ladies' Patriotic Association, which included seeing soldiers off and welcoming them back, visiting the sick and wounded, consoling the bereaved, and sending supplies to soldiers, exactly paralleled those of more elite organizations such as the Ladies' Volunteer Nursing Association. The Ladies' Patriotic Association, in addition to mobilizing women to support soldiers at the front, also provided a mechanism for women to join in the celebration of victory. In June 1905, for example, a special meeting was held in Tokyo to celebrate recent naval victories.[34]

The well-publicized activities of elite women on behalf of the war effort conveyed several messages about women's role in the new Japan. First, women who were wives and mothers could make legitimate contributions toward national goals outside the home as well as within. Their activities, which were extensions of traditional feminine responsibilities such as caring for the sick and the poor and providing clothing, could take them not only to public meetings but also to train stations and hospitals. In a few instances, officers of women's associations even left the capital to visit distant hospitals and military bases.[35] Second, these activities showed that women worked hard—a quality not always associated with the upper classes. Marchioness Ōyama wrote of her fellow members of the peerage, "You can not realize how earnest the ladies of our upper classes are unless you know their life intimately. They who never dressed themselves without maids waiting on them, they who never held in their hands anything heavier than their handkerchiefs, they who never went outside of their houses without two or three attendants, all come along to the hospital with their little lunch baskets and their bundles containing their nurses' uniforms."[36] Finally, the women of Japan, from the empress downward, were frugal in the national interest, contributing their wealth as well as their time to the war. The empress sent the chief of her bodyguard off to war, insisted on a reduction of her guard, and offered her valuables to the Bank of Japan. Even

32. Ibid., October 8, 1904.   33. Ibid., January 13, 1905.

34. Ibid., June 10, 1905.

35. For instance, Viscountess Matsudaira and Mrs. Hamao visited Sasebo on behalf of the Ladies' Patriotic Association; see ibid., February 5 and 9, 1904.

36. Ibid., May 26, 1905.

before the war was officially declared, a Kobe woman tried to donate her two gold rings. An elderly woman in the same city offered the substantial sum of ten thousand yen. The Baroness Mitsui and eleven other women of that family each subscribed ten thousand yen to the naval relief fund.[37]

While those Japanese women with leisure were conspicuously dedicating their time to the war effort, other women were working for wages as nurses in military hospitals. In fact, the activities of the Ladies' Volunteer Nursing Association originated as a means of legitimating, by the example of upper-class women, military nursing as a feminine activity.[38] The Japan Red Cross began formally training women as nurses in 1890. When the Sino-Japanese War broke out in 1894, they immediately dispatched twenty women to the military hospital at Hiroshima.[39] By autumn 1904 they had provided over two thousand female nurses in the conflict with Russia, and in October the army began accepting nurses from other training schools as well.[40] Press attention to upper-class women and the widows of officers created an impression that all women who became nurses did so because of self-sacrificing patriotism, a quality appropriate to women of all classes. It would seem, however, that the majority of the women working as nurses were merely trying to support themselves. The work was humble, the pay low, and women receiving the Red Cross three-year training had to promise to serve the army at any time for fifteen years after graduation.

When it came to the question of assistance to the families of soldiers at the front or those killed or wounded, the government made no mention of women's responsibilities as wives and mothers. The Home Ministry strongly advised against giving aid directly to the relatives of soldiers; instead the funds were to be donated to associations, which then provided either work for the adults or education for the children of such families.[41] The same ministry announced with pride that "at present, either at the centre or in local places, the utmost caution is taken to give relief by furnishing employment to those who need relief, so as to preserve and develop the spirit of independence and self-help in the heart of the relieved, and thus the abuses of giving out ready money are carefully avoided."[42] A commonsense hypothesis that many of those el-

---

37. Ibid., January 15 and February 10, 20, and 23, 1904.

38. Anna Hamilton, "Les Ambulancières japonaises," *Revue Christianisme social*, 1904, 526.

39. Chino, *Kindai Nihon*, 110.

40. Anita Newcomb McGee, "The American Nurses in Japan: An International Episode," *Century Magazine*, n.s. 47, no. 6 (April 1905): 903–4. Uchida, "What the Women of Japan Are Doing," 403, claims that ten thousand women volunteered to serve as nurses.

41. *Japan Times*, January 21, 1905.   42. Ibid., April 9, 1905.

igible for assistance must have been widowed mothers or wives with children is confirmed by the fact that the relief work provided was often sewing and laundering.[43] Their gender did not excuse these women from their duty to remain financially as well as spiritually independent. The establishment of a few day-care centers confirms that a woman could better be spared as a mother than as a wage earner.

BUREAUCRATIC IDEALS OF WOMANHOOD

Besides the Education Ministry, the body most instrumental in articulating state policy toward women was the Home Ministry; with its control of the prefectural governors, subordinate administrative appointees, and the police, it was the chief bureaucratic instrument for enforcing national policy at the local level. This ministry was responsible for community organizations for adolescents and adults, including philanthropic and patriotic associations for women. Its authority over hygiene and poor relief affected women as well. Finally, the Home Ministry controlled the police who were charged with enforcing the exclusion of women from political meetings and organizations.

The interest of the Home Ministry in women was integral to its general concern with asserting central government authority, both moral and political, over the towns and villages of Japan. This task naturally entailed as well the imposition of middle- and upper-class values on peasants and workers. One approach that the ministry took following the Russo-Japanese War was to encourage local Hōtokukai (Gratitude societies). These organizations had been founded by progressive landlords in the early Meiji era to encourage technical improvements, honesty, diligence, and communal cooperation, in the spirit of the Tokugawa agricultural moralist Ninomiya Sontoku. On November 26, 1905, Home Ministry officials held a celebration of the fiftieth anniversary of Ninomiya's death at a music school in Tokyo, and the next year they founded the Central Hōtokukai to draw together into a national organization the scattered local groups. The new society immediately began publication of an official magazine, *Shimin* (The subject).[44]

The pages of *Shimin* are a valuable source of information on how the Home Ministry bureaucrats who supported the Hōtokukai regarded

43. Ibid.

44. Carol Gluck, *Japan's Modern Myths: Ideology in the Late Meiji Period* (Princeton: Princeton University Press, 1985), 190–91; Chino, *Kindai Nihon*, 141–43. See also Kenneth B. Pyle, "The Technology of Japanese Nationalism: The Local Improvement Movement, 1900–1908," *Journal of Asian Studies* 33, no. 1 (November 1973): 51–65, esp. 61 for the relationship of the Hōtokukai to the Local Improvement Movement. Neither Gluck nor Pyle mentions that these movements had implications for women.

women. That these officials were concerned with women as well as with men was amply demonstrated by their sponsorship of the first Women's Hōtokukai meeting in Tokyo in December 1907.[45] The authors published in *Shimin* included educators and military men as well as Home Ministry officials. Although the opinions expressed on the proper role of women were by no means monolithic, they provide us with a sense of how officials were trying to shape the women of Japan.

A special issue on the family in 1909 featured articles by two prominent members of the peerage, Count Tokugawa Tatsukō and Baron Ishiguro Tadanori.[46] These men expressed the common wisdom on women—that is, women of their own class; their views will serve as a foil with which to contrast the opinions of the government officials who were endeavoring to mold Japanese women of all classes. Tokugawa began with an assertion that the household was the wellspring of the current era. Ladies should assist the male head of the household in all of his responsibilities, but their chief duties were to keep the house clean and beautiful and to educate the children. A woman should also cultivate good taste, leading her husband and children in song at the organ or piano, gardening, painting, or reading literature. As for Ishiguro, he expressed great satisfaction with his country wife, whom he had married at age seventeen. He stated emphatically that men and women have separate spheres: just as men have duties in politics and the military, so women are responsible for childrearing and household management. It would be a mistake for women to participate in politics or form local defense groups. He admitted that there were cases in which women helped their husbands with work, but he believed that an able, independent male would probably not ask for such help. Men went out to work and had no time to manage the home; therefore women, especially wives, had to do it. He himself would not have been able to be successful if his wife had been gadding about away from the home. Fortunately for him, except for the philanthropic activities appropriate to their status, his wife took not a step outside. For Ishiguro, however, it was not enough that wives stay home; they should be hard-working and frugal as well. Rather than sitting next to the charcoal brazier reading novels, they should fire the maid and save money by doing the cleaning themselves. Like Tokugawa, he thought women should lead songs around the piano.

As these references to the piano and organ make clear, both Tokugawa and Ishiguro were talking about the women of well-to-do households. Ishiguro may well have been directing his criticism to all womankind, but lazy wives and women who sent their children to relatives or remarried too readily after the death of their husbands exemplified

45. Chino, *Kindai Nihon*, 142.
46. Tokugawa Tatsukō, "Fujin no katei," and Ishiguro Tadanori, "Fujin no honmu wa katei ni ari," *Shimin* 4, no. 4 (May 28, 1909): 3–5 and 6–9, respectively.

vices that were available only to the wealthy. Ishiguro himself was not pleased with the public role upper-class women had played in the Russo-Japanese War, criticizing women who dressed in Western uniforms and went off to visit foreigners.

Ishiguro and Tokugawa spoke as members of the peerage. A better example of the ideal of feminine virtue endorsed by the Home Ministry can be found in the life stories of three paragons of virtue, which were recorded in various issues of *Shimin* (at least one written by an employee of the Home Ministry). The ministry's approval of these women is further indicated by the fact that two of the three heroines received special recognition from their prefectural governors.

Yamasaki Ichi of Saitama prefecture was the perfect model of filial piety. Her father had owned a mansion, agricultural fields, and a sake shop, but by the time Ichi was born he had become blind. Before Ichi was even twelve, her mother suffered a nervous breakdown. Ichi cared for her blind father, her younger sisters, and her mad mother. She married in 1891, but only five years later, her husband became ill. She nursed her husband and her father until their deaths, and continued to care for her unappreciative mother. The mother whined and scolded while Ichi did farm day-labor to supply her with sweets and sake; nevertheless, Ichi patiently informed her sympathetic neighbors that she would rather die than neglect her mother.[47]

Ichi was singled out for praise for at least two reasons. As we have seen, she carried out the duties of a daughter even when it was most unrewarding; neither of her parents had been able to care for her as a child, yet she continued to care for them even as the family fortunes declined and although her mother did not value her faithfulness. Her case was thus typical of a long tradition of exemplary commoners who were honored by governmental rewards and publicity in Japan as well as China.[48] The ruling class had traditionally preached filial piety and frugality to commoners; at one level, the retelling of Ichi's life reasserted these values. Ichi's story, however, is not simply one of loyalty unto death. Illness and madness may have taken their toll, but the family did not die of starvation. Ichi is praised equally for her devotion in nursing the sick and supporting family members through her wage labor. This tale thus exhorted the new Meiji generation to practice endurance, submission, sacrifice, industriousness, and self-reliance—all qualities equally as valuable in industrial development as in the preservation of the household.

A Home Ministry official, Ushio Shigenosuke, used the life of a second woman, "the virtuous Hana," to show *Shimin* readers how official

47. Ōkido Muneshige, "Kōjo O-ichi," *Shimin* 2, no. 6 (September 1907): 60–64.
48. On female models in China, see Mark Elvin, "Female Virtue and the State in China," *Past and Present* 104 (1984): 111–52.

sponsorship could transform self-denial into the uplift of the community and nation.[49] Shibata Hana was born in what is now Ibaraki prefecture in 1857. Her family was very poor, and from early childhood she worked for other families to contribute to the finances of her father's household. Sometime in her twenties she married a fisherman's apprentice, Koikeri Torakichi. Since Hana supplemented his earnings by continuing day labor and gathering firewood to sell, after ten years the couple was able to buy a fishing boat. Unfortunately, Torakichi was not suited to fishing and suffered a nervous breakdown, and in two short years all their property, including the boat for which they had worked so hard, passed into the hands of others. Despite Hana's constant care and prayers, Torakichi's condition worsened, and he disintegrated into imbecility. Hana eked out a bare existence for them, using spare moments to gather firewood and take in laundry to pay for her husband's medicine. Finding that if she left him alone the neighborhood children tormented him, she treated him like a baby, carrying him about on her back and even allowing him to try to nurse. To survive, she sold their furniture and worked while he slept. When in 1899 he finally died, her tears fell like rain. Thereafter, Hana's work as an agricultural day laborer and peddler of fish enabled her to live independently and entirely respectably. Since the couple had no heir to perform sacrifices for Torakichi's ancestors, in 1901 Hana adopted an abandoned three-year-old girl.

Private suffering was transformed into public virtue when the governor of Ibaraki, Mori Masataka, heard of this paragon of faithfulness and charity. He held a public ceremony to honor her. When her native village held a celebration for her, the governor attended and encouraged the villagers to maintain strict discipline in public morals, promote savings, and honor such a virtuous wife. The villagers soon formed the Maebama Moral Reform Savings Society for just these purposes. Among the moral reforms undertaken by the society were many suspiciously close to the heart of urban bureaucratic reformers: substituting a joint New Year's celebration for the formal visits that tradition required, abolishing the exchange of gifts on seasonal festivals such as girls' day and boys' day, and, in general, practicing greater austerity in local festivals. Parties to send off and welcome back soldiers were to be held at the local shrine, and only the village flag should be flown.[50] The society encouraged saving and discouraged smoking.

49. Ushio Shigenosuke, "Teijo Hana to Kyōfū Chochiku Kai," *Shimin* 3, no. 5 (July 7, 1908): 70–74. In 1938, Ushio would hold jointly the posts of home minister and education minister.

50. For an example of condemnation by the elite of extravagance in local festivals, see Inoue Kigorō, excerpted in Miyasaka Kōsaku, *Kindai Nihon shakai kyōikushi no kenkyū* (Hōsei Daigaku Shuppankyoku, 1968), 244–46.

Within months, the village was transformed. Crime virtually disappeared. The citizens were diligent in pest extermination, tax payment, weed pulling, and good housekeeping. To control erosion and to attract fish, society members planted three thousand pine seedlings along the shore. Most remarkable of all was the capital accumulated by the Maebama Moral Reform Savings Society. In three months of 1908, deposits averaged more than one per household as community spirit translated into hard cash. The society's propaganda stressed the interest accruing to even a tiny deposit over a decade. The proper deposit of savings was as important as the hard work that generated a surplus.

We have no reason to suppose that all or even any of the members of the savings society were women. In founding this society, however, Governor Mori linked the hard work of Shibata Hana for her family to the larger paradigms of village and national development. The millions of small depositors who used the postal savings system enabled the Japanese government to float bonds for heavy industrial and military development in an era when private banking and capital markets were still in their infancy.[51] The equation of feminine virtue with capital accumulation was high praise indeed for womanhood.

The third heroine from the pages of *Shimin*, Taniguchi Kiku of Kagawa prefecture, was singled out precisely because of her economy. Kiku is of particular interest in this canonization process because she represented the few (although probably the poorest of these) who were privileged to attend girls' higher schools. She lived in the dormitory during her entire four years at Takamatsu Girls' High School, never once returning to her home. When other girls went home, Kiku recorded in a notebook what she would have spent on round-trip transportation; she then deposited that amount in the postal savings system. She married soon after graduation. When her husband departed for the front as a second lieutenant in the Russo-Japanese War, Kiku worked hard to save more than ever, and she was able to contribute ten yen toward war relief. She had enlisted the help of her high school principal in making her donation, and through him her virtuous actions became known to Governor Onoda, who wrote her a postcard in praise of her wartime contribution. Her story is included in an article on women in the prefectures, and part of the significance of her virtue is not simply that she was engaging in economical and patriotic behavior, but that she was doing so in Kagawa on the island of Shikoku, far from the sophisticated women of Tokyo. We find here no mention of the piano or organ or novels or wasted time. Moreover, Kiku's frugality was practiced in a

51. William Lockwood, *The Economic Development of Japan: Growth and Structural Change, 1868–1938* (Princeton, New Jersey: Princeton University Press, 1954), 249, 252, 515.

modern way that would benefit the nation: whereas in the closing years of the Tokugawa era a samurai's wife had used scraps of worn quilts to make straps for clogs, the virtuous wife of an officer in the Russo-Japanese War made deposits in the postal savings service and contributed to war relief.[52]

Even though the rhetoric used to extol these three women invoked the past by labeling their actions as filial piety and feminine virtue or modesty, their contributions to their families cannot be dismissed as simply remnants of the traditional family system. Their virtues included working outside the home for wages and saving in the modern banking system. Filial piety may have been worthy of praise when Ichi was caring for her parents and thus obviating the need for poor relief; it was less important when Kiku was saving money by not visiting home.

Invoking the past was, of course, an effective means of legitimating the importance of hard work, endurance, and education as feminine virtues. Tomeoka Kōsuke, a founder of the *Hōtoku* movement, used the female members of the household of the sage Ninomiya Sontoku himself to illustrate the importance of these qualities. It seems that Ninomiya was married twice. At some point in his first marriage, a high-ranking samurai whose household had fallen into ruin summoned him to straighten out his finances. It took Ninomiya five years, but he was finally able to repay the debts of one thousand *ryō* and leave the samurai with three hundred *ryō* for himself. Of this sum, the samurai gave one hundred to Ninomiya, who, instead of keeping it for himself, divided it among the servants who had helped him during the five years. When he returned home after five years with no money, his long-suffering wife asked for a divorce. Though he tried to dissuade her, he finally agreed. Tomeoka concluded that this wife was not very wise, and he tells us that she fell into greater poverty. Ninomiya's second wife—without whom, Tomeoka tells us, the sage could not have achieved a fraction of his life work—could read the *Analects of Confucius* and proved that she could endure hard work and poverty. Ninomiya also provided his daughter, Fumiko, with the best education of the time: she learned to read and write and to sew and cook, as well as the fine arts of tea, poetry, and calligraphy.[53]

All three of the above women singled out as heroines were good wives, but, as it happens, none had children. Their service to family and

52. Maeda Ujirō, "Chihō ni okeru fujin katsudō no omokage," *Shimin* 4, no. 4 (May 28, 1909): 36–37. The example of the samurai wife is the mother of Matsukata Masayoshi; see Haru Matsukata Reischauer, *Samurai and Silk: A Japanese and American Heritage* (Cambridge, Mass.: Harvard University Press, Belknap Press, 1986), 27.

53. Tomeoka Kōsuke, "Joshi ni taisuru Ninomiya Ō no risō," *Shimin* 4, no. 4 (May 28, 1909), 61–62.

nation included broader familial responsibilities, such as caring for parents, siblings, and husbands. Moreover, the authors of *Shimin* presumed that the good of the nation might even require women's work outside the home. A prospectus for a girls' vocational school spoke of women's responsibilities for philanthropy, education, and industry.[54] Another author identified working in textile factories, selling railroad tickets, serving as telephone operators, and working in stores as employment appropriate to women, but cautioned that if wages in other fields were to rise too high, then those jobs also would become women's jobs because women could be paid less.[55]

Although bureaucrats assumed that women did far more than simply raise children, and honored women who were not mothers, they equally assumed that mothers were the primary caretakers of children, and they wanted the job done right. To these bureaucrats, correct childrearing practices were not those inherited unquestioningly from the past but rather those that conformed to the latest scientific knowledge and practice. When a physician contributed an article entitled "The True Principles of Childrearing," he seems to have been referring strictly to the proper nourishment of infants. He stressed that regardless of what cow's milk might do for cows, babies needed mother's milk. If, however, a mother suffered from beriberi, tuberculosis, or certain other communicable diseases, the mother's milk might actually harm a child. A carefully chosen wet nurse would be the next best option; only if no nurse were available should cow's milk be used.[56] Given the scarcity of cows in Japan, this article should be read as a warning on the dangers of sickly nursing mothers rather than as an attack on bottle feeding, which was not a widespread practice in Japan. Equal concern with the latest knowledge and practice was reflected in an article on the effectiveness of women home visitors in reducing the infant death rate in certain British cities.[57]

A number of articles by women, most of them educators, appeared in the pages of *Shimin*. In general, the opinions of these women were at least as conservative as those of Home Ministry bureaucrats. Tanahashi Ayako (1839–1939), who was the wife, daughter, and granddaughter of Confucian scholars, argued that in education as in life, nothing was more important than morals.[58] Miwada Masako, head of a private

54. Ōhashi Jūshō, "Okayama no gejo oyobi kōjō gakkō," *Shimin* 3, no. 8 (October 7, 1908): 49.

55. Mano Bunji, "Joshi no jitsugyō kyōiku," *Shimin* 2, no. 10 (January 1908): 33–34.

56. Segawa Shōki, "Makoto no ikujihō," *Shimin* 4, no. 4 (May 28, 1909): 61–62.

57. Amaoka Naoyoshi, "Fujin no eisei shisatsu," *Shimin* 4, no. 4 (May 28, 1909): 18–20.

58. Tanahashi Ayako, "Joshi kyōiku no hōshin," *Shimin* 4, no. 4 (May 28, 1909): 10–13.

school, was more in tune with the bureaucrats, bestowing equal praise on sincerity and thrift.[59] These writers were probably invited to contribute to this issue on the home in order to appeal to potential women readers; nevertheless, their publication here suggests not only government acceptance of accomplished women but also a desire to co-opt their prestige.

As might be expected from a publication closely associated with the government, there is no suggestion in these pages that women should be involved in politics. In fact, politics was rarely mentioned, perhaps in hopes that women would spend all their time and energy in constructive pursuits and leave the problem of power relationships between the sexes decently shrouded behind its figleaf of national progress. Still, one of the women educators who wrote for *Shimin* was Yajima Kajiko, a co-founder of the Tokyo Women's Reform Society whose criticism of the exercise of male privilege and of the repression of women in Japan has been praised in recent years as "incipient feminism."[60] Indeed, in 1909 Yajima had spent more than two decades in reform activities, and even more years as an educator. In an essay for a special issue of *Shimin*, she referred explicitly to raising the position of women in Japan. She proudly took credit on behalf of her society for inaugurating celebration of the empress's birthday, invoking the imperial institution not to justify women's repression but to assert the legitimacy of women's reform.[61] In the 1920s, Yajima even joined associations that advocated women's suffrage. The explanation for her inclusion in *Shimin* might well be that the government was in sympathy with the major issue pursued by the women reformers: the elimination of concubinage and prostitution. Government rhetoric about good wives implicitly conceded the point of reformers who had argued that Japan would not be able to equal the West until it provided proper respect for the institution of marriage.[62]

The articles in *Shimin* confirm the impression that women were ex-

59. Miwada Masako, "Katei no kōfuku to fujin no kokorogake," *Shimin* 4, no. 4 (May 28, 1909): 14–15. An educator in Tokyo since 1887, she died on May 3, 1927, at the age of eighty-six. Other women who contributed articles were Tsukamoto Hama, Miyagawa Sumiko, Yamawaki Fusako (1867–1935), and Yasui Tetsu (1870–1945). See also note 61 below.

60. Sievers, *Flowers in Salt*, 93.

61. Yajima Kajiko, "Chikyūsetsu no yurai," *Shimin* 4, no. 4 (May 28, 1909): 16–18. This special issue of the magazine was published on the empress's birthday, which may be another explanation for Yajima's inclusion. For further information on her life, see *Konsaisu jinmei jiten* (Sanseido, 1976). Kozaki Chieko, who in April 1921 succeeded Yajima as head of the Women's Moral Reform Society, also contributed an article.

62. Fukuzawa Yukichi, for instance, was most concerned with women's status within the marriage relationship; see *Fukuzawa Yukichi on Japanese Women*, trans. and ed. Eiichi Kiyooka (Tokyo: Tokyo University Press, 1988), 9, 29, 33, 48, and 142.

cluded from politics because of their social value, not because they were physically, mentally, or morally incapacitated. Their virtues were essential for the management of the home, the education of children, and even capital formation in the industrializing nation. Although some of the articles had a scolding tone, as if women might at times be just slightly foolish, there was not the least intimation that women were weak. Women ought to be strong enough to endure marriage to Ninomiya Sontoku, to support their husbands and parents through illness and poverty, and to run households when their husbands were absent at war. When times were particularly difficult, women ought to be strong enough to comfort and encourage their husbands, as had the wife of Kimura Shigenari (1593–1615), a samurai who died in battle.[63]

In the two decades between 1890 and 1910, the Japanese state pieced together a policy toward women based on two assumptions: that the family was an essential building block of the national structure and that the management of the household was increasingly in women's hands. The family relieved the state of responsibility for the old, young, and ill; taught acceptance of one's proper place in the social hierarchy; and performed as a more efficient economic and productive unit than the individual. The orthodox "good wife" was one who pursued whatever employment and education would serve her family and the society. Despite rhetoric about filial piety, frugality, and feminine modesty, these policies were not simply the preservation of past ways. As Japan passed from the nineteenth century into the twentieth, the ideal woman was one who attended girls' higher school, spent an appropriate amount of time on organized philanthropic and patriotic activities, and used the postal savings system. When Tomeoka Kōsuke wrote apologetically that in Ninomiya Sontoku's time there were no higher schools and therefore his daughter studied at home, the clear implication was that if Ninomiya had had the opportunity, he would have sent his daughter to higher school.[64]

Most important, the new state ideology based on gender, with its policies that applied to all women, gradually replaced the premodern differentiation of women by class. Whereas once only samurai women had been exhorted to be modest, courageous, and frugal, now these virtues were praised in all women. As the example of Ninomiya Sontoku's second wife reminds us, women of certain families in Japan had long enjoyed literacy; now literacy and formal education had become a duty of all women. Peasant women had always been hardworking and had contributed to household income through work outside the home. Now

63. The example is cited by Miwada, "Katei no kofuku," 15.
64. Tomeoka, "Joshi ni taisuru," 19.

even the wives of the wealthy could not justify sitting by the brazier reading novels. Shimoda Jirō, a teacher at the Tokyo Women's Higher Normal School, made peasant women a model for unproductive urban middle-class women: he suggested to his students that they visit the countryside, observe sericulture, and so discover their own productive powers.[65] An ideal woman who combined the cardinal feminine virtues of the various Japanese classes would be modest, courageous, frugal, literate, hardworking, and productive. This constellation of virtues was so appropriate for economic growth that we might term it a "cult of productivity."

The bureaucrats who shaped gender policy in these two decades acted in the interests of industrializing Japan. Was the experience of Japanese women, then, the same as that of women in the industrializing West? Certainly Confucian rhetoric on women's responsibility for the inner realm and male dominion in the outer corresponded neatly to the Western concept of separate male and female domains.

As the United States industrialized in the early nineteenth century, the true woman was characterized by piety, purity, submission, and domesticity.[66] The Japanese bureaucrats who defined the ideal woman at the turn of the century would readily have accepted this list. There were, however, subtle differences. Participation in institutional religion was a much more important expression of piety in America than in Japan. In the United States, where men courted their future wives rather than depending on arranged marriages, the resistance of sexual advances was the chief content of sexual purity; in our examples from Japan, feminine modesty was exemplified by self-supporting widowhood. American women were warned against marrying for money rather than love, something that would make no sense to a Japanese woman. The American virtue of submission contained an element of passivity and weakness somewhat different from the endurance required of Japanese women. Most striking of all is the absence from American domestic ideals of economic productivity and economic management. Although some American women, especially in the South, had considerable responsibility for supervising servants and distributing goods, little more was expected of the mythical true woman than to do the housework herself if vicissitudes in economic fortunes should deprive her of servants. Frugality was an American as well as a Japanese virtue, but systematic saving in banks and the accrual of interest were not part of the feminine mystique. It is hard to imagine an American woman, "more

65. Shimoda Jirō, "Tokai fujin to sangyō ryōhō," *Shimin* 4, no. 4 (May 28, 1909): 53–56.

66. The seminal article on this subject is Barbara Welter, "The Cult of True Womanhood, 1820–1860," *American Quarterly* 18 (Summer 1966): 151–74.

vulnerable, more infirm, more mortal than men," doing agricultural day labor to support her husband and parents.[67] The Japanese "cult of productivity," then, was significantly different from the American "cult of domesticity."

Japan's gender policies were also significantly different from Western policies at the turn of the century. In Great Britain, the content of domesticity had undergone a subtle shift from emphasis on a woman's importance as wife to a focus on her role as mother. A falling birthrate, the unfitness of many young men for service in the Boer War, and the exigencies of empire had drawn attention to the importance of women as the mothers of future soldiers and workers. High infant mortality and sickly children were blamed on the ignorance of working-class mothers. The prevailing assumption among those in power was that "mothers should be at home and that children should be with their mothers."[68] Policies to cope with this crisis included pamphlets on child-rearing, visits to homes, the provision of meals for needy children, and the supply of sanitary milk to mothers who could not nurse their babies. Certain articles in *Shimin* drew attention to these British concerns and thus indicate Japan's awareness of these policies, but declining population and the failures of mothers were not major Japanese concerns. Japan's population was in fact growing, a statistic often noted by British polemicists. In 1910, the Japanese government still valued a woman's productive power more than her ability as a mother.

In the West, where the separation of work and home increasingly confined women to the domestic sphere, women struggled to claim for themselves a place in the industrial world. "Cloaking themselves in the robes of millennial and philanthropic enthusiasm, they claimed the right to take the values of the Christian home into the world. That world, of course, was none other than the new commercial city complete with slums and brothels, factories, shops, and newspapers, schools and libraries."[69] Japan's industrialization differed from that of the original industrial powers precisely because Japan had advanced models from which to learn. The Meiji leaders, recognizing the value of women's economic and educational contributions, claimed the home as a public place. They also mandated from above institutions for which Western women had bitterly struggled. To take just one small example, no Japanese woman had to convince the military authorities that female nurses were useful; the Japanese military accepted Florence Nightingale's ar-

67. The exact quotation is from Ralph Waldo Emerson and is cited in ibid., 162.

68. Anna Davin, "Imperialism and Motherhood," *History Workshop* 5 (Spring 1978): 9–65; quote is from p. 50. For examples of articles relating to British concerns, see notes 56 and 57 above.

69. Tanahashi, "Joshi kyōiku," 12–13.

guments, and high-ranking men then recruited and trained nurses. Philanthropy and war relief were activities in which Japanese women could participate, but they could not claim these territories as their own.

Motherhood, however, was still a fairly vague concept in Japan in 1910. As Tanahashi Ayako's condemnation of young women who fantasized about marrying into a household without a mother-in-law reminds us, the good wife and wise mother was rarely privileged to live in a situation where she could care for only her husband and her children.[70] It is especially important to note that in the two decades prior to 1910, Japanese state policy placed much more importance on a woman's responsibilities as wife than on her function as mother. Only with the development of an articulate women's movement in the twentieth century did the definition of motherhood become an issue that reformist and feminist women could hope to influence.

70. Carroll Smith-Rosenberg, *Disorderly Conduct: Visions of Gender in Victorian America* (New York: Oxford University Press, 1985), 86. For the same phenomenon in England, see Martha Vicinius, *Independent Women: Work and Community for Single Women, 1850–1920* (Chicago: University of Chicago Press, 1985), 15–16.

EIGHT

Yosano Akiko and the Taishō Debate over the "New Woman"

Laurel Rasplica Rodd

In November 1911, a production of Henrik Ibsen's *A Doll's House*, starring the beautiful young actress Matsui Sumako (1886–1919) and directed by Shimamura Hogetsu (1871–1918), opened in Tokyo.[1] Although it was only a university production, the strong performance by Matsui and the explosive message of the play generated considerable attention from the popular press. *A Doll's House*, with its suggestion that marriage is not sacrosanct and that man's authority in the home should not go unchallenged, created an immediate sensation in a society where women had few, if any, rights.

In his review of the production, playwright Ihara Seiseien wrote that while many in the audience seemed unmoved when Nora deplored the sacrifice of wives for their husbands' honor, two women, Okada Yachiyo (sister of playwright Osanai Kaoru) and Hasegawa Shigure (herself a playwright), had pressed handkerchiefs to their eyes. Ihara recalled thinking at the time that these were "truly new women," inspired by Western theater models to reconsider women's lives.[2]

Ihara's term "new women" (*atarashii onna*) was soon taken up by others writing about women's new roles. In particular, women journalists writing for the general-interest magazines and new women's publications that flourished in the relatively liberal era of "Taishō de-

1. From about 1909 the Japanese new theater movement had been treating the conflicts in Japanese society, attempting to portray them in a realistic manner rather than with the traditional stylization of Kabuki, and bringing women actresses to the stage again after a three hundred year banishment.

2. Ichiko Teiji, ed., *Nihon bungaku zenshi*, vol. 5 (Gakutōsha, 1978), 438.

mocracy" carried the debate over the redefinition of women's roles into the public arena.[3] With the much-vaunted role of women as "good wives and wise mothers" now held up to vigorous scrutiny by women themselves, the state lost its monopoly over gender construction in Japan.

Among those who responded during the Taishō period to the challenge to redefine women's roles were four prominent women whose backgrounds, experience, and philosophies led them to argue widely differing positions. Yosano Akiko (1878–1942) advocated a feminism grounded in equal legal, educational, and social rights and responsibilities for women. Hiratsuka Raichō (1886–1971) propounded a doctrine of motherhood that called for state protection of and special privileges for mothers. Yamakawa Kikue (1890–1980) embraced a socialist view of history that traced women's subordination to the system of private property and so set the destruction of that system as her goal. Finally, Yamada Waka (1879–1957) held a more traditional view of women as "good wives and wise mothers."[4] The debate waged among these four women in magazines and newspapers over the course of the 1910s and early 1920s introduced much of the thought and many of the writings of Western feminist thinkers, touching as it did on such crucial topics as women's role in politics and in the home, the goals of women's education, women's rights within the family and the workplace, the need for women to control their own sexuality, and—the topic that most clearly reveals the differences in these women's thought—the part government should play in supporting women in their roles as wives and mothers.[5]

A major forum for the debate over the "new woman" was the literary magazine *Seitō* (Bluestockings), founded by Hiratsuka Raichō in Sep-

---

3. Even during the era of Taishō democracy women were excluded from the political process, denied even the right to attend public meetings. Education remained conservative, stressing child care and the family and serving as a foundation for filial piety and national virtue. Censorship of books and the popular press was constant.

4. The term *ryōsai kenbo*, coined by Nakamura Masanao to describe a model for women's roles adapted from the nineteenth-century West (i.e., that women should provide the moral foundation of the home, educating the children and acting as "better half" to their husbands), was taken up by one branch of the Japanese women's movement, led by Hatoyama Haruko, who saw it as providing women a sphere—the home—in which they would be preeminent. It was also adopted by the Meiji government, which instituted regulations in 1898 requiring each prefecture to provide at least one high school for women, with the goal of creating "good wives, wise mothers." In the official concept, women were to be educated not to exercise power at home, but to better carry out their responsibilities as childbearers and cogs in the patriarchal family system. See Sharon Sievers, *Flowers in Salt: The Beginnings of Feminist Consciousness in Modern Japan* (Stanford: Stanford University Press, 1983), 109–13, for a discussion of the political stands for which this term became the rallying cry.

5. See Kauchi Nobuko, ed., *Shiryō bosei hogo ronsō* (Domesu Shuppan, 1984), for a summary of these arguments and an edition of the major essays that made up these debates.

tember 1911 to encourage and advertise the creative talents of women. The maiden issue of *Seitō* had carried an anonymous translation of an article on Ibsen's *Hedda Gabler*, and the January 1912 issue included a supplement devoted to Matsui's performance as Nora in *A Doll's House*. The June issue carried a supplement on *Magda*, the Hermann Sudermann play, first performed in Japan in 1913, about a woman who defies her father's authority when she decides to become an opera singer. The *Seitō* articles about these plays were scholarly pieces incorporating references to both European and Japanese secondary sources. The author did not glorify Nora and Magda. Indeed, she took the position that Nora should not have abandoned her home and family for the goal of self-realization; and of Magda she wrote, "She cannot be called a true 'new woman.' "

From the beginning, however, *Seitō* was treated less as a literary than as a news event. Reporters delighted in the sensation they could cause by misreading the magazine and reporting fanciful versions of the activities of the women members of the Seitō group. Having undertaken to discuss "new women," Raichō and other members were soon being criticized as "new women who took Magda as their ideal and praised Nora," and *Seitō* was called "a nursery for Japanese Noras."[6]

At first the Seitō members shrugged off this misrepresentation, but after two incidents involving Odake Kōkichi attracted further malicious gossip about their activities, the attacks were viewed more seriously. Odake made headlines twice. The first time was when she accepted a "five-colored liqueur" (an exotic Western drink made by floating layers of different liqueurs one upon the other) at a bar while out soliciting advertisements for the magazine, and then published a story about a "beautiful young boy" who visited Raichō after having accepted such a drink. The press spread rumors that Raichō had taken a lover. (They would have created an even greater scandal had they realized it was Odake herself who was infatuated with Raichō.) The second time was when she agreed to her uncle's proposition that she, Raichō, and Nakano Hatsue accompany him to the Yoshiwara entertainment district to learn more about the lives of prostitutes in the brothels there.

Fanned by inflammatory headlines, such as "Seitō New Women, Seeking Equal Rights with Men, Spend Night of Pleasure with Yoshiwara Prostitute," opposition to the "new women" intensified.[7] Raichō's house was stoned, she received death threats, and many young women were pressured to resign from the group.[8] Far from being intimidated, Rai-

6. Cited in Yamamoto Fujie, *Kogane no kugi o utta hito* (Kōdansha, 1985), 572.

7. Ibid., 573.

8. Kamichika Ichiko, a student at the Women's English Academy, was forced to dissociate herself from the group to remain in school. Later she lost a job as a teacher after her

chō determined to launch a serious discussion of what the real "new woman" should represent. The January 1913 issue of *Seitō*, called "On the New Woman and Other Women's Issues," featured contributions by Raichō, Itō Noe ("The Path to the New Woman"), Iwano Kiyoko ("Men and Women are Equal as Human Beings"), Katō Midori ("About the New Woman"), Ikuta Hanayo ("The Liberation of the New Woman"), and others. Raichō's contribution was a translation of Havelock Ellis's introduction to *Love and Marriage* by Ellen Key (1849–1926), which she followed with a serialized translation of the entire book. The articles examined the role of women from various perspectives, and one (attributed to Ōsugi Sakae's wife, Yasuko) even sardonically asserted "I Am the Old Woman," meaning a woman created by Japan's educational system and traditional method of socialization.

The February 1913 issue, which continued the focus on the "new woman and women's issues," was censored because of an article entitled "The Solution to the Woman Question" by the socialist activist Fukuda Hideko, who advocated a revolution to liberate both men and women from irrational economic and social systems created by self-interested elites. Although many of the members of Seitō were uncomfortable with the new political focus of the magazine, the leaders stood firm in their determination to air these serious matters. They were summoned by the police again when the April issue carried an article by Raichō ("To the Women of the World") that challenged the ideal of the "good wife and wise mother" and attacked the Japanese marriage system for making women yield to power, not love, and legislating against the development of affection in marriage.

Attacks on the "new women," deemed "wild talk and nonsense" by Raichō, continued.[9] Soon other journalists entered the fray. In January 1913, *Chūō kōron* published a special issue with articles by "fifteen accomplished women," including Yosano Akiko and Raichō. The April issue countered with an article by an *Asahi* newspaper reporter entitled "Handling the New Woman." In June and July special issues dealing with the "woman question" appeared, and the magazine *Taiyō*, too, published a special number on the subject in June.

Although *Seitō* had been founded as a women's counterpart to the literary journal *Shirakaba*, and the first issue described its goal as "seeking the development of women's literature," by 1913, as the literary venture evolved into a forum for the advocacy of social and political change, the names of most of the early supporters from the literary world—among them Mori Shigeko, Hasegawa Shigure, Koganei Ki-

connection with the Seitō group was discovered. Many members around the country did resign. See ibid., 573.

    9. Ibid., 576.

miko, and Kunikida Noriko—disappeared from the magazine. Yosano Akiko, however, continued to publish regularly in *Seitō* until it ceased publication in February 1916.[10]

YOSANO AKIKO: ONE TYPE OF "NEW WOMAN"

Akiko had a stormy childhood. The strong-willed daughter of a Sakai sweet-shop owner who had wanted a son, she was exiled from the family until a younger brother was born. Nevertheless, her family allowed her almost as much education as any young girl could hope for in late-nineteenth-century Japan. She graduated from middle school, but then had to take her place at the counter in the shop, following in the footsteps of an elder sister who had married, and she was effectively sequestered in her home, as was traditional in Kansai merchant families. Fortunately, her father was a bibliophile, and Akiko had the run of his library of classics. She whiled away the tedious hours alone in the store with classical Japanese texts ranging from *The Tale of Genji* and *The Pillow Book* to the *Kokinshū* and *Shinkokinshū*.[11]

In her late teens, Akiko secretly began to write poetry and to publish it in the magazines of local literary societies. In 1900 she was thrilled to meet Yosano Tekkan, founder of the New Poetry Society and publisher of the journal *Myōjō*. The next year, in a move that foreshadowed the fearlessness with which she conducted her entire adult life, she ran away from her home in Sakai to live with him in Tokyo—even though he was still married to his second wife. She became notorious the following year upon the publication of her first volume of poetry, *Midaregami* (Tangled hair). Although written in the classical form of the thirty-one-syllable *waka*, the collection boldly explored her personal responses to the world, her youthful sensuality, and her newly awakened feelings of love for the man she was soon to marry.

As Akiko's reputation climbed, Tekkan's fell. His prickly personality led to the disintegration of the New Poetry Society, and he was forced to stop publishing *Myōjō* in 1908. Meanwhile Akiko, formerly the unknown poet and his disciple, now became the famous and prolific "mas-

10. Akiko's publications in *Seitō* were as follows: In 1911, 1:1, "Sozorogoto" (poem); 1:2, "Hitogomi no naka o ikitsutsu" (poem); 1:3, "Kaze" (poem); 1:4, "Waga ie" (ten *tanka*). In 1912, 2:1, "Yume" (poem); 2:2, "Mudai" (poem); 2:3, "Utsuriyuku kokoro" (essay); 2:9, "Parii zatsuei" (poem). In 1913, 3:1, "Parii zatsuei" (poem). In 1914, 4:2, "Dentō" (poem). In 1915, 5:8, "Mori no taiju" (poem); 5:12, "Tanka jusshu" (ten *tanka*).

11. Akiko's self-education in the Japanese classics later enabled her to contribute to the Yosano family's finances by offering public lectures and private classes, and she lectured at the Bunkagakuin on Japanese literature as well. As with most topics, she had original opinions, and this was in fact another source of conflict with her husband Tekkan, who believed in presenting the received critical opinion in such lectures.

ter" whom everyone clamored to meet. Requests for articles from a variety of newspapers and magazines led her to write enough essays to fill a second volume, which appeared as *Hitosumi yori* (From my little corner) in July 1911.[12] These writings were largely introspective, subjective, *zuihitsu*-like essays[13] on topics of interest to Akiko herself, her personal experiences (three are about childbirth)[14] or those of her family; but she was also interested in contemporary political reforms as they affected women, in particular the Constitution and the Imperial Rescript on Education, arguing that "women are people the same as men" and attacking contemporary theories of education designed to produce "good wives and wise mothers."

Akiko had become acquainted with Hiratsuka Raichō through the Accomplished Women's Society (Keishū Bungakukai), and in 1911 agreed to contribute a series of poems called "Wandering Thoughts" (*Sozorogoto*) for the premier issue of Raichō's journal *Seitō*. The first poem in this sequence, "The Day the Mountains Move," assured Akiko's voice in the women's movement in Japan, and retains its appeal for international feminism today:[15]

The Day the Mountains Move

The day the mountains move has come.
I speak, but no one believes me.
For a time the mountains have been asleep,
But long ago they all danced with fire.
It doesn't matter if you believe this,
My friends, as long as you believe:
All the sleeping women
Are now awake and moving.

12. After *Myōjō* folded in 1908, Akiko was freed from the work involved in its publication and had more time to write—as well as additional financial incentive to be productive. As her outlets for publication increased, so did the range of her thinking. Everything she came into contact with sparked creativity as she moved into her thirties.

13. *Zuihitsu* ("following the brush") refers to a genre that encompasses a variety of different styles of writing characterized by a loose organization that follows the flow of the author's thoughts.

14. In "Ubuya monogatari" (Tales of the delivery room), for example, Akiko writes vividly of the birth of her second set of twins, one of whom died during delivery. She concludes, "It is strange that among those men who debate women's issues, there are those who view women as being physically weak. What I want to ask these people is whether a man's body could bear childbirth. I have given birth six times, borne eight children, and have left seven new human beings in the world. Could a man suffer over and over that way?" See *Teihon Yosano Akiko zenshū*, 20 vols. (Kōdansha, 1979–81), 14:3–12 (hereafter referred to as *Zenshū*).

15. The poem was read at the 1985 meeting in Nairobi commemorating the United Nations International Year of Women.

Fig. 8.1. Akiko in the hat she bought in Paris. During her stay in Europe she wrote an article, "First Impressions of Paris," critical of the lack of social activism among French women. (Courtesy of Yosano Hikaru and the Nihon Kindai Bungakukan)

Fig. 8.2. An oil portrait of Akiko and Tekkan in Izu. The artist, Ishii Hakutei, was a lifelong friend who frequently accompanied the couple on their excursions in search of poetic inspiration. Ishii was studying in Paris during the couple's sojourn there, and he later taught with them at the Bunka Gakuin. (Courtesy of the Nihon Kindai Bungakukan)

Akiko had become a leading figure in the literary world, but Tekkan was by now nearly forgotten. The couple came close to divorce, but Akiko devised a solution: she would raise funds to send Tekkan to Europe to recover his spirits and his poetic inspiration. Her plan was successful, and Tekkan set off for Europe in the autumn of 1911. Akiko herself followed the next spring, eager to share his enjoyment of the "freedom and civilization" to be found in Parisian artistic circles.

Akiko's blind determination to undertake this journey, despite the almost insurmountable difficulties of finances and family arrangements, resembles her reckless but resolute flight from Sakai to Tokyo to join her lover in 1901. The European trip meant separation from her seven children, one of whom was not living at home, having been sent out as a foster child soon after her birth to ease the family's financial strain.[16] Though

16. In *Parii yori* Akiko described her child-care arrangements: "As I satisfy my love for my husband, I have begun to suffer as a parent. I worry more and more about the seven

the romantic biographers of the "passionate poetess" would have Akiko rushing to the side of her beloved, unable to bear their separation, love was not her sole motivation. Like many great artists, she was passionate for experiences of all sorts. Akiko's interest in social issues, individual rights, and education made her as eager as her husband (if not more so) to see with her own eyes the various European nations whose arts had first attracted them,[17] and especially to know more of the lives of women in those countries. Although she is best known as a poet, seven of the twenty volumes of her collected works are devoted to her highly opinionated essays, many of which concern the status of women.

In Europe Akiko had the opportunity to compare the situation of women and the women's movements there and in Japan.[18] Among the many articles she wrote, a lengthy piece entitled "My First Impression of Paris," commissioned by the French arts magazine *Les Annales*, is particularly interesting for her optimistic view on the future of the women's movement in Japan. Compared to the British and Japanese, French women, she felt, were somewhat lethargic in their efforts toward reform and overly accepting of such social evils as prostitution.[19]

In the months after her return to Japan, Akiko gave birth to her eighth child, named for Auguste Rodin; saw to the publication of a steady stream of poems and prose pieces; worked on her translation into modern Japanese of *The Tale of Genji*; and became involved in a major piece of work, her only novel. Serialized as *Akarumi e* (Toward the light) in the *Tōkyō asahi shinbun* during the summer of 1913, the book is

---

children I left behind in Japan. . . . My husband's younger sister came from her home to care for them in our absence, and the children have come to love her. Her letters report again and again that the children are well and safe. Each time I read one I feel a rush of relief, but still I cannot forget my concerns. . . . I who wasted away with yearning for my husband half of last year now feel myself growing even thinner as I pine for my children" (*Zenshū* 20:537).

17. The covers of *Myōjō* regularly featured contemporary Western-style illustrations, and the banning of the November 1900 issue for a nude illustration gave the journal a racy reputation. Tekkan and Akiko were close friends with a number of Western-style Japanese painters and greatly admired Auguste Rodin, whose home they visited and after whom they named a son.

18. For additional information about Akiko's European tour, see Laurel Rasplica Rodd, "Akiko in Europe," in the *Proceedings of the Seventh Annual Symposium on Asian Studies*, Fall 1985, 515–26.

19. Akiko returned from Europe with radical ideas. When Kobayashi Seiji, one of Akiko's publishers and a lifelong friend and supporter of the Yosano family, met her ship in Kobe in early 1913, he was shocked to find Akiko advocating a return to the fluid relationships between the sexes of the Heian period and comparing them to *ren'aishugi* (free love). He attributed Akiko's remarks to "hysteria," and related in his autobiography how he convinced her that she should spend a year researching the matter before publishing her opinion. Kobayashi's autobiography *Mōfu gojūnen* is quoted in Yamamoto, *Kogane no kugi o utta hito*, 525.

a fictionalized account of the domestic misery occasioned by Tekkan's depression following the collapse of the New Poetry Society and *Myōjō*, of Akiko's struggles to support their large family, and of her desperate search for some activity that would cure her husband's emotional paralysis.

During Akiko's period of furious activity following the couple's return from Europe, Tekkan too sought a new role for himself: he appealed to Mori Ōgai and other friends for a lectureship at Keiō University and considered the possibility of reviving *Myōjō*, but all his efforts failed. Although 1914 saw the publication of *Parii yori* (From Paris), a book of essays and travel pieces he and Akiko had written in Europe, and of a volume of his translations of European poetry, *Rira no hana* (Lilac flowers), his depression did not lift. Finally on December 24 he left Akiko, six months pregnant with their ninth child, Erennu, and there was again talk of divorce. Akiko's hopes for proceeding "toward the light" were fading, and she even considered suicide:

> yo mo hiru mo   all the night long
> ware o aware to   and all day too   I think
> omou nari   pityingly of
> tsui ni inochi mo   myself   until at last I come
> ayamachinubeshi   to think my life a mistake.[20]

"A Dialogue Between Two Women" tells of Akiko's feelings during those difficult months preceding the separation, and reminds us of the heroic amount of work she was undertaking to meet what she believed were her family responsibilities.[21] The essay is a fictional dialogue between a young single woman with no worries and a second woman in Akiko's situation:

> *Second woman:* . . . I have been suffering for four or five days. It's my work. I haven't enough strength to do all that has to be done, and if I miss work for even a day our family will starve. . . .
> *First woman:* Why not get *sensei* (Tekkan) to trade roles with you? You could get some rest and enjoy some reading.
> *Second woman:* Yes, I'm always thinking I'd like time to read and cultivate my thoughts. Recently I haven't even had time for magazines. But he is not being offered work. He'll work when the time comes. I have always felt that I don't want to force him to work for his existence the way I work.
> *First woman:* That's why he just becomes lazier.

20. *Zenshū* 3:148.
21. Included in Akiko's second volume of essays *Zakkichō* (Miscellaneous notes, 1915), the essay was originally serialized in the *Tōkyō asahi shinbun* during November 1914; it may be found in *Zenshū* 14:402–29.

Fig. 8.3. Yosano Akiko during the period of her most active participation in the women's suffrage movement. Akiko visited homes in the Kyoto area to campaign for her husband Tekkan's election to the Diet. This photo was first published in the May 1915 issue of *Fujin gahō*. (Courtesy of the Nihon Kindai Bungakukan)

Fig. 8.4. Yosano Akiko with her husband, Tekkan, and children (from right) Shigeru, Hikaru, Rin, Nanase, and Yatsuo. The photo, taken in 1915, appeared in the July 1916 issue of *Shinchō*. (Courtesy of the Nihon Kindai Bungakukan)

> *Second woman:* Maybe. But he is a poet, and even when I'm exasperated with him, I can think of his poetic genius and forget everything else. I want to respect him even more, and love him even more. The world may be turning away from him, but he is not giving up on himself: he retains his self-confidence. So his few disciples and I anticipate his future.

In 1915, despite attempts by Akiko and his friends to dissuade him, Tekkan decided to stand for election to the lower house of the Diet. On February 26 he left Tokyo to campaign in his home city, Kyoto, and Akiko joined him in touring the countryside by car, calling door to door. Although women could not vote, Akiko spoke to the wives, sisters, and mothers of voters and urged them to use their influence in electing a candidate who would advance the cause of women. Tekkan lost the election and found that his dreams of political life, like his other dreams, had failed. In August 1915 he published his last volume of poetry.[22] In the thick of the campaign Akiko had published a poem in *Taiyō* that explains her feelings of guilt at her own competence and success:

22. *Karasu to ame* (Crows and rain) includes poems written mainly in the period 1909–11; there are no new compositions.

kotogoto ni	in everything
kimi no kataki wa	my lover's rival is
onore zo to	none other than myself
mi o sainamu mo	how my wretched heart
ukigokoro kana	torments me with this sin.[23]

During 1915 Akiko produced numerous reflective essays. *Zakkichō* (Miscellaneous notes), published that May, contained essays on the women's movement, current events, politics, society, education, customs, home life, and other topics written since *Hitosumi yori*. In it we see how much Akiko had changed during those intervening four years. The emotional frankness of her poetry was now complemented by the open expression of opinions in her prose. In *Zakkichō* she criticized the poor output of poets who restrict their activities, asserting: "I myself flee the jail cell called 'poet' and want to live a brilliant life as a *person*. I don't care if I can't write poems or do any other particular thing, as long as I can live a life with a reason for living."[24] Her essays are heartfelt, not pieces merely dashed off to pay the rent or improve her reputation— although paying the rent was surely a consideration.

In March 1916, Akiko gave birth to another son, her tenth child, Ken. The family's financial worries increased. The next spring she and Tekkan made a "poetic pilgrimage" to Osaka, Kobe, and Kyūshū, ostensibly to give Akiko inspiration, but motivated in large part by the need to make money. As they traveled they sold a stock of rectangular and square display cards on which they had written their poems in their own calligraphy. Kobayashi Seiji, publisher and friend, recalls that prices were rising rapidly, and "the income of those who made their living by brush and pen was pitifully low."[25] One can easily imagine the difficulties of raising a family that now included ten children on the sales of poetry. And Akiko was not only overworked; she was pregnant again. In September she gave birth to Sun, who died a day later.

Akiko refused to give in to her grief and exhaustion. Her writing pace did not falter: she hid her manuscripts from her doctor in the hospital and kept working. In a steady stream of essays, Akiko refuted the traditional concept of *fushō fuzui* or *fushō fuwa* (the wife willingly following the husband's opinion), arguing that anyone whose eyes have been opened to the equality of men and women must be shocked by this old-fashioned ideal inculcated by educators who wished to repress women. Ironically, she herself was criticized by Itō Noe for being too yielding:[26]

23. *Zenshū* 3:148.

24. Ibid., 14:493.

25. Kobayashi's autobiography is quoted in Yamamoto, *Kogane no kugi o utta hito*, 557. Kobayashi noted that a manuscript page of some four hundred characters brought in about fifty sen.

26. Yamamoto, *Kogane no kugi o utta hito*, 584–85.

Fig. 8.5. Akiko and Tekkan in 1924. (Courtesy of Mori Fujiko)

her participation in the campaign for Tekkan's election, her numerous pregnancies, her respectful remarks about her husband, her shouldering of the family responsibilities, were all seen as signs of her subjugation. Akiko, however, replied that the distinction between subjugation and equality lay not in behavior but in choice. She chose to campaign for her husband, support his activities, bear their children, and support their family; Tekkan had not insisted on her participation. She and her husband were equals, and she proudly took complete responsibility for her life.

Akiko continued to find outlets for her writings, and her essays were collected regularly: *Zakkichō* was followed by seven more volumes, published between 1916 and 1921.[27] Her European travels with Tekkan were the springboard for these writings. The publication of "My First Impressions of Paris" in particular had awakened the interest of editors in Akiko's prose, leading to a flood of requests from the journalistic

27. *Hito oyobi onna to shite* (As a person and a woman) appeared in April 1916; *Warera nani o motomuru ka* (What are we seeking?), in January 1917; *Ai risei oyobi yūki* (Love, reason, and courage), in October 1917; *Wakaki tomo e* (To my young friends), in May 1918; *Shintō zassō* (Myriad grasses of the heart), in January 1919; *Gekidō no naka o yuku* (In immense excitement), in August 1919; and *Ningen reihai* (Worshipping humanity), in March 1921. During these years Akiko also published numerous volumes of poetry, annotated editions and translations of the classics, children's stories, and so on.

world.[28] In fact, during this decade Akiko was more famous as a *hyō-ronka* (commentator or essayist) than as a poet.

THE DEBATES OVER THE PROTECTION OF MOTHERHOOD

Akiko was joined by other women in the active print debate over women's roles, social change, and the future of the family that began with the 1912 *Seitō* issues on the "new woman." Because a central question was the role the government should have in determining women's roles, the advisability of state support for women with children gradually became the focus of the debate, which was often termed the *bosei hogo ronsō* (debate over the protection and support of motherhood). Yet participants also touched on, among other topics, emancipating love and marriage from traditional morality, securing women's political rights, combining work and home life, raising women's consciousness, guaranteeing equal access to work and equal earnings, educating children, providing vocational education for women, and improving the lives of middle-aged and older women.

Akiko became the obvious target for anyone else wishing to write about women in modern society because, beginning in January 1915, she had begun writing for the monthly magazine *Taiyō* a column entitled "One Woman's Notebook" in which she freely expressed her opinions on a wide range of social issues. In fact, the very start of the *bosei hogo ronsō*[29] may be dated to a January 1916 column in which she criticized both Tolstoy and Ellen Key for propagating "the idea that it was the mission and natural right of men to do both physical and mental labor, and that women's activity was of a secondary nature."[30]

Key's thought was often countered in Japan with that of the South African Olive Schreiner, whose *Women and Work* was translated in 1914. Whereas Key was most associated in Japan with the concept of "support for motherhood," Schreiner was seen as advocating economic independence for women. The two women were thus taken as banner carriers by two different groups of feminists in Japan. As Yamada Waka wrote in 1917:

28. From 1915 on Akiko wrote frequently for the *Yomiuri shinbun*, *Tōkyō asahi shinbun*, *Ōsaka mainichi shinbun*, *Yokohama bōeki shinpō*, *Taiyō*, *Shin Nihon*, *Shin kōron*, *Shinchō*, *Kaisō*, *Fujin sekai*, *Joshi bundan*, *Shukujo gahō*, *Jogaku sekai*, *Fujin kōron*, and other magazines and newspapers.

29. Sakaguchi Chie suggests in *Yosano Akiko: Sakai ga unda keu na kajin* (Osaka: Yamaguchi Insatsu, 1982), that the *bosei hogo ronsō* marked the beginning of real debates in Japan over women's nature and role.

30. Yosano Akiko, "Hitori no onna no techō," *Taiyō* 1916/1, quoted in Yamamoto, *Kogane no kugi o utta hito*, 593.

Today the women's movement has split into two roads. One branch asserts
that motherhood is a woman's heaven-ordained occupation, that a woman's world is the family, and that for a woman to leave the family and
compete with men degrades the woman and damages the family. The
other branch argues that women are human beings deserving all the
rights and privileges accorded men as well as the freedom to participate
equally with men in life.[31]

In her column Akiko, who, at thirty-eight, had just given birth to her
ninth child, wrote that motherhood was not the central or only feature
in her life, and should not determine her participation in other spheres.
She felt any human being should be allowed to take on as many roles as
she or he can manage. Was it necessary, she wrote, to have the division
of labor envisioned by Tolstoy for humans to live? Akiko accepted her
role as mother but argued that she was also someone's wife and someone's friend, a Japanese subject, and a human being of the world.
She could not live only as mother, or as wife, or as laborer, or as artist:
"I believe that making motherhood absolute and giving supremacy to
motherhood, as Ellen Key does, among all the innumerable hopes and
desires that arise as women undulate on the surface of life, serves to
keep women entrapped in the old unrealistic way of thinking that gives
a ranking to the innumerable desires and roles which should have equal
value for the individual." Akiko also took issue with Key's assertion that
having children is the goal of all human love. She believed children were
a welcome product of that love, but that the relationship of the couple
was equally important.[32]

Raichō responded in the May issue of *Bunshō sekai*, in an article entitled "About the Demand for the Protection of Motherhood" (*Bosei no
shuchō ni tsuite*), accusing Akiko of not really understanding Key's thinking.[33] Raichō agreed with Key's proposal that educational and political
equality for women was desirable precisely because they would better
prepare women for their roles as mothers. She quoted from Key's *Children's World* to show that, even though Key did not take up the issue of
women's roles, she did assert the right of free choice of occupation and
of individual life and did value individuality. Akiko replied with a somewhat sarcastic apology for not having had time to read Key carefully
enough and thanked Raichō for setting her straight. "I also feel relieved
to know that she, like me, does not solely value motherhood, but reveres
all the talents and abilities of women." At any rate, Akiko wrote, "in four
or five years child care should cease to consume me, and I will have

31. Yamada Waka, "Eren kei joshi no omokage," *Fujin Shinbun* 891–93 (June 15, 22,
29, 1917), quoted in Kauchi, *Shiryō bosei hogo ronsō*, 294.
32. Quoted in Yamamoto, *Kogane no kugi o utta hito*, 593–96.
33. *Bunshō sekai* 11:5 (May 1916), reprinted in Kauchi, *Shiryō bosei hogo ronsō*, 38–49.

more time for reading and writing. I am determined to give myself the chance to know more of the world."[34]

Akiko had deferred to Raichō's reading of Key, but Raichō kept watch on Akiko's pronouncements from then on, and her August column again drew Raichō's fire. Akiko had written of the concern that she and Tekkan felt for their children:

> We have given birth to many children without giving a thought to their future. Once they are born, a parent's love seeks to make them grow up happily, and one naturally develops ideas as a parent about the education one's children should have. But we have not even enough clothing and food for them, much less the money to realize our educational ideals, so we find we are parents without the ability to realize our goals. We think it unpardonable that parents' carelessness should have a harmful effect on their children's lives, and we are always ashamed of our lack of ability, feeling more strongly each day that we just want to raise them without doing them harm.[35]

Raichō quoted this passage in her article "On Birth Control" and criticized Akiko (calling her an intellectual woman who allowed her emotions to run away with her) for setting a bad example for the "ignorant, uneducated" lower classes among whom such thoughtless childbearing can cause grave harm and even death. She urged "enormous consciousness of the seriousness in human life of the act of procreation," but offered no practical advice, as birth control was still forbidden in Japan.[36]

34. Yosano Akiko, "Hitori no onna no techō," *Taiyō* 22:7 (June 1916), reprinted in ibid., 50–51.

35. *Taiyō* 22:10 (August 1916), reprinted in ibid., 51–55. In fact, the Yosano children were uniformly well educated, and several became prominent figures themselves as writers, teachers, or government servants. Akiko and Tekkan, according to the children's reminiscences, rarely pushed or helped with homework, but they made it clear that they expected their children to succeed. They refused to allow magazines or other products of popular culture in the house but encouraged the children to read good books. The children were also given responsibilities within the family: for example, they helped to carry manuscripts back and forth to publishers, collected payments, and were involved in their parents' work. This information was obtained from interviews and correspondence with Mori Fujiko (the youngest Yosano child), 1984–89. For additional information on Yosano family life, see such reminiscences as Yosano Uchiko, *Murasakigusa: Haha Akiko to satogo no watakushi* (Shintōsha, 1968); Yosano Hikaru, "Haha to kodomotachi," *Teihon Yosano Akiko zenshū geppō* 5 (April 1980): 6–8; Yosano Shigeru, "Chichi Tekkan to haha Akiko," *Shinchō* 5 (1950): 53–56; and Mori Fujiko, *Midaregami: Haha Yosano Akiko no zenshōgai o tsuisō shite* (Atsumi Shobō, 1968).

36. Quoted in Yamamoto, *Kogane no kugi o utta hito*, 597–98. Official policy in Japan encouraged population growth; population limitation was associated with socialist ideas. When Katō Shidzue and the magazine *Kaizō* invited Margaret Sanger to Japan to lecture in 1922, she was at first forbidden to land and then forbidden to speak about birth control in public meetings. It was not until 1934 that Katō was able to establish a birth control clinic; but in 1937 she was jailed, and the clinic was closed the following year.

Raichō demonstrated this "seriousness" by withdrawing from the "front" into her home life for some months after her husband was hospitalized with tuberculosis and she had given birth to her second child in September 1917. Akiko during this time published another essay entitled "Women's Complete Independence" (*Joshi no tettei shita dokuritsu*) in the March *Fujin kōron*, as part of a *zuihitsu*-like sequence of poems and prose fragments called "Records of the Purple Shadows" (*Shieiroku*).[37] Though only a few lines long, "Women's Complete Independence" summarizes Akiko's immutable striving for independence:

> I cannot agree with the European women's movements' demand for special economic protection from the state for women during pregnancy and childbirth. I, who feel that it is slave morality for women to be dependent on men because of their procreational role, must refuse dependency on the state for the very same reason. . . . I am convinced that couples, both the husband and the wife, must take responsibility for the economic needs of their families—and not just their present material needs, but their futures as well. I feel they should wait until they have enough earning power before marrying or having children. For example, even if the man has economic security, a couple should not marry until the woman, too, has security,

Akiko's concern that women not be parasites on society is reminiscent of Olive Schreiner's. What is astounding is her self-confidence and her independence: she refused to give in to occasional doubts that her poetic genius and her dogged round-the-clock work could support a family of twelve, even if her husband stopped contributing. Her talent and energy were her guarantee of earning power.

Raichō was impelled to respond: How many women in Japan had the genius and talent and spirit of a Yosano Akiko and could emulate her? How many women in those times of rising prices and discrimination against women in education and work could support themselves and their children? In the May issue of *Fujin kōron* she accused Akiko of being divorced from the physical and psychological realities of life.[38]

37. "Shieiroku," as published in *Fujin kōron* 3:3 (March 1918), has seven parts: "Misuse and Incorrect Use of Classical Japanese"; a poem, "Oh, 1918"; "A Woman's Face"; "The Meat Diet and War"; a poem, "Spring Grasses"; "Women's Complete Independence"; and a poem, "February Rain and Willows." "Women's Complete Independence" is reprinted in Kauchi, *Shiryō bosei hogo ronsō*, 85–86.

38. *Fujin kōron* 3:5 (May 1918), "Is the Demand for Protection of Motherhood a Kind of Parasitism?" (*Bosei hogo no shuchō wa iraishugi ka*), in Kauchi, *Shiryō bosei hogo ronsō*, 86–91. Raichō's own house had been bought for her and her family by her mother, who had also given Raichō her dowry to help her start *Seitō*. She had two children to raise, and her husband's earning ability was practically zero, while she herself wrote and earned little. Because of the war, prices were rising; this led to the rice riots of 1918. Raichō, although raised in an upper-middle-class family, lived in poverty after her mar-

Raichō believed that it was "absolutely impossible" for women—with the exception of a few like Akiko—to obtain economic independence without seeking special protection. The government had a duty to protect all mothers and children. Mothers were the source of life, and protecting them was necessary for the future of society and of all human beings. Women's economic independence was of course important, Raichō agreed, but Akiko's position would leave the majority of women unable to marry or have children because they had not received the vocational training that would allow them to be economically self-supporting.

> To set up an impossible ideal that cannot be realized in today's society, to demand a fantasy, to leave women of marriageable age, women who could bear healthy children, in the labor market single for their whole lives or for a long period of time, is not only, needless to say, a pity for the women themselves, but a great loss to society in various ways. . . . Is not the problem we must solve first that of encouraging women's vocational education, of broadening the work boundaries, of improving working conditions for women?

Akiko was not silent. She replied that she had not imagined that there could be an argument among young women against the ideal of economic independence.[39] She criticized Raichō for valuing motherhood unduly—over all other roles women can play—and she noted that the ideal of women working equally with men for support of their family was a hope for the future, not necessarily a call for immediate action. The urgent need was to change the individual and so revolutionize society, thus creating that society from which she expected so much. Akiko concluded with an appeal to the judgment of a third party, encouraging other women to join the public discussion.

Eventually a third commentator appeared, rescuing the debate from the personal emotions that had threatened to overwhelm the issues. Yamakawa Kikue was four years younger than Raichō and twelve years younger than Akiko. She had been in the audience eleven years earlier when Akiko spoke at a meeting of the Keishū Bungakukai under the auspices of Ikuta Chōkō of the Seibi Women's English School in Tokyo

---

riage. Akiko, however, was a competent household manager as well as a brilliant writer. Where Raichō failed to learn to cook and had to have meals brought in, Akiko herself was capable of producing regular meals as well as special treats. Normally, though, the cooking, cleaning, and child care in the Yosano household were the responsibility of various young girls who were sent to the Yosanos to help out in return for the "polish" that association with the family could give them. Akiko willingly added their training—in both practical matters and the arts—to her list of duties.

39. Yosano Akiko, "The Debate Between Mrs. Hiratsuka and Me" (*Hiratsuka-san to watakushi no ronsō*), *Taiyō* 24:7 (June 1918), reprinted in Kauchi, *Shiryō bosei hogo ronsō*, 96–105.

in 1907. Akiko's lectures on the eleventh-century novel *Tale of Genji* and on *waka* had attracted the young woman, who was studying to become a Japanese teacher. After the Keishū Bungakukai disbanded, Kikue had continued to study privately with Baba Kochō, reading Turgenev, Brandeis, and Ibsen in English. In February 1918 Kikue made her initial foray into journalism with an essay in *Chūgai* entitled "Women's Problems Viewed by a Woman,"[40] in which she analyzed the trends of the women's movement in Japan and criticized the idea that women should be educated to be "good wives and wise mothers." She wrote that "women's education is for their own sake. It is not for the sake of their husbands or their children, just as men are not educated for the sake of the wives and children they will have some day."

Kikue entered the *bosei hogo* debate in the September *Fujin kōron*, with an article "The Debate Between Mme. Yosano and Mme. Hiratsuka."[41] She addressed Akiko first: although Kikue recognized Akiko's "rationality and exhortations to vigor and strenuous effort as good stimulus to women of the middle class and above who are indecisive and indolent," she could not help feeling that Akiko overly valued personal effort in her belief that all social problems could be solved by the individual. Kikue argued that Akiko, who "stressed women's individuality and argued for freedom of education, expansion of the work world, economic independence, and women's suffrage," and Raichō, with her "emphasis on gender, her preaching of the evil influence that arises from equal opportunity for both sexes, and her demand for mother's rights," both presented "stopgap policies" in the face of "the calamity of current economic relationships." For Kikue, "the fundamental solution lies only in a revolution in the economic system that brought about women's problems." Kikue's goal was socialist economic reform as a prerequisite for social reform.

Akiko's startlingly modern demands for equality of opportunity and effort, Raichō's call for state welfare to support the family for the good of society, and Kikue's appeal for socialist revolution represent three of the paths the women's movement has taken in the twentieth century. A fourth path, one that sought no new ground, was represented by an article published in *Taiyō* in the same month as Kikue's call for socialism. Yamada Waka, too, addressed the motherhood issue in "The Problem of the Protection of Motherhood: On the Discussion Between Mme. Yosano and Mme. Hiratsuka."[42] Yamada had been a prostitute in America before she was rescued by a Japanese teacher who educated and mar-

40. Quoted in Yamamoto, *Kogane no kugi o utta hito*, 605–6.
41. *Fujin kōron* 3:9 (September 1918), reprinted in Kauchi, *Shiryō bosei hogo ronsō*, 132–47.
42. *Taiyō* 24:11 (September 1918), reprinted in ibid., 147–61.

ried her. In her essay, she urged the role for women as "good wives and wise mothers," for she believed that women should try to do all they could in the home to increase their husband's ability and effectiveness. On the future of the women's movement she wrote:

> Most theories not only forget the home and family, those things which set women apart as human beings, but they overemphasize individual freedom and make the mistake of advocating women's independence and women's equality with men. . . . The women's movement of the future will not demand equality with men, but will plan how men and women can live in harmony and how they can create a wholesome family and home. It is an empty argument to advocate that women should ignore their husbands and children to develop self [*jiga*]. . . . The women's movement should look forward to the perfection of the sacred mission of women, putting all the energy of body and spirit into the home.

Waka saw no loss of independence in a woman taking money from her husband or her nation for her work of motherhood; in fact, she wrote, "It is a woman's natural right as a mother to receive funds for her daily needs from her husband or from the state."

The contributions of Kikue and Waka brought new life to the debate over state support of motherhood. The fiercest attack on Waka came from Kikue in "A Criticism of the Feminist Theory That Stabs Women in the Back" in the August issue of *Shin Nihon*.[43] Kikue termed Ellen Key an old-fashioned social reformer who was still making "reactionary" distinctions based on gender, and wrote that Key's theories made it convenient for her followers to affirm the present conditions of life. In addition, she wondered why, if Waka "hoped to 'turn women's energy of body and spirit all back to the home and family,' she herself did not set an example" instead of engaging in journalism.

Akiko refused to bow to the attacks of Raichō or Waka as well. She accused them in her *Yokohama bōeki shinpō* (Yokohama trade news) column of presenting the conservative line as though it were new, writing, "I know from my own experience from my girlhood until today that it is possible for women, too, to work."[44] Akiko staunchly continued to argue for women's economic independence and against state protection of motherhood. In a piece for the April 20, 1919, *Yokohama bōeki shinpō*, "Childbirth and Ability," she even argued that in her experience childbirth aided productivity: "I can work my best just before giving birth." Before bearing Fujiko (the Yosanos' last child), she noted:

> In March I wrote almost twice as much as in a usual month. . . . In addition to feeling the responsibility to put aside the money needed for my

43. See ibid., 117–132.
44. *Yokohama bōeki shinpō*, October 20 and 27, 1918, reprinted in ibid., 161–68.

Fig. 8.6. Yosano Akiko reading her poetry at the Tsukiji Little
Theater, October 19, 1924. The photo was the frontispiece
of the December 1924 *Fujin gahō*. (Courtesy of the
Nihon Kindai Bungakukan)

Fig. 8.7. Akiko around 1933. (Courtesy of Mori Fujiko)

confinement by my own efforts, I feared that I might die in childbirth. Even a woman not as robust as I can increase her ability to work by exercising her body and soul in the face of such danger. The wise women of the future, who will forge themselves, will be always conscious of human independence, and will never think of giving up their pride and looking to the government for help or protection of motherhood.

Akiko looked forward to the time when Japan would have a system of insurance so that women could protect themselves against loss of income in cases of illness during or after pregnancy that prevented them from working. She proposed that women strive toward this goal, noting that she and her critics did not disagree on the ultimate goal: "the liberation and perfection of women—that is, their joining in the establishment of a cooperative life both better and higher for all human beings."

The debate over motherhood drew to an amicable close in 1919 when the participants agreed that they were all seeking women's liberation, even if they could not change each others' minds about the way to achieve it, and that the goal of their public debate was mutual encouragement to think deeply about society and women's roles. Raichō's final piece on the subject, "The Agony of Contemporary Housewives" (*Gendai katei fujin no nayami*), complained of the hardships of her own life and generalized from them: "Women suffer because they have irregular work hours that continue night and day all year long without holiday. When they are made to take on the heavy burden of labor outside the home in addition, what will become of them? Surely the majority of women will have nervous breakdowns and become invalids before they are middle-aged."[45] Akiko, who had eleven children and an unemployed husband and was continuing her remarkable productivity, surely was less than sympathetic, though she made no further effort to persuade her fellow feminists through essays. The debate over protection of motherhood, in the Taishō period at least, was over, but these women had set the stage for later public debate over women's roles and for women's active participation in society.

Yosano Akiko and other feminists turned their energies toward practical activism during the 1920s, seeking to change women's lives through education and political work. Raichō went on in late 1919 to found, with political activist Ichikawa Fusae, the organization later known as the Shin Fujin Kyōkai (New Women's Association), while Kikue's writings gave birth to the Marxist women's movement of the late Taishō and early Shōwa eras. Akiko continued to write at an astounding pace on an amazing variety of topics. She also devoted considerable energy to women's education. In 1921 she cofounded the Bunkagakuin, a school with an ideal of *jiyū kyōiku* (education for freedom or individualized education), where she taught until shortly before her death in 1942. By educating individual women for self-actualization and economic independence, she was working toward the realization of her vision of a new society in which husbands and wives would take equal responsibility for their households and each individual would receive an education that both was practical and encouraged development of individual talents.

Although Akiko's political activities were more peripheral than those of Raichō or Kikue, she lent her support regularly to the Shin Fujin Kyōkai and other political action movements.[46] In 1931 she wrote a song on women's suffrage on the occasion of the First All-Japan Women's Suffrage Rally. Speaking for all women in Japan, she promised to transform the nation "with our labor, our love, our beauty." The song was adopted by the postwar New Japanese Women's Alliance (later the League of Japanese Women Voters) in 1945, and is still sung regularly, a symbol of the new life these "new women" brought to social thought, and especially to the question of women's role in early-twentieth-century Japan.

45. *Fujin kōron* 4:1 (January 1919), reprinted in ibid., 207–13.
46. Ichikawa Fusae, "Yosano Akiko shi no omoide," in *Teihon Yosano Akiko zenshū geppō* 8 (March 1980), 3–6.

NINE

Middle-Class Working Women
During the Interwar Years

Margit Nagy

Although the Japanese prided themselves on having a unique family system that was the source of enduring national strength and unity, popular press accounts as well as statements by scholars and officials attest to the widespread concern over the apparent instability of the Japanese family in the 1920s. The rise in juvenile delinquency, the increase in the number of family disputes brought before the courts for settlement, and the perception that divorce was becoming more frequent seemed to portend undesirable social trends that already troubled Western industrialized nations.[1]

This chapter is dedicated to the memory of Yuri Takahashi (1944–1987), who aroused my interest in Japanese women's history and sustained my research efforts through the resources she shared and her dedicated action on behalf of Asian women.

1. Standard presentations in English, like Takeyoshi Kawashima and Kurt Steiner, "Modernization and Divorce Rate Trends in Japan," *Economic Development and Cultural Change* 9 (October 1960): 213–239, focus on a prewar steadily declining divorce rate as evidence that Japan managed to avoid the positive correlation believed to exist between a nation's industrial development and its divorce rate. In this view, the forces of industrialization and urbanization acted like a solvent on the traditional causes of divorce (the failure of the wife to conform to the ways of the household, her failure to produce a male heir, and so on) and promoted greater family stability over time. While the statistics for legal (registered) divorces do show a downward trend during the Taishō years, contemporaries observed family problems in Japan similar to what could be found in the industrialized West, where divorce appeared to be on the rise owing to financial difficulties faced by couples and also to women's growing initiative in terminating unhappy marriages. See, for example, *Tōkyō nichi nichi shinbun*, January 9, 1921, reprinted in *Shinbun shūroku Taishōshi* (Taishō Shuppan, 1978), 9:7–8 (a compilation of Taishō-era newspaper accounts, hereafter cited as *SST*); *Yomiuri shinbun*, June 8, 1921, in

Against this background of growing concern over the forces of familial disintegration threatening Japanese society, the entry of middle-class women into the work force came under the worried scrutiny of government officials and opinion leaders. Bureaucratic reports, on-site surveys, journalistic accounts, and personal narratives from this period reveal that the phenomenon of middle-class working women (*chūryū shokugyō fujin*) created profound anxieties about the future of family life and national unity, especially since the middle class was viewed as the bastion of social stability in an era of social and political turmoil.

In surveys, questionnaires, and news stories throughout the 1920s, numerous researchers probed the possible effects of employment on women's "mission in life" (*tenbun*) as wife and mother. They questioned whether a working woman would have lessened opportunity (or desire) to marry. They wondered, for that matter, whether her feminine virtue would still be intact when and if she did marry. They asked how married women could manage two full-time jobs—one at the workplace, the other at home—without both spheres being shortchanged. In terms of national impact, they explored the possible effect of middle-class working wives and daughters on male unemployment, and they asked how the middle-class family could serve as the role model for the lower class if it, too, sent its women to work to supplement the earnings of a household head. Finally, they worried about the possible adverse effects on the next generation of Japanese subjects if it were raised by working mothers.

These and other questions posed in the 1920s suggest that the discourse on the working woman of the middle class touched at the heart of a much larger debate over social values, the institution of the family, and the gender role of women. Unresolved tensions surrounding these women's entrance into the labor force disclosed a society in transition and struggling to reconcile changes wrought by modernization and urbanization with the late Meiji construction of women as good wives and wise mothers.

SST 9:212–13; *Miyako shinbun*, December 24, 1924, in *SST* 12:494; *Tōkyō nichi nichi shinbun*, June 7, 1925, in *SST* 13:246–47; and "Keishincho no sōdanjo e kuru fujin," *Fujin sekai* 6 (October 10, 1922): 19–22.

For a detailed comparative analysis of Japan's divorce system, see Hozumi Shigetō, *Rikon seido no kenkyū* (Kaizōsha, 1924), and the section on divorce in Hozumi's *Kekkon dokuhon* (Chūō Kōronsha, 1950), 181–221. Hozumi, a University of Tokyo legal expert in family law, thought that "invisible divorces"—separations that frequently terminated the common-law (*naien*) marriages prevalent in Taishō Japan—were as noteworthy as registered divorces.

THE MIDDLE-CLASS WORKING WOMAN DEFINED

Although much was written about the middle-class working woman in the interwar period, the terms "middle class" and "working woman" were never precisely defined either by writers of the time or by later scholars. It is therefore difficult to say exactly how many women belonged in this category or what kinds of work they did. Throughout this chapter, "middle class" (*chūryū kaikyū* or *chūsan kaikyū*) refers to urban salaried workers whose educational background and earned income, as a rule, put them above the working class, or laborers. According to this definition, the middle class was only an estimated 8.5 percent of the total population in 1920. During the Taishō era (1912–26), however, it increased notably in the cities. For example, the middle class of Tokyo grew from an estimated 5.6 percent of the work force in 1908 to about 21.5 percent by 1920.[2] Contemporary surveys of household budgets categorized such occupations as government official, teacher, policeman, and bank employee as middle class.[3] In my discussion on middle-class working women I use the term broadly to include women from skilled labor or shopkeeper family backgrounds who obtained white-collar jobs that the public considered to be middle-class employment.[4]

The term "working woman" (*shokugyō fujin*) was relatively new in the 1910s and 1920s and, as such, did not have a standard definition. True, *shokugyō fujin* had a "high-collar" nuance and thus was mainly used for women in the tertiary sector who held white-collar or professional jobs.[5] Even among government sources of data on working women of the interwar years, however, there was considerable variation. For example, *Living Conditions of Working Women* (*Shokugyō fujin seikatsu jōtai*), a survey conducted by the Hiroshima Bureau of Social Affairs in 1926, applied the term solely to the "intellectual laborers" (*chiteki rōdōsha*) among women in the labor force. These included female

2. Minami Hiroshi, *Taishō bunka* (Keisō Shobō, 1965), 183–87. For additional statistics on women in the labor force between the end of World War I and 1931, see Tazaki Nobuyoshi, "Josei rōdō nōshōruikei," in *Kindai*, ed. Joseishi Sōgō Kenkyūkaihen, vol. 4 of *Nihon josei seikatsushi*, 5 vols. (Tokyo: University of Tokyo Press, 1990).

3. For more details on the household budget survey, see Miyazaki Reiko, "Hyōjun seikatsushi no ashidori," *Shisō* 15 (1974): 13–28. Nakajima Kuni discusses the budget surveys of the middle class in "Taishōki no seikatsuron," in *Meiji kokka no tenkai to minshū seikatsu,* ed. Wakamori Sensei Kanreki Kinenkai (Wakamori Tarō Sensei Kanreki Kinenkai, 1975).

4. For a comparable phenomenon of women with "the desire to make a jump into middle class" in America during the 1920s, see Dorothy M. Brown, *Setting a Course: American Women in the 1920s* (Boston: Twayne, 1987), 109.

5. Kojima Tsunehisa, *Dokyumento hataraku josei hyakunen no ayumi* (Kawade Shobō Shinsha, 1983), 65.

teachers, office workers, telephone operators, midwives, and nurses, but excluded factory workers and domestic servants.[6] In another survey of working women carried out by the Kyoto Bureau of Social Affairs at about the same time, the term referred in a broad sense to "women and girls who were employed in mental or physical labor in some kind of occupation owing to the effect of the industrial revolution," but it was also "the general term for female workers in contrast to male workers."[7]

In addition to problems of definition, the imprecision of prewar statistics is a second obstacle impeding the study of middle-class women who were working for pay. Although the number of women in the labor force definitely increased from the Meiji through the early Shōwa (1926–31) years, no systematic statistical record exists. Certain industries employing female workers did keep reliable yearly data, of course; these include the Education Ministry (on women teachers), the Home Ministry (on midwives, nurses, and other licensed health care professionals), and the Postal and Railroad bureaus (on their female employees). At the same time, however, the number of white-collar working women in the private sector is largely a matter of conjecture and inference. Even the findings of on-site surveys of working women, which were popular among government entities during the interwar years, should be treated cautiously. The best approach is to take the numerical data as an approximation of reality.[8]

The data tell us first of all that middle-class working women were a clear minority of the total female population and even of the total labor force in Taishō–early Shōwa Japan. Of an estimated total female population of 27 million in mid-Taishō, women in the labor force numbered only 3.5 million. Nearly three-quarters of these employed women (2.6 million) were classified as manual workers, while the remaining one-fourth engaged in intellectual or mental work.[9] This was true even in

6. Hiroshima-shi, Shakai-ka, *Shokugyō fujin seikatsu jōtai* (Hiroshima, 1927), is quoted extensively in Kasahara Kazuo, ed., *Mezame yuku josei no aikan* (Hyōronsha, 1978); on the meaning of *shokugyō fujin*, see esp. 204–5.

7. Kyōto-fu, Shakai-ka, *Shokugyō fujin chōsa* (Kyoto, 1926), 1. The survey continues with a breakdown of female occupations based on the amount of knowledge or skill required in each.

8. Murakami Nobuhiko, *Taishōki no shokugyō fujin* (Domesu Shuppan, 1983), 54–55.

9. Tōkyō-shi, Shakai-kyoku, *Shokugyō fujin ni kansuru chōsa* (1924), 1–2 (hereafter cited as Tokyo, *Shokugyō fujin chōsa*). The survey was actually carried out in 1922 and included the major occupations for middle-class women: teacher, nurse, telephone operator, typist, office worker, and department store clerk. Murakami Nobuhiko draws heavily on this survey in his analysis of women and employment in Taishō Japan; see *Taishōki no shokugyō fujin*, 8ff. In 1925 the Tokyo Social Affairs Bureau published the same survey results

Tokyo, the political, educational, commercial, and financial center of Japan.[10]

Still, Taishō–early Shōwa records document a "marked increase" (*saikin ichijirishuku zōka*) in middle-class working women. The conspicuous growth in numbers of these workers held true both for teaching, originally a male profession, and for nursing, which from its beginnings in Japan was a female occupation.[11] The steady influx of women into teaching had begun around 1916–17—the World War I years of prosperity for Japan, when many men left teaching to take better-paying jobs in private industry.[12] As the demand for female education grew and the school-age population in the major cities swelled, educational leaders expressed their willingness to train women to be excellent teachers, with the anticipation that in the future, half of the teaching population would be female.[13] The newspaper *Ōsaka jiji* underscored the significance of this trend when it reminded teachers that "male shortage, female increase"(*otoko wa futtei, onna wa fueru*) typified not only the ratio of male to female teachers in Osaka for the 1917 school term, but also enrollments at normal training schools. Only half the usual number of males had applied to the area teacher training facilities; by contrast, at female normal schools 184 women vied for 80 positions in the preparatory course, 90 applied for 10 spaces in the regular first-year program, and almost double the allotted number sought to enter the second-year program.[14] Thus, a comparison of growth rates for female occupational sectors between 1920 and 1930 shows that the greatest increase was in the public servant (*kōmu*) category, with female teachers, especially at girls' schools, accounting for most of that gain.[15]

In nursing, the growth was even more conspicuous. With the World War I prosperity, a new health consciousness permeated the expanding middle class and spurred the development of medical treatment facilities requiring medical personnel, including nurses. Attracted by the rel-

---

under the title *Fujin jiritsu no michi* in *Kindai fujin mondai meicho senshū zokuhen*, vol. 7 (Nihon Tosho Sentā, 1982).

10. Tokyo, *Shokugyō fujin chōsa*, 6, 11.

11. Murakami, *Taishōki no shokugyō fujin*, 236. He notes that the only exceptions were the military men caring for the wounded during the Satsuma Rebellion of 1877.

12. Maeda Hajime, *Shokugyō fujin monogatari* (Tōkyō Keizai Shuppan, 1929), 30. Maeda, who was born in 1895, wrote this book as he was preparing to leave for Europe and America to study labor issues. After his return to Japan, Maeda served as mediator in labor disputes for many years.

13. Ichibangase Yasuko, "Taishōki no 'jokyōin' mondai," in *Taishō no joshi kyōiku*, ed. Nihon Joshi Daigaku Joshi Kyōiku Kenkyūjo (Kokudosha, 1975), 331.

14. *Ōsaka jiji shinbun*, March 5, 1917, quoted in Murakami, *Taishōki no shokugyō fujin*, 94.

15. Ichibangase, "Taishōki no 'jokyōin' mondai," 328–29.

atively high income and the fact that licensing was fairly easy to obtain, women flocked into the nursing field. Compared to the approximately thirteen thousand nurses at the end of the Meiji era (1911), by the last year of the Taishō period (1926) there were about fifty-seven thousand—better than a fourfold increase.[16]

Among female white-collar workers (typists, office workers, telephone operators) employed in government offices, a similar pattern emerges: sixteen thousand in 1920, and almost double that number by 1930, or some thirty thousand.[17] In the private sector, too, the unprecedented concentration of an estimated seven hundred female white-collar workers in the Marunouchi district of Tokyo, newly constructed after the great Kantō earthquake of 1923, gave the public the impression of sharp growth.[18]

Educational records of the graduates of girls' higher schools also indicate that an increasing number were seeking paid employment. Thus in 1917, only 3.4 percent of all girls' school graduates were working women; by 1921 that number stood at 5 percent, or 8,750 out of a total of 176,000 students at five hundred schools.[19]

MOTIVATIONS FOR EMPLOYMENT

Three basic reasons explain the increase in middle-class working women: economic necessity, awakened women's consciousness, and job availability. Economic need was foremost. The middle class initially had benefited greatly from the economic boom that Japan enjoyed during World War I. Urban salaried workers, the core of the middle class, had used their higher income to upgrade their life-style. They provided their families with better-quality food, leisure activities, and, for their daughters, often a higher education.[20] Beginning in mid-1917, however, complaints of "livelihood difficulties" multiplied among members of the middle class as the price of rice and other staples mounted and the Tokyo housing shortage pushed up rents. The postwar recession was followed in 1923 by a bank panic, when the Kantō earthquake destroyed

16. Maeda, *Shokugyō fujin monogatari*, 231–32. See also Murakami, *Taishōki no shokugyō fujin*, 244.

17. Kojima, *Dokyumento hataraku josei*, 65, cites from labor statistics based on the census data for 1920 and 1930 as given in Rōdō Undō Shiryō Iinkai, ed., *Nihon rōdō undō shiryō* (Chūō Kōron Jigyō Shuppan, 1962–), vol. 10.

18. Yoneda Sayoko, *Kindai Nihon joseishi*, vol.1 (Shin Nihon Shinsho, 1972), 181.

19. Murakami, *Taishōki no shokugyō fujin*, 71.

20. For a contemporary analysis of the connection between World War I economic prosperity and improved educational opportunities for women, see *Yomiuri shinbun*, February 19, 1915, in *SST* 3:78.

areas of Tokyo and its environs.[21] Before there had been sufficient recovery from these economic setbacks, Japan confronted the financial panic of 1927, and then began to feel the impact of the worldwide depression.[22]

By 1922 the middle class was already in financial trouble. A six-month survey of the household accounts of 397 salaried workers in Tokyo and five other major cities revealed that the necessities of life consumed most of their household income. Another finding showed that the income of the household head alone was insufficient to meet expenses.[23] Moreover, whereas in 1923 almost 82 percent of male university and professional school graduates found employment, by 1928 that number had slumped to 54 percent.[24]

As a partial solution to the financial problems of their families, middle-class daughters in growing numbers took jobs between the time they completed their education and their marriage. Their pay helped directly as supplementary income or indirectly as savings that would help defray upcoming wedding expenses.[25] The *Yomiuri* newspaper noted this trend in a May 31, 1919, column that called attention to the eighty graduates of girls' higher schools who staffed office jobs at the Postal Savings Bureau: "When we see that the majority of those [working] want to supplement their family incomes with whatever be their pay," the writer concluded, "there is no doubt that the world war and its aftermath has exerted some direct and indirect effect on the families of the middle class."[26] The Taishō educator and columnist Kawasaki Natsu also commented on the effect of the continuing recession on middle-class living standards: "It is a situation in which women, who, until now, moved on after girls' schools to flower arranging and sewing and who did not know the taste of poverty, are suddenly facing the storms of life."[27]

The various surveys on white-collar working women confirm these impressions of contemporaries: need was indeed pushing middle-class women into the labor force. Of the 900 respondents (teachers, typists, office workers, department store clerks, nurses, and telephone operators) in the 1922 Tokyo survey, more than half (471, or 53

21. Yoshida Kyūichi, *Nihon hinkonshi* (Kawashima Shoten, 1984), 293–94.

22. Ichibangase Yasuko, "Shōwa zenki no 'jokyōin' mondai," in *Shōwa zenki no joshi kyōiku*, ed. Nihon Joshi Daigaku Joshi Kyōiku Kenkyūjo (Kokudosha, 1984), 157.

23. Kyōchōkai, *Hōkyū seikatsusha, shokkō seikei chōsa hōkoku* (1925).

24. Maeda, *Shokugyō fujin monogatari*, 4.

25. See *Fujo shinbun*, March 26, 1915, reprinted in *Fujinkai 35 nen*, ed. Fukushima Shirō (Fujo Shinbunsha, 1935), 392–94; *Yomiuri shinbun*, October 16, 1917, in *SST* 5:359–60; *Hōchi shinbun*, October 27, 1917, in ibid., 374.

26. *Yomiuri shinbun*, May 31, 1919, cited in Murakami, *Taishōki no shokugyō fujin*, 70.

27. Kawasaki Natsu, *Shokugyō fujin o kokorozasu hito no tame ni* (Genninsha, 1931), 21.

percent) indicated that their work supplemented household income. An important minority (98 out of the 784 women who were single, widowed, or divorced, or 12.9 percent) worked because they were the primary breadwinners for the household: single women cared for parents, widows supported their children, and some of the divorced had both parents and children as dependents.[28] Family misfortunes prompted Gotō Matsuko, for example, to take a job. Her father had died suddenly while she was in school. Then the 1923 earthquake destroyed the store her mother had opened. As a result, after graduating from girls' schools in 1924, Matsuko became an office worker with the Electric Light Bureau to support her mother and two brothers.[29]

Economic need propelled married women into the labor force as well. At times their income provided a small cushion of savings for emergency use; at other times the second salary was so important to household finances that after a woman became pregnant, she tried to find someone to help with the housekeeping so she could keep working.[30] More than half of the 116 married women in the 1922 survey, in fact, had children. The majority of working mothers were teachers and had an average of two children.[31]

When the Central Employment Exchange of Tokyo surveyed 8,280 female employees of forty-five government offices, banks, companies, and stores in Tokyo and its environs toward the end of the decade, the results showed that the single greatest reason for women of any age to be employed was still the need to assist the family budget (2,822, or 46 percent).[32] Of course, this percentage was even higher when only the replies of the 633 youngest workers (eighteen years or under) were considered (433, or 66 percent).[33] Again, if the related motives of needing "to support others or oneself" are added to "supplementing household income," then 3,949, or 60 percent, of all those surveyed were in the labor force owing to economic necessity.[34]

Necessity, however, was not the only reason middle-class women worked. Some were attracted by the opportunities that a job offered. As in other industrialized countries, the awakening of women and the movement for their emancipation had also begun to influence Japan. In the words of the Tokyo 1922 survey, female employment was an ex-

28. Tokyo, *Shokugyō fujin chōsa*, 53–54. Of the 900 respondents, 67, or 7.5 percent, gave "other reasons" for working; 98, or 10.5 percent, gave no reason at all (p. 50).

29. Murakami, *Taishōki no shokugyō fujin*, 143–44.

30. Tokyo, *Shokugyō fujin chōsa*, 6.

31. Ibid., 47–48. Of the married teachers, 67 percent had children.

32. See Maeda, *Shokugyō fujin monogatari*, 32–33, for a statistical breakdown of employment motivation by worksite and age.

33. Ibid., 34.

34. Ibid., 32–33.

pression of the women's irrepressible aspiration for independence and self-reliance (*dokuritsu jiritsu*).[35]

At least for some of the unmarried women surveyed, employment guaranteed the economic independence that made the option of a single life possible. For them, there was no rush to get married. In reply to the 1922 question concerning the kind of marriage preparation the respondent was making, a telephone operator wrote: "I am making no marriage preparation, but I want to learn an occupation that will make me independent." An office worker responded, "I do not care for the married life and am making no preparation." A teacher declared, "I do not intend to prepare for the married life. I seek out refined interests and hobbies, and I save at least a little. I want to have comfort in my old age."[36] Among the other groups included in the survey—nurses, department store clerks, and typists—there were always at least a few who expressed a willingness to continue in the single state.

Of course, it was also true that the postwar economic recession discouraged male workers from marrying. Some of the surveyed women who gave lofty reasons for remaining single might well have been turning necessity into an ideal. Whether the aspiration for independence and self-reliance was in fact a second-best choice owing to lessened opportunities for marriage, or rooted in a romantic desire to escape from a confining family situation in pursuit of some glamorous ideal, or grounded in a realistic assessment of a particular work situation, seems to have varied with the individual. A spokesman for the Tokyo Central Employment Exchange, for example, in 1920 described the young women who daily came to his office seeking jobs: they were largely graduates of girls' higher schools who wanted something other than the boring life they were leading in families that had no financial worries.[37]

Middle-class women joined the labor force as well because of the greater availability of professional and white-collar jobs. These occupations had higher pay, better working conditions, and higher social prestige than the characteristic female jobs of domestic servant, factory worker, or agricultural laborer. With the steady growth of the tertiary sector since the Russo-Japanese War of 1904–5, thousands of clerical and sales jobs had been created in the expanding bureaucratic structures of government and private industry and within the developing distribution center. These developments in Japanese capitalism coincided with the raising of the compulsory educational level to six years in 1908, the expansion of girls' higher schools, and the creation of specialized training facilities, such as typing schools. Female graduates of these

35. Tokyo, *Shokugyō fujin chōsa*, 5–6.
36. Ibid., 99–100.
37. *Yomiuri shinbun*, November 12, 1920, in *SST* 8:411.

institutions had improved chances for employment that required more mental ability than physical strength.

Ironically, during the Taishō years public preoccupation with the "woman question" (*fujin mondai*)—the debate over the nature, status, and proper sphere of women—created new positions that from the outset women themselves filled. Newspapers put female reporters in charge of the new feature sections for women; established magazines like the *Taiyō* (Sun) used female writers for special issues on female employment and family problems. The birth of new periodicals geared to female readers (thirty-five during the decade of the 1910s alone) added to the demand for female journalists.[38]

In the public sector, official concern with social issues like the health of working women and their offspring, the rise in juvenile delinquency, and evidence of strain in family life also generated new jobs for women. On the national level, the Social Affairs Bureau of the Home Ministry one month after its establishment in August 1920 hired two female nonregular members with overseas training in social work to "observe places and situations that male officials failed to notice," with the aim of trying to "listen to the ideas of women from the standpoint of future legislation."[39] A year later the Home Ministry contributed two thousand yen to the newly founded social work department of Japan Women's College (Nihon Joshi Daigaku), which trained students for work with children and with female factory workers. Tanino Setsu, one of the first to graduate from the program, not only was hired by the Home Ministry, but went on to become the first female assistant factory inspector.[40]

Metropolitan government offices also began to hire qualified female personnel to deal with women's labor problems. Thus in 1920, a position for a person in charge of female labor (*fujin rōdō gakari*) was created within the labor section of the Tokyo Social Affairs Bureau. The woman director, Hayashi Katsu, assisted by a staff of ten female office workers, served as advisor on all matters related to women's labor problems. In 1921 she directed a survey of the conditions of two thousand factory girls in 317 medium to large Tokyo factories.[41]

---

38. See Margit Maria Nagy, " 'How Shall We Live?': Social Change, the Family Institution, and Feminism in Prewar Japan" (Ph.D. diss., University of Washington, 1981), 102–8; and Mitsui Reiko, ed., *Gendai fujin undōshi nenpyō* (San'ichi Shobō, 1963), for the Taishō years (1912–26).

39. *Tōkyō nichi nichi shinbun*, September 18, 1920, in *SST* 8:347.

40. *Hōchi shinbun*, August 11, 1921, in *SST* 9:278. On Tanino Setsu, see Mitsui, *Gendai fujin undōshi nenpyō*, 128.

41. *Yomiuri shinbun*, March 20, 1920, in *SST*, 8:106; Mitsui, *Gendai fujin undōshi nenpyō*, 94–95. These were factories employing more than fifty workers.

Job availability for middle-class women improved during the Taishō–early Shōwa years, in periods both of economic prosperity and of recession, as employers found they could hire women with skills comparable to men for about one-third the cost. When the lure of higher pay during the World War I business boom created a large-scale exodus of males from the teaching profession into the world of commerce, for example, officials quickly hired females as replacements.[42] The salary that males considered too low was quite attractive to female teachers, because the female labor market of that time still consisted primarily of low-wage, unskilled types of labor, and teaching was an occupation with comparatively high social status.[43] Similarly, during the postearthquake recession of 1924, the chief of transportation in Tokyo proposed replacing one-third of the seven thousand male conductors with females, arguing: "If we employ female conductors, we will realize a savings of 50 sen per person a day and 180 yen per person per year. With 2,500 women, the expected savings would be 350,000 yen."[44]

In sum, several factors in late Taishō and early Shōwa Japan accounted for the entry of growing numbers of middle-class women into the white-collar and professional labor force. No doubt, as the surveys of working women indicate, economic necessity and the desire to contribute to household finances figured prominently in the decision to seek employment outside the home. It should not be forgotten, however, that the times encouraged women to look to employment as a means of satisfying their desire for economic independence and self-fulfillment. Finally, during this era both private and public employers actively recruited women for white-collar jobs as a cheap source of competent labor. As was the case during the Meiji period, changes in the male labor market to a large extent determined the employment prospects for women in the 1920s.[45]

THE SOCIETAL RESPONSE TO MIDDLE-CLASS WORKING WOMEN

Taishō and early Shōwa society, and even middle-class working women themselves, responded ambivalently to the redefinition of the gender role for middle-class women. Attitudes toward women who worked for pay outside the home varied. On the one hand, Murakami Nobuhiko contends that society in the interwar years was relatively tolerant of

42. Nishi Kiyoko, *Shokugyō fujin no 50 nen* (Nihon Hyōron Shinsha, 1955), 20.

43. Ichibangase, "Taishōki no 'jokyōin' mondai," 333; Murakami, *Taishōki no shokugyō fujin*, 93–94.

44. *Yorozu chōhō*, December 9, 1924, in *SST* 12:482.

45. Ichibangase, "Taishōki no 'jokyōin' mondai," 338.

women in the labor force, and this, he argues, made it possible for middle-class women to seek jobs—something that their mothers and grandmothers could not have done except in teaching. Reflecting this permissive social atmosphere, women's magazines of the 1920s regularly featured articles on female employment for the largely middle-class readers.[46]

According to the testimony of a contemporary, the favorable shift in public opinion produced concrete results. The director of the Suidobashi Women's Employment Exchange observed in 1926 that in early Taishō, people had regarded the employment agency as a type of welfare agency. Only women who were somehow socially defective—widows with many children to raise or women unable to make a successful marriage—were his clients. By contrast, those coming in 1926 were "fine unmarried young women, including graduates of girls' higher schools."[47]

On the other hand, there is considerable evidence of negative public opinion—or at least ambivalence—toward female employment. Such feelings reflected anxieties about the impact of Japan's increased modernization and industrialization on the family. The Meiji leaders who had mobilized national resources in the single-minded pursuit of attaining equality with the industrialized West had assured the nation that Japan's unique family institution (*ie*) would enable Japan to avoid the social turmoil that had accompanied industrialization elsewhere. Though comforting, the prediction proved to have little basis in reality. The Rice Riots of 1918, in which an estimated seven hundred thousand people publicly protested, were followed in the 1920s by a series of organized protests against the status quo. Labor strikes, tenant-landlord disputes, and public lectures held to win sympathy for causes like women's suffrage and equitable treatment for the outcaste sector of society (*burakumin*) demonstrated that the traditional values of harmony and self-sacrifice could not buffer Japan from the social strains provoked by industrialization.

On the level of the family unit, "scientific" sources—on-site household surveys and statistics compiled by public and private social work agencies—as well as the testimony of experts on family law alerted the public to disturbing signs of family breakdown. For example, in the 1920s Japan had the world's highest number of illegitimate births (*shiseiji*) owing to the practice of common-law (*naien*) marriage, which was especially prevalent in the expanding urban areas.[48] Family disputes set-

46. Murakami, *Taishōki no shokugyō fujin*, 70–71.

47. *Miyako shinbun*, November 7, 1926, in *SST* 14:392.

48. See Hozumi, *Rikon seido no kenkyū*; and his *Kon'in seido kōwa* (Bunka Seikatsu Kenkyūkai, 1925), 50–52.

tled through lawsuits rather than within the family were also on the rise.[49]

The recollections of middle-class working women and the observations of government officials and social critics of the interwar years present vivid descriptions of the varied ways in which Japanese vented their anxiety. One common form, sexual harassment, stemmed from the view that employed women represented a deviation from woman's basic calling as wife and mother and must therefore be women of either low class or questionable virtue.[50] Young women on the electric trains of Tokyo reported sexual harassment from men with wandering hands who pinched their hips and fondled their breasts in the anonymity of the congested trains. One office worker, who described herself as something of a tomboy, complained that subjection to this daily humiliation was almost more than she could endure. The men felt free to engage in these improprieties, Murakami explains, since no proper woman—that is, wife and mother—rode the public transit during the rush-hour periods.[51]

Middle-class working women were also the object of demeaning remarks and attitudes. They were sometimes called "abandoned old women" (*obasuteyama*), which bespoke the popular fear that by postponing marriage in order to work a young woman ran the risk of ending up with no marriage prospects whatsoever when she did wish to marry.[52] One visiting nurse at the house of a nouveau riche (*narikin*) family overheard the children describing her and the maid as nobodies. In that same household the nurse was expected to do the laundry, clean house, and run miscellaneous errands for the family when she was not actually tending the patient.[53] Female teachers complained that their views were slighted by male colleagues and that they were accepted only if they smiled sweetly and did not contradict the men.[54] A typist quoted in the 1926 Hiroshima survey wrote that she had heard complaints from some people about working women who earn their income with a pen being talkative, disliking work, and not being competent. The typist objected, stating: "I don't think it is really like that at all."[55]

Another indication of the ambivalence toward women's expanded

49. See Nagy, " 'How Shall We Live?' " 204–5, for excerpts from the testimony of members of the Special Investigative Commission on the Revision of the Legal System (Rinji Hōsei Shingikai) on the need for a domestic court system. Kano Masanao, *Senzen. "Ie" no shisō* (Sōbunsha, 1983), 156–62, gives a valuable overview of this commission.

50. See the essay by Silverberg in this volume (chap. 11).

51. Murakami, *Taishōki no shokugyō fujin*, 144.

52. Cited in Kojima, *Dokyumento hataraku josei*, 66.

53. Murakami, *Taishōki no shokugyō fujin*, 251.

54. Nishi, *Shokugyō fujin no 50 nen*, 21.

55. Cited by Kasahara from the Hiroshima survey in *Mezame yuku josei no aikan*, 208.

opportunity in the public sphere appeared in the recruitment campaign of the Central Telephone Exchange. In 1920, badly in need of female operators, the exchange distributed handbills advertising job openings and emphasizing the appropriateness of the work for women who would be future wives. As a special incentive, the exchange established a branch of the Japan Women's Commercial School (Nihon Joshi Shō-gyō Gakkō), which offered many courses, including the time-honored accomplishments considered important for marriage preparation—tea ceremony and flower arranging—as well as career-enhancers like math, composition, and shorthand. Employees who attended classes from five to seven in the evening could expect to complete the entire program in two and a half years.[56]

Employer expectations of female workers also reflected the absence of a social consensus on women in the workplace. The 1926 Kyoto survey of 3,666 women in ten white-collar occupations included a question for employers on the strengths and weaknesses of their female employees. Over half of the 111 employers who described the positive traits of their women workers used words like "docile," "meek," and "gentle" or said that women's work was meticulous and exact. Other comments emphasized loyalty, patience, perseverance, and manual dexterity as commendable attributes.[57] The survey results contained some surprises, though. A minority identified the strengths of their female workers to be independence of spirit, the ability to adapt to the times, intelligence, and decisiveness.[58] The 104 employers who responded to the question about weaknesses of their female staffs listed twenty-four kinds of defects. The most common of these was the lack of continuous service; other complaints were that the women lacked a spirit of dependence or that they were indecisive—just the opposite of the opinions expressed in the first question on strengths.[59]

Taishō surveys on middle-class working women also indicate that the women themselves had doubts about their new roles as paid employees. When asked to comment on the "hopes and reflections of working women," the respondents focused on the personal conflicts they faced. For unmarried women, a recurring theme was the struggle to fulfill themselves without sacrificing their femininity, a quality they equated with being able to prepare adequately for the married state. For example, in the Kyoto survey of 1926, respondents insisted that their desire

56. Murakami, *Taishōki no shokugyō fujin,* 70.

57. According to Kyoto, *Shokugyō fujin chōsa,* 70, of a total of 111 respondents, 31 replies (28 percent) listed these attributes of women employees, while 28 replies (26 percent) noted these attributes of their work.

58. Ibid.

59. Ibid. Of a total of 104 respondents, 31 replies (30 percent) cited this defect.

was "not to lose their special virtue as females, but to develop it more and more"; to "cultivate accomplishments as a future housewife in a family and to fulfill their vocation as women"; and to "increase both in knowledge and virtue."[60]

For the married women in the 1922 Tokyo survey, tensions between their responsibilities as mothers and homemakers and their responsibilities as paid workers emerged as most salient. Women usually managed to fulfill their responsibilities at home while working full time by entrusting some of the housekeeping and childrearing to a member of the family or a maid. A working mother would typically set the table for her child's noon meal, then leave for work. Homeward bound, she would buy the side dishes for the evening meal, which she would cook with a family member or with the maid.[61]

The strain of trying to fulfill work responsibilities without neglecting family life permeates the following responses:

> When I think about the importance of my official responsibilities as a parent with a child, I regard my superficial knowledge with regret. I have an inquiring mind but I have no spare time. When I return home, I am pressured by the need to get clothing ready for the various seasons. I cannot rest even on holidays, because there is [always] some kind of meeting. I am pressed with my duties and have no time to spare, even to recover from my tiredness. Thus I have become isolated from my family. Nor can I teach the children [at school] adequately, as is my duty.

> I have two children, aged three and one. It takes me one hour to commute to school. My children, like goldfish, await my return. Without even changing clothes, I give them milk, and, going to the kitchen, I give directions to the maid. . . . [At times] I must entrust my sick children to someone I do not know and leave for work. The fact that I have no one I can feel secure with to be at home in my absence also pains me. My mind and my body are always tired.

> As a married working woman, I request that the hours of work be made a little shorter [for married women] than for unmarried women or males, or that a married woman be permitted to go home and await the arrival of her husband at least one hour before he returns.[62]

While contemporaries were personally experiencing the tensions surrounding the redefinition of the role of middle-class women, government officials and social critics searched for solutions to the issues raised by the entry of these women into the labor force. In the interwar years prior to 1937 they generally resisted the dogmatic approaches of indoc-

60. Ibid., 72–73.
61. Tokyo, *Shokugyō fujin chōsa*, 132–33. The 148 married women were 16.4 percent of the total surveyed.
62. Ibid.

trination and repression; it was, after all, not their intention to make social reality conform to the male-centered, authoritarian family model of the Meiji era, which had accorded inferior status to women in both family and society. Instead, recognizing the centrality of women to their major concerns of family stability and economic viability, they preferred to study actual conditions through on-site surveys and the like and to propose ameliorative measures that would help keep the family unit intact and economically healthy. Meanwhile, the search continued for ways of making the urban middle-class family (and woman) the bulwark against radical social and economic change and the role model for the lower classes.

Although some help was given to middle-class women in their new role as paid employees, the primary aim of the ameliorative measures was to render employment outside the home unnecessary, especially for the wife and mother. Thus in the 1920s and 1930s, when survey results and personal interviews convinced analysts that most women worked because of family need,[63] government officials and concerned individuals published employment guides and operated job exchanges to assist middle-class women in obtaining suitable jobs. From their expressions of concern about the possible relationship between the steady expansion of the female labor force and mounting male unemployment, however, it is clear that they viewed women's role as white-collar workers to be a double-edged sword for society.

Attempts to make the wife's employment unnecessary took two forms. One was to provide employment for the male household head through special sections for salaried workers at the public job exchanges; arrangements made by Tokyo employment exchange officials, who personally visited area factories and companies on behalf of their middle-class clients; and the creation of government projects (like the on-site surveys) that employed displaced white-collar workers.[64] A second method, represented by the Campaign to Improve Livelihood (Seikatsu Kaizen Undō), sought to rationalize home management by training homemakers to run their households with economic sense. Techniques of effective budgeting and wise selection of consumer goods presumably would enable these wives of salaried workers to respond creatively to their husbands' shrinking incomes. A further objective of the campaign was to inculcate in middle-class homemakers a

---

63. See Maeda, *Shokugyō fujin monogatari*; Taniguchi Masao and Ono Iwao, *Shokugyō fujin to jissai* (Tōgensha, 1931); and Ogata Tsuneo, *Shitsugyō mondai to kyūsai shisetsu* (Ganshōdō Shoten, 1926).

64. *Asahi shinbun*, November 9, 1923, and *Tōkyō nichi nichi shinbun*, December 2, 1923, in *SST* 11:473, 504–5; see also Shakai Fukushi Chōsa Kenkyūkai, ed., *Senzen no Nihon no shakai jigyō chōsa: Hinkon, seikatsu mondai, chōsashi kenkyū* (Keisō Shobō, 1982), 36–37.

broader societal view that would encourage them to make home management decisions based on the well-being not only of their own households, but of the family-state as well.[65]

This vision of women as "public-spirited rational homemakers" prompted the Home Ministry in 1926 to recruit leaders from middle-class women's groups for a Standing Committee on Women's Associations to Encourage Thrift (Kinben Shōrei Fujin Dantai Jōnin Iinkai). The committee was charged with studying various methods of economizing in households and also with promoting savings and a reduction in the use of imported goods in order to repay Japan's foreign debt in six years.[66] Meanwhile, one year earlier, a blue-ribbon commission charged with revising the family provisions of the Meiji Civil Code recommended that the rights of wives be expanded in order to eliminate a major cause of family conflict: the arbitrary actions of the household head.[67] In all these ways, the Japanese government in the 1920s attempted to bolster the middle-class family by keeping the wife in the home with expanded rights and broader responsibilities.

CONCLUSION

The story of the middle-class working woman in the Taishō–early Shōwa period is an important link in the redefinition of the gender role of women between prewar and postwar Japan. The unresolved tensions surrounding the entry of both married and unmarried middle-class women into the labor force reveal a society in transition. On the one hand, economic need and new white-collar and professional jobs provided opportunities for middle-class women to work for pay outside the home, activity that had previously been identified almost exclusively with lower-class women. On the other hand, personal narratives in the interwar years demonstrate that single women and their society were ambivalent about the compatibility of marriage preparation and employment, while married working women felt uneasy about the coexistence of family life and work life.

This uneasiness characterizes present-day Japanese society as well. While it has become commonplace for proper middle-class young women to work in offices before marriage and for middle-aged women

65. Nakada Tatsuko, "Taishō-ki no kateika kyōiku," in Nihon Joshi Daigaku Joshi Kyōiku Kenkyūjo (ed.), *Taishō no joshi kyōiku*, 96–97; Inoue Hideko, *Kasei shinron* (Bunkō-sha, 1934), 438, 444.

66. Chino Yōichi, *Kindai Nihon kyōikushi: Taiseinai fujin dantai no keisei kado o chūshin ni* (Domesu Shuppan, 1979), 251.

67. Nagy, " 'How Shall We Live?' " 204–9. These proposed revisions, though not enacted at the time, laid the foundation for the civil code adopted after World War II.

with grown children to return to the work force on a part-time basis, the majority of these women are not on a career path, and a young mother is still expected to devote herself to childbearing and homemaking. Nevertheless, despite a variety of obstacles, women who work outside the home now outnumber those who remain at home, and the number of women pursuing professional careers is rising.[68] It was perhaps in light of these trends that the editor of a special magazine issue on changing Japanese society advised readers "wish[ing] to predict the shape of Japanese society in the twenty-first century" to focus on the changing role of women—the "most dynamic sector of the population."[69] The same could have been said for middle-class working women in the interwar years.

68. Contemporary views include "Thwarting Women in the Work Place," *Japan Times*, November 21, 1986, 14; and "Japanese Career Women Program Draws Large Audience," *Bulletin: The Japan-America Society of Washington* 34, no. 4 (April 1990): 4.

69. Iwao Sumiko, "The Japanese: Portrait of Change," *Japan Echo* 15 (special issue) (1988): 2–6.

TEN

Activism Among Women in the Taishō Cotton Textile Industry

Barbara Molony

"Where are the organized women workers?" Alice Kessler-Harris asked in 1975.[1] Her question unleashed an unabating torrent of provocative studies of proletarian women in a number of countries, particularly in the United States and Europe.[2] This deluge of solid research notwithstanding, activist women, to paraphrase Anne Firor Scott, continue to be seen and not seen.[3] Pre–World War II Japanese women textile workers suffer the same, if not indeed a more pervasive, invisibility. When they are not generally overlooked, they are pitied as passive victims incapable of acting on their own initiative. When instances of activism are so obvious they cannot be ignored (as when silk reelers carried out a major strike in 1885), they are dismissed as unique, aberrant events. Women's failure to become the backbone of an enduring union move-

The research for this chapter was made possible by grants from the National Endowment for the Humanities, the Northeast Asia Council of the Association for Asian Studies, and Santa Clara University. I am indebted to independent scholars Suzuki Yūko and Watanabe Etsuji, who generously shared their time and expertise in labor and women's history; to Professors Nakamura Masanori and Nishinarita Yutaka, who offered me helpful materials and facilitated my research at Hitotsubashi University; and to the members of the Fusae Ichikawa Memorial Association, particularly Yamaguchi Mitsuko and Kubō Kimiko, who gave me access to their invaluable collection.

1. Alice Kessler-Harris, "Where Are the Organized Women Workers?" *Feminist Studies* 3 (Fall 1975): 92–110.

2. See Jacquelyn Dowd Hall, "Disorderly Women: Gender and Labor Militancy in the Appalachian South," *Journal of American History* 73, no. 2 (1986): 356, for an impressive list of studies inspired by Kessler-Harris's question.

3. Anne Firor Scott, "On Seeing and Not Seeing: A Case of Historical Invisibility," *Journal of American History* 71, no. 1 (1984): 7–21.

ment confirms the conventional view of them as passive. Their gender, it is argued—or, as one scholar suggests, their youth[4]—made them hard to organize.

Further research on women's collective action should modify this assertion. Even if the focus on collective action is limited to institutionalized, organized activism (that is, unions), we must ask whether structural factors like the organization of the factory itself or attitudinal factors like the hostility of male unionists, and not women's "nature" or "culture," explain the lower rate of female participation. Louise Tilly argues persuasively that proletarian women's lower rate of participation in collective action in nineteenth-century France needs "no special psychological or gender-attribute explanation": that is, a similar set of conditions may be used to predict men's and women's propensity to activism.[5] Societal constraints, restrictions by management on the economic independence of female workers, and, in certain circumstances, the workers' own views of what was appropriate behavior for women may have slowed female labor organization in Japan; yet when conditions for activism existed, women workers responded.

The question of activism, however, should not be limited to formal political or union actions. This chapter attempts to expand the definition of the term "activism" to connote the opposite of passivity. Thus, activism manifested itself as much in the decisions of rural Japanese women and girls to enter employment in the cotton textile industry as in their collective actions as workers. To understand why farm women would be motivated to enter the mills, one must examine general attitudes regarding appropriate behavior for women in the 1920s. To be sure, what women saw as suitable for themselves as women was itself in a state of evolution. As Teresa de Lauretis notes, "Self and identity . . . are always grasped and understood within particular discursive configurations. Consciousness is never fixed, never attained once and for all because discursive boundaries change with historical conditions."[6] The converse is equally true: women's contributions to the definition of gender helped produce shifts in their historical context.

Certainly the motives of the mill workers varied, and their perceptions of the choices available to them were affected by their individual circumstances. Yet these women shared many experiences, and their decisions were conscious ones within the limited bounds of their lives.

4. Andrew Gordon, *The Evolution of Labor Relations in Japan: Heavy Industry, 1853–1955* (Cambridge, Mass.: Harvard University, Council on East Asian Studies, 1985), 8–9.

5. Louise A. Tilly, "Paths of Proletarianization: Organization of Production, Sexual Division of Labor, and Women's Collective Action," *Signs* 7, no. 2 (1981): 416–17.

6. Teresa de Lauretis, ed., *Feminist Studies/Critical Studies* (Bloomington: Indiana University Press, 1986), 8.

Their socialization as farm girls created a shared consciousness of class and gender as these were constructed in the setting of Japan of the 1920s. Many were accustomed to wage labor, either their own or that of their neighbors or families. Moreover, they were probably aware of such common 1920s phenomena as tenant strikes, labor organizing, and the Taishō youth culture that distanced itself from the Meiji culture of older generations.[7] The women whose lives inform this study tell us that, in the 1920s at least, activism was compatible with women's notions of gender identity. Thus, as conscious actors, women helped to shape significant aspects of modern Japanese life, including labor-management relations and the remolding of farm women into proletarian women.

THE COTTON INDUSTRY IN JAPANESE INDUSTRIALIZATION

Surprisingly little attention has been focused on the Japanese cotton textile industry by scholars writing in English.[8] Yet cotton textile production was Japan's most important industry before the Second World War for several reasons.[9] First, cotton textiles accounted for 26.5 per-

7. See Silverberg's essay in this volume (chap. 11).

8. This neglect may be the result of scholars' desire to study industries viewed as glamorous and "important." Although capital investment per worker was higher in the cotton textile industry than in many heavy industries owing to the high cost of the huge spinning and weaving machines, women-dominated industries like textiles have been seen as traditional or backward rather than as part of a leading sector inspiring technological advances. Such attitudes have caused contemporary scholars to view textiles as a less worthy object of study.

9. While labor conditions and recruitment practices in the cotton and silk industries have many similarities, this paper focuses on the cotton textile industry. Silk filatures were more often located in rural areas, and silk workers' contracts were of shorter duration than those in the cotton industry; see Nakamura Masanori, *Rōdōsha to nōmin* (Shōgakkan, 1976), 81. Thus, silk workers may have had closer ties with their rural communities and families. Furthermore, the silk industry was less mechanized than the cotton, and although silk reeling probably required greater skill and dexterity than running the large cotton-spinning machines, silk reeling was technologically an extension of the kind of work farm women had traditionally done. Hence, silk reeling was often erroneously viewed—by both contemporaries and later scholars—as unskilled work suitable for young farm girls. See Gail Lee Bernstein, "Women in the Silk-Reeling Industry in Nineteenth-Century Japan," in *Japan and the World: Essays on Japanese History and Politics in Honour of Ishida Takeshi*, ed. Gail Lee Bernstein and Haruhiro Fukui (New York: St. Martin's Press, 1988), 54–77. The methods of remuneration for labor also differed: management in the silk industry fostered intense competition among workers, which inhibited cooperation and may have slowed the development of worker consciousness; see Nakamura, *Rōdōsha*, 97–98. Because of these differences, my observations concerning the active role of women mill workers is confined to the cotton-spinning industry, although further study may show the industries' differences to be more apparent than real. Moreover, I focus on spinning rather than weaving, since most weaving operations, except for those in large, vertically integrated cotton mills, were not carried out in the same plant as spinning. In Japan,

cent of all Japanese exports, and 14.5 percent of all industrial output, as late as 1935.[10] Second, the first large-scale private companies established after the Meiji Restoration were cotton-spinning firms; moreover, the textile industry was one of the first industries to benefit from government assistance.[11] Third, starting in the 1880s, cotton manufacturers banded together to form the Japan Cotton Spinners' Association (Dai Nippon Menshi Bōseki Dōgyō Rengōkai)—one of the earliest manufacturers' associations in Japan—which attempted, none too successfully, to control producers' access to labor.[12] Fourth, the "rationalization" process of studying standard motions and implementing efficient labor techniques that was so characteristic of the 1920s was most highly developed in large cotton textile firms.[13] Fifth, as in the United States and Europe, the industry was the leading employer in the early-modern manufacturing sector.[14]

For this study, the industry is particularly important for two additional reasons. First, young unmarried women predominated among cotton textile workers. Second, the migration of these women from the countryside to the urban mills had tremendous demographic and social implications: it fueled Japan's urbanization and created a link that permitted the social and economic integration of city and countryside in an era of rapid change.[15]

---

moreover, weaving was mechanized much later than spinning, and the scale of plants was smaller. See Sung Jae Koh, *Stages of Industrial Development in Asia: A Comparative History of the Cotton Industry in Japan, India, China, and Korea* (Philadelphia: University of Pennsylvania Press, 1966), 25. This situation was not universal: in Shanghai, for instance, weaving was done in the same plant as spinning; see Emily Honig, *Sisters and Strangers: Women in the Shanghai Cotton Mills, 1919–1949* (Stanford: Stanford University Press, 1986), chap. 6, for a description of the integration of mill operations.

10. Keizo Seki, *The Cotton Industry of Japan* (Tokyo: Japan Society for the Promotion of Science, 1956), 6.

11. Ibid., 15

12. Koh, *Stages of Industrial Development*, 66.

13. Seki, *Cotton Industry*, 29, 88.

14. Statistics for employment by industry tell the story: in 1931, cotton-spinning firms employed 54.1 percent of all industrial workers (82.4 percent of women industrial workers); in 1936, 39.6 percent (80.2 percent of women); and in 1938, 30 percent (81.2 percent of women). Agriculture employed four times as many women as industry did in that period, but 70–80 percent of the women employed in farming were married, widowed, or divorced, compared to 40–50 percent for industry. See Takada Jirō, ed., *Nihon rōdō kagaku kenkyūjo hōkoku: Fujin rōdō ni kansuru bunken shōroku* (Nihon Rōdō Kagaku Kenkyūjo, 1940), 2–8.

15. Until the 1890s, the early cotton industry recruited female workers from the urban poor and from middle- and lower-class families in villages near the urban textile plants; see Nakamura, *Rōdōsha*, 159–60. This situation changed after 1890, when workers came to be recruited from greater distances. It is frequently asserted that the income of these workers recruited from afar, remitted to their tenant farmer families, permitted the fam-

FROM FARM TO FACTORY

All industrializing societies have had to draw rural labor into factories.[16] In some cases, notably the United States, most of the jobs in the textile industries were initially held by young unmarried adult women, who only later were replaced by families including men and children. In other cases, such as England, child labor was used until prohibited by law. Many societies relied on kinship networks to supply labor, as well as to act as welfare organizations, in lieu of the state or the employer. Others developed a labor supply through paid recruiting agents, whose work was often facilitated by the decision of family members to go together to the mills. At least one society, China, developed half a dozen different recruiting methods, the most infamous of which was the coercive contract system whereby the "recruiter," who was really more like a gangster, promised to feed and lodge the young worker (at minimal cost) in return for her wages.[17] Thus, no single pattern of recruitment typified societies undergoing industrial revolutions: some developed paternalistic controls over workers, while others simply employed workers' labor. Nevertheless, all had to attract workers somehow to urban factory jobs. What motivated people in rural areas to move elsewhere for work in industry?

One of the most detailed studies of the migration of farm girls is that of Thomas Dublin on the textile mills of nineteenth-century Lowell, Massachusetts.[18] Dublin found that between 1830 and 1860, rural economic disasters predisposed young farm daughters to enter the mills. A significant minority of women, citing the value of selfless duty to their parents, took jobs in the hope of contributing to their families' total income. Most girls, however, cherished the wages they earned and kept them. Their families, in any case, were often too proud to accept a daughter's earnings. Moreover, most factory girls ceased being dependent on their families when they left home to live in carefully proctored, company-administered boarding houses. Thus Dublin found that the

ilies' survival and, by extension, the survival of the landlord-tenant system in pre–World War II Japan. This argument confuses the horse and the cart; it is more accurate to say that rural poverty, exacerbated by the tenancy system, induced many farm daughters to enter employment and to send their pay to their families.

16. See, for example, Thomas Dublin, *Women at Work: The Transformation of Work and Community in Lowell, Massachusetts, 1826–1860* (New York: Columbia University Press, 1979); Thomas Dublin, *Farm to Factory: Women's Letters, 1830–1860* (New York: Columbia University Press, 1981); Philip S. Foner, *The Factory Girls* (Urbana: University of Illinois Press, 1977); Tamara Hareven and Randolph Langenbach, *Amoskeag: Life and Work in an American Factory City* (New York: Pantheon Books, 1978); Hall, "Disorderly Women"; Honig, *Sisters and Strangers*; and Louise A. Tilly and Joan W. Scott, *Women, Work, and Family* (New York: Holt, Rinehart, & Winston, 1978).

17. Honig, *Sisters and Strangers*, 94–113.   18. Dublin, *Women at Work*.

real motivations of mill girls to work generally deviated from the selfless reasons often cited in contemporary moralistic writings: the girls had specific, personal reasons for wanting to earn money. Jacquelyn Dowd Hall found that American textile workers two generations later had similar reasons for seeking mill jobs. Most expected to help their families and to find some type of personal fulfillment. These young girls, four-fifths of whom were between the ages of fourteen and twenty-one when they went to work, "saw factory labor as a hopeful gamble rather than a desperate last resort."[19] That is, they made informed choices that served not only their families' interests but, significantly, also their own.

The influential study of women, work, and the family in England and France by Louise Tilly and Joan Scott contrasts with Dublin's findings for New England and Hall's for the rural South.[20] Nonelite women in Europe had always contributed to their families, even in the preindustrial era, either as part of the "family team" or as servants doing undifferentiated work as domestics and artisans in other's houses. Married women blended economic activity with reproductive work, often using the undesirable expedient of wet nurses to permit them to maximize their economic contribution to family subsistence. Child labor was taken for granted, especially after age seven or eight. As European industrialization began, factory work continued to be tightly integrated with the family economy; men, women, and children contributed all their earnings to the family.

The advent of industrialization and certain changes in farm conditions, such as the disappearance of the family farm in eighteenth-century England, accelerated the movement of women and children into wage work. Many rural families migrated to the cities to find mill work for their children. In other cases young women, especially those who had been hand-spinners before industrialization left them underemployed, migrated alone or followed a close relative.

Elsewhere, Tilly calls the trend toward female wage labor "proletarianization," which she defines as "the increase in the number of 'people whose survival depended on the sale of labor power.' " She adds that "although proletarianization was a common experience, how it occurred in given populations varied markedly, as did the timing of the process."[21] As we have seen, many women in Europe, both single and married, became "modern" wage earners to support the "family wage economy";[22] by contrast, American women workers showed greater indi-

19. Hall, "Disorderly Women," 362.   20. Tilly and Scott, *Women, Work, and Family.*

21. Tilly, "Paths," 402–3. Tilly's definition of "proletarianization" cites Charles Tilly, "Did the Cake of Custom Break?" in *Consciousness and Class Experience in Nineteenth-Century Europe*, ed. John M. Merriman (New York: Holmes & Meier, 1979), 29.

22. Alice Kessler-Harris objects to this interpretation; see her "Problems of Coalition-Building: Women and Trade Unions in the 1920s," in *Women, Work, and Protest: A Century*

vidual autonomy at an earlier stage in the development of the cotton textile industry in the United States. Gradually, however, the ties of unmarried European women to their rural families weakened as the number of
proletarianized, propertyless families unable to offer their daughters
dowries or inheritances increased. In both the United States and Europe
factory girls, especially those who made a large percentage of family income, were unlikely to return to their place of origin but instead would
marry "mechanics"—working-class men—from their new locale. Thus,
specific motives to work varied among individuals and societies, but in
both Europe and the United States women and girls themselves decided
to work in the mills. Some showed autonomy not only in deciding to
work but also in increasing the separation from their families—that is, by
retaining some or all of their wages or by remaining in the cities to marry.

In the case of Japan, most scholars have promoted the view that female
factory workers of rural origin, their major contributions to Japan's development notwithstanding, passively accepted their role in the textile
industry. Since the publication in 1925 of Hosoi Wakizō's *Jokō aishi* (The
pitiful history of women workers), the classic study of female employment in the cotton textile industry,[23] it has generally been thought that
young girls right out of elementary school were lured to work in the
mills by unscrupulous recruiters who offered their parents or guarantors a prepayment of at least several months' wages in return for a contract that effectively made the girls indentured laborers. The received
interpretation further asserts that the girls bowed to their fate because
of their underdeveloped consciousness as workers. The Japanese value
system, with its emphasis on filial piety and, for girls, on docility and
obedience, contributed to their passivity. According to this interpretation, most young women returned to their villages to marry after saving
for a dowry, and remained unsullied by their industrial experience.

This view of women's employment, from their passive recruitment as
short-term workers to their return home as dutiful daughters, has endured for a variety of reasons, including, of course, its resonance with
stereotyped images of women in Japan. Perhaps equally important, this
interpretation parallels another common assumption that needs reas-
sessment: that is, that the rise in labor activism in the 1920s was due
principally to the increase in male industrial employment. Let us now
look more closely at the received wisdom in an effort to revise the overall argument.

Farm girls of the 1920s played a major role in initiating and implementing the economic decision to leave the family to go to work, often

of U.S. Women's Labor History, ed. Ruth Milkman (Boston: Routledge & Kegan Paul, 1985),
135n.

    23. Hosoi Wakizō, *Jokō aishi* (1925; reprint Iwanami Shoten, 1954).

against parental wishes. Many did so, paradoxically, because they believed they could better serve their families' interests, as did the European women in the study by Tilly and Scott. Others did so for more personal reasons, as Dublin's study found of American women. In either case, the fact that they made the decision to enter the mills on their own belies their depiction as hapless pawns. After entering the factory, many attempted to overcome their disappointment with the abysmal conditions they encountered and made a second economic decision to transfer to a new factory. Whether or not their expectations of improved conditions were fulfilled—and usually they were not—it is significant that, contrary to the standard interpretation, a large number of new hires in cotton factories were not young, inexperienced girls right off the farm.[24] Rather, they were older, more skilled transfer workers who had already had several jobs.

Furthermore, not all female workers in the textile industry quietly accepted unhealthy labor conditions. By the 1920s, cotton textile workers, working in a highly mechanized and electrified industry, were, like other workers in the more modern industrial sector, staging successful strikes for improved conditions. Clearly many activists saw themselves first as workers and second, if at all, as farm daughters who would eventually return to the farm. The growing sense of personal autonomy that permitted the development of increased worker consciousness also helped to make employment in industry a viable option for young girls. Thus, labor actions and positive motives for employment can be seen as interrelated forms of activism among textile workers.

What of the argument that workers eventually returned to life on the farm, regardless of youthful expressions of labor activism? A significant minority did return—and many firms used this fact to keep from having to retain older girls and women whose wages should presumably increase with experience and seniority. The overwhelming majority of farm girls, however, either remained industrial workers throughout their teen years and often even after marriage to fellow industrial workers, or else retired at marriage to lead the life of urban working-class housewives. Even during the depression-ridden 1930s, only 22.5 percent of the mill workers of rural origin returned to the farm, and of these only a quarter were in registered marriages within a year of their retirement.[25] To be sure, nonregistration of common-law marriages before

24. Tanino Setsu, "Bōseki jokō taishokugo no kisu," in *Sangyō fukuri* 12, no. 11 (November 1937): 22–23. She found that 45.5 percent of workers who had left their jobs in spinning were employed in another factory one year later; of these, 22 percent were working in cotton spinning, 15 percent in silk reeling, and 13 percent in weaving.

25. Nakamura, *Rōdōsha*, 168. Nakamura states that just 6 percent returned to their villages to marry. Along these same lines, it is interesting that Kawasaki was the fastest-

fertility was proven was typical in many rural areas, a fact that probably skews the evidence. Nevertheless, even if all returnees did marry quickly, their numbers were fewer than those of women who went from factory to factory in search of better and more remunerative jobs.

The migration of farm women seeking employment, moreover, was not a new phenomenon that came only with modern industrial labor opportunities. In a study of one typical village between 1773 and 1868, Akira Hayami found that 74 percent of the women and 63 percent of the men at some time in their lives left the village to work. Many of the women were employed locally, but significantly, 25 percent of the women left their village permanently during those years. Thus, working women in the twentieth century were building on a long tradition of female migration.[26]

RECRUITMENT IN THE COTTON TEXTILE INDUSTRY

As Hosoi noted, most textile workers, especially after the turn of the century, were the daughters of poor farm families.[27] But virtually all young textile workers, rather than being forced against their will into the mills, expressed a desire to work. When questioned by researchers in 1927, most workers cited economic reasons for wanting to work in the mills: 17.2 percent wished to earn money for personal use, such as self-support or for their trousseaux, and 69.3 percent wished to contribute actively to family finances.[28] These responses parallel the conclusions of Dublin and of Tilly and Scott: the women believed their work contributed to personal or family well-being.[29] The 1927 survey is cor-

growing city in Japan in the 1920s; see Gary Allinson, *Japanese Urbanism: Industry and Politics in Kariya, 1872–1972* (Berkeley and Los Angeles: University of California Press, 1975), 82. I suggest that the presence of a large Fuji Bōseki plant in Kawasaki contributed to this permanent increase in population.

26. Akira Hayami, "Rural Migration and Fertility in Tokugawa Japan: The Village of Nishijo, 1773–1868," in *Family and Population in East Asian History*, ed. Susan B. Hanley and Arthur P. Wolf (Stanford: Stanford University Press, 1985), 115–22.

27. Nakamura, *Rōdōsha*, 159.

28. Izumi Takeo, *The Transformation and Development of Technology in the Japanese Cotton Industry* (Tokyo: United Nations University, 1980), 36. Elsewhere, surveys indicate similar motives. The following reasons for entering the mill were given by 2,000 workers: family circumstances (493); family finances (289); to earn money (189); to rise in life (146); to study (131); to associate with one's betters (96); to get away from home (82); to earn a living (77); to be with one's friends (66); to go to the city (54); and so on. See "Watakushitachi wa ikani shiitagerarete iru ka?" *Rōdō fujin* 4, reprinted in *Nihon fujin mondai shiryō shūsei*, vol. 3: *Rōdō*, ed. Akamatsu Ryōko (Domesu Shuppan, 1977), 238.

29. Transcribed interview with Yonematsu Kame in a publication of the Kawasaki Okinawa Kenjinkai, February 1983, 113. Yonematsu stresses her desire to help her family; she even returned a second time from Okinawa to Kawasaki to work at Fuji Bōseki.

roborated by the data I use in this study: published reminiscences and
personal interviews with seven retired women workers and two retired
male workers.[30]

What recruiters offered prospective workers varied from factory to
factory and from recruit to recruit, and women were often deceived into
believing conditions were better than they turned out to be. Most were
promised comfortable working conditions, good food, steady wages (at
least sixty sen per day, similar to wages offered Japanese women in
other jobs), and a prepayment ranging from about five to fifty yen.[31] A
large part of the prepayment was often retained by the worker's family;
a worker's acceptance of this condition was thus her implicit contribution to family welfare, similar to that seen in Europe. What seems to
have been of greatest interest to the young girls themselves, however—
at least in retrospect—was that the recruiters offered money to buy decent clothes and the opportunity to continue their education in factory-
operated schools. (Early Lowell workers also saw the mill as a route to
higher education.) Most women whom I interviewed mentioned these
highly personal desires to improve themselves even before citing their
desire to contribute actively to family finances. Clearly, then, the importance of personal autonomy was growing, and it played a major role in
many girls' decisions to enter the cotton industry.

By the 1920s, most school-age children were completing at least elementary education. The fact that many farm girls wished to continue
schooling is significant because school, perhaps subconsciously, was a
means of self-improvement and, through testing, of self-evaluation.
Former textile worker Kumagai Kikuko was attracted to Tōyō Muslin
by her expectation that she could continue her education there; she had
once hoped to become a teacher.[32] Yamanouchi Mina, a pivotal feminist

30. Because four of these individuals were labor activists, some argue that they
were atypical of workers in general. Yet none was an activist before entering the mill; all
were radicalized by the conditions of their employment. Furthermore, their activism
meant that they were perhaps bolder and certainly more articulate than their peers. The
latter joined the strikes led by the activists because the activists expressed sentiments
they shared. Thus, the activists' ideas are no less valid than those of more "typical"
workers.

31. Fifty yen was a significant part of a farm family's annual income, yet at least one
interviewee believed it was a typical payment; Kumagai Kikuko, interview, March 10,
1985. Gary R. Saxonhouse, in "Country Girls and Communication Among Competitors
in the Japanese Cotton-Spinning Industry," in *Japanese Industrialization and Its Social Consequences*, ed. Hugh Patrick (Berkeley and Los Angeles: University of California Press,
1976), 112, notes that daily wages for women entering jobs in cotton spinning were just
85 percent of those for women in agricultural work, but that women in textiles worked
300 days per year compared to 180 days in agriculture.

32. Kumagai interview. See also the three-part series featuring Kumagai Kikuko,
"Haha no rekishi," *Shin fujin shinbun*, December 4, 11, and 18, 1980.

activist in both the women's suffrage movement and the labor movement, cited her love of education in her autobiography.[33] Hosoi Wakizō's wife, Takai Toshio, noted in her recent autobiography that she, too, craved a life of study and personal freedom, even as she transferred from company to company, each as dirty as the last, each with its own peculiarly loathsome conditions.[34]

Of course, most workers who wished to take advantage of the "corridor schools" (classes were conducted in the corridors of the dormitories) found themselves too exhausted to study after their twelve-hour shifts ended. Yamanouchi, who tried to attend classes at Tokyo Muslin, noted that of the three thousand girls living in her factory's dormitories, only sixty had the energy to attend classes, and just thirty graduated from the program of study.[35]

Although women in textiles tended to have less education than those in some other occupations such as typing or office work, their level of schooling was consistently rising after World War I.[36] As girls stayed in school longer, and as legislation limiting child employment began to be enforced during the 1920s, the average age of beginning factory workers rose. With fewer vulnerable children under thirteen working in the mills, the incidence of disease decreased, producing a generally healthier, more vigorous work force.[37] Older girls were also less susceptible to family dominance in the decision to leave the farm.[38]

Factories seem to have preferred recruiting girls from great distances, thereby binding them more firmly to the dormitory and company. Fuji Bōseki, for instance, employed surprisingly large numbers of Okinawans in its Kawasaki and Hodogaya plants (probably at least one-fourth of the work force at Kawasaki), as well as numerous girls from the Tōhoku region in its Hodogaya plant.[39] Other large firms showed a similar preference. Female commuting workers had

---

33. Yamanouchi Mina, *Yamanouchi Mina jiden* (Shinjuku Shobō, 1975), 11.

34. Takai Toshio, *Watashi no "Jokō aishi"* (Sōdo Bunka, 1980), 46.

35. Yamanouchi, *Jiden*, 32.

36. Tōkyō Shiyakusho, ed., *Fujin shokugyō sensen no tenbo* (Tōkyō Shiyakusho, 1931), 81–82. Textile workers showed increasing levels of education outside Tokyo as well, as Allinson notes for Aichi in *Japanese Urbanism*, 45.

37. Kumabe Toshio, *Joshi rōdō no shokugyō gakuteki kenkyū* (Ōsaka: Ginkō Shintakusha, 1943), 371–75. It should be noted that even before World War I (in 1914) just 5.9 percent of the cotton textile work force were girls under fourteen, a decrease from 14.6 percent in 1897; Takamura Naosuke, *Nihon bōsekigyō shi josetsu* (Hanawa Shobō, 1971), 2:209; 1:301.

38. Yamanouchi, *Jiden*, 36.

39. Sunabe Matsumitsu, interview, March 12, 1985; Umezu Hagiko interview, March 11, 1985. Sunabe Matsumitsu, in an interview published in *Kuotari Kawasaki* 4 (1984): 8, says there were at least one thousand Okinawans at Fuji Bōseki.

a higher rate of absenteeism because of family responsibilities and could not be coerced to work as dormitory residents could.[40] Japanese women who lived at home were likely to think first about how best to blend work and family responsibilities, unlike workers living in dormitories.

Although many women workers, as boarders who came from poor families, were fairly vulnerable to layoffs, they were hardly incapable of making economic decisions about their employment. Some of these women had themselves initiated the decision to leave the farm for the factory. For example, Yamanouchi Mina's family was neither rich nor poor, but her parents had insufficient funds for an adequate dowry, having spent their money on her elder sisters. Nevertheless, she had to spend a week trying to persuade her reluctant parents to permit her to go to work.[41] Umezu Hagiko's family was quite poor, but she ran away from home and into the Hodogaya plant of Fuji Bōseki at age seventeen to support herself, rather than submit to her father's plan for her arranged marriage.[42] Both women, as well as Kumagai Kikuko and the Okinawan M.U. (I use her initials as she was reluctant to be quoted), later compared their families' resources favorably with those of the poor girls from places such as the Tōhoku.[43] They pitied those girls who relished the dormitory food they disdained. Interestingly, their comments about their poorer colleagues indicate their belief that many girls lacked the autonomy—the freedom to choose to work—that they felt they themselves enjoyed. The frequency with which these women declared their relative economic superiority suggests that this sentiment may have been fairly common even among the poorer girls, and that a sense of autonomy may have been more widespread than even contemporaries thought. Of course, it may also reflect fading memories or nostalgia for the distant past.

Although farm girls frequently chose to work in the mills, they did not always make their decisions on the basis of accurate information. A

40. Katsura Susumu, "Bōseki rōdō jijō," *Shakai seisaku jihō* 28, no. 12 (1922): 57. He notes that commuting women had an attendance rate of 83 percent, as compared with 90 percent for commuting men and 97 percent for dorm girls. Takai Toshio, *Watashi no "Jokō aishi,"* 26–27, notes a particularly cruel case of coercion by one nasty supervisor whose proximity made her excessively attentive to her workers. The supervisor constantly berated Takai for "laziness." Not permitted even to sit during work, Takai tired quickly. One day, her hand slipped and her finger was cut to the bone. In the process of being injured, she broke her thread, causing the supervisor to say Takai deserved her injury because she was so stupid as to break her thread.

41. Yamanouchi, *Jiden*, 11–12.

42. Umezu interview, March 11, 1985; published interview with Umezu Hagiko in Shin Nihon Fujin no Kai, *Haha no rekishi* (Sōdo Bunka, 1978), 99.

43. M.U. interview, March 13, 1985.

number of female factory workers recalled their dismay at discovering the public's negative perceptions of them.[44] These perceptions had both class and gender components. Class bias appears in an example reported by one retired worker of the public criticism of workers as "pigs."[45] Workers' sexuality was also a major issue.[46] For example, during the 1920s both proponents and opponents of the abolition of night work for women couched their arguments in terms of women workers' morality. Proponents claimed that night work made women potential victims of foremen and male workers lurking in the dimly lit corners. Opponents made the women themselves the agents of their undoing by claiming that workers with too much free time would engage in *warui asobi* (bad play).[47] The public's fear of women's sexuality, however, was not echoed among the workers themselves, who must have been unaware of these negative attitudes before entering the factory. Otherwise it would have been difficult for them to choose textile work.

Young farm girls were equally unaware of labor conditions before signing their contracts. This is natural, given that few of their elder sisters or cousins returned to the countryside to tell tales of hard work and low pay, and as a result the ability of recruiters to disseminate information about the mills was quite extensive. By the 1920s, large companies generally preferred to rely on recruiters to bring in new workers, although smaller firms often hired women and girls directly at the plant. Recruiters signing up workers in the countryside could negotiate with both the girls' families and the girls themselves—thereby adding at least some element of coercion to their contracts. They could also secure the support of guarantors: after all, girls arriving alone at the factory gate were unlikely to be backed by guarantors or other institutions of societal control. Indeed, many large firms had policies prohibiting the hiring of workers without guarantors. Takai Toshio found, for example, that although she was often successful in gaining employment with smaller firms by promising managers she would work diligently, she was repeatedly turned back at the gate of Tokyo Muslin because she lacked a guarantor. Even if she had maintained close ties with her relations in the country, of course, none would have been able to guarantee Takai's

44. Shin Nihon Fujin no Kai, *Haha no rekishi*, 100.

45. Takai, *Watashi no "Jokō aishi,"* 46.

46. Elite attitudes in the West also scorned women's employment. Hall's study of activist textile workers in the American South in the 1920s notes that "respectable" folk viewed them as bawdy and sexually threatening; see "Disorderly Women," 374–75.

47. Janet Hunter, "Factory Legislation and Employer Resistance: The Abolition of Night Work in the Japanese Cotton-Spinning Industry," in *Japanese Management in Historical Perspective*, ed. Tsunehiko Yui and Keiichiro Nakagawa (Tokyo: Tokyo University Press, 1989), 251–52.

loyal, long-term service, as she had a history of frequent job changes. Eventually she secured the guarantee of the old man who guarded the gate and was able to begin work at Tokyo Muslin.[48]

Takai's experience in seeking employment was typical in the cotton textile industry. A 1927 survey of 21,852 female workers showed that company-designated recruiters brought in 62.8 percent of all new recruits, while only 8.3 percent were hired at the company, and 5.6 percent were introduced by family members.[49] My sample of interviewees shows a similar pattern. All had some contact with a special recruiting agent, at least for their initial employment; subsequently they often obtained jobs themselves by applying at the factory gate. Kumagai Kikuko was first informed by relatives about Tōyō Muslin, but then dealt with a recruiter. Umezu Hagiko approached a recruiter herself when she wished to flee an unwanted marriage prospect. Hanashiro Uta also approached a recruiter in Okinawa.[50] Yamanouchi Mina's aunt, who turned to her brother—Mina's father—for assistance after her divorce, decided to work in textiles to support herself. Afraid of failing because of her poor literacy, she asked her young niece Mina to accompany her and help her in her chosen job. Though interested in further schooling, Mina agreed to go, and the two approached a local recruiter. Mina secured her parents' approval after one week, and the recruiter then proceeded to make arrangements for the trip to Tokyo.[51]

In Okinawa, M.U. also negotiated with a recruiter, but her story had an unusual twist. Her father, a recruiter in addition to his regular oc-

48. Takai, *Watashi no "Jokō aishi,"* 43–44. Takai was not alone in desiring job mobility: many women escaped from their prisonlike dormitories, although police officials cooperated with company managers in capturing them. See Saxonhouse, "Country Girls," 97–125; and Nakamura, *Rōdōsha*, 164. Others used clever tricks such as claiming, falsely, to be married. Marriage changed a woman's legal household, which invalidated previous contracts. See Nakamura, *Rōdōsha*, 103–4. Frequent changes of employment in active search for higher wages is documented by Honig for Shanghai workers in *Sisters and Strangers*, 178.

49. Izumi, *Transformation and Development of Technology*, 30. Small numbers were also hired through employment exchanges and worker supply or protection unions. Whereas the former supplied only token numbers of workers to industry, the latter were slightly more important. These unions (*jokō kyōkyū kumiai* and *jokō hogo kumiai*) were associations of (male) local notables who mediated their daughters' and neighbors' labor exchange by arranging placements and looking after their welfare. See Janet Hunter, "Recruitment in the Japanese Silk-Reeling and Cotton-Spinning Industries, 1870s–1930s," in *Proceedings of the British Association for Japanese Studies*, vol. 9, ed. J. Chapman and D. Steeds (Sheffield, 1984), 73–75; Sawaki Kin'ichi, "Jokō kishukusha kanri ni kansuru gutai hosaku," *Jokō kenkyū* 4, no. 1 (1928): 128–29.

50. Kumagai interview; "Haha no rekishi" articles; Hanashiro Uto, interview, March 16, 1985.

51. Yamanouchi, *Jiden*, 12.

cupation, was accustomed to collecting groups of young girls and sending them to Fuji Bōseki in Kawasaki. Like most other recruiters, he painted a rosy picture of employment and offered prepayments and new clothing to attract new workers. M.U.'s young friends were the beneficiaries of these payments and clothes, and M.U. wished to receive them as well. But her father demurred, not wanting to send his own daughter off to the job he tried to urge other girls to accept. M.U. eventually prevailed, taking her mother with her, later to be followed by her father.[52] This story appears to be unusual in the Japanese context, though fairly representative of the European situation. Further research should tell whether it is indeed an example of the daughter's growing role in affecting economic decision making in the family.

Although most workers operated through recruiting agents, all recruiters were not alike; thus potential workers' abilities to make employment decisions were affected in different ways. Recruiters fell into several categories: those hired by the mill as salaried employees; placement and recruiting agents under special contract to a mill; recruiters paid a commission for each girl hired; and mill workers sent out to bring in new recruits.[53] Mill workers were most likely to present an accurate view of conditions in the factory, while recruiters working on commission were least likely. Many recruiters were otherwise employed, using their positions as recruiters to earn supplementary income. The pay was quite good: a recruiter could make several yen per girl hired, and many signed up groups of ten to twenty twice a year. On average, the company spent around thirty yen to attract each worker;[54] costs included prepayments and loans, train and ship fares, an allowance, clothing expenses, and the recruiter's fees. Thus, recruiters could significantly affect the relationship between workers and their employers.

CONDITIONS IN THE MILLS

Workers' responses to conditions in the mills, like their decisions to seek employment there, reflected a growing sense of personal autonomy and decreasing attachment to their rural origins. A few days after her parents and guarantor signed her contract, a new worker joined a group of other girls to travel with their recruiter to the mill.[55] Upon arrival, the

52. M.U. interview.

53. Izumi, *Transformation and Development of Technology*, 30–34; Katsura, "Bōseki rōdō jijō," 44–50.

54. Katsura, "Bōseki rōdō jijō," 45–46. Hunter, "Recruitment," 220n., cites lower costs (five to twenty-five yen) for recruiting each worker.

55. Kumagai interview.

recruiter left, and the girls moved into the dormitory.[56] The first three-month period was often considered a training period and, compared to later work, was something of a honeymoon: work hours were shorter and night work rare. Forced savings and repayment of debts did not begin until the probationary period ended.[57]

Conditions varied from factory to factory, but most big mills shared certain characteristics. Large buildings filled with long machines (and without chairs) formed the economic center of the factory complex. Dormitory buildings with rows of rooms, each accommodating ten to twenty girls per alternating shift, constituted its residential center. Many interviewees recall that dorm rooms had just one mat for two persons.[58] Alternating shifts (usually 6:00 A.M. to 6:00 P.M. and 6:00 P.M. to 6:00 A.M.) shared bedding, a practice that spread not only annoying pests like lice, but also serious diseases such as tuberculosis.[59] (By comparison, early New England boarding houses held eight or ten girls in one room, with two girls to a bed.) A dining hall and a large but dirty bath adjoined the dormitories. Meals were usually served four times a day, at 6:00 A.M., 12:00 noon, 6:00 P.M., and midnight, to permit workers on both shifts to eat. All the women interviewed recalled factory food as generally tasteless and lacking in nutrition.

Girls' salaries were extremely low. Many firms promised around sixty sen per day in wages, but not all offered that amount; in many cases, eighteen or twenty sen was more common.[60] (This was about one-tenth the wage of a contemporary New England worker.) To repay her pre-payment, a worker under contract often agreed to monthly deductions of about one yen from her already low income.

Worst of all were the conditions of labor itself. A twelve-hour day, alternating every week between the day and the night shifts, was exhausting. Lack of chairs prevented the workers from resting even dur-

56. This differs from the most common patterns in Shanghai as described by Honig, *Sisters and Strangers*. In Japan, the salient relationship was between employer and employee, whereas in Shanghai the recruiter often continued his parasitic relationship with the recruit.

57. Yamanouchi, *Jiden*, 13.

58. Nakamura, *Rōdōsha*, 160; Yamanouchi, *Jiden*, 23, notes that Tokyo Muslin supplied just fifteen mats for twenty-three people.

59. Takai, *Watashi no "Jokō aishi,"* 44. Hirose Yoshihiro, "Fujin rōdō mondai ni tsuite," *Shakai seisaku jihō* 14 (1924): 60–67, also describes mill conditions.

60. Hosoi, *Jokō aishi*, 132–33. Hosoi also cites (71–72) an advertisement for employment at Tokyo Muslin, which promised workers spectacular benefits including a starting salary of sixty sen per day, thirty yen per month after three months, and fifty to sixty yen per month after six months. The ad further asserted that workers could expect to save one hundred to two hundred yen per year, and would enjoy cheap but nutritious and delicious meals in the dormitories.

ing their fifteen-minute morning and afternoon breaks.[61] Girls were expected to operate large machines for hours. Although in many factories machines could be turned off individually while workers took necessary toilet breaks, stopping work was strongly discouraged.

Holidays were infrequent, four days off per month being typical in the 1920s. On rest days, girls rose late, wrote letters, washed, and, if free of debt to the factory, went to movies or other entertainments nearby.[62] Restriction of physical mobility for workers with outstanding loans was a major source of tension for factory workers.

Despite this gloomy picture of mill life, there were some positive aspects. Workers tried to make the best of their grim situation, either through enjoyable friendships or through labor activism to improve their conditions. Dormitory life provided girls with camaraderie, which was reinforced in some companies by the practice of seating room groups together at meals. Distasteful though the dirty bath may have been, girls also forged friendships while bathing. These kinds of friendships could be useful later when activist leaders planned strikes and other job actions.

One form of activism involved simply transferring to another employer. Most women who left a firm sought alternate employment in shops, offices, domestic service, and, most commonly, other factories. Almost half of the women who resigned (or escaped) from a cotton textile mill were reemployed by another factory, especially one making textiles.[63]

Another response of women workers to unhealthy and oppressive labor conditions was labor activism in the traditional sense of the word— that is, engagement in strikes and other forms of organizing. Japanese mill workers, like American workers in the mid-nineteenth century,[64] were depicted as selfless daughters of the soil with no abiding interest in labor activism. But neither group fits its stereotype. In Japan's case, mill workers staged labor struggles to shorten the workday, to raise wages, to end the confinement of workers whose contractual prepayments had not yet been repaid, and to improve food and lodging in the dormitories.[65] A significant number of workers surely believed their fu-

61. Yamanouchi, *Jiden*, 30.   62. Hanashiro interview.

63. Tanino, "Bōseki jokō taishokugo no kisu," 22–23.

64. Dublin, *Farm to Factory*, 10. American mill workers were more accepting of mill conditions in the early years of industrialization, but as pay and hours began to deteriorate with technological advances that accelerated the pace of work, they increasingly engaged in strikes. Wages for New England workers may be found in Robert G. Layer, *Earnings of Cotton Mill Operatives, 1825–1914* (Cambridge, Mass.: Harvard University Press, 1955), 17–42.

65. Makise Kikue, *Hitamuki no onnatachi* (Asahi Shinbunsha, 1976), 55–56.

ture to be as workers rather than as daughters returning to the farm; after all, organized strike activity would have been seen as superfluous by workers who expected their time in the mills to be a limited ordeal before they returned to their real role as farm women.

Labor activism was conditioned by the workers' own experiences. Male workers, most of whom were commuters and thus unaffected by dormitory conditions, often struck for such abstract rights as the freedom to unionize. Women workers, in contrast, struck mainly for improvements in working and living conditions.[66] Workers at Fuji Bōseki, for example, went out in 1927 for higher wages, overtime for night work, special sick rooms, twenty-four-hour on-call physicians, and, most important in some strikers' memories, better food.[67] Some also struck in the late 1920s for reasons that were particularly gender-specific, including maternity leave and, in at least one case, "freedom of marriage."[68]

Women workers' living arrangements also influenced how their strikes were organized. Planning could occur practically under the noses of the supervisors because workers ate, slept, and bathed together, and even if they socialized with one another after hours, they did not arouse suspicion. These experiences may help to account for the enthusiastic and militant involvement of large numbers of women workers in the massive textile strikes of the 1920s, despite their extremely low rates of union membership (only 3.7 percent of union members were women, and only 1 percent of women workers were unionized, compared to 16 percent of male workers).[69] Close living quarters thus made union membership unnecessary for women to be active in staging successful strikes.

Activism often paid off.[70] Fuji Bōseki, for instance, decreased its workday to eleven hours after the workers struck in 1925.[71] Most firms improved food and dormitory arrangements, and many offered pay raises, though these tended to be smaller than what was demanded.

In addition, social welfare advocates joined with working-class women and some government reformers to push for abolition of night work for women and children. After 1929, late-night (11:00 P.M. to 5:00 A.M.) work was prohibited for women, thereby shortening the hours of both

66. Hasegawa Kōichi, "Honpo ni okeru fujin rōdō undō no sūsei to sono kentō," *Shakai seisaku jihō* 135, reprinted in Akamatsu, *Nihon fujin mondai shiryō shūsei* 3:465.

67. Watanabe Etsuji and Suzuki Yūko, *Tatakai ni ikite* (Domesu Shuppan, 1980), 168–69.

68. Hasegawa, "Honpo ni okeru fujin rōdō undō no sūsei," 465.

69. Ibid., 459–60.

70. It paid off for most workers, though militant leaders often risked their jobs; see Watanabe and Suzuki, *Tatakai ni ikite*, 171.

71. Umezu interview, March 11, 1985.

TABLE 10.1.   Frequency of Strikes

	1924	1925	1926	1927	1928	1929	1930
Male Participation Only	200	163	303	219	259	361	577
Female Participation Only	19	30	22	26	21	34	38
Joint Participation	114	100	170	138	117	181	291
Total	333	293	495	383	397	576	906

SOURCE: Hasegawa Kōichi, "Honpo ni okeru fujin rōdō undō no sūsei to sono kentō," *Shakai seisaku jihō* 135, in Akamatsu Ryōko, *Nihon fujin mondai shiryō shusei*, vol. 3: *Rōdō* (Domesu Shuppan, 1977), 465.

shifts and radically altering the pattern of shared bedding in dormitories.[72]

Although grim working conditions continued to characterize the cotton textile factories, the various reforms gained during the 1920s helped promote worker recruitment. Furthermore, rising expectations of a decent workplace strengthened workers' commitments to their chosen jobs while intensifying their belief that activism could indeed produce positive results. Beginning in the late 1920s, then, strikes became more frequent (table 10.1). Increasingly independent young women were ready to accept the greater autonomy offered by the mills as reforms were implemented. Also, as rising levels of education in the 1920s made women workers more literate, new inspiration was found in the writings of such critics as the socialist feminist Yamakawa Kikue and playwright Henrik Ibsen.[73] Women were also more physically vigorous because they left school later and were therefore older.[74] By the end of the decade, gradual reforms in the workplace together with higher educational achievement had produced workers with attitudes and expectations at the time of recruitment that were markedly different from those of their predecessors in the textile industry.

Nevertheless, women remained outside the mainstream of union activity, as their low rates of union membership indicate. The structural

72. Kitaoka Hisashi, "Bōsekigyō no shinyagyō kinshi to sōtan mondai," in *Shakai seisaku jihō* 114 (March 1930): 1–16.

73. Umezu interview; Takai, *Watashi no "Jokō aishi,"* 47.

74. E. Patricia Tsurumi, "Female Textile Workers and the Failure of Early Trade Unionism in Japan," *History Workshop* 18 (Fall 1984): 3–28. Tsurumi questions the notion that education, which attempted to instill a respect for hierarchy and an acceptance of industrial paternalism, inhibited factory girls' activism during the Meiji period because, she notes, so few textile workers were educated at that time (see pp. 10–12). If we accept Tsurumi's assertion, we see a remarkable shift in the effects of education from the Meiji to the Taishō period, when education sparked activism. See also Allinson, *Japanese Urbanism*, 85, which notes that higher levels of education produced nondocile female workers, a condition deplored by their employer, Toyota.

characteristics of women's working and living conditions that aided communication may also have impeded formal organization by fostering a sense of vulnerability. Louise Tilly suggests that as European working women became less vulnerable, they became more militant. Married workers felt less threatened by the effects of job loss; indeed, as the percentage of the European work force that was married increased, so too did female militancy.[75] Japanese employers attempted to curtail militancy by housing women workers in dormitories. While dorms facilitated transmission of information and ideology, which fueled militancy once a strike began, they were also a way of maintaining workers' vulnerability: a dismissed worker lost more than just a job.

Male unionist opposition also impeded women's participation in formal collective actions. As in other countries, male workers shored up their limited gains vis-à-vis their employers by distancing themselves from the needs of women workers: in short, their own job security and higher wages depended on subtle collusion with employers' oppression of women workers.[76] Moreover, many men opposed the creation within unions of women's sections because, they said, these would focus women workers' attention on their "special interests" and divert it from the "real business" of the union.[77] A combination of ignorance of women workers' needs, hostility toward women, and self-importance is evident in this conflation of male workers' interests with those of the larger group.

When women did strike, however, they were no less active than the better-organized men. The striking textile workers of Tōyō Muslin in 1930, who took their demonstrations to the streets and even stopped the trains in their area, could certainly not be characterized as passive workers.[78] Such labor activism paralleled the less structured "activism" of young farm women who decided to leave for the mills.

CONCLUSION

Women workers were taking an increasingly active role in seeking and maintaining their employment in the cotton industry when Hosoi Wakizō wrote his influential book about them in 1925. As we have seen, Hosoi's approach had serious limitations. Although deplorable conditions did exist, his emphasis on oppression offers an incomplete picture of

75. Tilly, "Paths," 411.

76. Hunter, "Factory Legislation," 255–56.

77. Taniguchi Zentarō, "Nihon rōdō kumiai Hyōgikai shi," in *Nihon rōdō kumiai Hyōgikai shi*, vol. 4, pt. 1; and vol. 5, pt. 1; reprinted in Akamatsu (ed.), *Nihon fujin mondai shiryō shūsei* 3:426–31.

78. Watanabe and Suzuki, *Tatakai ni ikite*, 179.

changing recruitment and employment patterns. In particular, his view suffers from the tendency to treat the workers merely as the victims of exploitation. Such an approach fails to account for changes in workers' attitudes toward and relations with their families and their social environment during the half-century (1877–1925) covered in *Jokō aishi*. While Hosoi's depiction of factory girls may have been accurate for the Meiji period, it fails to consider changes that must surely have affected women workers later on, such as the evolution of industrial capitalism and the development of male labor-management relations; the growth of the regulatory power of the state; the expansion of education for all segments of society, including rural girls; and the sense, even among some rural girls, that they did not completely share their mothers' values, particularly after the social changes that transformed Japan in the post-World War I (late Taishō) period.

The theory of female passivity is perhaps most evident in histories of the Japanese labor movement in the late Taishō period, which frequently attribute the rise of union activism to the increasing percentage of men in the industrial work force. Until recently most analysts have overlooked the origins of labor activism among female workers, though interestingly, scholars on both sides of the Pacific have now begun to modify the theory of Japanese women's passivity in the area of worker organization and strike activities.[79]

Labor activists, of course, developed a worker consciousness during their period of employment, with their experiences helping to mold their identity. But even rural girls and women newly entering urban employment made active choices about their work situation.

Two major developments during the 1920s affected women's attitudes toward their employment, making them more favorably disposed to work. First, within the workplace working conditions gradually improved, particularly with the upgrading of dormitory, food, and recreational services following major strikes and, after 1929, the enforcement of the prohibition against child labor and the elimination of late-night work for women. Second, outside the workplace higher levels of education and the desire for learning instilled in female workers a greater sense of self-confidence. The challenge to previous definitions of gen-

79. Some of these works use a predominantly feminist approach, others a more traditional Marxist labor-historical approach. They include ibid.; Watanabe Etsuji and Suzuki Yuko, *Undō ni kaketa onnatachi* (Domesu Shuppan, 1980); the documents collection edited by Akamatsu Ryōko, *Nihon fujin mondai shiryō shūsei;* Sharon Sievers, *Flowers in Salt: The Beginnings of Feminist Consciousness in Modern Japan* (Stanford: Stanford University Press, 1983); and E. Patricia Tsurumi, "Problem Consciousness and Modern Japanese History: Female Textile Workers of Meiji and Taishō," *Bulletin of Concerned Asian Scholars* 18, no. 4 (1986): 41–48; and E. Patricia Tsurumi, *Factory Girls* (Princeton: Princeton University Press, 1990).

der by Taishō middle-class feminist workers and activists described by
Rodd, Nagy, and Silverberg in this volume (chapters 8, 9, and 11),
though not explicitly articulated by the women in my study, also undoubtedly helped to motivate changes in working-class women's attitudes. In sum, the 1920s was a period of significant change in the composition, conditions, and consciousness of the female work force in the
cotton textile industry as older, better-educated, and more autonomous
and activist workers from rural backgrounds sought to determine their
own economic and social conditions while contributing to the industrial
and demographic development of Japan.

ELEVEN

The Modern Girl as Militant

Miriam Silverberg

Where can you folks clearly say that there is a typical Modern Girl?
KATAOKA TEPPEI

Let's get naked and while we're at it work our damnedest.
HAYASHI FUMIKO

The Modern Girl makes only a brief appearance in our histories of pre-war Japan. She is a glittering, decadent, middle-class consumer who, through her clothing, smoking, and drinking, flaunts tradition in the urban playgrounds of the late 1920s. Arm in arm with her male equivalent, the Modern Boy (the *mobo*) and fleshed out in the Western flapper's garb of the roaring twenties, she engages in *ginbura* (Ginza-cruising).[1] Yet by merely equating the Japanese Modern Girl with the flapper we do her a disservice, for the Modern Girl was not on a Western trajectory.[2] Moreover, during the decade when this female, a creation of the

Earlier versions of this essay were given at the Berkshire Conference on the History of Women, June 1987; and at the conference "Women in 'Dark Times': Private Life and Public Policy Under Five Nationalist Dictatorships in Europe and Asia, 1930–1950" in Bellagio, Italy, August 1987. I am grateful to the participants of the Bellagio conference for their responses, to Fujita Shōzō for introducing me to the women of *Nyonin geijutsu*, and to my students at Hamilton College for helping me to take a closer look at the Modern Girl.

1. See Peter Duus, *The Rise of Modern Japan* (Boston: Houghton Mifflin, 1976), 187–88; the segment devoted to the Modern Girl in Umino Hiroshi, ed., *Modan Tōkyō hyakukei*, special issue of *Taiyō*, "Nihon no kokoro" ser. no. 54 (Heibonsha, 1986), 126–28; and the entry in Tsuchida Mitsufumi, ed., *Meiji Taishō fūzokugoten* (Kadokawa Shoten, 1979), 325–26.

2. For an analysis of how the flapper as emblematic of sales mania displaced the "social mother" of the preceding era, see Mary Ryan, *Womanhood in America: From Colonial Times to the Present* (New York: Franklin Watts, 1983), 220–23. To equate the *moga* with the flapper would be to engage in the specialized brand of Orientalism documented in Chandra Talpade Mohanty, "Under Western Eyes: Feminist Scholarship and Colonial Discourses," *Feminist Review*, no. 30 (Fall 1988): 61–88.

mass media, titillated her Japanese audience, she was not easily defined. Who was this "Modern Girl"? Why did she do what she did? These two questions, raised by the Japanese Modern Girl's contemporaries, are also the two problems posed in this chapter.

The Modern Girl was a highly commodified cultural construct crafted by journalists who debated her identity during the tumultuous decade of cultural and social change following the great earthquake of 1923. By asking first of all who she was, I am concerned with the representation of the Modern Girl as the Japanese cultural heroine of the 1920s, and not with the actual beliefs or practices of young women of that era. (In this essay, therefore, I do not call the heroine by her nickname, *moga*, for to do so would be to deny her the full respect that is her due. It would also depart from the practice of her time, when most commentators spelled her name out in full, as *modan gaaru*.) The second question has been appropriated from the title of the hit movie of 1930, *What Made Her Do What She Did?* (*Nani ga kanojō wo sō saseta?*). In this saga of an orphan turned criminal, based on a play by Fujimori Seikichi, the heroine withstood varied forms of servitude, including domestic labor for a lecherous government official, before she took her revenge by setting fire to a Christian institution for wayward young girls. According to Fujimori's stage directions, published in 1927, at this moment the curtain was to fall on the electrically lit query, "What made her do what she did?" floating above the flames.[3] The movie audience, which included members of the new salaried middle class, off-duty groups of geisha, and working men and women who had crowded into Asakusa, the honky-tonk night-life neighborhood of Tokyo, to watch the show had to formulate their own answers to this question—just as the historian must do when asking why the Modern Girl moved so vigorously through the closing years of the 1920s. To answer this question, the Modern Girl must be made a part of the political economy and sociocultural transformations of her time.

DEFINING THE MODERN GIRL

The first documented reference to the Modern Girl appeared in August 1924 in the title of an article in the woman's magazine *Josei*. The author, Kitazawa Shūichi, established the character of the Modern Girl as apolitical but militantly autonomous, neither an advocate of expanded rights for women nor a suffragette; yet at the same time, she had no

3. The movie directed by Suzuki Jūkichi drew unprecedented crowds when it opened in 1930. For a discussion of its appeal, see Tanaka Junichirō, ed., *Nihon eiga hattatsu shi*, vol. 2: *Musei kara tookii e* (Chūō kōronsha, 1968), 178. "Nani ga kanojo wo sō saseta" first appeared in the January 1927 issue of *Kaizō* and was staged by the Tsukiji Theater in April of that year. I am working from Fujimori Seikichi, *Nani ga kanojo wo sō saseta* (Kaizōsha, 1927), pp. 1–160.

intention of being a slave to men. This self-respecting modern girl had liberated herself from age-old traditions and conventions, and now, suddenly, without any argument or explanation, she had stepped out onto the same starting line with man in order to walk alongside him. Kitazawa saw a reconstruction of gender accompanying this reordering of power, but he did not bemoan the fact that woman was becoming more like man both spiritually and physically, for what woman had lost in grace she had gained in a newfound animation.[4]

Nii Itaru, who is usually given credit for coining the term *modan gaaru*, followed with his "Contours of the Modern Girl" in a 1925 issue of another woman's magazine, *Fujin kōron*.[5] He provided a character sketch of someone who, like Kitazawa's Modern Girl, was highly animated. She was also "brightly breezy" and shockingly fond of the double entendre and other erotic come-hithers. One young woman, for example, after a single meeting with the author, had sent him a note that read, "I am lonely sleeping all alone today. Please come visit." Nii reported that he did not know how to interpret this message, but he was convinced that all contemporary young women were in the process of changing for the sake of "liberation and freedom of expression." Nii admitted that the contemporary young Japanese woman was aggressive and erotic, but was she in fact a "Modern Girl" like her European counterpart, the modern young woman, whom he likened to a bouncing ball of reason, will, and emotion, thrown at full force? And was the anarchistic Modern Girl a creature to be lauded as the proletarian emblem of revolutionary possibility, or should she be reviled as one final expression of a decaying class, owing to origins in the wealthier strata of society? Nii offered his readers choices, but he would not take a stand.[6]

Nii's ambiguity set the tone for Japanese mass journalism. From 1925 until the early 1930s writers attempted to flesh out the contours provided by Nii, in such print media as a cartoon series about a Modern Girl and a Modern Boy entitled "Mogako and Moborō," in sensational newspaper articles, in questions and answers in advice columns, and in special issues of popular magazines aimed at men and women.[7] While

4. Kitazawa Shūichi's article is cited in Satō Takeshi, "Modanizumu to Amerikaka: 1920 sen-kyūhyaku nijūnen wo chūshin to shite" in *Nihon modanizumu no kenkyū*, ed. Minami Hiroshi (Tōkyō Bureen Shuppan, 1982), 41–42; Ueda Yasuo, "Josei zasshi ga mita modanizumu," in ibid., 135–36; and Barbara Hamill, "Josei: Modanizumu to kenri ishiki," in ibid., 215–16.

5. Nii Itaru, "Modan gaaru no rinkaku," *Fujin kōron*, April 1925, 24–31. Nii's colleague, Ōya Sōichi, is responsible for attributing the origin to Nii, but Nii gave credit to Kitazawa; see Hamill, "Josei," 229.

6. Nii, "Modan gaaru no rinkaku," 24–5, 29–31.

7. Maeda Ai notes how the term *modan gaaru* won out over the label "woman of the new era" (*shin jidai no onna*) in *Kindai dokusha no seiritsu* (Yūseido, 1972), 214–15. Ueda, "Josei zasshi," 115–30, follows what he terms the discourse on the modern girl through

ambiguity remained, a composite picture of a Modern Girl does emerge from a select reading of articles written by journalists and feminist critics of the 1920s.

First and foremost, the Modern Girl was defined by her body and most specifically by her short hair and long, straight legs. In a brief disquisition entitled simply "Woman's Legs," the proletarian writer Kataoka Teppei argued that, while other eras of Japanese history had been graced by sightly legs (which nobody had noticed), the preponderance of beautiful legs among contemporary young women had to be explained. His answer: the legs of the Modern Girl were a product of the ability of the human spirit to shape the human form; her legs symbolized the Modern Girl's growing ability to create a new life for woman. The author ended his polemic with the hortatory appreciation of the modern girl in motion: "Onward! Dance! Legs! Legs! Legs!"[8]

Discussion of fashion is always talk about the female body, as another article, "Studies on the *Moga*," made blatantly clear. In the course of his attempt to define the Modern Girl, Kiyosawa Kiyoshi emphasized the significance of her protruding buttocks by repeating how the traditional function of the obi ("to hide the ass") had been abandoned by the modern girl, who wore her obi high.[9] The preoccupation with the clothing of the Modern Girl also confirms Rosalind Coward's thesis that "women's bodies, and the messages which clothes can add, are the repository of the social definitions of sexuality."[10] According to Kataoka, the Modern Girl's simple hairstyle was the outcome of a strategic decision to facilitate violent hugging, and her boldly colored and patterned clothing expressed her attraction to the fleshly vitality exuded by the Westerner. This Modern Girl went after the physical pleasures of love (*ren'ai*), which meant that she sought "fleshly" stimuli in "flirtation," an activity that had spread from the United States to England, France, and Japan. (The author spelled "flirtation" in English after he had transliterated it into the Japanese syllabary reserved for imported terms.) The Modern

---

articles published in *Josei* from 1924 through 1928. He cites the cartoon series, penned by Tanaka Hisara, as beginning in the September 1928 issue of *Shufu no tomo*; see p. 127. For a commentary on the manufacture of the *moga* via the reinforcing "advertisements" of newspapers, magazines, and the movies, see Hoshino Tatsuo, "Modaan shinbun zasshi eiga mandan," in *Kaizō*, June 1929, 42–45.

8. Kataoka Teppei, "Onna no kyaku" (October 1926), in *Kindai shomin seikatsushi*, ed. Minami Hiroshi, vol. 1: *Ningen seken* (Sanichi Shobō, 1985), 175–77; quote 177.

9. Kiyosawa Kiyoshi, "Modan gaaru no kenkyū," in ibid., 143–58; on female buttocks, 143–44.

10. Rosalind Coward, *Female Desires: How They are Sought, Bought, and Packaged* (New York: Grove Press, 1985), 30; see this volume generally for insightful analysis associating fashion with the historical construction and representation of the female body.

Girl was flirting, the author explained, when she went for a shoulder or a hand in a crowded train and then pulled back, protesting with a polite "Oh, excuse—it was just that it was oh so crowded" when her motions were met with anger. This mixed message was also projected in dance halls and theaters, where the Modern Girl went after man's physical rather than spiritual beauty.[11]

For Kataoka, as for other male writers, to talk about the Modern Girl's body and clothing, and thereby her sexuality, was to underscore her promiscuity. In contrast, the feminist journalist and critic Kitamura Kaneko, in an essay called "Strange Chastity," defended the Modern Girl from a double standard, pointing out the obvious contradictions in the public outcry at woman's indiscretions. For a woman to have played around with a man was considered bad: but if there were women who had transgressed with men, there had to have been men who had played around with women.[12] Kitamura refused to define the Modern Girl as sexual transgressor. But like Kiyosawa, who saw woman as moving closer to man spiritually and physically, and like Kataoka, who celebrated new, separate cultures for men and women and claimed that gender distinctions were based on the differing attitudes toward love held by men and women, she accepted that what it meant to be feminine and what it meant to be masculine were being called into question.[13]

The intimate relationship between efforts to conceptualize the *moga* and the cultural reconstruction of gender is made clear in a section of Kiyosawa's Modern Girl essay called "Man's Education and Woman's Education." According to the author, gender differentiation in 1920s Japan began at birth, as baby girls were put into red kimono, and baby boys were swaddled in kimono decorated with images of the mythical peach-boy. At age six or seven, the boy child was reprimanded for the unmanly behavior of crying with the rebuke, "What is this—and you a boy. . . !" By the time the boy and girl were adults, they had been educated for entirely different societies; they were like two races separated

---

11. Kataoka Teppei, "Modan gaaru no kenkyū" (September 9, 1926), in Kataoka, *Modan gaaru no kenkyū* (Kinseidō, 1927); reprinted in Minami (ed.), *Kindai shomin*, 170, 163–64, 172. The term *ren'ai*, used to translate the Western term "love," was, like the words for philosophy (*tetsugaku*) and society (*shakai*), a Meiji invention. Two Chinese characters—*ren* (or, in the Japanese pronunciation, *koi*), alluding to feelings of deep affection between a man and a woman, and *ai*, meaning to be drawn to something and yearn for it or feel a tenderness toward it—were combined to create the new word, which could only apply to a yearning for a member of the opposite sex; see Tanaka Sumiko, ed., *Josei kaihō no shisō to kōdō*, prewar vol. (Jiji Tsūshinsha, 1975), 166.

12. Kitamura Kaneko, "Kaiteisō" (1927), in Minami (ed.), *Kindai shomin*, 128–42, esp. 131–34.

13. Ueda, "Josei zasshi," 135; Kataoka, "Modan gaaru no kenkyū," 161, 168; Kitamura, "Kaiteisō," 133.

by a broad river, living according to differing moral standards. Kiyosawa gave the Modern Girl's resolution to this predicament: let the boy
and girl start at the same place.[14]

Although the Modern Girl's bold gestures crossed gender boundaries, they were, according to her creators, unquestionably female. Her
cultural identity, however, was less certain. Nii had begged the issue in
his "Contours of the Modern Girl" when he claimed that European ways
had been integrated into daily life in Japan, while simultaneously refusing to equate the Modern Girl with her Japanese sisters.[15] Kiyosawa also
separated the Modern Girl of Europe and the United States from the
Japanese Modern Girl, by suggesting a distinction between the function
and the intent of the latter. Whereas both sets of Modern Girls stood "in
the vanguard of a changing age to battle old customs," the author feared
this had not actually been the goal of the Japanese version, whose short
hair might not in fact be an emblem of resistance but the "mark of decadence" of a woman still content to live by the actions and decisions of
men.[16]

Was the Japanese Modern Girl Japanese? Europeanized? Cosmopolitan? To the artist Kishida Ryūsei, who defined the short-haired Modern
Girl by her body, clothing, and rapid style of walking on Ginza, she was
all of the above. While she appeared for the most part in Japanese-style
clothing, the face of this beauty, originally that of a Japanese person,
had been harmonized to become, in a most natural fashion, a Western-
style face. The Modern Girl was not indulging in the forced European-
ization of an earlier era; rather, Kishida concluded, she was part of a
process whereby "all material civilization would . . . inevitably Euro-
peanize Japan." Japan was not to lose its identity; only after it had been
thoroughly Europeanized could Japanese culture become non-Euro-
pean.[17]

An alternate resolution to the ambiguity in the Modern Girl's cultural
identity was embodied in Naomi, the polymorphously perverse heroine
of Tanizaki Junichirō's fictional *A Fool's Love*, whose exploits were serialized in the *Ōsaka asahi shinbun* and *Josei* during 1924 and 1925.[18] In
the story, a nondescript young engineer becomes obsessed by the body

14. Kiyosawa cites in romanized letters a "Dr. Meyrick Booth," published in the "Hib-
bert Journal"; "Modan gaaru no kenkyū," 152, 155–56.

15. Nii, "Modan gaaru no rinkaku," 24.

16. Kiyosawa, "Modan gaaru no kenkyū," 156–57.

17. Kishida Ryūsei, "Shinko saiku Ginza dōri," in *Kishida Ryūsei zenshū*, vol. 4 (Iwanami
Shoten, 1979), 295–97. This essay was serialized in the evening edition of the *Tōkyō nichi
nichi shinbun*, May 24 through June 10, 1927.

18. *Chijin no ai* was serialized in the *Ōsaka asahi shinbun* from March through June
1924, and in *Josei* from November 1924 through July 1925; the version cited here is from
Tanizaki Junichirō zenshū, vol. 10 (Chūō kōronsha, 1967), 1–302. For an English translation,
see Tanizaki Junichirō, *Naomi*, trans. Anthony H. Chambers (New York: Knopf, 1985).

and costuming of his child-bride, whom he has rescued from her labors
as a café waitress. As Naomi's body and desires mature, he is overwhelmed by her sexuality, and both confused and enticed by her constantly shifting persona, which challenges fixed notions of gender and
culture.

Naomi's bold transgressions across gender and culture boundaries
identify her as a Modern Girl and illustrate Coward's explication of how
social definitions of both female and male sexuality are projected onto
women's bodies, while "men are neutral."[19] This is the case in Tanizaki's
melodrama. Naomi's play with a fixed gender identity, expressed in
cross-dressing, is transformed into a power play involving the final shift
in a mistress-slave relationship. By the end of the story, the heroine has
taken on male language to challenge the authority of her former mentor. In response, her husband's speech does not become feminized, in a
role reversal, but rather infantilized: he responds to her demands that
he do whatever she desires of him with the acquiescent monosyllabic
grunt of a domesticated male child.[20]

Naomi's chief desire is to act and look Western, an aspiration at first
encouraged by her mentor, who calls his Mary Pickford–look-alike protégée a "Yankee girl."[21] Although her upward mobility into the ballroom
society of the genteel dance hall challenges class distinctions, and her
affectation of male speech threatens the narrator, her appearance as a
Westerner who is not Western (captured in the ambiguity of her un-
traceable name, "Naomi," which appears Eurasian but may not be) is her
most militant statement.[22] Naomi's identification with Pickford, Gloria
Swanson, and Pola Negri remains titillating only as long as the hero is
attracted to the *haikara* Western life-style, which is epitomized in the
"culture house" chosen by the young couple for its Western architecture
and furnished with imported goods aimed at a "simple life."[23] In the
end, he is drawn back to a "pure" Japanese-style house, and to a traditional notion of marriage and family. The ballroom dancing scenes are
revealed to be battle sites of East-West confrontation: Naomi appears as
an unrecognizable apparition in white face, and the author's real con-

19. Coward, *Female Desires*, 30.

20. For a passage describing how the hero poses Naomi in various guises, and for the
role reversal, see Tanizaki, *Chijin no ai*, 45, 294. I am grateful to Lucy North for the concept of "mistress-slave relationship."

21. It is noteworthy that Tanizaki chose "Yankee girl," an unambiguously pejorative
term that implied an unreflexive copying of Western mores, over "Modern Girl." For a
discussion of the term "Yankee girl," see Ueda, "Josei zasshi," 136–37.

22. Tanizaki, *Chijin no ai*, 264.

23. Tanizaki uses the Meiji term *haikara*, derived from the transliteration of "high collar," to mean fashionably Western, rather than *modan*, or "modern." The *bunka jūtaku*, or
"culture house," was the term for the Western structures erected for the new middle class
during the post–World War I era.

cern turns out to be his discomfort with anything that "smells" Western and is therefore a threat to the authentic Japanese family. Tanizaki projected this fear onto a Modern Girl.[24]

While journalists grappled with the Modern Girl's purported sexual activity, her gender identity, and her cultural identification, they were almost unanimous in proclaiming her unquestionable autonomy. Charges of promiscuity leveled against the Modern Girl, according to Kitamura, stemmed from the new, public nature of woman's activity. She summed up these charges in a composite sketch:

> She went for a walk with a man in Nara Park; I spotted a glimpse of her at a Dotonbori café; she was kicking up her heels at the dance hall; I discovered her going into the movies. When I watched her walking she was moving her left and right legs one after the other; I saw her yawning and decided she was tired out from waiting for a man; she'd decorated her hat with a flower—I wonder who she got it from. She sneezed, she must be run down from being with a man; etc.; etc.; etc.; etc.; etc.; etc.; etc.[25]

Kitamura noted that while sins are committed in the dark, the so-called disgraceful conduct of the Modern Girl was conducted in broad daylight. The Japanese woman was no longer secluded in the confines of the household, but was out in the open, working and playing alongside men. This was her real transgression: she would not accept the division of labor that had placed her in the home.[26]

The trumpeted promiscuity of the Modern Girl, who moved from man to man, was thus but one aspect of her self-sufficiency. She appeared to be a free agent without ties of filiation, affect, or obligation to lover, father, mother, husband, or children—in a striking counterpoint to the state ideology of family documented in the Civil Code and in the ethics texts taught in the schools.[27] According to one critic, the Modern

24. Tanizaki, *Chijin no ai*, 126, 264.

25. Kitamura, "Kaiteisō," 131.

26. Of course, women workers in the textile industry constituted 71 percent of the work force in private industry by 1910, as E. Patricia Tsurumi has documented, but this social reality was not reflected in official ideology regarding woman's place within the family. Kano Masanao suggests that in addition to separating the two parts of the compound word *kokka* into its constituitive *koku* or *kuni* (nation) and *ka* or *ie* (family) in order to posit an analogy between the two terms, historians of the construction of modern Japanese ideology might recognize how men have been placed within the nation and women within the family. See E. Patricia Tsurumi, "Female Textile Workers and the Failure of Early Trade Unionism in Japan," *History Workshop* 18 (Fall 1984): 5; and Kano Masanao, *Senzen. "Ie" no shisō* (Sōbunsha, 1983), 5.

27. For the assessment that the *moga* was unfettered by tradition or fatalism, and "more than anything respected herself," see the August 1924 issue of *Josei* (Woman), cited in Ueda, "Josei zasshi," 135. The introductory coda to the Civil Code, which explained that Japanese law differed from Western civil codes because the familial nature of the society

Girl had not simply abandoned motherhood: she was anti-motherhood. Even Hiratsuka Raichō, the feminist theorist of the World War I era, agreed. Although she portrayed the Modern Girl as the daughter of the New Woman and as someone who had the power to create the future because of her thought, emotion, action, and everyday life, Raichō did not imagine her having any daughters of her own.[28]

The autonomy of this Modern Girl who "strutted down the street" en route to and from work derived from her economic self-sufficiency. Kataoka surmised that the term *modan gaaru* had originated as a substitute for the vague reference "that sort of woman" which had been attached to the urban working women employed by stores and businesses after the First World War, and Kitamura warned that "it would be problematic to mistake the short skirts and the ability to endure chilled legs as the be-all and end-all of the Modern Girl," because the work and the morals of this "new working woman" differed from those of the "old household woman."[29] According to Kitamura, this heroine's livelihood positioned her beyond the reach of state and family: "Since the old morals have been broken and new morals have not yet come about and new standards of chastity have not been established, working women, in their system of thought, are a nomadic people. Nomadic people have neither laws nor national borders. All they can do is move as their convictions move them."[30]

Although Tanizaki's Naomi remains a consumer whose appetite for moving pictures and carefully chosen foreign and domestic order-in delicacies is matched only by her desire for a large assortment of male companions, the Modern Girl, according to many accounts, was not merely a passive consumer of middle-class culture, for she was depicted as producing goods, services, and new habits. She thereby differed from the New Woman of the previous era, who had exhibited resistance to outmoded traditions but had offered no new model for an everyday life.

---

displaced any notion of individuality, and the fourth book of the code, the *Book of Relatives*, placed woman in a patriarchal web. For an example of the subjugation of woman within the family in the ethics textbooks, consider the elementary school catechism verse about the soft-spoken, filial bride and mother-to-be who, with soft voice, engages in her needlework and cleaning; see Suematsu Kenchō, *Shōgaku shūshin kun*, pts. 2 and 3 (Seikasha, 1892), cited in *Nihon fujin mondai shiryō shūsei*, vol. 5: *Kazoku mondai*, ed. Yuzawa Yasuhiko (Domesu Shuppan, 1978), 369–70. See also Carol Gluck, *Japan's Modern Myths: Ideology in the Late Meiji Period* (Princeton: Princeton University Press, 1985), 120–27.

28. Hiratsuka Raichō, "Modan gaaru ni tsuite," *Dai chōwa*, May 1927, reprinted in *Hiratsuka Raichō chosakushū*, vol. 4 (Ōtsuki Shoten, 1983), 282–84; and Hiratsuka Raichō, "Kaku arubeki modan gaaru," *Fujin kōron*, June 1927, reprinted in ibid., 290–97.

29. Kataoka, "Modan gaaru no kenkyū," 164; Kitamura, "Kaiteisō," 135.

30. Kitamura, "Kaiteisō," 131.

The cerebral New Woman had been romantic rather than realistic; she had wielded ideals, not economics; she had imitated male habits instead of attempting to create a separately bounded life for women. In contrast, the Modern Girl was more interested in shaping the materiality of everyday existence.[31] It cannot be emphasized too much that the Modern Girl was not "just looking," to employ Rachel Bowlby's evocative term for the commodified woman who is at the same time a customer in a newly rationalized consumer culture.[32]

Authors agreed that the self-sufficient successor to the New Woman was definitely in the vanguard of the new modern age—the postearthquake era of economic, social, and cultural reconstruction. There was also a general consensus that this "free-living and free-thinking" Modern Girl was making history in part because she was making her own money.[33] The Marxist feminist Yamakawa Kikue, however, dissented. In a scathing essay entitled "Modern Girls, Modern Boys," Yamakawa depicted the Modern Girl as a passive figure who lay supine on a beach and afterwards strolled through town, still clad in her bathing suit.[34] While she disagreed with the right-wing press reports that the Modern Girl and Modern Boy (who could be found Ginza-cruising or at the movies or theater) were part of a communist conspiracy to weaken the children of the privileged through dissipation, she concurred that youth's dissolution marked a historic turning point: the behavior of these girls who painted themselves in bright colors and walked half-naked beside boys in kettle-shaped hats and flared pants was reminiscent of the antics of the "degenerate customs and the ephemeral epicureanism" of functionaries in the closing years of the feudal era in Japan. Their lack of interest in anything but sensual pleasures signified the fate of a ruling class in decline.[35]

31. Kiyosawa, "Modan gaaru no kenkyū," 157–58; Kataoka, "Modan gaaru no kenkyū," 161–65.

32. Rachel Bowlby, *Just Looking: Consumer Culture in Dreiser, Gissing, and Zola* (New York: Methuen, 1985), 18–34.

33. The notion is Kataoka's; see "Modan gaaru no kenkyū," 164. The terms *sentan* and *senei*, meaning "vanguard" and "radical," were commonly applied to the *moga*; on this issue, see Minami (ed.), *Nihon Modanizumu*, x.

34. Unlike other writers who either marginalized or ignored the Modern Boy altogether, Yamakawa placed no greater emphasis on the Modern Girl than on her male partner; see Yamakawa Kikue, "Modan gaaru, modan booi," *Keizai ōrai*, September 1927, reprinted in *Yamakawa Kikueshū*, 11 vols., ed. Tanaka Sumiko and Yamakawa Shinsaku (Iwanami Shoten, 1981–82), vol. 4: *Musankaikyū undō no fujin undō 1925–1927*, 268–71.

35. Exhibiting a revolutionary optimism, Yamakawa also drew a second parallel: the interests of the decadent girls and boys were undoubtedly very similar to the diversions enjoyed by the Russian nobility and landowners who were thrown off their land by the roughened hands of the ignorant muzhiks. See ibid., 269–70.

Yamakawa's prurient definition, which was consistent with the inability of early-twentieth-century Marxism to come to terms with questions of gender or sexuality, ignored the ambiguities and contradictions present in representations of the Japanese-but-Western Modern
Girl. In contrast, other writers did attempt to reconcile images of
gleeful consumerism and sexual play with the Modern Girl's identity
as a wageworker who, having abandoned confining tradition, exhibited
strains of resistance. To do this they resorted to a twofold definition, determining that there were Modern Girls—and then there were
real Modern Girls. According to Kiyosawa, the real Modern Girl lived
outside Japan, whereas the Japanese Modern Girl was a colorful but
apolitical and anti-intellectual imitation.[36] In "One Hundred Percent
Moga," Ōya Sōichi, the leading critic of popular culture of the 1920s,
offered three contemporaneous versions of the Modern Girl. The
first was crafty, manipulative, and intellectualizing. She was free to
go out, even to sleep out, and maintained no boundaries between
friends and lovers. She was a consumer, not a producer; she was like
a mannequin. The second type was group-oriented, productive, and
possessed of a self-consciousness. But only the third girl was "one
hundred percent *moga*." She was identified as the daughter of heroic
leftist activists who had been imprisoned countless times; she thus had
no sense of family other than the police, the jails, and the streets. Liberated from the traditions related to so-called female morality, she
articulated the authentic language, gestures, and ideology of the new
era.[37]

Hiratsuka Raichō's two versions of the heroine appeared in "The
Modern Girl as She Should Be." The first was a young woman with time
and money to fashion herself a brightly colored ensemble of Western
clothing with matching hat in order to attend the cafés on Ginza. This
seemingly liberated woman, however, was not free: she was the object
of man's physical desires, and while she might appear upbeat, she was
in fact depressed. The real Modern Girl, in contrast, would have a social
conscience. Although Hiratsuka could not find such a Modern Girl in
Japan in the 1920s, she predicted that such women would appear, not
from among the "fashion slaves" but from within the ranks of working
and laboring proletarian women who had organized as "social women."

36. Kiyosawa, "Modan gaaru no kenkyū," 153–57.
37. Ōya Sōichi, "Hyaku paasento moga," *Chūō kōron*, August 1929, reprinted in *Ōya
Sōichi zenshū*, vol. 2 (Eichōsha, 1982), 10–17. Hamill has concluded that the distinction
between a (progressive) "real modern girl" and a "real" modern girl interested only in
clothing and makeup was present in almost all accounts of the Modern Girl; see Hamill,
"Josei," 210.

The model for such a Modern woman was Takamure Itsue, the anarchist feminist.[38]

In sum, the discourse on the Modern Girl was more about imagining a new Japanese woman than about documenting social change. For this reason, as Kataoka Teppei admitted, despite repeated themes there is no clearly defined image:

> When we say the Modern Girl exists in our era we are not in particular referring to individuals named Miss So-and-so-*ko* or Mrs. Such-and-such-*e*. Rather, we are talking about the fact that somehow, from the midst of the lives of all sorts of women of our era, we can feel the air of a new era, different from that of yesterday. That's right; where can you folks clearly say there is a typical modern girl? That is to say that the Modern Girl is but a term that abstractly alludes to one new flavor sensed from the air of the life of all women in society.[39]

The Modern Girl resisted definition, but this did not mean that pundits did not keep trying to confine her. In the January 1928 issue of *Shinchō*, although the members of a roundtable discussion on various facets of modern life agreed to talk about urbanization and new forms of "articulation, expression, language, gestures, writing, and clothing," they could not set aside the topic of the Modern Girl: they were obsessed by the desire to enclose her in one all-encompassing meaning. In the course of their conversation these critics determined the following about the *moga*: (1) she was not hysterical; (2) she used direct language; (3) she had a direct, aggressive sexuality—she checked to see whether a man was compatible; (4) she scoffed at chastity—changing men, for her, was like putting on a clean white shirt; (5) she could be poor—clothing was now inexpensive; (6) she was liberated from the double fetters of class and gender; (7) she was an anarchist; (8) she accosted men when she needed train fare; (9) she had freedom of expression—which she got from the movies; and finally, an indirect commentary on the autonomy of this persona, (10) the *mobo* (Modern Boy) was a "zero."[40]

The women writers of *Nyonin geijutsu* (Women's arts), the journal for and by women that appeared with rare exception from July 1928 through June 1932, did not use the term "Modern Girl," but their unabashed celebration of female creativity, sexuality, and autonomy was a potent contribution to the process of representing and thereby defining her.[41] The magazine, advertised by well-heeled live mannequins at ma-

38. Hiratsuka Raichō, "Kaku arubeki modan gaaru," *Fujin kōron*, June 1927, reprinted in *Chosakushū* 4:290–97.
39. Kataoka, "Modan gaaru," 173; the suffixes *-ko* and *-e* are endings of female names.
40. "Modan seikatsu mandankai," *Shinchō*, January 1928, 123–47.
41. The story of the woman who committed suicide after being called a Modern Girl may be apocryphal, but the strategic decision of these women not to wield the label "Mod-

jor shopping intersections, was premised on a shrewd analysis: namely, that media manipulation of woman could be subverted through mass marketing of a self-consciously glossy journal produced by women cultural revolutionaries.

The tone of the journal was set on June 20, 1928, the day before the first issue appeared, when the leading women thinkers of the day, clad in both kimono and Western dress, seated themselves at the Rainbow Grill in Ueno and invited the press to photograph them.[42] (The women, conscious of the power of self-representation, had adopted the Japanese male tradition of initiating political and intellectual projects in semiprivate environs but had chosen a more modern and less sex-specific site than a geisha house.) The agenda for the new magazine was set in the inaugural issue in a manifesto by Yamakawa Kikue entitled "An Examination of Feminism."[43] Yamakawa placed women's culture in the context of economic advances and women's demands for equality in suffrage, education, and work. Her reference to women's demand for autonomous actions or freedom of activity constituted yet another rephrasing of the discourse on the Modern Girl's creation of her own separate and unprecedented everyday life, by a woman who was representing herself as a producer of culture.

The writers for *Nyonin geijutsu* denied boundaries erected in our histories (and in their own Japanese political culture) by proving that women on the left could unite to construct a multifaceted critique of women's place. Such writers as Sata Ineko, whose sympathies lay with the Japanese Communist party, and the noncommunist but avowedly Marxist Yamakawa Kikue joined with the anarchist Yagi Akiko and numerous other female (and a few male) writers, poets, and critics to demand a cultural space wherein women would not be treated like the live mannequins that had just appeared on Ginza. (In an article about these women in department store show windows, Yagi called this new job the most extreme example of the commodification of a human being as an item for sale.)[44]

---

ern Girl" is in part explained by Hiratsuka Raichō's remembrance that no woman in short hair and Western clothes would call herself a "Modern Girl," just as the Seitōsha activists of her generation had actively resisted the label of "New Woman"; see Hiratsuka, "Modan gaaru ni tsuite," 283.

42. Ogata Akiko, *Nyonin geijutsu no sekai* (Domesu Shuppan, 1980), 38–39.

43. Yamakawa Kikue, "Feminizumu no kentō," *Nyonin geijutsu* 1, no. 1 (July 1928): 2–7, reprinted in *Yamakawa Kikueshū*, vol. 5: *Doguma kara deta yūrei*, 167–74.

44. Yagi Akiko, "Kotoba: Hyōgen," *Nyonin geijutsu* 2, no. 1 (January 1929): 104–6. This theme may have been influenced by an essay by Yamakawa that I quote and discuss in the conclusion to my book *Changing Song: The Marxist Manifestos of Nakano Shigeharu* (Princeton: Princeton University Press, 1990). For Yamakawa's biting critique of the commodification of women, see Yamakawa Kikue, "Keihin tsuki tokkahin to shite no onna,"

Nyonin geijutsu used the weapons of the numerous magazines produced for mass circulation during the late 1920s—pictures and photographs, essays, fiction, theory, and roundtable discussion—and drew on both indigenous and foreign sources to champion women's liberation. The writers, unlike their male counterparts who were nervous about the cultural identity of the Modern Girl, made no attempt to distinguish "authentic Japanese" experience from imitations of the West. In addition to articles on Edo life and on domestic politics, the journal included writings by such thinkers as Alexandra Kollontai (whose works were causing a great sensation in Japan owing to rumors that they advocated "free love"),[45] Katherine Mansfield, Bronislaw Malinowski, and Langston Hughes.

The writers for *Nyonin geijutsu* talked about more than just art and theory. The women's magazines of the 1920s featured articles on love and romance, and so too did *Nyonin geijutsu*, in a series of pieces published in its earliest issues. One representative discussion was the "Roundtable Discussion of Other Angles on Love."[46] The fourteen women participants in the event, which was subtitled "Feelings and Sensations of Jealousy/Chastity and Love, Adulterous Love/The Eternal Nature of Love/Love in a Three-sided Affair and in a Multisided Affair/Sexual Desire and Love," were tough, cynical, and, like the Modern Girl as represented in the media, realistic. The political activist Kamichika Ichiko questioned whether strong feelings leading to a marriage based on love could last fifty years into the marriage. It was well and fine, she noted, if one had the time, but she was busy with her family and her work; there was no time for the cultivation of love. Another discussant claimed that only unattainable love was eternal.

Unlike the imagined Modern Girl, the modern women on the panel were confronting actual issues of bonding, relating, and reproducing. Yet significantly, in the process of defining the militant as a Modern Girl, these women, like so many of the women who appeared in *Nyonin geijutsu* as either writers or the subjects of articles, defined themselves as being out in public. They openly expressed their feelings about both love and work. While they may have eschewed the label "Modern Girl,"

Fujin kōron, January 1928, reprinted in *Yamakawa Kikueshū*, vol. 5: *Doguma kara deta yūrei*, pp. 2–8.

45. Kollontai's works were translated between 1927 and 1936 as follows: *Red Love*, trans. Murao Jirō (Sekaisha, 1927); *A Grand Love*, trans. Nakajima Hideko (Sekaisha, 1930); *Great Love*, trans. Uchiyama Kenji (Sekaisha, 1930); *Working Women's Revolution*, trans. Ōtake Hakukichi (Naigaisha, 1930); *Motherhood and Society*, trans. Ozawa Keishi (Logosu Shoin, 1931); and *Women and the Family System*, trans. Yamakawa Kikue (Seibunkaku, 1936).

46. "Tahōmen renai zadankai," *Nyonin geijutsu* 1, no. 3 (September 1928): 2–22. A picture of the discussants is on p. 20 of the article.

the sentiment that women should move out of the household and into the streets was familiar to the readers of *Nyonin geijutsu*. An example is available in the large print promoting a nationwide contest for the best lyrics for a "Woman's March":

> Women have already kicked off their heavy shackles and escaped from the dungeons of their darkened hearts. What lies before us now is for us to pour into the streets like rain in a sun-shower. What is left is the deafening roar of the factories, the tips of the spires of thought attacking the heavens. Lining up with all peoples we move forward into the world of all living things. Friends, at times like these we need a song that will sing, exhort, exalt, and push forward for us.[47]

The image of a Modern Girl on the road was publicized in "Letters from a Trip to Kyūshū," co-authored by Yagi Akiko and Hayashi Fumiko—whose *Hōrōki* (Tales of wandering), a sensational "diary" of her travels as a working woman spurred forward by desire, was currently being serialized in *Nyonin geijutsu*.[48] The travelogue opened with Yagi's expression of concern over Hayashi's drinking. Hayashi, in turn, boasted of the romance and whiskey she had enjoyed with a "tall, modern" fan in Nagoya, and of her behavior toward the soldier on the train whom she had pinched so as to terminate moves that were not fast enough. This document about wine, men, and song—an update of *Tōkaidō hizakurige*, the Edo classic about the picaresque antics of two déclassé warriors—produced by two women writers on the road, proved that adventure was not gender-bound.

In other words, Hayashi Fumiko, the lusty author-heroine of *Tales of Wandering*, who was busy punctuating her autobiographical account of a down-and-out woman drifter with lyrical references to dancing naked women, was not an idiosyncratic anomaly. Rather, the Modern Girl's protest, expressed through sensuality and mobility, could be communal.

But *Nyonin geijutsu* was not all about art, love, and exploration. Articles on women factory workers, and especially on labor in the Soviet Union, increased in later issues of the journal. The magazine's final six months contained a series on the notorious Tōyō Muslin strike of 1930, which had culminated in street-fighting.[49] This strike also produced fictional heroines in a series of short stories published by Sata Ineko in 1931, one year after Sata had stood in support outside the factory walls,

47. "Zen josei shinshutsu kōshinkyoku wo tsunoru," *Nyonin geijutsu* 2, no. 8 (August 1929): 2–3.

48. Yagi Akiko and Hayashi Fumiko, "Kyūshū tabidayori," *Nyonin geijutsu* 2, no. 9 (September 1929): 70–81; *Hōrōki* was serialized in nineteen installments between October 1928 and November 1930 in most issues of *Nyonin geijutsu*.

49. Nakamoto Takako, "Tōyō Mosu dai ni kōjō" (parts 1–4), *Nyonin geijutsu* July–December 1932.

listening to the sound of the strike drums. Her four-part narrative, which appeared in disparate sources in the mass media, recounted violence both among the young women workers and between them and the hired thugs of the "justice corps." Sata also presented propaganda produced by both sides, including letters to fathers and brothers appealing to the power of patriarchy.[50]

Like Tanizaki's A Fool's Love and Hayashi Fumiko's epic Tales of Wandering, Sata's stories presented a militant as a Modern Girl guilty of transgressing in both spoken language and body language. In her stories, class struggle and not cultural definitions were at stake when the teen-age activists refused to stay in their designated place as obedient workers. These young women were in the streets, but they did not dance, shop, or strut to work. Instead they were brawling as only men could. They used the rough male word for "I," ore, to refer to themselves, threatened to smash dishware, and literally wrestled physically over issues of ideology. Like most Modern Girls in the media they expressed sexual desires—they did take time to flirt with male co-workers—but this pastime was a secondary diversion. The abiding concern of the modern young women in Sata's stories, as in the articles in the closing issues of Nyonin geijutsu, was that they be allowed to continue to produce. They wanted above all to work.

What begins to emerge from the above overview of the varied commentary on the Modern Girl is that men and women writers for the popular press who talked about a new kind of woman believed that this cultural heroine was defining her own options and her own sexuality (along with the sexuality of the mobo—who was so inconsequential that his name did not have to be spelled out). This modern young woman transgressed by crossing boundaries erected by class, gender, and culture. Her resistance was usually not organized, but nevertheless it was political, as observers like Kataoka acknowledged, arguing that, as distinct from her predecessors in the Japanese women's movement, the New Woman, "like the grand waves of the Pacific Ocean," drew those before her into her activity. She had neither a leader nor an organization, but hers was the first nationally based movement of women; hers was the first voice of woman's resistance.[51]

The Modern Girl, in other words, was militant. The only article in Nyonin geijutsu with the term "Modern Girl" in its title hints at this equa-

50. See Sata Ineko, "Kanbu jokō no namida," Kaizō, January 1931; "Shōkanbu," Bungei shunjū, August 1931; "Kitō," Chūō kōron, October 1931; and "Kyōsei kikoku," Chūō kōron, January 1931; reprinted in Sata Ineko zenshū, vol. 1 (Kōdansha, 1977), 219–78. Sata has explained that the women workers asked her for aid, and that she had been outside the dormitory in Kameido during the strike; interviews with Sata Ineko, in Tokyo, October 1982; and in Karuizawa, August 1986.

51. Kiyosawa, "Modan gaaru no kenkyū," 158.

tion of women's transgressions across class, sex, and culture lines on the one hand with political action on the other. The heroine of this brief commentary, "The Modern Girl in Jail," is imprisoned for soliciting funds for an after-hours school for working girls. When she is placed in a cell with other women, her "crime" of organizing is not distinguished from the petty criminal acts of the other imprisoned women. They are all political prisoners.[52]

Although interviews with survivors of the Tōyō Muslin strike indicate that the street-fighting did not last long because the girls could not hold out against the strength of the state-backed company, the image of them as street-fighting women has persisted.[53] The same cannot be said for the Modern Girl. We have lost the picture presented by the journalists of the 1920s of an unattached woman who expressed her private desires for sex and for work in public places, thereby challenging the assumption that she belonged in the home. An interrogation as to why the Modern Girl did what she did—or in other words, why she was once represented in the way she was—contributes to an explanation of both the appearance and the disappearance of this pugnacious and lustful, multifaceted heroine.

WHY DID THE MODERN GIRL DO WHAT SHE DID?

In order to begin to explain why this Modern Girl did what she did *when* she did, we must contextualize her representation within a history of Japanese women of the 1920s and 1930s that sees women as consumers, producers, legal subjects, and political activists. For the Modern Girl appeared during a historical juncture when Japanese women were acting in all of these capacities.[54]

First of all, the talk about the Modern Girl's clothed (and disrobed) body cannot be divorced from documented social change in woman's

52. "Ryūchijō no modan gaaru," *Nyonin geijutsu* 2, no. 12 (December 1929): 77–81.

53. See Watanabe Etsuji and Suzuki Yūko, eds., *Tatakai ni ikite: Senzen fujin rōdō undō e no shōgen* (Domesu Shuppan, 1980), 194–214; and Rōdō Undōshi Kenkyūkai and Rōdōsha Kyōiku Kyōkai, eds., *Nihon rōdō undō no rekishi* (Sanichi Shinsho, 1960), 179–94.

54. In this sense the Japanese "Modern Girl" was not unlike the "New Woman" of Weimar Germany. In the words of Atina Grossman, "This New Woman was not merely a media myth or a demographer's paranoid fantasy, but a social reality that can be researched and documented. She existed in office and factory, bedroom and kitchen, just as surely as in cafe, cabaret, and film. I think it is important that we begin to look at the New Woman as producer and not only consumer, as an agent constructing a new identity which was then marketed in mass culture, even as mass culture helped to form that identity"; "Girlkultur or Thoroughly Rationalized Female: A New Woman in Weimar Germany," in *Women in Culture and Politics: A Century of Change*, ed. Judith Friedlander, Blanche Wiesen Cook, Alice Kessler-Harris, and Carroll Smith Rosenberg (Bloomington: Indiana University Press, 1986), 64.

material culture during the 1920s. Articles in women's magazines devoted to sewing Western-style clothes, for example, suggest some shift
toward non-Japanese dress. The magazine with the reassuring title of
"Housewife's Friend" (*Shufu no tomo*), which was aimed at the housebound married woman, had run its first series on making Western clothing in 1917, and by 1923 such articles as "How to Make a Convenient
House-Dress" were promoting Western attire as a stylish commodity.
Nevertheless, the daughter of the poet Hagiwara Sakutarō recalls how
neighborhood housewives had jeered, "Modern Girl," when her
mother—inspired by the author Uno Chiyo—first appeared in Western
clothing in 1927. It would appear that many were not as quick to accept
new fashions as they were to make use of a new media label.[55]

The social history of the affective life of a real-life Modern Girl during the 1920s is even more difficult to recount. Were young women in
fact as animated and promiscuous as they appeared in the claims of Nii
and others who suggested that the Modern Girl's gestures mirrored
movie imagery? To what extent did the bravado of the women intellectuals in *Nyonin geijutsu* reflect the self-assertive attitudes toward the opposite sex and toward sex reported in the media? One recorded exchange between a man and a woman on a commuter train in 1930
provides an illustration of brazen behavior that matches the accusations
of critics who caught (or lauded) the Modern Girl accosting helpless
men: A woman of thirty riding on a train was accused by a well-dressed
stranger of acting shamelessly for a wife and of threatening the national
good, because her permanent wave was "no good" and her powder too
thick. The woman's reaction was immediate and relentless. "Excuse me,
but how do you know whether or not I'm someone's wife," she retorted.
She then demanded his business card, threatened to visit his house that
very day, and followed him off the train when he attempted to retreat.[56]

As noted by the witness to this incident, the woman protagonist was
undoubtedly en route to the "Marubiru," the office building in the financial district of Tokyo famous for its female clerical workers in Western
dress. Beginning in 1923, these women workers could have their hair
permed at Japan's first beauty parlor, and, according to contemporary
sources, by 1924 women constituted 3,500 of the 30,000 white-collar
workers commuting to the Marunouchi district. By the second half of the

55. Ueda, "Josei zasshi," 120. The renovation and expansion of department stores between 1924 and 1930 is also an index to changes in consumer behavior. Hagiwara's rem-
iniscence is from Hagiwara Yōko, *Chichi: Hagiwara Sakutarō* (1959); reprinted in *Nihon no
hyakunen*, 10 vols., ed. Tsurumi Shunsuke (Chikuma Shobō, 1961–64), vol. 5: Imai Seiichi,
Shinsai ni yuragu, 165.

56. Minakami Takitarō, "Teitō fukkōsai yokyō," *Mita bungaku*, May 1930, reprinted in
ibid., 166–68.

1920s, approximately 8,200 women were employed at secretarial and service jobs in Japan's urban centers.[57]

During the 1920s, at the same time as the Modern Girl was being defined, journalists and state officials were surveying the Working Woman. A comparison of the six categories used in the 1924 "Survey Regarding Working Women," one of the many surveys released by the Tokyo Social Affairs Bureau, with the categories used in "A Modern Girl Mental Test," published in *Fujokai* (Woman's world), reveals that the discourse on the Modern Girl and the response to the Working Woman were part of the same social and economic history. While the six headings used by the Tokyo officials were teacher, typist, office workers, storekeeper, nurse, and telephone operator, the "Modern Girl Mental Test" had also included bus conductors, café waitresses, and urban women producers of services who could not be classified as middle class and who came from working-class backgrounds.[58] Although the term *shokugyō fujin* was usually used to distinguish white-collar women employees from their sisters in the factories, the meaning of "Working Woman" remained ambiguous. As late as 1932 a commentator, who had read several works on the "working woman problem" in order to put the café waitress in a sociological perspective, still could not find a clearly defined concept to fit the label.[59] Kon Wajirō's typology of the Working Woman in his 1929 *New Edition of the Guide to Greater Tokyo* also illustrated the blurring of class distinctions when he included in his list women bus conductors, chauffeurs, women company representatives,

57. Kon Wajirō, ed., *Shinban dai Tōkyō annai* (Chūō kōronsha, 1929; reprint Hihyōsha, 1986); and Kiyosawa Kiyoshi, *Modan gaaru* (1926); both cited in Tsurumi (ed.), *Nihon no hyakunen*, vol. 5: Imai, *Shinsai ni yuragu*, 162.

58. The appearance of a number of surveys, by such pundits as Yamakawa Kikue and by government officials such as the unidentified gentleman who in 1931 ruefully admitted that Ibsen's Nora had been a prophet, aimed at scientifically analyzing this new social phenomenon, and was one index of the widespread concern over the definition of the Working Woman. See Yamakawa Kikue, "Gendai shokugyō fujinron," in *Nihon fujin mondai shiryō shūsei*, vol. 8: *Shichō* (part 1), ed. Maruoka Hideko (Domesu Shuppan, 1976), 334–44; Nagy's essay in this volume (chap. 9); and Maeda, *Kindai dokusha no seiritsu*, 225–26.

59. The term *shokugyō fujin* has come to be associated with a middle-class response to the creation of thousands of jobs in the expanded tertiary sector after the Russo-Japanese War and accompanying the economic boom during the First World War. See, for example, Margit Maria Nagy, " 'How Shall We Live?': Social Change, the Family Institution, and Feminism in Prewar Japan" (Ph.D. diss., University of Washington, 1981), 118–38; and Murakami Nobuhiko, *Taishōki no shokugyō fujin* (Domesu Shuppan, 1983). In many instances, however, the Working Woman was associated with the Modern Girl or the working-class woman. See Kataoka's contention ("Modan gaaru no kenkyū," 164) that the term "Modern Girl" originated as a means of referring to the *shokugyō fujin*; and Obayashi Munetsugu's query, "Is the Café Waitress a Working Woman?" in " 'Jokyū' shakaishi," *Chūō kōron*, April 1932, 151–62.

journalists, women office workers, women shop clerks, gasoline girls, women who handed out advertisements and matchbooks, the elevator girl (newly being paid), and the mannequin who had first appeared in 1928 (and was now found even in the provinces!).[60]

A living counterpart to the imaginary Modern Girl emerges from these various surveys. She is the single or married Japanese woman wageworker who was forced into the work force by economic need following the end of the economic boom of the World War I years.[61] The omnipresent working-class café waitress in novels and stories of the late 1920s and early 1930s is therefore a better indication of the Modern Girl's true identity than the phantom figure of an aimless, mindless consumer frequently depicted in our history textbooks.

While woman's new position as producer was reflected in allusions to the Modern Girl's economic autonomy, there was also an actual social corollary to her representation as free from family obligations. The struggle of Tanizaki's hero to redefine his marriage with Naomi occurred at the very time that scholars and state officials, in response to the emergence of the "small" nuclear family, were actively considering the reconstitution of the modern Japanese family.[62] Commentators on the Modern Girl have all ignored the fact that the discourse on this threatening woman reached its height just when the government was debating revision of the Civil Code, having recognized that the "law ignoring women," as Oku Mumeo had called it, was not working.[63] Inasmuch as the denial of civic responsibility to women had been premised not on a biological determinism but on a notion of the woman's proper place within the family, changes in family life resulting from woman's newly expanded economic roles authorized an institutionalized ideological shift. By 1924, faced with the rise of wife-initiated divorces in urban Japan, pundits were openly lamenting the destruction of the family sys-

60. Kon Wajirō (ed.), *Shinban dai Tōkyō annai*, 281–82, 291–92.

61. Margit Nagy's essay in this volume (chap. 9) documents the entry of married women into the work force in the 1920s. For the monthly expenditures and income of the average salaryman, see Tsurumi (ed.), *Nihon no hyakunen*, vol. 5: Imai, *Shinsai ni yuragu*, 156–58. The consumption of the salaried worker must be placed in this context of depressed food and housing prices that were part of the overall crisis of Japanese capitalism. When the world depression hit in 1929, the economy had not recovered from the shocks of the post–World War I depression, the aftereffects of the earthquake of 1923, the run on banks during the panic of 1927, or the recession following the panic. By 1931, when Japan went off the gold standard, the country was in the midst of a severe depression.

62. Kano, *Senzen. "Ie" no shisō*, 112–15.

63. The words are from the title of a critique by Oku Mumeo written in 1923, cited in *Nihon fujin mondai shiryō shūsei*, vol. 5: Yuzawa (ed.), *Kazoku mondai*, 28. Murakami goes in this direction when he notes the contradiction between the emphasis on love and romance in the Taishō era and the reality of the legal system that was challenged by women's new engagement in education and work; see Murakami Nobuhiko, *Taishō joseishi* (Rironsha, 1982), 1–4.

tem; and by 1925, proposals challenging key provisions of the Civil Code, which in 1898 had granted full power to the male head of household, were under active consideration by the Rinji Hōsei Shingikai, a special investigative committee established in 1919 to revise the family provisions of the Meiji Civil Code. Women's competence was acknowledged in the proposed changes that would seemingly eliminate the requirement of parental consent before marriage, make divorce easier for women, expand the parental rights of women, and grant women the right to manage their own property.[64]

The Modern Girl's notoriety thus corresponded historically with the transition in state policy toward women's position within the family. An equally important historic conjuncture was the simultaneous appearance of the ostensibly apolitical Modern Girl and women's political groups. The displacement of the term "husband-wife quarrel" (*fūfu-genka*) by the more evocative "family struggle" (*katei sōgi*) indicates the extent to which family reality belied state ideology in the 1920s, and corroborates Sharon Nolte's suggestion that various interrelated political "configurations" during the interwar years may have served "to form a collective impression of rising politicization among women."[65]

Numerous militant feminist organizations emerged during the 1920s after the establishment of the liberal New Woman's Association (Shin Fujin Kyōkai) in 1919 and the Red Wave Society (Sekirankai), the first Japanese socialist woman's organization, in 1921. In 1922, the ban on women's right to attend political meetings was lifted. The League for Women's Suffrage (Fusen Kakutoku Dōmei) was well established by 1925, and as a result of the establishment of left-wing political parties following the promulgation of universal male suffrage in that year, women joined such auxiliary women's associations as the Kantō Women's Federation of the Labor-Farmer party. Women were also active in both wings of the labor movement; in the tenancy movement; in the Organization of Women's Consumer Unions (Fujin Shōhi Kumai Kyō-

64. For excellent documentation of the debate regarding revision of the code and the discourse surrounding the debate, see Nagy, " 'How Shall We Live?' " 198–219, 255. See also *Nihon fujin mondai shiryō shūsei*, vol. 5: Yuzawa (ed.), *Kazoku mondai*. For an article from 1924 on the destruction of the family which listed the end of the family as an economic unit, the power of the state, and the extension of individualism as three reasons for the collapse of the patriarchal system, see Kawada Shirō, "Kachōsei kazoku soshiki no hōkai Kazoku seido hōkai no kiun," in ibid., 438–53.

65. Sharon Nolte, "Women's Rights and Society's Needs: Japan's 1931 Suffrage Bill," *Comparative Studies in Society and History* 28, no. 1 (October 1986): 18–19. While Murakami has argued that education and the increase in number of Working Women, more than their organized protest movements, served to liberate women from the family system enshrined in the Civil Code, the role of the widespread organization of women in a variety of political interest groups in changing the attitudes of women and men cannot be ignored; see Murakami, *Taishō joseishi*, 2. For a use of the term *fūfu sōgi*, see Kitamura, "Kaiteisō," 137.

kai), established in 1928; and in such professional organizations as the Association of Typists (Taipusuto Kyōkai); the Society of Working Women (Shokugyō Fujinsha), which began publishing its own journal, *Working Woman* (*Shokugyō fujin*), within months of the establishment of the society; the Mannequin Club, organized by Yamano Chieko in 1929, six years after the opening of her beauty parlor in the Marunouchi Building; and the militant Federation of Café Waitresses (Jokyū Dōmei), which had chapters in major cities.[66]

The struggle of these women was as multifaceted as the Modern Girl's many guises. The political work of organized women during the 1920s encompassed the journalistic endeavors of activist leaders such as Yamakawa and Hiratsuka, the organization of lecture series, the lobbying of state officials, the formation of study groups dedicated to women's issues and of labor schools to educate proletarian women, and the use of leafletting and tea parties to influence politics. Women workers also took organized action over such issues as the woman worker's freedom to leave her dormitory to go out into the streets. By the end of 1928, 12,010 women had joined the labor movement, were solely responsible for 21 actions, and had participated in 138 of the 397 labor struggles of the year. The Tōyō Muslin Strike of 1930 was one of 329 instances of labor strife where women were active participants, and the Florida Dance Hall strike of the same year, one of the 38 strikes organized solely by women, illustrates how class conflict took place not only on the factory floor, but also in the places of play where working women served consumers.[67]

CONCLUSION: WHY THE MODERN GIRL DID WHAT SHE DID

The Modern Girl is rescued from her free-floating and depoliticized state when her willful image is placed alongside the history of working, militant Japanese women. Then the obsessive contouring of the Modern Girl as promiscuous and apolitical (and later, as apolitical and non-working) begins to emerge as a means of displacing the very real militancy of Japanese women (just as the real labor of the American woman during the 1920s was denied by trivializing the work of the glamorized flapper). But whereas the American woman worker by the mid-1920s had allowed herself to be depoliticized by a new consumerism, the modern Japanese woman of the 1920s was truly militant. Her militancy was articulated through the adoption of new fashions, through labor in new arenas, and through political activity that consciously challenged social,

66. For an excellent chronology, see *Nihon fujin mondai shiryō shūsei*, vol. 10: *Kindai Nihon fujin mondai nenpyō*, ed. Maruoka Hideko (Domesu Shuppan, 1980).
67. For detailed statistics, see ibid.

economic, and political structures and relationships.[68] The Japanese state's response encompassed attempts to revise the Civil Code, consideration of universal suffrage, organization and expansion of groups such as the Women's Alliance (Fujin Dōshikai) and the nationwide network of *shojokai* (associations of young girls), censorship, and imprisonment of leaders. The media responded by producing the Modern Girl.

Yet the Modern Girl must have represented even more, for the determination that talk about the Modern Girl displaced serious concern about the radical nature of women's activity does not fully address her multivalence (figs. 11.1–11.4). Why, in other words, was she Japanese *and* Western, intellectual *and* worker, deviant *and* admirable?[69] An answer is suggested by Natalie Davis in "Women on Top," which argues that the "unruly woman" in early-modern Europe, who whored, tricked, and traded, served both to reinforce social structure and to incite women to militant action in public and in private.[70] The culturally constructed figure of the Japanese Modern Girl certainly meets these two

68. Lois Banner notes that the flapper sent a mixed sexual message and makes the important connection between the flapper's play and the experience of the working woman: "The cultural focus on fashion and after hours activities in the lives of these women glamorized the working world for women while trivializing it"; Banner, *American Beauty* (Chicago: University of Chicago Press, 1983), 279, 280. See Rayna Rapp and Ellen Ross, "The 1920s: Feminism, Consumerism, and Political Backlash in the United States," in Friedlander et al. (eds.), *Women in Culture and Politics*, 52–61.

69. One way of dealing with the complexity of the contemporary woman's multifaceted image was to liken her to a colorless proteus who has been liberated from the darkness of her household, to take on the hues of its environment; see Kitamura, "Kaiteiso," 135–36. Three historians have looked beyond the stereotype of the modern girl to see a discourse constituted by contradiction. Satō, "Modanizumu," 26, 41–43, who likens the Modern Girl to the flapper, traces a shift from the Modern Girl as emblematic of woman's new customs to the Modern Girl as girl juvenile delinquent. Ueda, "Josei zasshi," 137, notes a multiplicity of definitions in his discussion of the relationship of women's magazines to a Japanese modernism. Hamill, "Josei," 208–25, like Ueda, talks in terms of a discourse, in a wide-ranging essay covering the working woman, women's education, advice columns, and women's magazines. Adopting the term *modan gaaru ron*, she analyzes the coexistence of positive and critical assessments of the Modern Girl. She attributes the pejorative aspects of the discourse to the impact of Marxism on intellectuals who could only see the "Modern Girl" as an expression of faddish mores, and to sensationalism in the mass press. In conclusion, she sides with the position of Hirabayashi Hatsunosuke to emphasize that the Modern Girl signified "the emergence of a new consciousness for women" breaking loose from traditional power relationships.

70. Natalie Zemon Davis, "Women on Top," in *Society and Culture in Early Modern France: Eight Essays* (Stanford: Stanford University Press, 1975), 143–45. While Davis's claim that a topos of sexual inversion placing woman on top in a hierarchy of power relationships was a "resource for private and public life" is far from definitive, and my discussion here has argued that the representation of the Modern Girl followed rather than encouraged political actions, the influence of the media on the actions of Japanese women during the interwar era deserves serious attention.

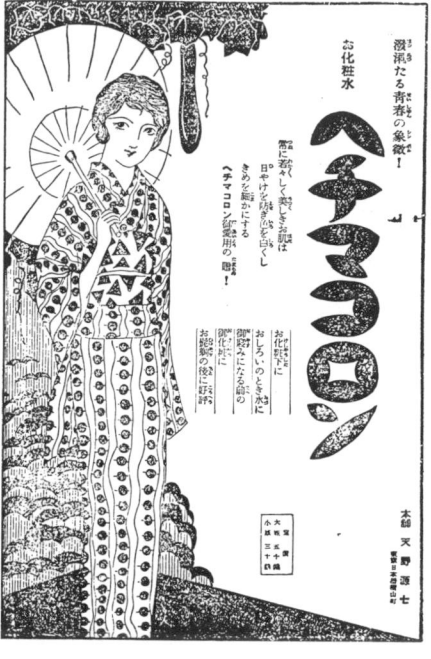

Fig. 11.1.
From *Nyonin geijutsu*, July 1929.

Fig. 11.2.
From *Kaizō*, September 1921.

Fig. 11.3.
From *Fujin no tomo*, April 1930.

Fig. 11.4.
From *Nyonin geijutsu*, August 1928.

requirements. Like the disorderly woman on top, the Modern Girl as multivalent symbol questioned relations of order and subordination and at the same time, through her cultural gender play and promiscuity, served "to explore the character of sexuality."[71]

Of course, the Japanese Modern Girl is no more a copy of her premodern European sister than she is of her kinetic American contemporaries, but the term *namaiki*, meaning cheeky, bold, or brazen, which recurs in Sata Ineko's prewar writings and which she still likes to use in mock-critical reference to herself, is a powerful analogue to the notion of woman as "disorderly." The connotations of this word are not violent, but they are certainly aggressive and transgressive: the person who is *namaiki*, like the *moga*, dares to take liberties. The symbol of a *namaiki*, uppity Modern Girl, who crossed gender and class boundaries and transgressed sexually, may indeed have spoken to those who demanded expanded social, sexual, and economic liberation for women and men. In this sense, she was admirable. But conversely, the Modern Girl did what she did because woman's new place in public as worker, intellectual, and political activist threatened the patriarchal family and its ideological support, the deferring woman who was presented in state ideology as the "Good Wife and Wise Mother." Inflected in this fashion, she was a threat. Finally, the Modern Girl, who was both Japanese and Western—or possibly neither—played with the principle of cultural or national difference. Seen in this way, she highlighted the controversy over adoption of non-Japanese customs in everyday life and called into question the essentialism (as opposed to the European physiological determinism) that subordinated the Japanese woman to the Japanese man. This thesis was indeed offered by the feminist Kitamura, who claimed that "labor struggle, tenancy struggle, household struggle, struggle between man and woman" were inevitable and had recently been joined to a new battle: "a struggle over good conduct" that pitted Japanese against Western behavior and used the Modern Girl to work out the struggle.[72]

This, then, is the significance of the Japanese Modern Girl in the broadest context of prewar Japanese history. The Modern Girl stood as the vital symbol of overwhelming "modern" or non-Japanese change instigated by both women and men during an era of economic crisis and social unrest. She stood for change at a time when state authority was attempting to reestablish authority and stability. The Modern Girl of the 1920s and early 1930s thus inverted the role of the Good Wife and Wise Mother. The ideal Meiji woman of the 1870s, 1880s, and 1890s had

71. Ibid., 150. In this way the Japanese Modern Girl is also akin to her American sister, the flapper, for as Paula Fass has shown, young women, even more than men, symbolized disorder and rebellion in the United States during the 1920s; see Fass, *The Damned and the Beautiful* (New York: Oxford University Press, 1977), 6, 22.

72. Kitamura, "Kaiteisō," 137.

served as a "repository of the past," standing for tradition when men were encouraged to change their way of politics and culture in all ways.[73] In contrast, the Modern Girl served critics who wanted to preserve rather than challenge traditions during a time of sweeping cultural change.

The Modern Girl as un-Japanese and therefore criminal was the real subtext to such press headlines as "Modern Girls Swept out of Ministry of Railroads," and "Conquering the *Moga* and *Mobo*." The sensational press coverage in 1925 of the trial of a "vanguard *moga*" in short hair and Western clothing accused of murdering a delinquent foreigner with whom she had been consorting illustrated both sexual and cultural transgression.[74] This story and others like it served a dual function: they registered unease with non-Japanese customs and at the same time denied the existence of the political activity of Japanese women. The Modern Girl's crime, in other words, was a culturally colored crime of passion; it was not a politically motivated thought crime. Thus, a father in the 1920s could beg his leftist son to become a Modern Boy or even a Modern Girl as long as he did not "go red."[75]

The most graphic example of the Modern Girl as cultural transgressor, one that signaled an end to her ubiquitous presence, was presented in a series of ink drawings constituting a history of Japanese mores during the modern era, published in the pages of *Chūō kōron* in 1932. In the first image, a reference to Meiji society, two women in kimono gossip under a parasol as men in Western military garb drive behind them in a horse and carriage. The following five sketches (with only one small exception) elaborate on the demure figure in kimono. Only in the image standing for 1932 does one of four figures wear Western dress; a second reclines decadently on a lounge, and a third sits undemurely with her legs spread and her elbows exposed. It is, however, the illustration accompanying the title of this piece of image-journalism that reveals the intensity with which tradition was being defended by the early 1930s. Alongside the painterly calligraphy of the title is a woman in kimono sheathed in fur; above her head is a large gun, pointed at the characters for "modern traditions" (fig. 11.5).[76]

The Modern Girl stood for a contemporary woman, but, like Naomi,

73. Sharon Sievers, *Flowers in Salt: The Beginnings of Feminist Consciousness in Modern Japan* (Stanford: Stanford University Press, 1983), 17, quoting Hanna Papanek's theory.

74. Satō, "Modanizumu," 41–42. I do not agree with Satō's notion of a two-stage development of the term "Modern Girl," which would have her stand first for Western customs and then later for criminal actions. The positive and pejorative connotations of her transgressions from the mid-1920s into the 1930s must, I think, be further explored.

75. Ichikawa Koichi, "Ryūkōka ni miru modanizumu to ero guro nansensu," in Minami (ed.), *Nihon modanizumu*, 267.

76. Itō Shunsui, "Jidai fūzoku e toki," *Chūō kōron*, April 1932.

時代風俗粧ひとつ　伊東深水

Fig. 11.5. From *Chūō kōron*, April 1932.

she was also an emblem for threats to tradition, just as the Good Wife and Wise Mother had stood for its endurance: To talk about the Modern Girl was to talk about Modernity. During the 1920s, her defenders, who saw her at the vanguard of a new imperial reign—the Shōwa era— were optimistic. One, who placed her appearance at 1926, saw her evolving toward complete fulfillment. This journalist predicted that future historians writing the history of prewar men and women in Japan would call the year when the term *modan gaaru* appeared in magazines and newspapers "1 A.D."[77] But such forecasts did not prove true. By the outset of the Pacific War, boundaries reifying gender and culture (and denying class) were imposed as women were legally forbidden to dress in men's clothing, women's magazines were placed under tight controls, all vestiges of Western decadence, including permanent waves, were outlawed, and intellectuals expounded on "the overcoming of modernity."

Only further research will show to what extent the Modern Girl, whose identity in our historical representations has been split into the dual images of a Working Woman and a middle-class adolescent at play, expressed a new set of gestures. Such work could explicate how Japanese men and women during the 1920s and 1930s translated expressions and actions experienced in such sites as the Hollywood movie into their own class cultures in the course of their daily lives. For now we can conclude that confusions and fantasies about class, gender, and culture were projected onto the Modern Girl before she was displaced by yet another embodiment of the Good Wife and Wise Mother, characterized by renewed ties of filiation with "tradition," state, and patriarchy.

77. Kitamura, "Kaiteisō," 139, used the term completion (*kansei*) to connote fulfillment. Regarding the notion of periodization see Kiyosawa, "Modan gaaru no kenkyū," 158.

TWELVE

Doubling Expectations: Motherhood and Women's Factory Work Under State Management in Japan in the 1930s and 1940s

Yoshiko Miyake

Why did the Japanese government resist mobilizing women for war work despite the acute labor shortage that resulted when male workers were drafted during the Pacific War? It was not until August 1944, when a scarcity of raw materials and a series of air raids had already interrupted production, that the wartime cabinet decided to implement compulsory conscription of women for the munitions industry. Even then, the conscription ordinance applied only to widows and unmarried women between the ages of twelve and forty and specifically excluded those women "pivotal [*konjiku*] to a family"[1]—that is, women in their procreative years whose roles as housewives and mothers were indispensable for family cohesion. The mobilization of Japanese women for war work, while "greater than in the case of Germany . . . [was] far less than the strenuous effort in Britain."[2]

1. "Joshi kinrōdōin no sokushin ni kansuruken" (Jikankaigi kettei) (September 13, 1943), in *Nihon fujin mondai shiryō shūsei*, vol. 3: *Rōdō*, ed. Akamatsu Ryōko (Domesu Shuppan, 1977), 478–80.

2. Jerome Cohen, *Japan's Economy in War and Reconstruction* (Minneapolis: University of Minnesota Press, 1949), 272. Mobilization of women in Great Britain was more comprehensive than in any other belligerent country except Soviet Russia. Under the mandatory registration of women between the ages of eighteen and fifty, women were required to work at least part time. To facilitate the mobilization of married women, the government took such major steps as the relocation of war factories to areas where labor reserves were available, the establishment of day-care facilities, the provision of canteen services, and the elimination of the requirement that professional women retire upon marriage. As a result, out of a total of 17.25 million women between fourteen and sixty-four years of age, about 7.3 million worked either in paid employment or were drafted

The failure to utilize women's labor effectively in armaments production illustrates the dilemma faced by the Japanese government, torn as
it was between the need to produce more weapons and the need to re-
produce more men for combat and colonization. This reason alone,
however, is inadequate to explain why public policy in wartime Japan
limited women's role primarily to childbearing.[3] In this chapter I argue
that the Japanese government, like other nationalist dictatorships during the Second World War, promoted population growth not only to
assure a supply of soldiers and colonists for imperialist expansion, but
also to associate ideas of fecundity and productivity with the power of
the state.[4] In the case of Japan, the government assigned women to reproductive roles for the primary purpose of revitalizing the family system, which formed the basis for the ideology of Japanese nationalism,
known as *kazoku kokkakan* (family-state ideology). The government's pro-

into auxiliary military service. See Alva Myrdal and Viola Klein, *Women's Two Roles: Home
and Work* (London: Routledge & Kegan Paul, 1956), 51–54.

In the United States, the mobilization of women was set into motion after the bombardment of Pearl Harbor. At the wartime peak in July 1944, 19 million women were employed, an increase of 47 percent over the March 1940 level. The increase in the wartime
labor force was marked by the recruitment of a great number of married women, since
the reserve of single women had been exhausted by 1943. Now, for the first time in American women's labor history, married women outnumbered single women in the work
force. To promote the recruitment of women workers, many discriminatory practices
were temporarily suspended. See Karen Anderson, *Wartime Women* (Westport, Conn.:
Greenwood Press, 1981); Ruth Milkman, *Gender at Work* (Urbana: University of Illinois
Press, 1987); and Sherna Gluck, *Rosie the Riveter Revisited* (Boston: Twayne, 1987).

In Germany, the official Nazi image of women as "Mothers of the *Volk*" prevented the
wartime government from systematically mobilizing women's labor, as in the United States
and Great Britain. (From the mid-1930s, about 7 million women were in the work force.)
Even when the labor shortage became acute, Germany managed to compensate by introducing a large number of foreign workers, although some women were unofficially mobilized for war work. See Leila Rupp, *Mobilizing Women for War: German and American Propaganda, 1939–1945* (Princeton: Princeton University Press, 1978); Renate Bridenthal,
Atina Grossman, and Marion Kaplan, eds., *When Biology Became Destiny: Women in Weimar
and Nazi Germany* (New York: Monthly Review Press, 1984); Renate Bridenthal, "Beyond
Kinder, Küche, Kirche: Weimar Women at Work," *Central European History* 6, no. 2 (June
1973).

3. See Thomas Havens, "Women and War in Japan, 1937–45," *American Historical Review* 80 (June–December 1975). Because the author fails to locate the history of the family
system from the mid-Meiji forward within the dynamics of patriarchy, his argument examining the state's control of women's reproductive roles goes no deeper than a description of conflicting policies toward women.

4. See the papers on racially selective pronatalism and the restructuring of gender
roles employed by the Nazi, Franco, Mussolini, and Chiang Kai-shek regimes, presented
at the conference "Women in 'Dark Times': Private Life and Public Policy Under Five
Nationalist Dictatorships in Europe and Asia, 1930–1950" (organized by Claudia Koonz
and held in Bellagio, Italy, in 1987). This chapter is a revised version of the paper presented at that conference.

natalist policy at a time when women's labor was desperately needed resulted in a dichotomized view of women's roles: women were treated either as mothers to be mobilized on a mass scale in patriotic associations or as draft labor to be organized in munitions factories. These two roles, however, shared the same origin: the state's definition of the woman's place.

Throughout Japan's modern history, as in other industrializing Western societies, there has been an interaction between two kinds of female labor as women's reproductive roles shaped their productive roles, and vice versa.[5] This is true of women's work in farm households, where the majority of women in the prewar population lived, as well as of women's work in the industrial labor force. Women did not choose either of these roles on their own; rather, their options were manipulated by the state. Because women's reproductive roles were integral to the preservation of the family system, which was the basis of the state's rule, the state promoted the slogan *ryōsai kenbo* ("good wife, wise mother") to advertise women's importance in the home. At the same time, the process of industrialization, promoted in another slogan, *fukoku kyōhei* ("rich country, strong army"), drew from the countryside a great number of single young women who were only temporary workers destined to marry and become reproducers of the next generation of the family system. Any attempt to analyze women's roles in modern Japan, therefore, should integrate these two kinds of women's work—reproductive and productive—and show how they interacted. By examining this interaction we can see how women's housework, stemming from their reproductive roles, provided the basis for reproducing the social relations of the capitalist mode of production.

The analysis of women's role in the modern period should also include the changing and occasionally competing demands of capitalism and the state, for whereas industry demanded women's cheap labor, the state looked on women's increasing entry into the work force as a potential threat to the institution of the Japanese stem family (*ie*), which was expected to buttress the ruling order.[6] In wartime, these competing demands proved irreconcilable. The state failed to balance women's two roles; indeed, although women were enjoined to produce more children, the population did not immediately grow, and although women

5. Louise A. Tilly and Joan W. Scott, *Women, Work, and Family* (New York: Holt Rinehart & Winston, 1978), explores women's entry into the industrial labor force, viewed from the interaction between their domestic and reproductive functions and productive labor during the course of French and British industrialization.

6. See "Joshi kyōiku ni kansuru rinji kyōiku kaigi no tōshin," a report published by the *Rinji Kyōiku Kaigi* (Special Commission on Education) in 1918, reprinted in *Nihon fujin mondai shiryō shūsei*, vol. 4: *Kyōiku*, ed. Mitsui Tametomo (Domesu Shuppan, 1975), 513–16.

were mobilized to work in factories, the economy did not meet wartime production needs. Moreover, the unmarried women who were drawn into the factories were forced to work grueling hours under miserable conditions to make up for the labor shortage. The glorification of motherhood and the victimization of female factory workers were two sides of the same coin.

WOMEN AS SUBJECTS OF THE SHŌWA VERSION OF FAMILY-STATE IDEOLOGY

The family-state structure of the Meiji state first took shape in the 1880s, when family-state ideology advocated the merging of the individual stem family with state power and cast the emperor as the great father of his subjects. This ideology was reflected in both the Meiji Constitution (1889), which defined Japanese people as subjects of the emperor, and the Imperial Rescript on Education (1890), which taught schoolchildren filial piety and loyalty to the state. The implementation of the Meiji Civil Code (1898) gave final legal substance to an ideology that functioned to sustain the patriarchal family as the basic unit of the ruling order of the state. This ideology considered the family to be a part of the state apparatus for exercising power—contrary to the notion in civil society that the family is a "private" institution.

By the 1920s, however, family-state ideology was on the wane. Capitalist economic development after the mid-Meiji period had undermined the *ie* as a kinship organization and as a labor organization for agricultural production. The development of individualism and the notion of the family as part of the private sphere, and not as a public institution dedicated to state ends, further eroded the family-state concept of the nation. Throughout the 1930s, starting with Japan's military aggression in Manchuria in 1931, the widespread draft of men for the expanding war effort and the migration of labor from the villages had accelerated the loosening of the family system, and as the war effort intensified many villages consisted not of intact families, but mainly of women, with the only males being either the very young or the very old.

In the absence of men, women were called on to mend the weakening family system. In the 1930s, as Kano Masanao points out, the emphasis thus shifted from father to mother.[7] Indeed, *The Cardinal Principles of*

7. Kano Masanao, *Senzen. "Ie" no shisō* (Sōbunsha, 1983). In her chapter, "Ōmikokoro to hahagokoro," in *Josei to tennōsei*, ed. Kanō Mikiyo (Shisō no Kagakusha, 1979), 65–81, Kanō Mikiyo also points out the shift in the discourse on women in wartime journalism, which praised motherhood, in contrast to the focus of the media in the 1920s on sexual equality.

the National Polity (*Kokutai no hongi*, 1937), *The Truth of the Subject* (*Shin-min no michi*, 1941), and *The Guidelines for Home Education* (*Senji katei-kyōiku shidō*, 1942), were all published by the Ministry of Education as a means of advocating the family-state structure of Japanese society and emphasizing woman's crucial role in preserving the family system. According to these documents, woman's role in preserving the family system was a crucial analogue to the male role of soldier fighting the "sacred war" for the Japanese family-state. Whereas the late Meiji government had strengthened the legal power of the father as household head and played up his role as rigid moral authority (following the definition in the Meiji Civil Code), the Shōwa version of family-state ideology, in an attempt to preserve the cohesion of the family system, focused on the imagery of fecundity and warmth of blood relations associated with mothers. The popular image of a soldier fighting well to die calmly, encouraged by his benevolent mother, conveyed a pervasive message to the Shōwa people: Imperial Japan would exist forever as long as her family system continued. The state's pronatalist policy thus acknowledged the instrumentality of motherhood as a means to preserve and revitalize a family system on the wane. During the war, in short, a dominant view of women emerged in terms of their "motherhood-in-the-interest-of-the-state" (*kokkateki bosei*).[8]

Women were called on to serve the state in a number of ways. First, they were urged to have large families. Government propaganda, expressed in such slogans as "Be Fruitful and Multiply for the Prosperity of the Nation," was intended to make women more willing to send their sons to the front in the belief that their honorable deaths would bring recognition to the family. An elderly woman farming in the heart of the Hida mountains commented on her drafted son in the following way:

> I am not sure whether my eldest son was of much help to the corps, but fortunately he has been sent back home safely. I have sent my second son to the service, and I hope he'll fight well for the nation. I wouldn't be regretful even if he gets killed at the front, since he is the second son. I only hope he will do his best. When he left, he said to me, "If I die doing distinguished service at the front, please take my death as an expression of filial piety."[9]

8. Nakajima Kuni renames the emerging discourse on motherhood in this period "motherhood-in-the-interest-of-the-state" (which refers to the title of Mori Yasuko's book, published in 1945). Nakajima argues that the state's direct control over motherhood had its roots in the mid-Meiji concept of *ryōsai kenbo*; see Nakajima Kuni, "Kokkateki bosei—senjika no boseikan," in *Kōza: Joseigaku*, ed. Joseigaku Kenkyūkai (Keisō Shobō, 1984), vol. 1: *Onna no imēji*, 235–63.

9. Ema Mieko, *Hida no onnatachi* (Mikuni Shobō, 1942), 31. Ema's ethnography of women in the Hida mountains—where joint families accommodating several generations

In short, her first son's duty was to be the family's heir and preserve their lineage, but other sons could satisfy their duty to the family by nobly serving the state.

In addition to encouraging women's fertility through propaganda and awards for women who had borne numerous children, the government drew women into the service of the state by organizing them into a variety of government-sponsored patriotic associations. Neighborhood associations (*tonari gumi*), composed of five households, were created after the 1938 National Mobilization Law (Kokka Sōdōin Hō) as the smallest unit of state administration, designed to buttress the declining family system in urban areas by exerting more control over the private lives of families. They relied on women for daily wartime activities, such as food rationing and fire drills in the event of air raids. Patriotic associations were unified in 1942 into a single Greater Japan Women's Association (Dainihon Fujinkai), which, only one year after its creation, numbered as many as nineteen million female members over the age of twenty.[10]

The most significant effort to promote the state's discourse on women was the Mother-Child Protection Law (Boshi Hogo Hō) in 1937. This first maternal protection law in Japan was aimed at helping poor, single mothers raise children less than thirteen years old by providing welfare and medical assistance and the like.[11] In the face of escalating mother-child suicides during the years of deepening economic depression, the government decided to legislate aid to single mothers by responding to the feminist demand for maternity protection legislation,

lived under one roof, unaffected by the rapid industrialization that was sweeping the nation—reflected the wartime discourse on women. That is, she glorified women as mothers by linking them to the fertile soil and life energies. The dignity, self-confidence, and benevolence emanating from the mistress of the joint family in the nostalgic world that had been lost was much more attractive to the readers than the feminist slogan of sexual equality and individualism.

10. Mitsui Reiko, ed., *Gendai fujin undōshi nenpyō* (Sanichi Shobō, 1963), 169. Concerning the history of the patriotic women's associations dating back to 1901, see Chino Yōichi, *Kindai Nihon fujin kyōikushi* (Domesu Shuppan, 1980). Fujii Tadatoshi, *Kokubō fujinkai* (Iwanami Shoten, 1983), documents the history of a major wartime women's patriotic association.

11. This legislation opened up an avenue for rescuing illegitimate children by undermining conservative forces that insisted on preserving the family system as defined in the Meiji Civil Code. From mid-Taishō to 1939, attempts to revise the Civil Code aimed at closing the gap between, on the one hand, the notions of the family and marriage as they had been shaped in people's lives and, on the other, their definition in family register laws established in the Meiji period. During the war, the status of a common-law wife and her illegitimate child became an issue in determining who was entitled to receive death benefits of military personnel killed in battle. To relieve drafted men of the anxieties over their own families at home, the government carried out a series of reforms that recognized de facto marriage practices. The Mother-Child Protection Law came into existence in this historical context.

first voiced in 1934. The government's rapid drafting of such laws shows the state's awakening concern with women as mothers.[12]

The shift to a mother-centered family ideology is important for a number of reasons. First, it demonstrates the changing nature of family-state ideology: the Shōwa version was not merely a revival of the Meiji version. It also helps revise the one-sided picture of the operation of family-state ideology conceived by postwar scholars, who have associated it solely with coercive state power, expressed in such forms as the compulsory military draft and the deaths of soldiers at the front, or in the efforts of the thought police (tokkō) to eliminate "unpatriotic, dangerous thoughts." The distorted picture results from the analytical emphasis of conventional studies on the political and economic aspects of this period, to the neglect of the family and women. An analysis of the history of the family and women's position, however, helps to explain why women became the target of state policies that appeared solicitous and benevolent when seen against the violence and repression elsewhere in the society.

In addition, study of the state's female-centered ideology provides insights into the reasons why feminists collaborated with war policies.[13] Ichikawa Fusae, who had led the Women Suffragist's League (Fusen Kakutoku Dōmei), played a significant role in mobilizing women after 1937. How ironic that someone who led a movement against the state to claim women's rights ended up rallying women around the idea of serving that state! Yet the state's emphasis on women as the subjects of family-state ideology appeared to Ichikawa and other women as a step forward in their fight for sexual equality, because "for the first time"[14] women were being given an officially acknowledged role outside the home—even if that role merely allowed them to join patriotic associa-

12. In 1926 the government had named similar legislation "Child Relief Law" with the word "mother" eliminated. See Fukushima Shirō's editorial "Boshi hogo hō gikai tsūka," *Shūkan fujo shinbun*, March 28, 1937, reprinted in *Nihon fujin mondai shiryō shūsei*, vol. 2: *Seiji*, ed. Ichikawa Fusae (Domesu Shuppan, 1977), 491–92. See chap. 8 in this volume for a discussion of the debate over the protection of motherhood in the early Taishō period.

13. Numerous leftist men, Kano Masanao argues, both voluntarily and involuntarily collaborated with state policies, but in these cases the motives for collaboration were more individualistic, and cannot be explained by a single interpretation. By contrast, the analysis of women's cooperation with state policies, as he suggests, required that the state focus on women in order to organize the home front. See Kano Masanao, "Fasshizumuka no fujin-undō: Fusen kakutoku dōmei no baai," in *Kindai nihon no kokka to shisō*, ed. Ienaga Saburō Kyōju Tōkyō Kyōiku Daigaku Taikan Kinenronshu Kankō Iinkai (Sanseidō, 1979), 306–27.

14. As the construction of the *ryōsai kenbo* ideal for women's education shows, the Meiji state acknowledged women's role as mothers and housewives in maintaining the family system. But in public life, women were excluded from all legal and political rights enjoyed by men. Wartime feminists viewed the pronatalist policies as the "state's first recognition of women's roles" in society.

Fig. 12.1. Housewives entertaining off-duty soldiers. The women wear white aprons and sashes emblazoned with the name of a major women's patriotic association. (Courtesy of Marujusha)

tions and to come out to the train stations to send soldiers off to the front. Moreover, in the 1930s and 1940s the state was acknowledging women as mothers and for the first time was asking for their cooperation.

The state was also able to seduce women in part because feminists produced no systematic critique of the imperial system, a critique that would have worked against collaboration. For example, when Kōra Tomi was called to the National Cooperation Council (Kokumin Chūō Kyōryoku Kaigi; also called the Family Council, Kazoku Kaigi), which was established in conjunction with the Imperial Rule Assistance Association (Taisei Yokusankai) in 1940, she expressed her joy this way: "I greatly appreciate the honor bestowed upon women by the invitation [as family members] to this historically significant family council. I am grateful for the emperor's mercy in permitting women who have been insignificant and useless to attend the council meeting to present their views of women and children."[15]

Flattered by the state's attention, feminists took the initiative by helping to organize women on the home front, recruiting them for the

15. Cited in Suzuki Yūko, *Feminizumu to sensō: Fujinundōka no sensō kyōryoku* (Marujusha, 1986), 58–59.

Greater Japan Women's Association, mobilizing them for factory work, and urging them to save money or to buy war bonds. In so doing, they thought that they could demonstrate women's abilities.[16]

Mori Yasuko, who wrote *Motherhood in the Interest of the State* (*Kokkateki bosei no kōzō*) in 1945, was one of the women deceived by the state's recognition of women as mothers. Unlike feminists who worked in the political arena in wartime, she was an unknown academic studying German philosophy, and therefore her book, which strongly echoed the state's appeal to women to be patriotic mothers for a "sacred war," has gone largely unnoticed.[17] Yet a careful reading of her account reveals the way in which she and other feminists succumbed to the state's instrumental use of women.

Mori had begun her pursuit of the goal of gender equality "under the influence of liberalism in the last years of Taishō."[18] Yet, like other feminists, she was mistaken about the state's commitment to motherhood (not to mention her flawed interpretation of Japan's war of aggression against China starting in 1931 and the ensuing Pacific War as a "sacred war"), and she was inspired to formulate the thesis that women could gain social recognition by becoming mothers and carrying on the historical mission assigned by the state.

According to Mori, women were progressing on the road to liberation in the 1930s and 1940s because the state had given them the task of restructuring the family system. In contrast to the women suffragists of the 1920s, Mori argued for preserving the status quo by retaining the family system, with women at the center of that family. Her analysis was rooted in distinctions between femininity and masculinity that were, in turn, based on anatomical differences. Women and men, she believed, both played indispensable roles comparable to the base and apex of a triangle: the base could not take form without the apex, and the apex could not stand without the base. Given their reproductive roles, women were at the base of the triangle, providing daily order and stability, while men, as the apex with their adventurous and innovative tendencies, gave shape to the family.

This argument was relatively progressive regarding woman's status, in the sense that it saw women's and men's roles in the family as equally important.[19] Writing at a historical turning point for Imperial Japan—

16. Ichikawa Fusae, *Ichikawa Fusae jiden: Senzenhen* (Shinjuku Shobō, 1978), 434–35.

17. See Miyake Yoshiko, "Ningen no ne wa kazoku no naka de tsuchikawareru—Mizoue (Mori) Yasuko-san ni kiku," in *Joshi kyōiku mondai* 11 (1982): 174–85. This article is the first critical review of Mizoue's failed attempt to create a woman-centered analysis of the family.

18. Mori Yasuko, *Kokkateki bosei no kōzō* (Dōbunkan, 1945), 1.

19. This view was propagated to improve women's status, which had been defined by the Confucian notion that women were inferior to men simply because they were born

the start of the Pacific War—Mori pressed for the utilization of half of the human resources that had been wasted by the Confucian assertion of women's inferiority. The starting point for reform, she suggested, was the restructuring of gender relations within the family. The problem, however, lay in Mori's view of the father. As a representative of the state's rationality, from which stemmed the morals and ethics shaping human behavior, he was to shape the family. Since the Japanese family was a miniature of the state, without the father's role individual families could not merge with the state and, therefore, could not be considered part of the society. By describing the father in such terms as "the revered commander to deliver the state's rationality" and the mother as "the loyal subject," Mori's argument lost whatever democratic, egalitarian overtones it may potentially have had. Moreover, to elaborate on her view of the woman's role in the family, she revived all the old female virtues, such as self-sacrifice, subservience, and benevolence—words that only highlighted the image of the rigid moral father as a reincarnation of the state's will. Embellished with the old-fashioned language used in the Meiji period to create loyal Japanese subjects and subservient women—for example, "women must be modest" and "each one must do his or her own duty as a subject of the emperor"—her discourse on motherhood in the interest of the state ultimately extolled benevolent mothers loyal to the state's dictates.

Although Mori's book harked back to certain themes familiar in Meiji ideology, there were several significant differences. For one thing, Mori's image of the benevolent mother was not an exact replica of the mid-Meiji ideal, for she emphasized that the female and male roles were equivalent in value (although, it is true, she also described subservient mothers as responsive to the dictates of moral fathers).[20] In other words,

---

female. Contrary to the views of many writers in later years, *ryōsai kenbo* was not synonymous with Confucian teachings about women and was not a legacy of feudalism. The term, as used in discussions among intellectuals, such as members of the Meirokusha (Meiji Six Society), meant the creation of a new womanhood suitable for Japan's modern society. However, its meaning was distorted when Confucianism became an official doctrine in the mid-Meiji period. The *ryōsai kenbo* ideal thereafter taught women the virtue of subservience to men and confined them within the family. Relatively progressive educators then explored ways to raise women's status within the family by restructuring gender relations based on sexual differences rather than challenging the family system. See *Meiroku Zasshi: Journal of the Japanese Enlightenment*, translated and with an introduction by William R. Braisted (Cambridge, Mass.: Harvard University Press, 1976).

20. For Mori, this argument was not contradictory. She reinterpreted the traditional ethic of maternal self-effacement in a positive light because she viewed motherhood as the highest expression of women's potential. In her view, even though women were *seemingly* subservient to the dictates of moral fathers, this was not because they were inferior; instead it was the expression of confidence and strength, gained through motherhood. This sort of argument was accessible to the Japanese reader familiar with the common wisdom

in the Meiji version of family-state ideology, the morality of the father was superior in value to the mother's benevolence, but in the Shōwa version the virtues of benevolence and moral rectitude were equally important. Moreover, Shōwa mothers were in Mori's view raised in status because they were publicly recognized by pronatalist policies. The Shōwa mother was regarded as the mother of the nation, while the Meiji mother had been recognized merely as the mother *within* the family. Mori's woman-centered analysis demonstrated that women had become the cornerstone of the family system in this period, a perspective epitomized by such statements as "The family community in its structure can be compared to a mother's body" and "It is the mother who lays the foundation for the family."[21]

Mori's redefinition of the female role captures the history of the Japanese women's movement in the prewar period. Rather than challenging a family system that supported the male-centered, authoritarian state, she decided to support the status quo of the family system and to redefine women's role within it. Instead of opposing state ideology, she embraced the idea of women serving the state, as long as the state recognized this service and rewarded it with praise. In this way, Mori and other feminists joined the chorus glorifying the image of motherhood that the state had created, and guided women to take up their positions on the home front. Now that the state had recognized women's maternal contributions as comparable to soldiers' contributions, women willingly demonstrated their capabilities.

WOMEN'S REPRODUCTIVE ROLES:
REVITALIZING THE FAMILY SYSTEM

In the "Outline for Establishing Population Growth Policy" (*Jinkō seisaku kakuritsu yōkō*), written in January 1941 and issued the next year, women's reproductive roles were brought under the direct control of the state.[22] As a tentacle of family-state ideology, the "Outline" extended into the intimate areas of women's lives, constituting them as loyal subjects of Imperial Japan.

Before examining this document, we need to take a brief look at the process by which this pronatalist policy came into effect. In the National Mobilization Law of 1938, which organized the home front, article 1

expressed in such proverbs as "A talented person knows to be modest" and "Still waters run deep."

21. Mori, *Kokkateki bosei*, 228.

22. Kōseishō Jinkōkyoku, "Jinkō seisaku kakuritsu yōkō" (1942), reprinted in *Nihon Fujin mondai shiryō shūsei*, vol. 6: *Hoken: Fukushi*, ed. Ichibangase Yasuko (Domesu Shuppan, 1978), 166–68.

defined national mobilization as "the policy for controlling resources both human and material in order to make efficient use of them." The Welfare Ministry, established two months before this law, was geared toward achieving the same goals, in compliance with the strong wishes of the military authorities. The Ministry of Welfare took the initiative in promoting the slogan "Healthy Nation, Sturdy Soldiers," and in allocating the work force for production of wartime necessities—even though its declared aim was to better national welfare.

The Ministry of Welfare issued two important mandates in sequence in 1940 and 1941. One was the National Eugenics Law (Kokumin Yūsei Hō, established in 1940 and promulgated in 1941), and the other was the "Outline for Establishing Population Growth Policy." The National Eugenics Law demonstrated the state's determination to secure "quality control" of the population by providing two significant stipulations: the sterilization of those identified as having hereditary diseases, and the prohibition of birth control for the healthy. The "Outline for Population Policy" begins with a discussion of the urgent importance of increasing the quality of the population in the name of the imperial mission to construct the "Greater East Asian Co-Prosperity Sphere" (*Dai tōa kyōei ken*). It goes on to outline the specific means for increasing the birth rate and decreasing the mortality rate by reducing the average marriage age by three years, to twenty-five for men and twenty-one for women, and by stipulating an average of five children per couple as the goal during the next ten years. The following policies were recommended to increase the domestic population from seventy-three million to one hundred million (excluding Japan's imperial territories) within twenty years:

1. The family system should be strengthened and *unsound thoughts eliminated* [emphasis added].
2. Matchmaking or marriage consultation should be actively offered by public bodies or municipal agencies.
3. Marriage expenses should be minimized and a loan system established.
4. The existing school system should be reformed out of consideration for population policies.
5. Girls' high schools and girls' community schools should provide the knowledge and techniques of childrearing and hygienics needed to foster sound mothers who are aware of their national mission of motherhood.
6. Only women under the age of twenty should be employed, and the working conditions and employment conditions that hinder early marriage should be modified or improved.
7. Tax policies should be modified in accordance with population policies. They should be designed to lessen the burden for people with many dependents and to increase taxation on single persons.

8. A family allowance system should be introduced to lessen the burden of medical expenses, education expenses, and other family expenses. For this purpose the state must implement a special budget, called "resources for assisting families with straitened finances."

9. Big families should be given preferential treatment in receiving rationed goods, awards and bonuses.

10. Pregnant women and their babies should receive protection by the systematic improvement of maternity hospitals and baby hospitals. Ways should be devised to secure rationed medical material necessary for childbirth.

11. Artificial methods of birth control, such as contraception and abortion, should be prohibited, and special efforts should be made to eliminate venereal diseases.

The significance of the proposals expressed in the "Outline" can be summarized in the following three points: First, the state implemented a pronatalist policy to revitalize the family system, which was the axis for preserving the ruling order of Imperial Japan. The maintenance of the family system was linked not only to bearing more children, but also to eliminating "unsound" thoughts. This was in harmony with the aim of the Peace Preservation Law (Chian Iji Hō) of 1925, which tightened censorship over "unsound" and "antisocial" liberal and communist thought by adding capital punishment and lifetime imprisonment for such "crimes," along with preventive custody of leftists. Second, by confining women's role to their reproductive capacities, the state denied women the autonomy to define their own destiny by deciding for themselves whether or not to bear children, a choice that had been promoted by the feminist movement since the 1910s. Higher taxation imposed on single persons was one penalty for their failure to contribute to the state's interests. Third, by this population policy the state acquired a rationale for its intervention in "private" issues, such as marriage and birth, and thereby furthered its advocacy of family-state ideology, which merged the private sphere into the public realm.

The ideas included in the "Outline" were promoted by a variety of government-sponsored events. In November 1940, for example, 10,622 families who had produced over ten children were recognized and rewarded for their contribution to national goals. The Ministry of Welfare also issued a report entitled "On the Rewarding of Excellent Families with Many Children" that explained how these families were chosen.[23] They had met demanding criteria: all the children were legitimate and born of the same parents, and none of the children had died except for unavoidable reasons, including war or natural calamities. In the course of selection, the ministry confirmed its recognition of the important role

23. Kōseishō Shakaikyoku, "Yūryō tashi katei no hyōshō ni tsuite," reprinted in ibid., 153–65.

of farming households in producing "human resources": 65 percent of the awardees were farm families. It also turned out that 65 percent were classified as middle income. Half of the mothers were between twenty and twenty-five years old when they gave birth to their first child, and 48 percent were between fifteen and twenty. (The median age difference between husband and wife was five years.) This survey became the basis of ensuing population policies that intervened in people's daily lives. For example, marriage consultation at new public agencies for matchmaking, authoritatively called "Eugenics Marriage Counseling Centers," and publications such as *Ten Instructions for Marriage* (*Kekkon jukkun*) and *Guidelines for Home Life in Wartime* (*Senjika katei seikatsu no kokoroe*) emphasized the significant role of mothers in producing the next generation of Imperial Japan.

How did the women feel when praised as part of the nation's "child-bearing corps" (*kodakara butai*)? One woman said: "Nothing but eleven girls. But I can feel proud of myself for the first time." Another confessed: "I didn't make an effort, but they just came. I am embarrassed to be praised for distinguished service."[24] Despite their embarrassment, they were obviously pleased to have their worth as women recognized. This is understandable, if one considers that in earlier times women had blamed themselves for not preventing more pregnancies than their family's finances could afford. Farm women, despite their important contributions to farming, had been vulnerable to criticism as long as their mothers-in-law were alive, because they were at the bottom of the family hierarchy. Frequent pregnancy slowed down their work and left them open to charges of being too sexually active. With the new pronatalist policy, the state drew out such nameless women and publicly honored them.

The state's recognition of fecund women in wartime Japan invites further speculation. This reward system provided women with an opportunity to reconstitute themselves as subjects of Imperial Japan. Although educated as the emperor's subjects in school, women did not have the same opportunity to relate to the state directly as men did through their military experiences. The state acted on men and women differently to elicit loyalty. Conventional studies of family-state ideology highlight solely the state's coercive power; yet actually, the state used varying modi operandi. The compulsory military draft, the Peace Preservation Law, and the National Eugenics Law represented violence or repression, while the Mother-Child Protection Law ostensibly conveyed a tender, nurturant image. The fecund women honored by the state can be put in the latter category, too, even if what awaited them was news

24. *Tōkyō Asahi* (October 19, 1940) and *Katei* (December 1940), cited in Suzuki Sumuko, "Umeyo sodateyo kuni no tame," in *Jūgoshi nōto*, no. 6, ed. Onnatachi no Ima o Toukai (JCA Shuppan, 1982), 106–7.

of their son's death at the front. Solicitation and violence, benevolence and moral rectitude, reward and punishment, life and death, were all inseparably woven into family-state ideology. With this diversity the state was able to obtain and maintain its full hegemony. The state's intervention into women's reproductive roles by pronatalist policies, in conjunction with other repressive state policies, restructured the family system so that it could function as an arm of the state.

WOMEN'S MOBILIZATION FOR WARTIME PRODUCTION

Although the state hesitated to mobilize women for war work, fearing that the family system might be threatened by the incompatibility of women's reproductive roles and their working life, young single women were finally mobilized in late 1944. The number of married women in the work force also increased, reflecting the need to supplement family income in the face of the spiraling inflation that afflicted the wartime economy.[25] Especially after Japan's entry into the Pacific War in 1941, when the government began indiscriminately drafting skilled male workers, production became increasingly dependent on women workers, as well as on students, Koreans, and some Chinese.[26]

Despite this influx of new workers into heavy industry, however, the government made little effort to help employees adjust to their new work. Although the munitions industry constituted a newly opened work arena for women, the government did not urge employers to provide job training, create work environments appropriate for women, or raise wage levels. In contrast with the mobilization of women workers in Great Britain and the United States, where such incentives as equal pay for equal work were given, in Japan the government sought to inspire women primarily with the slogan of "Labor in the Service of the State."[27] The result was the abuse of women in the workplace.

25. Like Jerome Cohen, who complains of inaccuracies in statistics of this period, I was unable to obtain reliable figures indicating the proportion of married women in the entire female work force. However, the 1928 governmental survey computing married women as one-sixth of the total of female workers suggests the overall progression of the female work force. See Tatewaki Sadayo, *Nihon rōdōfujin mondai* (Domesu Shuppan, 1980), 128.

26. Jerome Cohen, *Japan's Economy*, 308, provides statistics on the estimated supply of laborers to meet planned allocations, 1940–44. "Kyōkō to sensōka ni okeru rōdōryoku shijō no henbo" in Hazama Genzō, ed., *Kōza: Nihon shihonshugi hattatsushiron*, vol. 3: *Kyōkō kara sensō e*, ed. Kawai Ichirō, Kinoshita Etsuji, Kamino Shōichirō, Takahashi Makoto, and Hazama Genzō (Nihon Hyōronsha, 1968), 302–4.

27. Service in a factory was said to be a way for women to cultivate feminine virtues. Kirihara Yoshimi, a labor scientist, argued that schooling alone was not enough for contemporary women to prepare to be good wives, but experience with factory work would equip them for a good marriage. See Kirihara, *Joshi kinrō* (Tōyō Shokan, 1944) and *Senji rōmu kanri* (Tōyō Shokan, 1943).

TABLE 12.1.   Changing Number of Workers by Industry and Sex
(in thousands)

	1931		1936		1941	
	Male	Female	Male	Female	Male	Female
Metals	81	8	232	21	375	50
Machinery	144	10	412	37	1,215	158
Textiles	175	766	232	868	176	723
Miscellaneous	285	59	395	115	487	227
Total	767	886	1,450	1,134	2,496	1,227
	(46.4%)	(53.6%)	(56.1%)	(43.9%)	(66.2%)	(33.8%)

NOTE: Only plants with over five employees are covered.
SOURCE: Tsūsanshō Chōsatōkeibu, *Kōgyō tōkei 50-nenshi, Shiryōhen* 1 (Ryukei Shosha, 1979), cited in Kojima Tsunehisa, *Dokyumento: Hataraku josei 100-nen no ayumi* (Kawade Shobō-shinsha, 1983), 108.

Women first entered heavy industry in the 1930s and early 1940s. Previously, female labor, concentrated almost exclusively in the textile industry, had dominated the modern sector of the economy, with women constituting the majority of all industrial workers. With the shift from light to heavy industry, including heavy machinery, aircraft production, and chemical industries (table 12.1), men became the majority of the industrial labor force. After the start of the war in China in 1937, however, women began performing unskilled jobs in these male-dominated industries, as well as filling the increasing number of clerical jobs that opened up in the Japanese economy as a whole.[28] By February 1944 there were 13,246,000 women in the civilian labor force out of a total 31,657,000 workers (table 12.2). Although the total number of women in the labor force in the following year did not increase by much, the percentage of females rose as a result of the continuing decline in the male labor force.[29]

Tanino Setsu, the first woman factory inspector in Japan, meticulously recorded the changes in women's employment in the 1930s in a series of articles.[30] Her observations, summarized below, provide important information on the situation of women workers in that decade:

1. *Increase in female labor force.* According to a 1935 survey, females made up 36 percent of the total population working in manufacturing,

28. The female clerical work force, only 12.3 percent of all clerical workers in 1937, increased rapidly; by 1942 it had doubled, and by 1947 it had grown about fivefold. See Shimazu Chitose, "Sengo joshirōdō no tokushitsu," in *Kōza: Rōdō mondai to rōdō hō*, vol. 6: *Fujin rōdō*, ed. Ōkōchi Kazuo and Isoda Susumu (Kōbundō, 1956), 57.

29. Mitsui, *Gendai fujin undōshi nenpyō*, 176.

30. These articles, which originally appeared in the late 1930s, are reprinted in Tanino Setsu, *Fujin kōjō kantokukan no kiroku*, 2 vols. (Domesu Shuppan, 1985).

TABLE 12.2. Changing Numbers in Labor Force by Sex and Industry (in thousands)

	Oct. 1, 1930			Oct. 1, 1940			Feb. 22, 1944		
	Total	Male	Female	Total	Male	Female	Total	Male	Female
Agriculture & Forestry	14,131	7,735	6,396	13,842	6,619	7,223	13,376	5,569	7,807
Fishing	568	515	53	543	476	67	464	380	84
Mining	316	217	45	598	529	69	805	681	124
Manufacturing & Construction	5,876	4,428	1,448	8,132	6,178	1,954	9,494	4,743	2,251
Commerce	4,906	3,406	1,500	4,882	3,006	1,876	2,364	1,127	1,237
Transportation & Communication	945	907	38	1,364	1,214	150	1,650	1,385	265
Government & Professional	1,762	1,369	398	2,195	1,515	680	2,900	1,895	1,005
Domestic Service	802	92	710	709	39	670	473	58	415
Miscellaneous	71	64	7	218	154	64	131	73	58
Total Civilian Labor Force	29,377	18,787	10,590	32,483	19,730	12,753	31,657	18,411	13,246
		(64.0%)	(36.0%)		(60.7%)	(39.3%)		(58.2%)	(41.8%)

SOURCE: Ōhara Shakai Mondai Kenkyūjo, Nihon rōdō nenkan: Bekkan Taiheiyō sensōka no rōdōsha jōtai, cited in Kojima Tsunehisa, Dokyumento: Hataraku josei 100-nen no ayumi (Kawade Shobōshinsha, 1983), 120.

mining, and transportation-communication, which demonstrates that women workers were playing a significant role in heavy industry after 1937. In 1939 the rate of increase in the number of women workers was 432 (over a base rate of 100 in 1924), whereas for men the rate was 311. Female employment in the machine industry grew from 9.8 percent of the total work force in 1935 to 13.6 percent in 1939. Notably, women began to engage in such difficult jobs as milling, cutting, turning, and grinding, work that had hitherto been the exclusive province of male mechanics.

2. *Reasons for the increase in women's employment.* According to Tanino, the number of women workers in the 1930s increased for many reasons. In addition to the shortage of male workers, mechanization created numerous unskilled jobs. Tanino argued that women were suited for repetitious, unskilled work owing to their biological and psychological characteristics; thus, the mass production system at munitions factories was amenable to women's labor. Furthermore, employers quickly lost their fear of an excess of female workers in the labor force. Indeed, they saw them as leverage to reduce the wage standards for male workers. Because most women participated in the industrial work force to earn supplementary income before marriage, employers could hold women's wages down. For example, in an engine plant the daily wage for twelve-year-old females and males started with forty sen for the former and fifty sen for the latter. The longer an employee worked, the more the wage differential increased. Similarly, when war production ceased employers could send women home without causing an unemployment problem. Finally, women were motivated to work in the machine industry out of the patriotism stimulated by wartime conditions.

3. *Changing composition of the female work force.* The majority of women workers in the machine industry were twenty years of age; 17.3 percent of them were married. In workplaces that required a degree of physical labor, most of the employees were married women. In the machine industry, female workers were mainly the daughters of merchants, artisans, white-collar workers, and industrial workers in urban areas, whereas in the textile industry they had been recruited from the countryside. This difference in background explains differences in their living situations: most workers in the machine industry commuted from home, whereas textile workers tended to live in company-run dormitories.

4. *High turnover of women workers in the machine industry.* The high turnover rate of females in the machine industry (47 percent quit within six months) was caused by hazardous working conditions and a long workday that sometimes amounted to eleven or twelve hours with only a thirty-minute lunch break. Many women complained of difficulties

with their menstruation, including irregularity and cramps due to stand-up work over long hours. As a result, the machine industry was characterized by a higher rate of absenteeism and more reports of sickness and injuries than the textile industry, which, by the 1930s, had improved working conditions in response to growing public concern over mill owners' arbitrary exploitation of their female workers.

Based on these observations, Tanino, in a 1940 article, appealed to employers to reform women's working conditions, arguing for job training, higher wages, and the delineation of certain work as inappropriate for women out of consideration for their future childbearing functions.[31] Yet despite her pleas, during the next five years until the end of the war working conditions for women continued to decline, even though the number of women workers in heavy industry increased. (Men's working conditions declined as well.) Throughout 1942, the average workday was recorded as eleven hours (in 1931, when Japan had not yet recovered from the depression, it had been reduced to ten hours). Workers' real wages continued to decline owing to spiraling inflation, plummeting in 1941 to 79.1 percent of the 1934–36 average, and in 1945 to 41.2 percent.[32] The decline continued throughout the late 1940s during the economic rehabilitation period following the war, with workers' living standards becoming even worse.

In addition to this general deterioration in working conditions, women suffered both a discriminatory wage rate amounting to 30.6 percent of male wages and special hardships resulting from their lack of training for their assigned jobs.[33] After Japan's entrance into the Pacific War, the government redeployed both male and female workers to designated "important industries," such as iron and steel, mining, and aircraft- and shipbuilding, and away from such "nonessential industries" as textiles. In 1943, still facing a labor shortage, the government decided to mobilize women for heavy industry. The National Railroads took the lead in hiring women, immediately increasing the number of female employees from 20,000 to 100,000.[34] Women not only took over as ticket examiners, but also worked as switchmen, replacing men who had been drafted for military service. Also in 1943, the government issued a special ordinance eliminating clauses in the 1923 Factory Act, which had prohibited women or children under sixteen years of age

31. Tanino Setsu, *Joshirōdō ni kansuru hōkoku* (Shōwa Kenkyūkai, 1940), reprinted in ibid., 131–78.

32. *Gendai Nihon shihonshugi taikei* 4:97, cited in Kojima, Tsunehisa, *Hataraku josei no 100-nen ayumi* (Kawade Shobōshinsha, 1983), 122.

33. Kawahigashi Eiko, "Nihon shihonshugi to joshi rōdō," in *Joshi rōdōron*, ed. Takenaka Emiko (Yūhikaku, 1983), 84.

34. Mitsui, *Gendai fujin undōshi nenpyō*, 173.

from working in hazardous, harmful jobs and from taking night shifts
from 10:00 P.M. to 4:00 A.M. (Wartime Special Ordinance for the Factory Act, or Senjika Kōjōhō Tokurei). Women could now engage in the
most dangerous pit work in mines (in fact, they had begun to work in
the pits as early as 1940).[35] As a result, the number of women employed
in mining dramatically increased from 25,000 in 1936 to 120,000 in
1944.[36] The Wartime Factory Act also revived women's night work,
which had been prohibited after a twenty-year-long struggle by progressive bureaucrats, labor reformers, and trade unionists to regulate
textile entrepreneurs, who had wanted to run the mills twenty-four
hours a day.

Numerous injuries and deaths resulted from the substitution of female workers lacking adequate training.[37] According to Tanino's survey,
moreover, the female workers who took sick leave for tuberculosis accounted for some twenty-six out of every thousand workers in heavy
industry, a higher rate than in the textile industry.[38] As organizing efforts were suppressed, workers had no choice but either to succumb to
employers' dictates for a long workday and dangerous jobs or to quit.[39]
Quitting was the only possible expression of resistance for workers who
were deprived, by a series of administrative ordinances, of the freedom
to move from job to job.[40]

The working conditions in the textile industry before the passage of
the factory act were sufficiently deplorable to create great concern
among reformers. Then, however, the issue had only affected girls
of country origin, whereas in the 1930s and 1940s the new workers
were women from urban families; for this reason working conditions for women became a topic of widespread popular discussion,
as reflected in a series of publications on the management of women

35. Tanino, *Fujin kōjō kantokukan*, 129.
36. Kojima, *Hataraku onna*, 117. The number of female mine workers dropped between 1930 and 1936 but rose steeply thereafter.
37. Mitsui, *Gendai fujin undōshi nenpyō*, 173.
38. In 1913, in his classic publications *Kokka eiseigakujō kara mitaru jokō no kenkō mondai*
and *Jokō to kekkaku*, Ishihara Osamu, M.D., called public attention to the high death rate
among women operatives. According to his calculation, twenty-three of one thousand operatives died of tuberculosis every year—more than three times the rate of the general
public in corresponding age brackets. This investigation forced the implementation of the
1911 Factory Act.
39. The Sanpō Association (Sangyō Hōkokukai) was formed in 1940, based on a broad
coalition of workers' representatives, bureaucrats, politicians, and intellectuals, along with
some managers. Rather than advocating workers' rights, it promoted harmony in the
workplace and industrial service to the nation.
40. See Hattori Eitarō, "Kokubō kokka to shakai seisaku no dōkō: Rōdōryoku haichi
ni kanrenshite," *Kaizō* 9, no. 8 (August 1940): 49–59.

workers.[41] Some authors, for example, brought up the issue of equal pay for equal work as an incentive for raising production.[42] But it is questionable whether this discussion actually benefited women workers.[43] Rather, the idea of "service for the nation" justified many employers' efforts to further drive workers without improving working conditions.

The 1942 Control of Management of Important Plants Ordinance (Jūyō Jigyōjō Rōmu Kanri Rei) illustrates the government's tendency to separate maternity protection from women's overall working conditions. The impetus for this policy was concern with population growth.[44] The ordinance obligated the employer to set up day-care facilities in plants with over two hundred workers, if the Welfare Minister deemed it necessary. The government's lead in providing working women with day-care facilities paralleled similar attempts in rural areas across the country in order both to raise productivity and to alleviate infant mortality.[45] Curiously, however, the first maternity protection ordinance for working women contained a clause that waived regulations governing work hours for women and children under sixteen who were doing hazardous jobs.[46]

This inconsistency in government policy regarding women's labor ran through most state policies of this period. The government was

41. Nakajima Kuni notes that both the discussion of women's labor and their mobilization peaked in 1943, with a considerable number of publications describing ways to manage female workers being published in this period. In addition, the greatest number of publications with the word "women" in their titles was published in wartime Japan. See Nakajima, "Senjika no boseiron: Joshi kinrōdōin tono kanren de," in *Namae Yoshio sensei kanreki kinen rekishi ronshū kankōkai* (Namae Yoshio Sensei Kanreki Kinen Rekishi Ronshū Henshū Iinkai, 1978), 117–118.

42. Kirihara Yoshimi, *Joshi kinrō*, 251, for example, argued that equal pay for equal work was unrealistic because women's physical strength was not comparable to men's. He emphasized that if women improved their job skills in order to serve satisfactorily in the workplace, employers would recognize their abilities and so raise wages (although contemporary women workers were not seen as working for money).

43. For example, according to a report on thirty-one factories inspected by the police office, only three had sufficient toilet facilities for women, three had some but not enough, and the rest were not equipped at all. See Murakami Nobuhiko, *Nihon no fujin mondai* (Iwanami Shoten, 1978), 171.

44. See Satō Akiko, "Joshi kinrōdōin no jittai," in *Jūgōshi nōto*, no. 8 (1983), 250–53; and Mitsui, *Gendai fujin undōshi nenpyō*, 171.

45. Day-care facilities for the busy farming season increased to 16,538 in 1938, compared to 4,882 in 1933; Tatewaki Sadayo, *Nihon no fujin* (Iwanami Shoten, 1957), 149. In 1934 the government also increased the number of visiting health workers in charge of maternity care, in order to lower the world's highest stillbirth rate of 1.7 deaths per 1,000 population.

46. Satō, "Joshi kinrōdōin," 252; and Mitsui, *Gendai fujin undōshi nenpyō*, 171.

apparently unable to devise methods for raising productivity other than by neglecting working conditions. Yet the end result of exploiting unskilled labor was to reduce still further the efficiency of production. Faced with this dilemma, the government merely continued to appeal to women to devote themselves all the more to the state.[47]

MILITARY CONSCRIPTION OF WOMEN

The contradiction between the two different tasks of preserving the family system and solving the labor shortage was also apparent in the military conscription of women. By the end of 1941, the conscription of unmarried women between the ages of fourteen and twenty-five, as well as of men between fourteen and forty, became legally possible through a series of ordinances (the Revised Work Registration Ordinance, the Control of Turnover Ordinance, the Revised People's Conscription Ordinance, and so on). At this point, however, women were urged only to organize themselves into patriotic labor corps (*aikoku hōkokutai*) to assist with war work at school, in the workplace, and in the neighborhood. Women were also obliged to do thirty days' factory work a year (the Ordinance for Cooperation with the National Patriotic Labor Corps). As late as the spring of 1944, Welfare Minister Koizumi Chikahiko spoke against the drafting of women: "Although in Germany and among enemy countries women are conscripted," he said, "out of consideration for the family system, we will not draft them."[48]

Nevertheless, faced with the acute shortage of labor needed for maintaining war production, in the fall of 1944 the cabinet announced its decision to draft women. The national registration system had already expanded to include men twelve to sixty years old and women twelve to forty years old; now women of those ages were urged to organize themselves into a women's volunteer labor corps (*kinrō teishintai*) so that they could give one to two years' service in the munitions industry. The "Outline for Reinforcement of Women's Volunteer Corps" (*Joshi teishintai seido kyōka hōsaku*), issued in March 1944, and the "Ordinance on Women's Volunteer Labor Corps" (*Joshi Teishin Kinrō Rei*),

47. See Minoguchi Tokijiro, "Joshi dōinron," *Kaizō* 12, no. 3 (March 1943), reprinted in *Nihon fujin mondai shiryō shūsei*, vol. 3: Akamatsu (ed.), *Rōdō*, 491–97. This article was written to urge women to enter the labor force, but it also presented the government position that women's reproductive roles were more valuable than their roles in the industrial labor force. The author, a member of the committee for cabinet population planning policies, merely appealed to women's sentiment to serve the nation through their labor, derogating "Japanese women's inclination to stick to the family."

48. Mitsui, *Gendai fujin undōshi nenpyō*, 170–71.

issued in August of the same year, finally made women's industrial service compulsory for one year.[49]

Efforts to draft women (who were informed on white notices, in contrast to the red pieces of paper received by men) did not go well. Less than 7 percent responded to draft notices received from the Police Office in May 1944.[50] Because working conditions in the textile industry were poor, factory work became stigmatized, and women, unless they were strongly patriotic, were hesitant to work in factories. Another "Ordinance on the Women's Volunteer Corps" was issued in June to facilitate the draft by strengthening the compulsory overtones, and thereafter, the mobilization of women began in earnest. But even as late as August 1944, "women who are pivotal to a family," that is, women whose roles as housewives and mothers were indispensable for family cohesion, were exempted from the draft in order to preserve the family system.

Even after mobilization became compulsory, with a maximum penalty of up to one thousand yen or a year in prison for evasion, a substantial number of women still did not register. The daughters of upper-class families were able to avoid compulsory work by working instead as office girls at companies run by their fathers or relatives. Women unprotected by their parents' "considerate" arrangements, however, were drafted through neighborhood associations. By monitoring local residents' lives, these organizations forced people to bow to state policies. In this sense, the Japanese draft of women, called "volunteering," actually functioned as a club to drive daughters of less privileged middle-class families into the labor force.[51]

Middle-class parents were anxious about sending their daughters to the factories, being well aware of the decadent sexual morals of "mill girls" and the poor working conditions in the textile industry. The state's patronage worked to remove these anxieties. Thus, the "Guidelines for Plants Receiving Women's Volunteer Corps" (*Joshi teishintai ukeiregawa sochi yōkō*)[52] advised employers to be careful "to reduce the risk of undesirable incidents that might happen to female workers by making them commute in groups and by adapting staggered commut-

49. Both documents are reprinted in *Nihon fujin mondai shiryō shūsei*, vol. 3: Akamatsu (ed.), *Rōdō*, 480–81, 484–86.

50. Mitsui, *Gendai fujin undōshi nenpyō*, 173.

51. "Joshi kinrōdōin sokushin ni kansuruken" was aimed at turning unemployed women and daughters of the leisure class into an industrial labor force, but the slow draft of domestic servants suggests the importance of preserving class privileges even at the expense of labor mobilization. In 1940 there were 100,000 fewer domestic servants than in 1930, and by February 1944 an additional 230,000 were eliminated, with some 600,000 remaining; see Cohen, *Japan's Economy*, 292.

52. Reprinted in *Nihon fujin mondai shiryō shūsei*, vol. 3: Akamatsu (ed.), *Rōdō*, 481–84.

ing hours from male workers." It also suggested that employers provide marriage consultation. This paternalistic attitude merely remained rhetorical; it did not improve working conditions, partly because the government did not take further steps to enforce its requirements. In any case, given the wartime shortages of raw materials that seriously affected production, employers could not afford to improve working conditions.[53] Nevertheless, paternalistic rhetoric on the part of the government helped the Women's Volunteer Corps successfully organize daughters of a certain section of the middle class, partly with the assistance of feminists who supported the women's draft.[54]

When a Women's Volunteer Corps was allotted to a factory, the plant was registered as conscripted, a designation that denied freedom of mobility to the rest of the workers. In March 1944, 201,487 women were mobilized through Women's Volunteer Corps, and more than 472,000 in August 1945.[55] These numbers were relatively small, in that the rural female population was exempted in order to maintain food production.[56] Yet nearly four million working women and their male co-workers in war firms were frozen in their jobs by state decree in 1944.[57] Most of them were workers redeployed from the textile industry and other miscellaneous industries, or shop clerks, and they were forced to work unprotected from the increasing number of air raids until the end of the war. Accounts written by women in volunteer corps convey the stressful life in the munitions factories. Despite an intensified work regimen, though, somehow they found ways to alleviate shortages in raw materials, to allay their fears about bombardment, and to survive malnutrition. But cessation of menstruation, a prevalent complaint, was one indication of their extreme stress.[58]

The Toyokawa Women's Volunteer Corps (Toyokawa Joshi Teishin-

53. See Adachi Kimiko, "Senji keizaika no fujinrōdō mondai," in *Gendai fujin mondai kōza*, ed. Ōba Ayako et al. (Aki Shobō, 1969), 2:18–35.

54. Women's organizations appealed strenuously to mothers to send their daughters to the "front for increasing production"; Mitsui, *Gendai fujin undōshi nenpyō*, 173. Feminist Oku Mumeo and progressive educator Hani Setsuko played an active role in drawing daughters from middle-class families into women's volunteer corps; see Suzuki, *Feminizumū to sensō*, 76–100, 162–86.

55. *Nihon fujin mondai shiryō shūsei*, vol. 3: Akamatsu (ed.), *Rōdō*, 487. At the defeat of Japan, 1,920,000 students mobilized by students' volunteer corps were working along with women's volunteer corps in factories and agriculture; see Kojima, *Hataraku onna*, 120.

56. By August 1945, the Ministry of Agriculture estimated that fewer than two-thirds of the farming households included able-bodied male workers; see Irene Taeuber, *The Population of Japan* (Princeton: Princeton University Press, 1958), 340.

57. This figure is cited in Havens, "Women and War in Japan," 923.

58. Ibid., pp. 924–25. This article cites several women's journals and recollections on factory life in wartime. See also Kajinishi Mitsuhaya, Tatewaki Sadayo, Furushima Toshio, and Oguchi Kenzō, *Seishirōdōsha no rekishi* (Iwanami Shoten, 1955).

tai) was the most tragic case of women workers in the munitions factories.[59] In the face of Japan's difficult war situation at the front and the
acute labor shortage at home, the Toyokawa Women's Volunteer Corps,
which worked at the Toyokawa Naval Arsenal in Aichi prefecture, had
been urgently formed in the fall of 1944 by drawing on women between
fourteen and forty from several towns in Ishikawa prefecture. These
women had been engaged in housework or employed as maids or waitresses when they were chosen out of the registration list as "women engaged in nonessential industries." Most were unable to evade the compulsory draft because their parents had not placed them in safer jobs
beforehand, though some patriotically volunteered to do this dangerous
work against their parents' will. On August 7, 1945, the U.S. Army
dropped three thousand bombs on the arsenal, killing 2,477 persons
(almost all civilians) and injuring over 10,000 of the 50,000 total employees. Women accounted for about 1,000 of the total deaths;[60] most
of them were members of the Women's Volunteer Corps. Another significant group of victims comprised male students organized by the
corps.

The survivors' notes tell us how the young women endured the demanding, dangerous work and a dormitory life governed by a strict regimen, which included chronic hunger and censorship of letters to prevent the divulgence of military secrets, by convincing themselves that
they were serving the nation. Meanwhile, their notes reveal that they
envied their cohorts who were sent home to be married, and that a considerable number of girls became mentally deranged from the frequent
ringing of the air raid alarms.[61]

These women obviously bore the brunt of the state's lack of realistic
policies for maintaining war production. Even before the main weight
of the U.S. strategic air attack was delivered, Japanese war production
had come to a standstill, with access to essential industrial raw materials
shut off by the Allied forces.[62] To continue the war, the government
chose to overcome this shortage of materials by relying on labor-inten-
sive production—a strategy familiar to Japanese entrepreneurs who had
survived world competition at the turn of the century by using women
workers as disposable hands in the textile industry. The second time
around, however, this approach completely failed. The victimization of

59. See Tsuji Toyoji, *Aa Toyokawa joshi teishintai* (Kōyō Shobō, 1963).
60. Ibid., 203.
61. Marriage provided a legitimate excuse for women to be released from their compulsory service. Some successful examples of the women who quit work on the pretense
of marriage are recorded in Fukuchi Hiroaki, *Okinawa jokō aishi* (Okinawa: Ryūkyū Shuppansha, 1985).
62. Cohen devotes most of *Japan's Economy* to proving this thesis.

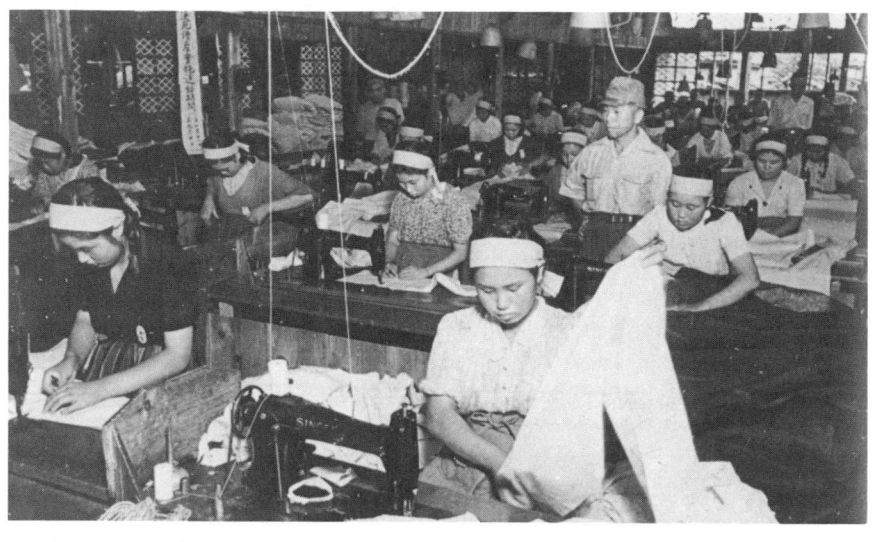

Fig. 12.2. Members of a women's volunteer corps work under a man's supervision in a factory. (Courtesy of Otsuki Shoten)

women workers in heavy industry in the 1930s and 1940s can be called, with deliberate irony, the "Shōwa version of the pitiful history of the mill girls."[63]

CONCLUSION: THE LEGACY OF THE STATE'S MANAGEMENT OF WOMEN

The postwar government fired about three million women in 1945 in order to open their jobs for returning soldiers; Japanese women were thus again forced to work only in the textile industry.[64] Yet for several reasons, women's wartime experiences merit attention if we are to understand long-term changes in gender relations in the workplace.[65] First, the entrance of women into a wide range of jobs previously monopolized by men served to undermine the sex-segregated labor mar-

63. Yoshimi Kaneko, "Fasshizumuka no joseitachi," in *Nihon fasshizumu to josei*, ed. Yoshimi Kaneko (Godo Shuppan, 1977), 220.

64. Mitsui, *Gendai fujin undōshi nenpyō*, 176. The figure of 5,250,000 women engaged in nonfarming industries at the war's end shrank to 2,310,000 by December 1945.

65. Pioneering studies such as Tanabe Teruko, "Dainiji taisenka ni okeru dairyūshon no kenkyū (1)," in *Meiji Daigaku Tankidaigaku kiyō*, no. 11 (Meiji Daigaku Tanki Daigaku, 1967), 143–98; and Takenaka Emiko, "Kyōkō to sensōka ni okeru rōdōshijō no henbō," in Hazama (ed.), *Kōza*, vol. 3: Kawai et al. (eds.), *Kyōkō kara sensō e*, 271–331, situate the broad extent of women's entry into wartime labor markets as a point of departure for changing gender relations in the postwar workplace.

ket, because it now became possible to calculate sex differentials in wages by occupation; when women were segregated in the textile industry, such comparison had been impossible. It is true that the wartime government kept women's wages at a lower level than men's, which reinforced the belief that women's husbands and fathers should provide for them. Nevertheless, the massive military conscription of men, coupled with the entrance of unskilled women into the previously male-dominated labor force, lessened these sex differentials, raising the female wage rate from 30.6 percent of men's wages to 46.5 percent during the period from 1936 to 1945.[66] In addition, the removal of sexual barriers in order to raise productivity, and women's demonstration that their capabilities compared favorably with men's, gave impetus to the postwar working women's movement for equal employment opportunities. The 1947 Labor Standards Law (Rōdō Kijun Hō) provided the legal basis for this ongoing movement.

As a result of women's entry into the labor force and men's conscription into the military during the 1930s and 1940s, gender relations within the family began to change well before the Occupation reforms of the immediate postwar period. Although the wartime government had tried to bolster the family as an ideological arm of the state by keeping women out of the workplace and out of the military, the numbers of women, married and unmarried, who eventually entered the labor force to help family finances was sufficiently high to dramatically alter gender relations within the family.[67] The 1948 legal reform of the family system under the Occupation authorities ratified these ongoing

66. Kawahigashi, "Nihon shihonshugi to joshi rōdō," 84.

67. Such changes have been sporadically noted in studies on urban and rural families of this period. See, for example, Ōkōchi Kazuo's argument against the postwar government's plan to "send women back home" and in favor of women's right to work, in his article "Joshi to shitsugyō," *Nihon shihonshugi to rōdō mondai* (Kyōto: Hakujitsu Shoin, 1947), 109–15. The fact that the majority of 3,070,000 women, the number calculated by the government as *not* in need of jobs, worked to help family finances worsened by the inflationary spiral during the war suggests resulting changes in the daughter-father and wife-husband relationships in urban lower-middle-class and working-class families. Daughters may have obtained a certain degree of autonomy from their fathers owing to their economic gains and broadening social life. After getting a well-paying job in a munitions factory, one wife was so cheered that she would tap her chopsticks on her rice bowl to accompany songs when she became relaxed after a cup of wine at supper. This was a big change from her image as a beaten wife and miserable bride. See Ōtake Hitoko, "Zoruge jiken no koro" in *Jūgoshi nōto*, no. 7 (1982), 122–29.

As for rural families, Watanabe Yōzō notes the undermining of the male power in work groups as well as in the family, due to men's wartime absence. Watanabe argues that this favorably affected the status of wives, who then took responsibility for farming. See Watanabe, "Ie no kaitai to sono fukkatsu," *Sekai*, no. 142 (October 1957): 125. This transformation of farm women's active involvement in farming is also recorded in Teruoka Gitō, *Rōdōryoku no saihensei* (Kagakukōgyōsha, 1940), 213.

changes by replacing the *ie* with the nuclear family. In place of the absolute power of the father/head of the family as defined in the Meiji Civil Code, the postwar family gave equal standing to husband and wife: no longer was the wife legally defined as incompetent.

Married women continue to contribute significantly to Japan's labor market, accounting for two-thirds of the total female working population. Yet despite wartime gains, women still confront barriers to their equal integration into the work force. A big wage differential—in fact, the biggest among the advanced countries—characterizes present-day Japan, where women's wages amount to only 51.8 percent of men's.[68] Furthermore, progressive practices temporarily implemented in the wartime workplace, such as the full-time employment of married women and the promotion of women to supervisory positions, have not yet become widespread in the contemporary workplace. Women are still expected to retire upon marriage and to return to work only on a part-time basis in order to supplement their husband's income after their children are old enough to be put in day care. These women, who account for over 20 percent of the entire female work force,[69] acquiesce to poor working conditions and gain no assistance from trade unions.

The inability to change women's working conditions stems from the belief—shared by trade unions, the state, and women themselves—that women's real identity lies in the family. Supported by the operation of family (rather than family-state) ideology, the contemporary state's goal is to discourage women's full-time employment in order to preserve the nuclear family. This is evident in a series of reports issued by the government's advisory committee, emphasizing women's responsibility for childrearing and care of the old and infirm, and advising women to work only on a part-time basis.[70] The 1986 Equal Employment Opportunity Law (Danjo Koyō Kikai Kintō Hō) further discourages women's full-time employment by neglecting to question a sexual division of labor that places the entire responsibility for housework on women; it likewise fails to force employers to improve working conditions, which

68. Rōdōshō Fujin-Shōnenkyoku, ed., *Fujin rōdō no jitsujō* (Rōdōshō, 1985), 48.

69. Compared to the proportion of part-time workers in other advanced countries, this figure is not astonishingly high. However, the term "part-time," which suggests a worker with freedom to control her working hours, may actually serve to mask the exploitation of her labor in the workplace. Indeed, many surveys show that a considerable number of part-time female employees work almost the same number of hours as full-time workers, while receiving much less compensation.

70. The government's view of women as homemakers is consistently expressed in a report by the Katei Seikatsu Shingikai (Special Commission on Home Life), 1968; a report by the Keizai Shingikai (Special Commission on Economy), 1963; and a 1979 proposal by the Liberal Democratic party to solidify the material basis for family life, entitled "Katei kiban no jūjitsu ni kansuru taisaku yōkō."

hitherto were arranged exclusively for male workers utterly free from household responsibilities. The law, because of its many loopholes, obviously does not benefit part-time workers who are at the bottom of job hierarchies.[71]

Without women's childbearing, childrearing, and housework, the contemporary family would surely disintegrate and cease to meet the economy's demand for reproduction of a labor force. Moreover, without women's care of the elderly and infirm, the state would have to increase social welfare expenditures. Greater sharing of these responsibilities between husband and wife would also interfere with the kind of total dedication of male workers to the workplace that characterizes the Japanese employment system. In short, the stability of the nuclear family is still crucial to the maintenance of social relations mandated by the postwar capitalist system. Thus far, the contemporary state seems more successful than the wartime state in balancing women's reproductive roles with their productive labor.

71. Dashing the hopes of the women's movement and the committee representing workers' interests, the Japanese government did not create an antisexual discrimination law. Instead the government limited its goals to promoting equal employment opportunity for women by partially revising the existing Law to Increase the Well-Being of Working Women (Kinrō Fujin Fukushi Hō). The efficacy of the new law is suspect for several reasons. First, the law does not specify punishment for the employer's discriminatory practices, but merely expects him to uphold the ideas of the law, assisted, in part, by administrative advice. Second, when this legislation was passed, the 1947 Labor Standards Law regulating women's overtime, night, and hazardous work was deceptively undermined: that is, the Equal Employment Opportunity Law removed women's legal protection, in the name of equality. The government's (also the employer's) concept of equality is most controversial, for it is based on the equality-versus-protection premise that if women want equality, they must give up legal protection and work as men do. The equality that Japanese women are seeking, however, is not the kind achieved by exposing themselves to the same working conditions as men, such as long working hours (Japanese men work an average of two hundred to four hundred hours more per year than Western workers). The new law seriously affects women workers, dividing them into two categories: a minority of women who enjoy well-paying jobs thanks to their commitment to the same working conditions as men; and the majority of women, including part-time workers, who cannot work long hours owing to their household responsibilities. The latter group represents the bottom of the job hierarchy. Despite these significant problems, the new law represents a milestone for Japanese employers in that it expresses their intention to incorporate women workers selectively into the mainstream of industry, rather than segregating them as peripheral workers in clerical and menial jobs. See, for example, *Hōgaku seminā*, special issue no. 25: "Josei to hō" (Nihon Hyōronsha, 1984); and Nakajima Michiko, ed., *Hataraku onna ga mirai o hiraku* (Aki Shobō, 1984).

THIRTEEN

Women and War: The Japanese Film Image

William B. Hauser

Although feature films dealing with war, either as conscious wartime propaganda or as postwar efforts at apology or rationalization, have obvious consequences for men, they communicate to and about women as well. War films, as both official and unofficial statements about society at war, include important messages not merely on military service, patriotism, and nationalism, but also on women, the family, and the special roles that women must play to hold a culture together during the turmoil of international conflict.[1] Such messages were found in German films of the Second World War. Joseph Goebbels, minister for popular enlightenment and propaganda, summed up the role of women under National Socialism in 1929: "The mission of women is to be beautiful and to bring children into the world. . . . The female bird pretties herself for her mate and hatches eggs for him. In exchange, the mate takes care of gathering food, and stands guard and wards off the enemy."[2]

The Japanese government, likewise, had specific, though broader, propaganda objectives for feature films. Government agencies used films to project appropriate and inappropriate standards of social conduct during and after the Pacific War. And in the immediate postwar

1. For a discussion of women as portrayed in Hollywood combat films, see Kathryn Kane, *Visions of War: Hollywood Combat Films of World War II* (Ann Arbor, Mich.: UNI Research Press, 1982), 16–20.

2. As quoted in David Welch, *Propaganda and the German Cinema, 1933–1945* (Oxford: Oxford University Press, 1983), 66.

period, the Allied Occupation authorities used films for purposes of democratic socialization.[3]

The use of feature films as primary sources for an analysis of women in wartime Japan has obvious methodological drawbacks. Films reflect a limited viewpoint and do not necessarily represent any consistently definable body of opinion. Yet the power of films and their impact on the viewing audience is undeniable. There is a growing awareness that films have much to offer as sources of social and cultural history. As J. A. S. Grenville has suggested, "Film evidence is important . . . and if properly handled will illuminate and enrich the study of the twentieth century."[4]

Films often include serious social or cultural messages. Recent American concerns with the stereotyping of women, blacks, native Americans, Asians, and others in Hollywood movies strengthen the sense that film roles convey more than merely story content. In fact, films show the audience how each of these groups fits into American society and can help either reinforce or change social attitudes.

A similar case can be made regarding Japanese films made during and after the Pacific War. In this essay I shall explore the clues they offer on attitudes toward women in wartime and postwar Japan.[5]

WOMEN IN WARTIME FILMS

Women play a variety of roles in Japanese wartime films.[6] In most, they are background figures, holding the family together, supporting their husbands and sons when they are called into the military, and preserving family solidarity when the men go off to war. Indeed, most war films either exclude women altogether or cast them in purely supporting roles. Yet even in these limited portrayals, the formal expectations of women in wartime are reflected. They are to be steadfast and true. They

3. For Japanese wartime film censorship policies, see Joseph L. Anderson and Donald Richie, *The Japanese Film: Art and Industry* (Rutland, Vt.: Charles E. Tuttle, 1959), 128–30; Joan Mellen, *The Waves at Genji's Door: Japan Through Its Cinema* (New York: Pantheon Books, 1976), 138–40; and Tadao Sato, *Currents in Japanese Cinema* (Tokyo: Kodansha International, 1982), 100–104. See also Gregory J. Kasza, *The State and the Mass Media in Japan* (Berkeley and Los Angeles: University of California Press, 1988), 232–51.

4. J.A.S. Grenville, *Film as History: The Nature of Film Evidence* (Birmingham, Eng.: University of Birmingham, 1971), 3, quoted in David Welch, *Propaganda and the German Cinema*, 3.

5. Kathryn Kane has made a similar point about the value of genre studies in her discussion of Hollywood combat films; see *Visions of War*, 8–10.

6. The author has seen all the films discussed in this paper. Collections at the Motion Picture Division of the Library of Congress, Washington, D.C., and the Japan Film Center in Tokyo were used extensively. Screenings at the University of Rochester and the Japan Society of New York added additional titles. All plot summaries are from the author's viewing notes.

should accept their fate and that of their loved ones. They should do whatever is called for to protect the integrity of the family and the community. War has social costs, but in wartime women must ensure the maintenance of the family and the community and minimize the disruptions to everyday life. As Joan Mellen has noted, one of the aims of government propaganda was to "exalt . . . purely Japanese tradition." Nothing was more basic to this tradition than the role of women in the family.[7]

Official policy on war films was evident in Home Ministry directives that specified appropriate themes. Violence and the horror of war were to be avoided, as were scenes of close fighting. Films were to reinforce the morale of the conscripted men and their families as well as eliminate tendencies toward individualism. Of major importance was the emphasis on self-sacrifice and service to the national cause. Films were to provide models for appropriate social conduct and educate the Japanese public to their proper roles.[8]

Given that women are rarely the central focus, women's roles in war films are often shallow and superficial. One example is the wife in Sado Take's *Chocolate and Soldiers* (*Chokoreto to heitai*, 1941). This deeply moving film depicts small-town life and the need for all Japanese to accept their fate and do their utmost for the welfare of the state. Mr. Saeki, a good family man and army reservist, is called to active duty and goes off to war. His wife (played by Sawamura Sadako) is left to care for their two young children and make do during his absence. The details of their home life add a quality of realism that involves the audience in the intimacy of their everyday lives. Prior to her husband's departure, Mrs. Saeki attempts to get him to complete some unfinished house repairs. Realizing he will be gone for a long time and may never return, she attempts to put their affairs in order. Visiting a neighbor who embroiders for extra income, Mrs. Saeki discovers that she can augment their meager income by doing piecework at home, work that will not disrupt her primary role as a housewife and mother.

On their last night before his departure, Saeki asks his wife to do her best while he is away. He hopes all will go well during his time in China. He is uneasy about fulfilling his role as a family man while in battle and concerned about his family's welfare. While he has confidence in Mrs. Saeki's abilities, he also asks her brother to watch out for his wife and children. He urges his children to mind their mother, study well, and grow up to be strong. Having asserted his hopes for his children, Saeki goes off to the war. A fatalistic man, he knows he has no choice but to serve his country. In similar fashion, Mrs. Saeki knows she has no choice

7. Mellen, *Waves at Genji's Door*, 139–40.
8. Anderson and Richie, *Japanese Film*, 128.

but cheerfully to send her husband off to war. In the months that follow, Mrs. Saeki presides over her children and household and a new routine emerges. When notified by telegraph of her husband's death, she resolutely tells her son Ichirō that he is now the man of the household. Mrs. Saeki's stoic acceptance of her husband's death is striking.

> In her 1944 discussion of this last scene, Ruth Benedict exclaimed: Does the wife break down? Does she weep? Does she faint? Are there hysterics? Not in a Japanese film. She reads the letter quietly, braces herself as she lifts her eyes to the skies, then calls the little son to tell him his father is dead. The only weeping which accompanies the memorial service is that of the friends who weep for pity and admiration of Seki's [sic] gallant wife and son.[9]

The Saekis' future seems bleak, but they accept it willingly and without question. When Ichirō wins a candy wrapper contest, having collected wrappers sent by his father from the front, he is awarded a scholarship to assure his future education and, thereby, the survival of the family unit. The town, the neighbors, and even the candy company will all look out for the Saekis' interests, now that the man of the house has been sacrificed to the national cause. The understated acting by all the performers in this film enhances the impact on the audience. As movie director Frank Capra noted, "We can't beat this kind of thing. We made a film like that maybe once in a decade."[10]

Similar themes are apparent in *Airplane Drone* (*Bakuon*, 1939), directed by Tasaka Tomotaka. Here the primary theme is the support of a rural community for the pilot son of the village headman, Mr. Yoshida. The women in the film, including Mrs. Yoshida, the Yoshidas' daughter, Fusako, and their son's fiancée Michiko, all represent the preservation of conventional community life despite the disruptions caused by war. This lyrical film climaxes with an impressive flying demonstration by the son, Tarō, who flies his plane, purchased for the Air Corps by his home prefecture, over the village to show his thanks for their contributions to the war effort. While most of the film is directed at Mr. Yoshida's bumbling and often humorous efforts to inform his constituents about the forthcoming overflight, the fears and concerns of the women characters are also expressed.

Mrs. Yoshida quietly supports her son Tarō's dedication to pilot training and the nation, even though she knows the risks entailed, having already lost her eldest son to the war. She worries about Tarō while taking pride in his accomplishments. Fusako, an ebullient and light-

9. Ruth Fulton Benedict, "Japanese Films: A Phase of Psychological Warfare," Foreign Morale Analysis Division, Office of War Information, Washington, D.C., March 30, 1944, 4.

10. As quoted in ibid., 11.

hearted young woman, is proud of her brother and tries to ignore the implications of his military service. Michiko, Tarō's fiancée, expects to marry into the Yoshida family but worries that she might be left a war widow. Despite the apparent innocence of their village setting and the bucolic surroundings, they all acknowledge the potential costs of the war. While never dwelling on the war theme, the film makes it obvious that all the characters are ready to sacrifice when necessary. The women are both realists and fatalists, prepared to enjoy what they have, but anticipating that they may face future suffering. They represent social stability and the maintenance of the family. They reflect the pride in service and the community support for the national cause. They acknowledge the risks, yet refuse to be broken by their fear of the unknown. In a quiet and understated manner, women are shown as basic to the preservation of family and community continuity. Joseph Anderson and Donald Richie view this film as setting the pattern for "home front" films made during the war.[11]

The 1937 film *Song of the Advancing Army* (*Shingun no uta*) provides additional examples of women supporting their men at arms. The main theme is the reconciliation of friendship between Tōyama Jiro, a factory owner's son, and Mr. Andō, a union leader in the father's plant. Rejecting the class tensions that had alienated them from each other, they head off together to serve in the same army unit at the front. Although they are the combatants, it is the solidarity of Mrs. Andō and Jiro's geisha girlfriend, Oyuki, that concerns us here. Mrs. Andō is left to fend for herself on her husband's limited army salary. As the war drags on she is impoverished and sells flowers on the streets of Tokyo. Encountering Oyuki, she finds a new friend and supporter. Oyuki aids her financially and helps her obtain a job in the teahouse where she works.

Although both women in this film are concerned about their men in the army and, as such, are sisters in arms, a clear distinction is made between roles for single and married women. Mrs. Andō must stay home and care for her young son, but Oyuki has other options. Although she is a talented entertainer, her skills are less valuable to a country at war. Accepting the special needs of wartime Japan, she volunteers to serve as a nurse at the front, taking on risks like those the men bear. After asking her boss to give Mrs. Andō her accumulated earnings, she heads off to support the war effort. The film thus suggests that wives and mothers are uniquely responsible for the important tasks of preserving the family and assuring future generations of young Japanese. They may work, but they must stay on the home front. Single

11. Anderson and Richie, *Japanese Film*, 136.

women, like Oyuki, can make personal contributions to the war effort by becoming frontline nurses. All women should support the national cause and recognize the important assistance that other women make to the defense of the state.

Sister Goes to the Front (*Ane no shuppei*, 1940) develops this theme directly. The film is about rural Japanese farmers and their children. Taguchi Setsuko is a navy nurse, and her younger sister, Hideko, is in nurse's training. Because Setsuko is soon to leave for the front, Mr. Taguchi worries about her and fears that Hideko will also go off to war. In contrast to her father, Setsuko encourages Hideko and urges her to study hard and dedicate herself to the national cause. When Setsuko departs, Mr. Taguchi both fears for his daughter and takes pride in her contribution to the war effort. It is not only sons who can serve a nation at war. Ruth Benedict's analysis of this film emphasizes that service, by both men and women, incurred the risk of suffering and death: those who served were heroic because, despite "loving life, home, peace, [and] beauty, they renounce all when called to fight."[12]

This film reinforces traditional family values, even while encouraging women to play supporting roles in the military. In a parting letter to her boyfriend, Setsuko explains that although she is eager to serve as a navy nurse, she hopes to return to the village and marry. She accepts her obligations to the nation, yet, despite her medical training, she has conventional aspirations for rural family life. The social implications are obvious: war requires special sacrifices and all should do their utmost for the war effort. Nevertheless, traditional social values remain the same: women's primary roles are in the family and the community, and they should return to these roles once normalcy returns. Sacrifice is required from all Japanese, but conventional social roles must be resumed once the conflict is concluded.

A film with a different approach to the issues of family commitment and sacrifice is *Eighty-eight Years After the Opening of Japan* (*Hachijūhachinenme no taiyō*, 1941), directed by Takizawa Eisuke. The focus is on the Uraga shipbuilding yards, where naval ships are under construction, and at issue is the conflict between Fukami Kōkichi and his wife. Kōkichi is a trained musician who is out of work owing to the war. His family has worked for generations as shipbuilders in Uraga, and he wants to return home and find a job building warships. His wife, however, wants him to dedicate himself to his music: he is, after all, an artist and must struggle to preserve his musical talents. Torn between his musical career and his wife, on the one hand, and his family heritage and the national

12. Benedict, "Japanese Films," 4.

need, on the other, Kōkichi is unsure where to turn. His only opportunities in music are in nightclubs, as there are no orchestral positions. Because such work compromises his musical principles, he decides instead to go back to his roots. The transition to shipbuilding proves difficult, and he finds the job of welder's assistant overwhelming. Determined to succeed, though, he struggles on, despite the continued opposition of his wife. She objects to the sacrifice of his musical talents, feeling that the preservation of his artistry is more important than the national need. In time, however, she sees the error of her ways. They accept their sacrifice and are welcomed back into his family and the shipyard. Nothing must impede Japan's war production needs.

In *A Story of Instruction* (*Shidō monogatari*), the subject is training railway engineers for the army. This 1941 film, by Kumagai Hisatora, narrates the story of Seki, an elderly engineer suddenly assigned to train military railway engineers. Private Sagawa becomes his apprentice, but only three months are allotted to convert the young college graduate into a seasoned railway man. Seki, a widower, lives with his three daughters; his eldest daughter, Kuniko (Hara Setsuko), runs the household. As a patriotic young woman, she encourages her father and Sagawa. Knowing that her father wants to present Sagawa with an expensive foreign book as a present, she sells one of her kimono to obtain the necessary funds. Times are hard, but Kuniko does her all to support the war effort. Kuniko and Sagawa become friendly, and she invites him for dinner to celebrate the completion of his studies; in a further act of sacrifice, Sagawa is given the only serving of fish, an example of how civilians must provide the best possible support to the men in uniform. Civilian support and encouragement are necessary if Japan is to win the war. Both men and women can contribute to the national cause.

Toward the Decisive Battle in the Sky (*Kessen no ōzora e*, 1943) is about the training of navy fighter pilots at the Tsuchiura training base. Living near the airfield, the Matsumuras often entertain the recruits, who hunger for civilian company and home-cooked meals. The Matsumura daughters, Sugie and Shigeko, love to watch the planes fly, while their younger brother Katsuro dreams of becoming a pilot. He is frail and small, and failed his induction physical. The young airmen urge him on and help him to prepare for his next examination. While the emphasis is on the airmen, the important role of Mrs. Matsumura and her daughters in encouraging their progress and providing social and emotional support is obvious.

An important theme here and in many other films is the family-style character of the military. Mitamura, the drill instructor, cares about his trainees and treats them like younger brothers, even as he drives them to excel. Yet for all the familial qualities of the navy, civilian reinforcement must also be provided. The military takes care of the training, but the emotional support and encouragement are reinforced from elsewhere. Families owe their allegiance to all young men in arms, not just their own loved ones. The Matsumuras illustrate how simple contributions like sharing meals and offering a glimpse of home life can help the national cause.[13]

WOMEN IN POSTWAR FILMS

The Japanese surrender in 1945 ushered in a new era for the film industry. Government censorship was initially eliminated and then replaced by new standards established under the Supreme Commander of the Allied Powers.[14] Occupation policies regarding feature films aimed to eliminate support for nationalism and militarism and encourage viewers to support the new democratic reforms. These goals, together with the strong response of Japanese filmmakers to the abolition of wartime controls, led to dramatic new themes.

No Regrets for Our Youth (*Waga seishun ni kui nashi*, 1946), directed by Kurosawa Akira, is a bold statement on feminist independence. The heroine, Yagihara Yukie (Hara Setsuko), is transformed in the film from a naive schoolgirl into the fiercely loyal wife and widow of an oppressed antiwar radical. Based on the Takikawa Incident of 1933, the film focuses not on the Kyoto University law professor who was forced to resign for his antiwar "communist" teachings but on his daughter, Yukie. Initially confused by her father's views and notoriety, she nevertheless falls in love with one of his most radical students, Noge (modeled on Ozaki Hotsumi, who was executed in 1944 for his participation in the Sorge spy ring).[15] Their growing relationship and Yukie's dedication to him, despite the risks associated with his cause and the stigma of his radical political activities, are at the core of the story.

13. Omitted here is any discussion of the so-called National Policy Pictures, which present explicit roles for Japanese, Chinese, Korean, and Manchurian women in areas occupied or controlled by Japan. These films encouraged active support of Japan's efforts to expel the West and create a Greater East Asian Co-Prosperity Sphere. Films representative of this theme include *Daughter of Asia* (*Ajiya no musume*, 1938), *Song of the White Orchid* (*Byakuran no uta*, 1939), *China Night* (*Shina no yoru*, 1940), *Vow in the Desert* (*Nessa no chikai*, 1941), and *Cherry Blossom Country* (*Sakura no kuni*, 1941). Each of these films emphasizes the good intentions of the Japanese in mainland Asia and the problems encountered convincing the local population of Japan's fundamental goodwill.

14. For film censorship policies under the Supreme Command of the Allied Powers (SCAP) during the Allied Occupation of Japan, see Anderson and Richie, *Japanese Film*, 160–64; and Mellen, *Waves at Genji's Door*, 167–69.

15. For the historical Ozaki, see Chalmers Johnson, *An Instance of Treason: Ozaki Hotsumi and the Sorge Spy Ring* (Stanford: Stanford University Press, 1964).

The power of this film and of its heroine is effectively summarized by Donald Richie:

> Rarely in the history of cinema has a woman's character been shown in all its fullness, its contradictions, its perversities, and its strengths—and almost never has it been suggested, as Kurosawa does in this picture, that (stronger than most men) she has the strength to discard training, society, her "place," and instead realize herself, forge herself, make herself into an intensely living human being. "I want to find what it is to live," she says. This is just what she does.[16]

Yukie rejects her middle-class background and self-indulgent tastes and suffers the hardships of social isolation and police repression with Noge. After his imprisonment and execution for antiwar activities, she moves in with his impoverished parents in a farm village where they are shunned and vilified by their neighbors for their son's crimes against the state. Through her dedicated labors she helps them survive in a hostile village community and transforms herself into an outstanding farmer. When the war ends and Noge's efforts against the war come to be seen as heroism rather than treachery, the parents are welcomed back into the village. Yukie stays with them, drawn by the honest hardships of life on the soil and the new, more egalitarian social values of the village.

While representative of the new enthusiasm for democratic social values, this film is iconoclastic in its approach to social issues. Although the liberal ideals of the university are lauded and the military condemned for its suppression of antiwar thought and actions, the peasants' brutality is also graphically presented and condemned. It is Yukie who enables Noge's parents to survive and to regain their pride and place in the community. She emerges from her ordeal as a confident and mature woman.

In Hara Setsuko's Yukie, Japanese women found a heroine with a zest for life and a determination to succeed on her own terms, whatever the cost.[17] Yet the image she projected was threatening to male viewers; in the view of most critics, she was too strident and went too far. The film, moreover, condemns not just the government, but Japanese social values, and encourages women to assert their independence and realize their own personal ambitions.[18] Kurosawa, the director, was roundly

16. Donald Richie, *The Films of Akira Kurosawa* (Berkeley and Los Angeles: University of California Press, 1970), quoted in *Japan at War: Rare Films of World War II* (film program) (New York: Japan Society, 1987), 18.

17. For another analysis of this film, see Richie, *Films of Akira Kurosawa*, 36–42.

18. In her analysis of this film, Audie Bock (Japanese Film Directors [Tokyo: Kodansha International, 1978], 167) calls Yukie "Kurosawa's most attractive postwar heroine."

criticized for his portrayal of Yukie and for his focus on the need for social as well as political change in Japan.

Another aggressive, self-confident woman is found in the 1946 film *The Victory of Women* (*Josei no shōri*). Mizoguchi Kenji, a director whose prewar films illustrated the victimization of women in Japanese society, embraced with enthusiasm the use of films to assert new roles for postwar Japan.[19] In this, the first postwar film completely under the control of Occupation authorities, we have an assertive yet moving effort to promote an improved position for women in Japanese society.

The film centers on Hiroko (Tanaka Kinuyo), a determined young woman lawyer fighting to defend a classmate whose poverty in the aftermath of the war led her to smother her baby. Hiroko's position is complicated by her engagement to antiwar activist Yamaoka Keita, who was imprisoned for his criticism of the wartime government. Now released from prison for medical reasons, Yamaoka is dying. Hiroko is torn between spending time with him and defending her friend, Asakura Tomo. Yamaoka urges her to stand up for what she believes and pursue the case. His enthusiasm is particularly strong because the prosecutor, Kono, is the man who sent him to prison; yet Kono is also Hiroko's brother-in-law. He stands for the conservative, authoritarian values of prewar Japan, she for the progressive and modern democratic values of the postwar era. Kono is anxious to use the case to restore his reputation as an attorney and preserve his job in the Prosecutor's Office. He pressures Hiroko to drop the case. Having helped her through law school, he demands that she respect his wishes and withdraw. Her sister, Michiko, seconds Kono's appeals, while their mother supports Hiroko and urges her to follow her own conscience and not worry about the appeals of her sister and brother-in-law.

Just as Kono and Hiroko represent the prewar and postwar legal systems, Michiko and Hiroko represent prewar and postwar women. Michiko, the elder, married sister, has dedicated her life to serving her husband and has little sense of her own independence and self-worth. Hiroko, in contrast, refuses to break her engagement to the imprisoned Yamaoka, despite severe pressure from Kono. She is determined to make her own decisions as an independent woman and legal professional. She sees in herself and Yamaoka the spirit of a new egalitarian Japan and pushes on despite the opposition she encounters. Tomo embodies the plight of women struggling to survive the economic and social dislocation of the immediate postwar era, and Hiroko is resolved that her friend, unlike so many other Japanese women, will not be sacrificed to poverty and insensitive laws.

19. *Japan at War*, 28.

During the trial (which is never resolved), Hiroko makes an impassioned plea for women's rights, presenting a strong case for Tomo's acquittal. She also convinces Michiko that the old ways are no longer appropriate and that she should assert herself as a postwar woman and leave her oppressive and abusive husband. Hiroko passionately argues that women should no longer be dominated by men. Kono represents the worst aspects of traditional Japanese attitudes toward women and their subservient position in the family. By the end of the film, Michiko sees in her younger sister a model of independence. She determines to create a new life for herself, one in which she can make her own decisions and not be dominated by her husband. The sisters unite in a common purpose, leaving viewers with great hopes for women's rights in postwar Japan.[20]

Several films of the Occupation period provide additional examples of strong women struggling to survive and protect their cultural or humanitarian values under difficult wartime or postwar conditions. Two examples are *Morning with the Ōsone Family* (*Ōsone-ke no asa*, 1946), directed by Kinoshita Keisuke, and *Ball at the Anjō House* (*Anjō-ke no butōkai*, 1947), directed by Yoshimura Kimisaburō. In both films the women are among the strongest characters portrayed. In the Ōsone family, it is the mother who refuses to concede her cosmopolitan cultural values in the face of ultranationalism and war. As a widow with three sons and a daughter, she is under great pressure from her brother-in-law, an army general. He despises her Western-style education, the cultivated upbringing she has given her children, and her lack of support for Japanese ambitions in Asia. Her elder sons play the piano and paint, and only the youngest has the martial values the general respects. Yuko, her daughter, is in love with the young radical Manari, a disciple of her liberal academic father. It is his values, not her uncle's, that she respects. When Manari is jailed for his antiwar writings, Yuko decides to wait for him, rejecting the more conventional marriage candidates presented by her militant uncle.

The war is hard on the Ōsone house. All three sons are inducted into the army; one dies in the conflict, and the youngest commits suicide in despair after Japan's surrender. Mrs. Ōsone berates the general for teaching her youngest son about *bushidō* and militarism, and for the death of her other son in battle. She rejects his gifts of food and blames herself for not having challenged him more aggressively during the war.

20. Bock, *Japanese Film Directors*, 44, sees Hiroko as an unattractive model and terms her a "severe, pedantic, lonely heroine . . . who shows precious little that is attractive in her encouragement of others to follow her lead." The American and Japanese women who saw this film when I screened it in Rochester in 1987 reacted much more positively, calling the film inspiring and a bold feminist statement.

She asks him how much suffering he has caused. How many thousands of men has he killed? When the eldest son returns alive and Manari is released from prison, the future of the Ōsone family and of Japan seems assured. They have suffered and lost both loved ones and possessions, but they, like the nation, will endure. It is their cosmopolitan and democratic values that will assure the future of Japan.

Ball at the Anjō House is set in the immediate postwar period. The peerage has been abolished and the Anjō family, a noble and formerly wealthy house, is facing bleak prospects. They are deeply in debt, about to lose their house, and unsure of where to turn. The youngest daughter, Atsuko, serves as the source of strength and rationality in the household. She encourages her father to accept an offer for their property from their former chauffeur, Toyama, now a wealthy trucker. Forget the past and look to the future, she tells him. Her older siblings, Akiko and Masahiko, want a last fling and schedule a dance to signal the end of the noble family tradition. By the end of the ball, Mr. Anjō has acknowledged and married his geisha mistress, Chiyo; Masahiko has rejected his rich fiancée and acknowledged his love for the house maid, Kiku; and Akiko has recognized the loyalty and devotion of Toyama, and stops rejecting his amorous advances. Throughout the film it is Atsuko who holds them all together, who comforts and counsels her father and siblings, and who alone among them looks to the future with enthusiasm. The new, democratic Japan has promise. While it will challenge their ingenuity and force them to redefine their social and economic objectives, they all can make the transition successfully.

One of the most important post–Occupation period films is Kinoshita Keisuke's *Twenty-four Eyes* (*Nijūshi no hitomi*, 1954). The character of Miss Oishi, the young schoolteacher played by Takamine Hideko, represents the best in the Japanese humanitarian tradition. As the film develops, her naive first-grade pupils from 1928 are inexorably drawn into the jingoistic nationalism that pervades prewar Japan. Miss Ōishi is increasingly confused by the intrusion of nationalism and war rhetoric into the school and into her life. From the beginning of the film, as a professional woman in a rural and socially conservative Shōdo Island setting, she stands for decency, modernity, and the ideals of education for social betterment. Her objectives are to assist her students in escaping poverty through education. She is saddened and frustrated by the loss of many of the young girls to service-industry jobs or death by tuberculosis, and the fascination of the boys with the coming war in the Pacific. All of the things she stands for and believes in are compromised and undermined by ultranationalism and war. Eventually she resigns her position and withdraws into her family.

Even within her family Miss Ōishi finds disappointment. Her sons, like her male students, view her as a coward for her stance against the war. Her merchant seaman husband willingly goes off to the navy, despite the risks and the forced separation from his wife and children. Wartime poverty and deprivation lead to the death of her daughter, who falls from a persimmon tree she had climbed for a rare bit of fruit. A widow at war's end, Miss Ōishi returns to the school and finds some of her pupils are the children, nieces, or nephews of her original class of first-graders. A generation has passed, and they are reminders of those fresh, young, innocent faces she met as a new teacher. At a reunion with the seven survivors of her first class of twelve, she weeps with them for their suffering and for the loss of their classmates in the war. Was it all necessary? Couldn't it have been avoided? Her message is clearly about the futility of war and the failure of the naive and "good Japanese" like herself to steer Japan away from national catastrophe. Miss Ōishi and her former students represent the best that might have been if the war had not intervened. She weeps for the heavy costs entailed in convincing Japanese leaders of their folly.

The Human Condition (*Ningen no jōken*, 1958–61), directed by Kobayashi Masaki, is perhaps the most powerful of the postwar Japanese films on the Pacific War. Set in China and concerned with the period from 1943 to the postwar internment of Kwantung army survivors in Siberia, this three-part, ten-hour film depicts the transformation of Kaji (Nakadai Tatsuya), a dedicated leftist humanist, from a caring, social idealist into a savage brute concerned only with his own definition of justice and individual survival. The film illustrates the all-corrupting impact of war and militarism. Not even the most dedicated humanitarian can survive the brutalization and dehumanization of military life and warfare. That this gentle, educated, and humane visionary is condemned by war to metamorphose into an unprincipled and vulgar monster is a chilling reminder of how thoroughly war dehumanizes the human spirit. "In many ways," one critic suggested, remarking on its great power, "this is a revolutionary film."[21]

Kaji's conversion, through his inability to alter the brutal military and capitalist systems that dominate his life, is the principal emphasis of the film, yet a host of other characters are also developed. The women portrayed offer a range of images, from the ideal Japanese wife to the well-intentioned whore. Most prominent is Michiko, Kaji's girlfriend and then wife. As part 1 of the trilogy opens, Michiko is pursuing him, anxious to marry and make a life together. Having followed him to Man-

21. Richard N. Tucker, *Japan: Film Image* (London: Studio Vista, 1973), 98. Tucker further states that in this film the director, Kobayashi, "stood up and shouted that . . . there is no justification for any system, social, commercial, or military, to impose its will upon the individual."

churia, where they both work for a Japanese mining company, her sole objective is to become his wife. The possible impositions of the war are irrelevant to Michiko. Kaji, however, is reluctant to marry, being convinced that conscription is inevitable: he does not want to leave a wife behind when he goes into the army. Michiko loves him enough to bear his child, whether or not they marry, but he is too honorable to take advantage of her devotion. Only when he is offered a draft deferral in exchange for implementing his labor utilization plan at the company's mine does he decide they can marry and consummate their relationship.

Michiko is so enamored of Kaji that the deprivations of the mining camp are unimportant. She does her utmost to provide a warm and supportive home environment, but is frustrated when Kaji proves increasingly unwilling to share with her his concerns about his job. For her, principles are less important than the pragmatic details of life: providing good meals and protecting her husband from his often self-destructive tendencies to challenge his superiors and the *kenpeitai* (military police).

The contrast between their superficially idyllic home life and the life of the POWs he supervises dramatically illustrates the power of the Japanese over their Chinese subordinates. In their home life, Michiko creates what Joan Mellen terms a "moral oasis."[22] She is focused exclusively on providing every comfort for Kaji. She is human and vulnerable. When her plans for a long weekend with Kaji in Harbin are foiled by an incident at the mine, she goes off alone to visit a girlfriend. There she is advised to dedicate herself to serving Kaji's every need, whether or not he fully confides in her and shares his problems with her. She must be a good wife, a perfect helpmate, and suppress her other concerns. When his efforts to protect the Chinese prisoners from abuse threaten the sanctity of their life together, Michiko urges him not to sacrifice her and their happiness together on behalf of his charges.[23]

In part 2, when Kaji's plans for humanizing conditions at the mine are finally rejected, he is drafted into the army and goes off for military training. Michiko refuses to let go of her husband, however, and visits him at the training camp. Kaji is both ridiculed and envied by the veteran soldiers and the other trainees, for Michiko's visit is unprecedented. When allowed to stay one night together in a storage building, they spend the night in tender lovemaking. As dawn approaches, Kaji asks her to stand naked in the morning light so he can remember her female perfection when he is in the desolate wilds of Manchuria. She offers all of herself to him and cries that she has nothing more to offer. Michiko is an idealized Japanese wife, completely dedicated to support-

22. Mellen, *Waves at Genji's Door*, 182.
23. This is characterized rather differently in ibid.

ing her husband's every need. On parting, both appreciate that they may never meet again.[24]

Michiko never reappears in the film, and in Kaji's imagination she is transformed from a real person into the personification of the Japanese womanly ideal. In the final minutes of part 3, when Kaji is struggling to survive in the desolate wastes of Manchuria, wandering alone in his quest to return to Michiko and a normal community, it is his love for her that drives him and gives him his only source of strength. His love is one of the few remaining elements of his original character, and illustrates that a noble warrior can also be sustained by the love of a woman.[25]

When Kaji becomes sick and is hospitalized in part 2, he encounters two sharply contrasting female stereotypes in the army nurses. One is young, attractive, and empathic. He is strongly drawn to her and feels guilty about this threat to his fidelity. Yet his loneliness enables him to transfer some of his attachment to her. The other woman, a tough, elderly head nurse, is the female version of the insensitive military authority figure. She brutalizes the patients, acting like the army veterans who brutalized the recruits and soldiers of lower rank or less seniority. In this characterization, the army is shown as all-corrupting. There is no place to escape from the rigors of military life; beauty and kindness have no place in the Japanese army. Even women are corrupted by the inhumanity of military life and war.

At the end of part 2 and the beginning of part 3, the Japanese positioned along the Manchurian-Mongolian border are being crushed by Russian armored divisions. It is August 1945, and the Soviet Union has entered the war against Japan. Kaji and the remnants of his squad endeavor to return to rear areas in search of safety. Just as the war and the military have brutalized and dehumanized Kaji, so too are women despoiled by the war. Japanese civilians attempting to flee are raped and brutalized by both Russian and Japanese soldiers. The Russian troops are shown as animals, gang-raping women and throwing their exhausted or lifeless bodies from moving trucks. The Japanese soldiers justify their predations on their own nationals as legitimate because the women have already been violated by the Russians and have nothing more to lose. Seeing Michiko in each of the rape victims and fearing for her safety, Kaji is revolted by both the Russians and his unprincipled Japanese associates.

24. This scene, with its limited nudity, was censored by the Japanese Movie Morality Committee, even though it was an integral part of the emotional relationship between Kaji and Michiko; see Joan Mellen, *Voices from the Japanese Cinema* (New York: Liveright, 1975), 141–43.

25. Sato, *Currents in Japanese Cinema*, 35.

When, in part 3, he is joined in his quest for safety by civilian stragglers, another set of stereotypes is presented. On the one hand are the good colonists with their wives and families. Some are gentle, others cruel in their selfish struggle to survive; one mother is willing to compromise the safety of the whole group to obtain food for her dying baby. Among the most noble and democratic of the civilians are two prostitutes. Sent to Manchuria to satisfy the needs of the military and civilian workers, they are grateful for Kaji's assistance and egalitarian treatment and willing to follow his every order. Selfless and interested in the survival of the whole band, they stand in sharp contrast to the self-centered "good Japanese" settlers, most of whom view them and Kaji with contempt. This reversal of roles, where harlots are noble and their critics and social betters fundamentally evil, illustrates the contaminating impact of war on all citizens. Colonial exploitation has infected most of the civilians, just as military life has perverted Kaji and his army followers. The film directly and passionately attacks the subversion of humanity by militarism, war, and colonial expansion.[26]

CONCLUSION

Among the most obvious differences between wartime and postwar films is the changing support for the war effort. In wartime films, women actively or passively support the war effort and rarely challenge the induction of their husbands and sons into the military or war production jobs. Some are willing to work in war industries or volunteer to serve as nurses at the front. Others merely endure, quietly accepting their fate as one aspect of service to the national cause. Examples of these attitudes are seen in *Sister Goes to the Front, Chocolate and Soldiers,* and *Airplane Drone,* among others.

In contrast, postwar films present female characters, like Miss Ōishi in *Twenty-four Eyes* and Mrs. Ōsone in *Morning of the Ōsone House,* as questioning the war and challenging the nationalist and expansionist claims of its supporters. In both films, the women's arguments against the war are apolitical: their objections are socially or culturally oriented and naive. Even Yukie, in *No Regrets for Our Youth,* is essentially apolitical, despite the strongly political stance of her husband. Thus, while women may take positions against the war, they do not take political positions that oppose the government or their male associates. Even Hosokawa Hiroko in *The Victory of Women,* the most outspoken and liberated woman character we have discussed, argues women's rights from a social and economic rather than a political perspective. She champions

26. Bock, *Japanese Film Directors,* 252.

equal opportunity and an egalitarian society, despite the fact that her fiancé was jailed as a political radical. Women have new opportunities in postwar Japan, but the films analyzed here minimize the scope of these new openings and limit the intrusion of women into the realm of political discourse. Women can oppose the war, object to virulent ultranationalism, and decry the drafting of their husbands and sons into the military, but they do so for what are primarily social and cultural reasons. Social change is advocated, but the consistently apolitical message suggests a timidness about the new areas in which women were expected to participate.

More impressive than the contrasts are the continuities between wartime and postwar films. In both, the preservation of the family is emphasized as the most appropriate concern for the women. Noge Yukie in *No Regrets for Our Youth* dedicates herself to her deceased husband's parents. Her goal is to ensure their survival and reintegration into their community, even if this involves great cost to herself. Hosokawa Hiroko in *The Victory of Women* argues that women must be protected from exploitation and oppression; male domination in law or in the family can no longer be tolerated. Miss Ōishi in *Twenty-four Eyes* is transformed into a conventional wife and mother, and by the end of the film her spirit is broken. She has abandoned the Western suit she once wore and dresses now in kimono. She accepts her fate, albeit unhappily, and wonders why such suffering was necessary, without really questioning the fundamental causes that brought the war about. Her primary concerns lie with the preservation of the family and with her students' abilities to reach their full potential.

Some critics view *Twenty-four Eyes* as a simplistic tear-jerker precisely because of this failure to confront the underlying political issues of the war period. Tadao Sato, for instance, sees Miss Ōishi as "weak, because she drops out of the picture at the most important time, when she should be questioning the responsibility of teachers for indoctrinating their pupils with war-time ideology."[27] For him, Miss Ōishi is a passive victim of the war and the film too sentimental. Joan Mellen is also critical of the film: "Kinoshita oversimplifies its political dimension by making Miss Ōishi abandon her protest against Japanese imperialism to become a simple pacifist who hates war because it kills people."[28]

These analyses miss one of the basic points illustrated by this and most other films on the war theme: women do not *belong* in the realm of politics. Women may object to the war and to the pointless destruction it brought to Japan, but their opposition should be social and cultural, not political. The protection of the family and the community is

27. Sato, *Currents in Japanese Cinema*, 109–14.
28. Mellen, *Waves at Genji's Door*, 169–73.

what should concern women: leave political discourse to the men. The patronizing attitude projected by Miss Ōishi's rural school principal is found in most of the films that place women in wartime roles. Indeed, this viewpoint is consistent in both wartime and postwar movies. While the postwar constitution provides enhanced social *and political* rights for women, none of these films confronts the issue of women's liberation in the political realm. They advocate social change and a broader social, cultural, and economic role for women in the family and the community, but beyond that they do not go.

Even in *The Human Condition*, a radical attack on Japanese wartime values and policies, the female protagonist, Michiko, is presented as a paragon of the good Japanese wife. She dedicates herself to her husband, abandoning her job and her friends to support Kaji's every need. When she asserts her independence and wants to share his concerns as an equal, both Kaji and her girlfriend discourage her. Her frustrations are presented as inappropriate behavior for a good wife: she can be loyal and even courageous in her support of her man, but she must subordinate herself to his needs, even while attempting to protect him from his own demons. The contrast here between Michiko—the aggressive, but still conventional, wife—and Kaji—her moral, humane, and revolutionary husband—is striking. Males can be heroic, but women should stay in the background and be nurturing and supportive. When, during their final night together, she cries because all she has to offer is herself, he wishes for nothing but to see her naked body in the morning light. The scene reveals the limitations imposed on women's roles both in wartime and in postwar Japanese society. If Michiko is unconventional, she is unconventional within the bounds of a traditional family orientation. She wants to bear Kaji's child, not join his crusade to humanize the Japanese army and end the economic exploitation and brutalization of the Chinese. She is an idealized wife, but an apolitical Japanese women.

War films are admittedly a limited vehicle for analyzing women's roles in wartime and postwar Japan, especially since all the films discussed here were directed and produced by men. At the very least, however, they do say a great deal about male attitudes toward women in this era. One point is repeatedly made in each of the films: women should focus on their family and community obligations and leave the political realm to men. That this theme is still prevalent in films produced as late as fifteen years after the war speaks volumes about the "democratization" of Japanese society in the Occupation period and beyond.

Afterword

Jane Caplan

When Gail Bernstein suggested that I write an afterword to this collection to set it in the context of current thought in women's history, I was intrigued by the idea, if also somewhat daunted by the potential scale of the task. It offered a challenging opportunity to reflect on the current status of women's history, and it seemed nicely consistent with the self-reflective and critical quality that has marked feminist studies as an academic discipline. I also knew that reading the essays would introduce me to a field of history with which I, as a European historian, was largely unfamiliar, and that it would open new perspectives on the history of women and the social organization of gender.

What I was less prepared for was the complex dialectic of recognition and difference that emerged as I read, a dialectic that has forced me to think beyond what I originally envisioned as a straightforward, if demanding, exercise in contextualization. I found myself tracing in the essays a helix of interlocking tensions, which circulated on the central figure of difference but in several guises: the master figure of the difference of women in the order of gender; the figure of difference represented by the contrast between Japanese and Western European history; and the figure of difference that sets Japan apart from other so-called non-Western societies in the pattern of colonial occupation, dominance, and hegemony that has so powerfully shaped the modern world. The essays forced me to confront my vantage point as an English woman academic schooled in European history, and to question the

Thanks to Gail Bernstein for encouragement, and to Mary Poovey for her critical reading of a first draft of this Afterword.

project of construing a history of "others" in relation to the West's over-whelming master discourses of history and emancipation: a confronta-tion from which we who stay within the purview of the master discourse are all too frequently exempted.

Similar challenges seem to face Western historians of Japan, includ-ing those who, whatever their individual ethnic affiliation, write from the position of the West. Some of the contributors to this volume delib-erately locate their discussion of Japanese women's history in the perti-nent literature on American and European women's history. Others do not offer such an explicitly comparative dimension, but do draw on the chronological categories and social terminologies produced in and for the history of the Western world, such as the preindustrial and indus-trial eras, or the public and private spheres. In the first instance, a nonspecialist such as myself is invited to reflect on what is similar and different in the history of Japanese women by comparison with America or Europe. I begin with this comparative perspective, therefore, before moving on to the more difficult question of how the history of Japanese women may be studied in relation to a historiography of Western women that is presently at a crux of unity and pluralism. Hovering in the back of my mind will be the question of how to confront the Hob-son's choice between revitalizing and homogenizing women's experi-ence—to which I will return below.

I propose to focus on three interrelated issues that emerge from these essays on Japanese history and that seem most salient to the com-parative study of women and gender: first, the ideological subordina-tion of sex to gender in Tokugawa codes; second, the wife/mother dis-tinction in traditional ideology; and third, the place of the family or household in state policy in Meiji and modern Japan. Each of these top-ics stimulates thoughts on the specificity of Japanese experience that could also lead back to a reconsideration, and perhaps a remodeling, of Western models.

The ideological subordination of sex to gender, articulated in Jenni-fer Robertson's essay, is a richly rewarding formulation that can readily be contrasted with the modern Western subordination of gender to sex. This formulation of the relationship makes it possible to ask crucial questions about the historical contingency of sex/gender definitions, and about the conditions under which the relationship may change. The To-kugawa cultural order, in which the male Kabuki impersonator became a pattern of a "female-likeness" from which women's very anatomy dis-qualified them, epitomized this priority of gender over sex. As Robert-son points out, women's achievement of the female gender was thus no more than "tantamount to their impersonation of female-like males."

The Shingaku movement represented a bid to force sex and gender into a closer fusion, on the basis of a teleological achievement of the natural or originary state (the "original heart") of maleness or femaleness. The Shingaku conception of gender can be compared with that in modern Western bourgeois culture, from which the priority of gender over sex has also been evicted since the Renaissance. Instead of gender determining the authority of sex, gender in the West has been subjected to a rigid discipline of sex that established and grounded a naturalized (and eventually scientized) hierarchy of gender roles.

The Tokugawa order of gender and sex also appears in the ideological dissociation of the roles of motherhood and childbearing on the one hand from femaleness and wifehood on the other, and the origins of its later renegotiation can be located in the Meiji state's "Good Wife, Wise Mother" campaign at the turn of the nineteenth century. In the preindustrial Japanese *ie*, or household, the contribution by women to peasant and craft production was at least as important as their reproductive and nurturing activities, if not more so; indeed, as Kathleen Uno explains in her essay, men were often closely involved in the rearing and training of children. This allocation of roles and significance to women as members of the productive household unit rather than merely as mothers was also characteristic of preindustrial Western Europe; so, too, was the capacity of women to take over the conduct of household or enterprise as widows or daughters. In Europe, the shift to an order of sex and gender that privileged biological sex, aligned gender roles with biological capacity, and constructed a social morality centered on women's status in the family originated in the early-modern period, becoming the sponsoring ideology of the late-eighteenth- and early-nineteenth-century bourgeoisie. A parallel transition apparently did not begin in Japan until the Meiji "Good Wife, Wise Mother" campaign, and it never secured the same apotheosis of motherhood and domesticity.

Yet to emphasize a chronological sequence that aligns Japanese experience against that of the West is misleading, for it occludes the point that this transposition of women's roles took place in a specific structural context that had great significance in shaping modern Japan, namely, the autonomy and power of the state from the Meiji period onward in shaping family policy. In their essay, Sharon Nolte and Sally Ann Hastings point out that while the state-sponsored process of forced industrialization in Japan has been widely explored and theorized, the historians have ignored the state's policies of gender construction. This formulation lends itself to a structural comparison between Japan and the West. The political "underdevelopment" of Japan, notably the absence of the institutional and ideological networks of bourgeois liberalism, obliged the Meiji state to erect its own ideological state apparatuses to effect a policy of national and economic development—a policy that in the West was carried out through the operations of far more diverse and dispersed political and social institutions. The substance of this political "underdevelopment" had profound consequences for the relationship between the family and the state, epitomized in the Japanese state's designation of the home as a public place. Nolte and Hastings contrast this notion to the Western model of the home as a moral sanctum from which women then issued forth to moralize the world. The Western vision presumed a balance between public and private interests, but in Japan, by contrast, the state marched into the home to claim women for the state's own purposes.

Japan, in other words, lacked the crucial distinctions between state and society, between public and private, on which the institutions of the pluralist bourgeois political order developed in the West; hence, the notion of politics as the sphere in which legitimate collective interest might be pursued was also absent. It also lacked an inherited indigenous discourse on "the rights of man," which formed the substantial ideological foundation of Western liberalism and was the partial source of bourgeois women's claims to emancipation there. The extension of political rights to men in late-nineteenth-century Japan thus took place in the context of an attenuated concept of politics. The political was construed as the sphere of private interests, while the deprivatized family was construed as the locus of public interest and the public good. For women, the formalized codification of law had contradictory effects. On the one hand it eventually offered them a range of rights as women and wives, but on the other it eclipsed a previously diverse and flexible range of local and customary activities and behaviors.

In Japan, therefore, the ideological and the institutional sources of national legitimacy were soldered to each other far more rigidly than was the case with the more diversely articulated Western polities. Yoshiko Miyake explains how feminists in the Shōwa period could be attracted by state policies that conceded them a previously unlegitimized status, even in the contexts of coercive and depoliticizing policies of social organization and severe political repression—a conclusion that echoes the study of fascist manipulation of gender in interwar Europe. Several of the other essays in part 2 suggest that the discourses on women's emancipation that arose within this framework were more or less challenging depending on how far they reached beyond the hierarchy of gender alone to a confrontation with the figure of modernization/Westernization.

The form of "making sense" of Japanese women's history that I have been pursuing up to this point culminates in a logical movement of convergence in which the arbitrary comparison of feudal Japan and medieval Europe is retrospectively legitimized by an eventual "modernization" of Japan that is also a "Westernization." The inevitable vocabulary of economic and political "underdevelopment," of "lack" and "absence," discloses the fact that the story was all the time a story about the authority of the master subject to set the terms in which it would be written. This is what Gayatri Spivak calls "the subject of the West [which is also] the West as Subject."[1] I want therefore now to try and deconstruct the terms in which I have told this story, and so dislodge the Western subject of history from its privileged and hegemonic pedestal.

What can feminist historians writing from the vantage point of the West use to understand the history of women in other parts of the world? To begin with, one can, as I have done here, select what is recognizably the same or different vis-à-vis the history of Europe or of postconquest America and offer this in the privileged categories of explanation that are already familiar to the Western reader. Whether this history is represented as one of resemblance or difference, of imitation or resistance, of constants or variables, the hierarchy of the comparison and the authority of the West will be left to constitute the yardstick of interpretation. Alternatively, one might pursue the residual quest within feminism for a universal history of women, or at least a history in terms of common categories of analysis and explanation that will parallel a shared history of patriarchal exploitation. Here, however, one confronts the impossibility of developing a single adequate language in the face of the irreducible diversity of local circumstance, itself subdivided, as Anne Walthall's essay here emphasizes, by further specifications of class, time, and so on.

The more appropriate and timely tasks for feminist historians seem to me to be threefold. First, we must account for the real imbrication of women's lives across national and cultural boundaries in the modern world system; this in turn is linked to the challenge to build feminist practices that are appropriate to differently positioned women. Second, we must develop specific and pluralist histories of the cultural construction of women in different parts of the world that reject universalizing categories and explanations and that try to resist homogenizing accounts, whether of "the West" or "the Third World." And third, although those of us who inhabit the postimperial cultures can neither escape our vantage point nor evade its hegemonic claims, we can at least attempt a critical self-consciousness about the position from which we write. This involves both the multiplicity of possible vantage points and

---

1. Gayatri Spivak, "Can the Subaltern Speak?" in *Marxism and the Interpretation of Culture*, ed. Cary Nelson and Lawrence Grossberg (Urbana: University of Illinois Press, 1988), 271.

the related willingness to accept that the grounds for and the truth of arguments, including arguments for women's claims, are not epistemologically susceptible to final proof.[2]

These projects are obviously already under way, and certainly in greater numbers and variety than I am aware of.[3] Yet what is the effect of deconstructing the dualistic structure of analysis inherent in the dichotomies "West/Japan" and "male/female"? An inversion of the "self/other" hierarchy of the West over Japan, or of the male over the female, will not of itself undo the implied power relationship, because the two sides of the term are mutually constituted and depend on each other. In any such dualism, the unity of the privileged term is conserved only by the power of its owner to impute its own undesirable elements to the inferior half of the pair; this renders the former an effect of the latter rather than an autonomous term. Edward Said has explored this move in his well-known study of orientalism, arguing not only that the Western discourse on orientalism was a "discipline by which European culture was able to manage—and even produce—the Orient," but also that "European culture gained in strength and identity by setting itself off against the Orient as a sort of surrogate and even underground self."[4]

The same move can be followed in terms of the gender relations studied in this collection. Both the Shingaku movement and the *moga* debate discussed by Robertson and Silverberg respectively established a splitting that distributed behavioral characteristics and roles along a gendered axis, enabling men to conserve their own claims to a unitary and coherent identity only by exporting incoherence and contradiction to women. This inauthentic division renders male discourses about women alternative vehicles for discourses that are actually about men. By extension, if, in talking about women, men are engaged in the displaced contemplation of themselves, we would be ill advised to draw direct conclusions about women from advice books written by men; rather, we will need to probe them more critically as the vehicles of a masculine ideology that is intent on obscuring its own origins and grounding.[5]

To avoid reifying such dualisms means refusing to erect any entity as

2. See Mary Poovey, "Feminism and Deconstruction," *Feminist Studies* 14, no. 1 (Spring 1988): 51–65.

3. See, for example, the discussion and references in Chandra Mohanty, "Under Western Eyes: Feminist Scholarship and Colonial Discourses," *Feminist Review* 30 (1988): 61–88; and, for an ambitious attempt at a world-scale analysis of women, Maria Mies, *Patriarchy and Accumulation on a World Scale: Women in the International Division of Labour* (London: Zed Books, 1986).

4. Edward Said, *Orientalism* (New York: Vintage Books, 1979), 3.

5. For a clear statement and other examples of this, see Isobel Hull, "Feminism and Gender History" in *Central European History* (forthcoming).

a fixed and homogeneous standard against which to measure the other. Instead, we could allow the dialectics of difference with which this Afterword began to remain in tension, disclosing the insufficiency of either side of the comparison in isolation from the other. As an example of this revisionary move, the unsatisfying choice of depicting women as either passive or active, both sides of which are reductionist and one-dimensional, could be reworked if the individual subject were deconstructed; in other words, the ostensible coherence and unity of the subject or agent would be unraveled and revealed as something that is actually plural, internally contradictory, and overdetermined by mutual influences beyond its control and consciousness. More significantly in terms of the subject of this collection, the location of Japan as a third term between the imperializing Subject and the colonized Other may also assist in the deconstruction of the West/East dualism, an issue that is here directly confronted in Miriam Silverberg's essay, with its analysis of the way in which the *moga*, or modern girl, directly "played with the principle of cultural or national difference."

The critical study of Japan's history, especially its history of women and gender construction, can thus act as a powerful solvent to the dualist straitjacket that homogenizes and reduces the real diversity of histories, cultures, and positions even as it attempts to question the power relations that produced them.[6] The essays in this collection will help us to think ourselves beyond conventional dualisms that seem so self-evident, it takes an act of willful resistance to recognize them for the artifacts they are.

6. This is the purpose of some recent work by feminist historians, notably Joan Scott, *Gender and the Politics of History* (New York: Columbia University Press, 1988); and Denise Riley, *Am I That Name?* (Minneapolis: University of Minnesota Press, 1988).

Glossary of Japanese Names and Terms

atarashii onna	"new woman"
atotori	heir
bakufu	military administration of the shoguns
bantō	head clerk, apprentice
bunjin	scholar of Chinese studies
bunke	branch house; junior branch of main house
chōnin	merchants, townsmen
daimyō	feudal lord
dekasegi	migrant work
gonin gumi	five-household association
honke	main house
ie	stem-family household
jokun	precepts for women
kanreki	sixty: the traditional age of retirement
kazoku kokkakan	family-state ideology
koku	a measurement: 1 *koku* = 47.654 U.S. gallons; 5.119 U.S. bushels
Meiji	period between 1868 and 1912
mobo	"modern boy"
moga	"modern girl"
mon	family crest
mukoyōshi	son-in-law in a matrilocal, matrilineal marriage; adopted son-in-law
Obasuteyama	literally, "old woman–abandoning mountain"
obi	wide sash worn around kimono and tied in back
onnagata	male Kabuki actors who perform as women
onnarashisa	female-likeness

ryō	unit of currency
ryōsai kenbo	"good wife, wise mother"
sake	rice wine
samurai	feudal military class
shafu	housewife
shikigin	dowry
shokugyō fujin	working women
Shōwa	period between 1926 and 1989
shūmon aratame chō	population registers compiled annually by village headmen from the mid–seventeenth century to 1872
Taishō	period between 1912 and 1926
Tokugawa	period between 1600 and 1868
yobai	night visits
yome	bride; daughter-in-law

Contributors

Gail Lee Bernstein, Professor of History at the University of Arizona, is author of *Japanese Marxist: A Portrait of Kawakami Hajime, 1879–1946* (1976) and *Haruko's World: A Japanese Farm Woman and Her Community* (1983), and co-editor with Haruhiro Fukui of *Japan and the World: Essays in Japanese History and Politics* (1988). She is currently doing research on the history of a Japanese family.

Jane Caplan is Professor of History at Bryn Mawr College, where she teaches mainly in the field of German history and European women's history. She is the author of a book and several articles on the state and the civil service in modern Germany, and of articles and reviews on the history of women and sexuality. Her current research is on the history of identity documentation in Europe.

Laurel L. Cornell, Assistant Professor of Sociology at Indiana University, is a demographer and social anthropologist who works on population, gender, and family relations in early-modern Japan. Her work has appeared in *Signs, Journal of Family History*, and *Annales de démographie historique*.

Patricia Fister is Associate Professor of Art History and Curator of Oriental Art at the Spencer Museum of Art, University of Kansas. She is author of *Japanese Women Artists, 1600–1900* (1988) as well as numerous articles on Japanese art.

Sally Ann Hastings is Assistant Professor of History at Purdue University. She is nearing completion of a book on the impact of national movements on local organizations in Tokyo in the early twentieth century. Her most recent research explores the role of women educators in the making of modern Japan.

William Hauser is Professor of History at the University of Rochester. He is author of *Economic Institutional Change in Tokugawa Japan: Osaka and the Kinai Cotton Trade* (1974) and co-editor with Jeffrey P. Mass of *The Bakufu in Japanese History* (1985). He is currently working on a history of Osaka and on the cultural images of war in Japanese films.

Joyce C. Lebra is Professor of History at the University of Colorado. She has authored *Jungle Alliance: Japan and the Indian National Army* (1971); *Okuma Shigenobu: Statesman of Meiji Japan* (1973); and *The Rani of Jhansi: A Study of Female Heroism in India* (1986), and edited *Japan's Greater East Asia Co-Prosperity Sphere: Readings and Documents* (1975); *Women in Changing Japan* (1976); *Chinese Women in Southeast Asia* (1980); and *Women and Work in India* (1984).

Yoshiko Miyake is completing her dissertation on Japanese women's labor history, 1868–1990, in the History of Consciousness program at the University of California, Santa Cruz. She has written widely on women's issues in Japan, contributing to such major Japanese periodicals as *Asahi Jānuru* and *Shisō no kagaku*, and has also worked as an editor of periodicals devoted to the development of a women's movement and women's studies in Japan.

Barbara Molony is Associate Professor of History at Santa Clara University. She is author of several scholarly articles on economic and business history, the "Introduction" and "Afterword" to *Facing Two Ways: The Story of My Life* by Baroness Shidzue Ishimoto (1984), *Technology and Investment: The Prewar Japanese Chemical Industry* (1990), and, with Kathleen Molony, *Ichikawa Fusae: A Political Biography* (forthcoming, Stanford University Press).

Margit Nagy is Associate Professor of History and Intercultural Studies at Our Lady of the Lake University, San Antonio, and President of the Japan-America Society of San Antonio. She is author of *Remembering the Alamo Japanese-Style: Shigetaka Shiga's Monument as Tribute to Alamo Heroes* (1989) and is currently revising her doctoral dissertation on Taishō working women for publication.

Sharon Hamilton Nolte was Assistant Professor of History at DePauw University. Her publications included *Liberalism in Modern Japan: Ishibashi Tanzan and His Teachers* (1987) and a number of articles and book reviews. At the time of her death, she was about to begin writing a book on Japanese women and the state.

Jennifer Robertson, who has lived in Japan for seventeen years, is Assistant Professor of Anthropology at the University of California, San Diego. Robertson has published articles on historical and contemporary Japanese culture in *Anthropological Quarterly; Politics, Culture and Society; Peasant Studies; Monumenta Nipponica*; and *Genders* and has a forthcoming book, *The Making of Kodaira: Being an Ethnography of a Japanese City's Progress*. Her current research is on gender attribution, construction, and performance in Japan.

Laurel Rasplica Rodd is Associate Professor at Arizona State University, where she teaches Japanese language and literature. Author of *Nichiren: Selected Writings* (1980) and *Kokinshu: A Collection of Poems Ancient and Modern* (1984), she is currently writing a biography of Yosano Akiko.

Miriam Silverberg, Assistant Professor of History at the University of California, Los Angeles, is author of *Changing Song: The Marxist Manifestos of Nakano Shigeharu* (1990), which won the John King Fairbank prize of the American Historical Association in 1990. She is writing a cultural history of prewar Japan.

Kathleen S. Uno is Assistant Professor of History at Temple University, where she teaches Japanese history and comparative women's history. She has published several studies on modern Japanese women's and children's history, and is currently completing a book entitled *Childhood, Motherhood, and the State in Early-Twentieth-Century Japan*.

Anne Walthall is Associate Professor of History at the University of Utah. In addition to articles in *American Historical Review, Journal of Social History, Journal of Asian Studies*, and *Monumenta Nipponica*, she is author of *Social Protest and Popular Culture in Eighteenth-Century Japan* (1986) and *Peasant Uprisings in Japan* (forthcoming, University of Chicago Press).

Index

Abortion, 72, 279
Accomplished Women's Society (Keishū Bungakukai), 180
Adoption, 3, 6, 23, 54–55, 138, 140n.12, 142, 144, 145, 148, 166
Adultery, 8, 63–64
aikoku hōkokutai (patriotic labor corps), 288
Airplane Drone (*Bakuon*; film), 299–300, 311
Akira Hayami, 225
akujo (evil woman), 105
amadera (nunneries), 100
Anderson, Joseph, 300
Arimatsu Hideyori, 156
Arisugawa, Princess, 160
Ariyoshi Sawako: *The Doctor's Wife*, 65
Artisans, 2, 21, 22, 25, 29, 31, 34, 38n.70, 89, 96
Asahi shinbun, 178, 183, 244
Asai Kio, 103–4, 106
ashibumi (foot treadle), 138
Association of Typists (Taipusuto Kyōkai), 260
atarashii onna (new women), 175. *See also* New Woman

Baba Kochō, 194
Bachnik, Jane, 54
Bacon, Alice Mabel: *Japanese Girls and Women*, 42, 62

bakufu (shogunal military administration), 89, 91, 94, 102, 106
Ball at the Anjō House (*Anjō-ke no butōkai*; film), 306, 307
Bandai Kumiko, 104, 106
Banner, Lois, 261
bantō (head clerk), 142, 145, 148
Benedict, Ruth, 299, 301
Bernstein, Gail Lee, 315
Bird, Isabella, 32–33
Birth control, 12, 191, 278, 279
Bluestockings (*Seito*), 8–9, 14. *See also Seitō*
Book of Filial Piety, 93
bosei hogo ronsō (debate over the protection and support of motherhood), 189–98
Bowlby, Rachel, 248
bōzu (lit. "shaved head"; Buddhist priest), 99
Brandeis, Louis, 194
Buddhism, 5, 61, 66, 69, 89n.4, 99, 100, 101, 102, 132
bugyō (shogunal commissioner), 137
bunjin (scholars of Chinese arts and letters), 5, 108–30
bunjinga (*nanga*; literati painting), 108, 128. *See also* Ema Saikō
Bunkagakuin, 198
bunka jūtaku (culture house), 245n.23
bunke (branch houses), 142, 144, 145

bunmei kaika ("civilization and enlightenment"), 37
Bunshō sekai, 190
burakumin (outcasts), 210
bushidō, 153, 306

Campaign to Improve Livelihood (Seikatsu Kaizen Undō), 214
Capra, Frank, 299
Childbearing, 65, 180, 191, 216, 295; freedom from, 5, 128; vs. sexuality, 97;
and the state, 11–12, 192, 317; and
womanhood, 3; and women workers,
285. *See also* Motherhood; Mothers
Child labor, 36, 221, 222, 234, 237
Childrearing, 18, 27, 28, 45, 95, 164,
182n.16, 190–91, 193n.38; and financial management, 95n.24; in Great
Britain, 173; men and, 21, 30–33, 39;
mothers and, 13, 40; and the state, 7,
169, 278, 294, 295; and womanhood,
3. *See also* Work, reproductive
Children, 22, 44–45, 82–84, 173, 190; dependent, 36, 40; and divorce, 61, 136;
education of, 26, 36, 37, 38; as workers, 25, 34–35, 39
China, 108–9, 113, 124, 232, 282; factory
workers in, 221, 232n.56. *See also*
Women: Chinese
chiteki rōdōsha (intellectual laborers), 201
Chocolate and Soldiers (*Chokoreto to heitai*;
film), 298–99, 311
chōnin (townspeople), 89, 96
Chūgai, 194
Chūō kōron, 178, 264
chūryū kaikyū (*chūsan kaikyū*; middle class),
201
chūryū shokugyō fujin. *See* Working women,
middle-class
Civil Code, Meiji (1898), 8, 11, 43, 95n.26;
and patriarchal family, 246n.27, 270,
271, 272n.11, 294; revision of, 215,
258, 259, 261, 272n.11
Concubines, 97–98, 170
Confucianism, 109, 113, 169, 172; classics
of, 31, 168; and filial piety (*see* Filial piety); and hierarchy, 2; and inferiority
of women, 4, 8, 30, 275n.19, 276; and
patriarchy, 34n.58, 90n.6, 91, 95, 100;
and political suppression of women,
151; and Shingaku movement, 89n.4;

"six virtues for women" of, 94,
276n.19. *See also* Neo-Confucianism
Constitution of the Empire of Japan
(1889), 152, 154, 270
Control of Management of Important
Plants Ordinance (Jūyō Jigyōjō Rōmu
Kanri Rei), 287
Cornell, Laurel L., 4, 53
Coward, Rosalind, 242, 245

daimyō, 48, 97, 103, 109n.3, 113, 126,
134, 153
danjo no shobu no arasoi (sexual antinomy),
90n.6
dansho (certificates), 104
Daughters, 165, 231, 289, 290n.54,
293n.67; in merchant families, 138,
140, 142, 144, 148; in Tokugawa peasant families, 44–52, 67, 68, 87
Daughters-in-law, 4, 5, 6, 26, 52–64, 66,
77, 80–82, 84, 95, 106, 141
Davis, Natalie Zemon: "Women on Top,"
261
dejokunin (outdoor artisans), 29–30. *See also*
Artisans
dekasegi (migrant work), 132, 134
de Lauretis, Teresa, 218
Depression, worldwide, 205, 224, 258n.61
Divorce, 8, 60–61, 100n.41, 136, 168, 184,
199, 200n.1, 258, 259
dokuritsu jiritsu (self-reliance), 207
Domesticity, cult of, 7, 12, 17, 19, 154, 172
Dore, Ronald P., 46
Dōtoku mondō (Moral dialogues; Jion-ni
Kenka), 99, 102. See also *Kenka hogushū*
dōwa (parables), 105–6
Dublin, Thomas, 221, 224, 225
Durkheim, Emile, 79

Education, 235n.74, 259n.65, 278; compulsory, in Meiji period, 7, 36, 39, 40,
153, 157–58, 176n.4, 237; and factory
work, 226–27, 235n.74; in Tokugawa
period, 25–26, 26n.30. *See also* Women,
education of
Eighty-eight Years After the Opening of Japan
(*Hachijūhachinenme no taiyō*; film), 301–
2
Ellis, Havelock, 178
Ema Ransai, 109, 128
Ema Saikō, 5, 6, 31n.52, 108–30

Empress of Japan, 160, 161
en (attachment), 97
enkiridera (temple for severing marital connections), 60
Entrepreneurs, female, 6, 134–37. *See also* Tatsu'uma Kiyo
Equal Employment Opportunity Law (Danjo Koyō Kikai Kintō Hō; 1986), 294, 295n.71
Equality for women, 294–95, 312; vs. protection, 295n.71
Explanation of the Six Womanly Virtues (Sung dynasty), 93

Factory Act (1923), 285–86
Family, 1, 2–3, 10, 12, 272, 275–77; changes in, 258; in 1920s, 199–200; nuclear, 11, 294, 295; preservation of, 10, 17, 269, 271, 289; revitalizing, 277–81, 295; in wartime, 297–98, 300, 301, 302, 303, 312; women's rights within, 176. *See also* Households, heads of; *ie*
Family Council (Kazoku Kaigi). *See* National Cooperation Council
Family-state ideology, 10, 11, 171, 215, 268, 270–77, 279–80, 293–94, 318
Fass, Paula, 263n.71
Fathers: and child care, 31–33, 37, 95; and daughters, 31, 100, 101, 293n.67; of Meiji period, 25, 32; and the state, 276, 277; of Tokugawa period, 31–33
Federation of Café Waitresses (Jokyū Dōmei), 260
Femininity, 2, 10, 212–13; definition of, 8
Feminists: debates of, 176, 198; and history of women, 315–21; and labor activism, 237n.79; and motherhood, 3n.4, 11, 174, 198, 272; in 1920s, 226–27, 242, 243, 247, 248, 250, 259, 263, 272n.9; and politics, 151, 152, 155, 170; in postwar films, 303, 306n.20; in Shōwa period, 318; in Taishō period, 9, 176; and war policies, 273–75, 277, 279, 290. *See also* Women's movement
Filial piety, 3, 24, 65, 165, 168, 171, 176n.3, 223, 270, 271
Films, 296–313; censorship of, 297n.3, 303, 310n.24; women in postwar, 303–11, 312; women in wartime, 297–303, 311, 312, 313

First All-Japan Women's Suffrage Rally (1913), 198
Fister, Patricia, 5, 31n.52
Folklore, 71–72, 76
Four Books, 93
France, 56, 64, 157, 183
Frederic, Louis, 51
fūfugenka (husband-wife quarrel), 259
fugen (wifely words), 97
Fuji Bōseki, 227, 228, 231, 234
Fujimori Seikichi, 240
fujin (women's room), 96, 97, 104
Fujin kōron, 192, 194, 241
fujin rōdō gakari (person in charge of female labor), 208
Fujokai (Woman's world), 257
Fukazawa Shichirō, 72
fukō (wifely merit), 97
fukoku kyōhei ("rich country, strong army"), 37, 269
Fukuda Hideko, 178
fushō fuzui (*fushō fuwa*; the wife willingly following the husband's opinion), 187
futoku (wifely morality), 97
fuyō (wifely etiquette), 97
"Fūzoku-chō" (Record of customs), 57
fūzoku torishimari (lit. "supervision and control of traditional manners and customs"), 91

Gender, 1–2, 93, 96, 243, 315, 318; definition of, 2, 89n.5, 218, 235–38; and division of space, 96, 102; in Meiji period, 7, 152–53; vs. sex, 2, 90, 91, 92, 316–17; in Taishō period, 9; in World War I era, 8; in World War II era, 268n.4, 293
Germany: mobilization of women in World War II, 267, 268n.2; role of women in Nazi, 296
Geronticide, 72–77, 84, 87
ginbura (Ginza-cruising), 239, 248
Goebbels, Joseph, 296
gonin gumi (five-household association), 137
Gotō Matsuko, 206
Gotō Shōin, 126
Great Britain: wartime mobilization of women in, 267n.2, 281; women as mothers in, 173

Greater East Asian Co-Prosperity Sphere
(*Dai tōa kyōei ken*), 278, 303n.13
Greater Japan Women's Association (Dai-
nihon Fujinkai), 272, 275
Greater Learning for Women (Onna daigaku),
91, 92, 94
Grenville, J. A. S., 297
Grossman, Atina, 255n.54
"Guidelines for Plants Receiving Women's
Volunteer Corps" (*Joshi teishintai ukeire-
gawa sochi yōkō*), 289
Gyokudō, 115
Gyokurin, 110, 111, 120, 121

Hagiwara Sakutarō, 256
haikara (fashionably Western), 245
Hakuōsha poetry society, 124
Hakushika brewery, 140–42, 146, 147, 148
Hakutaka brewery, 145
Hall, Jacqueline Dowd, 222, 229n.46
Hanashiro Uta, 230
Hara Setsuko, 304
Hardacre, Helen, 49
Hasegawa Shigure, 175, 178
Hastings, Sally Ann, 7, 8, 317, 318
hatamato (high ranking retainers), 48
Hatayama Haruko, 176n.4
Hauser, William B., 12, 68
Hayami Akira, 52, 67
Hayashi Fumiko, 239, 253; *Hōrōki* (Tales
of Wandering), 253, 254
Hayashi Katsu, 208
Heian jinbutsu shi (Who's Who in Kyoto),
126
Higuchi Ichiyo, 31n.52
Hirabayashi Hatsunosuke, 261n.69
Hiratsuka Raichō, 177–78, 180, 192, 193,
194, 195, 247, 251n.41, 260; "About
the Demand for the Protection of
Motherhood" (*Bosei no shuchō ni tsuite*),
190; "The Agony of Contemporary
Housewives" (*Gendai katei fujin no na-
yami*), 197–98; "The Modern Girl as
She Should Be," 249; "On Birth Control," 191; and state protection of
motherhood, 176, 190
Hirose Chiyo, 55
hōkōnin (indentured servants), 50
honke atotori (heir to the main house), 142
honshin (original heart), 89, 90n.6, 94

honshin hatsumei (discovery of "original
heart"), 94
Hosoi Wakizō, 227; *Jokō aishi* (The pitiful
history of women workers), 223, 225,
232n.60, 236–37
Hōtokukai (gratitude societies), 163–64,
168
Households, heads of, 3, 24, 138, 205,
214, 215; legal authority of, 8, 259,
271; men as, 33–34, 40, 67, 74, 136;
succession of, 6, 144, 148; women as, 4,
13, 24n.25, 43, 55, 68, 136–37. *See also*
Family; *ie*
Housework: men's participation in, 21–22,
33–34, 39
Hughes, Langston, 252
The Human Condition (Ningen no joken;
film), 308–11, 313
hyōronka (commentator or essayist), 189

Ibsen, Henrik, 194, 235; *A Doll's House*,
175, 177, 257n.58; *Hedda Gabler*, 177
Ichikawa Fusae, 198, 273
ie (stem-family household), 3, 6, 11, 72;
conflict in, 76–77; continuity of, 23, 24,
25, 31; corporate nature of, 22, 23–30,
34, 140n.12; division of labor in, 3–4,
17–41; and industrialization, 210, 270;
under Occupation, 293–94; productive
work of, 25, 317; use of term, 22n.18;
wealthy, 25, 26, 28, 164; and working
women, 269. *See also* Family; Households, heads of
Ienaga Saburo, 70
Ihara Saikaku, 90
Ihara Seiseien, 175
Ikuta Chōkō, 193
Ikuta Hanayo, 178
Illegitimate births, 210
Imamura Shōhei, 72
imonbukuro, 159
Imperial Rescript on Education (1890),
270
Imperial Rule Assistance Association
(Taisei Yokusankai), 274
Industrialization: and cotton industry,
219–20; and divorce, 199n.1; and fam-
ily, 210; and Meiji state, 7, 152n.3, 154,
317; and proletarianization, 222, 223;
and silk industry, 214n.9; women's role

in, 38, 40, 94, 151, 152, 172, 173, 222, 269, 272n.9
Infanticide, 72, 73, 92
Inoue Kiyoshi, 70
Inoue Nihei, 144
Ise monogatari, 93
Ishida Baigan, 88, 89, 90, 94, 99, 101, 102, 103
Ishida sensei goroku (The analects of Teacher Ishida, 1740s; Ishida Baigan), 103
Ishiguro Tadanori, Baron, 164–65
Ishihara Osamu, M.D., 286n.38
ishiki (*mentalité*), 20, 39
ishokunin (indoor artisans), 29–30. *See also* Artisans
Itō Noe, 178, 187
Iwano Kiyoko, 178

Japan Cotton Spinners' Association (Dai Nippon Menshi Bōseki Dōgyō Rengōkai), 220
Japanese Communist party, 251
Japan Red Cross, 160, 162
Japan Women's College (Nihon Joshi Daigaku), 208
Japan Women's Commercial School (Nihon Joshi Shōgyō Gakkō), 212
Jiafan (Exemplary household; Sima Guang), 98n.34
jiga (self), 195
jinrin o midashumasu mono (corrupting public morals), 92
Jion-ni Kenka, 5, 6, 99–103, 106
jitsugaku ("practical school" of Confucianism), 91
jiyū kyōiku (education for freedom, or individualized education), 198
jochū (maidservants), 105
jokun (precepts for women), 46, 91, 92, 93, 107, 113, 151, 172
joruri (ballad drama), 91
Josei, 240, 242n.7, 244
Juvenile delinquency, 199, 208, 261n.69

Kabayama Sukenori, 158
Kabuki, 5, 90, 91, 105n.60, 106, 107, 175n.1, 316
kabu licensing, 147
Kaibara Ekken, 30, 89, 91, 94, 95; *Onna*

daigaku (Greater learning for women), 28n.39, 91, 94; *Wazoku tojikun* (Traditional Japanese precepts for children), 95
Kaizō, 191n.36
Kamichika Ichiko, 177n.8, 252
Kamimura, Vice-Admiral, 159, 161
Kan-in, Princess, 161
Kano Masanao, 273n.13
Kanō Mikiyo, 270
kanshi (Chinese-style verse), 108
Kantō earthquake (1923), 204–5, 206, 209, 240, 258n.61
Kantō Women's Federation of the Labor-Farmer party, 259
kata (model of existence), 89
kata ni yoru kokoro ("the heart that conforms to the model"), 90
Kataoka Teppei, 239, 242, 243, 247, 250, 254
katei sōgi (family struggle), 259
Katō Midori, 178
Katō Shidzue, 191n.36
Kawasaki Natsu, 205
kazoku kokkakan. See Family-state ideology
Keishū Bungakukai, 193, 194
Keller, Evelyn Fox, 2
Kelly, Joan, 40
Kenka hogushū (Kenka's scribblings; Jion-ni Kenka), 99, 102, 103
Kessler-Harris, Alice, 217
Key, Ellen, 195; *Children's World*, 190, 191; *Love and Marriage*, 178, 189, 190
kijo (ogre woman), 105
Kimura Shigenaki, 171
Kinoshita Keisuke, 72, 306, 307, 312
kinrō teshintai (women's volunteer corps), 288, 290–91
Kirihara Yoshimi, 281n.27, 287n.42
Kishida Ryūsei, 244
Kitamura Kaneko, 243, 246, 247, 263
Kitazawa Shūichi, 240, 241
Kiyosawa Kiyoshi, 242, 243, 244, 249
Kiyoura Keigo, 156
Kobayashi Masaki, 308
Kobayashi Seiji, 183n.19, 187
kodakara butai (childbearing corps), 280
Koganei Kimiko, 178–79
Koikeri Torakichi, 166
Koishi Teien (pen name; Genzui), 115

Koizumi Chikahiko, 288
Kojiki, 90n.6, 131
kōjo (filial woman), 105
Kokinshū, 179
kokkateki bosei (motherhood-in-the-interest-of-the-state), 271
kokoro (*shin*; heart-mind), 88, 90n.6
kokugaku (nativism), 65, 90n.6
Kollontai, Alexandra, 252
komori (part-time or live-in nursemaids), 27
kōmu (public servant), 203
Konjaku monogatari, 72
Konohana Sakuya Hime, 131, 132n.1
Kono Mitsuko, Dr., 134, 135
Kon Wajirō, 257
Kōra Tomi, 274
Kōsaisha (poetry society), 126
kōsha (colleges), 96
kōshi (lecturers), 104–5
koshu. *See* Households, heads of
Kumagai Hisatora, 302
Kumagai Kikuko, 226, 228, 230
Kumazawa Banzan, 89
Kunikida Noriko, 179
Kurosawa Akira, 303, 304–5
Kurozumikyō, 34n.58
Kurozumi Munetada, 34n.58

Labor Standards Law (Rōdō Kijun Hō, 1947), 293, 295n.71
Labor unions, 217–19, 227, 233–36, 259, 260; and strikes, 233–36, 253–54, 255, 260. *See also* Textile industry, Taishō; Women: activist
Ladies' Patriotic Association, 160, 161
Ladies' Volunteer Nursing Association, 160, 161, 162
Law on Associations and Meetings (Shūkai Oyobi Kessha Hō; 1890), 154–55, 156, 157
Law to Increase the Well-Being of Working Women (Kinrō Fujin Fukushi Hō), 295n.71
League for Women's Suffrage (Fusen Kakutoku Dōmei), 259
Lebra, Joyce Chapman, 5, 6
"Letters from a Trip to Kyūshū" (Yagi Akiko and Hayashi Fumiko), 253
Living Conditions of Working Women (*Shokugyō fujin seikatsu jōtai*), 201
Local Improvement Movement, 163n.44

Maebama Moral Reform Savings Society, 166–67
Maeda Hajime, 203n.12
Maejima Zengorō (pseud: Seibi), 65–66
Malinowski, Bronislaw, 252
Mansfield, Katherine, 252
Marriage, 5, 23n.20, 50, 51, 52–64, 101, 102, 113, 170, 175, 178; age differences in, 53, 82n.23; and class, 53–54; and dowries, 59n.57; and female-likeness, 94, 97; and legal contracts, 230n.48; in 1940s, 278, 280, 290; and remarriage, 62; and sexuality, 56, 64; in Taishō period, 207. *See also* Merchants: and marriage
Marxism, 248, 249, 251, 261
Matsui Sumako, 175, 177
Matsunaga Hyōshi, 62
Meiji Constitution (1889), 152, 154, 270
The Meiji Greater Learning for Women (Meiji onna daigaku), 156
Meiji period, 72, 202, 204, 214, 219, 237, 270; change in, 35–39, 69, 70, 94, 137, 147, 154; households in, 23–24, 136, 210; reforms of, 6–7, 18, 35–39, 151, 154; role of fathers in, 25, 32, 271; state policy toward women (1890–1910), 8, 9, 13, 151–74, 200, 259, 276, 277, 316, 317, 318; state prohibition of women's political activity in, 154–57, 163, 164
Meiji Restoration (1868), 35, 151–52, 154, 220
Meika gafu (Book of paintings by famous masters), 115
Meirinsha (Shingaku college), 96
Meirokusha (Meiji Six Society), 276n.19
mekake (concubine), 98
Mellen, Joan, 298, 309, 312
Men: attitude toward women in labor unions, 236; and childrearing, 21, 30–33, 39, 317; and gender differentiation, 40, 320; and household division of labor, 21–22, 33–34, 39. *See also* Fathers; Households, heads of
Mencius, 89n.4
Merchants, 6, 21, 22, 25, 28, 29, 38n.70, 68, 90, 96, 179; children of, 34; as fathers, 31, 32; and marriage, 144; status of, 2, 88, 89. *See also* Sake industry; Women: in family business

Mill, John Stuart: *The Subjection of Women*, 155
Ministry of Education, publications of, 270–71
Ministry of Welfare, 278, 279, 287
Mino fuga (compilation of verse), 126
Miscellaneous Lessons on Filial Piety (Sekiguchi Tōemon), 47
Misogyny, 91–92, 98, 102
Mitsui, Baroness, 162
Miwada Masako, 169–70
Miyake, Yoshiko, 11, 12, 318
miyamizu (special spring water), 138–39, 147
Miyashita Michiko, 52, 53
mobo (Modern Boy), 239, 250, 254, 264
moga (*modan gaaru*; modern girl), 11, 12, 14, 239–66, 320, 321; defining, 240–55, 261n.69; origin of term, 247
"Mogako and Moborō" (cartoon series), 241
Molony, Barbara, 10, 11
mon (family crest), 136
Mori, Princess, 161
Mori Masataka, 166, 167
Mori Ōgai, 184
Mori Shigeko, 178
Mori Yasuhiko, 53
Mori Yasuko: *Motherhood in the Interest of the State* (*Kokkateki bosei no kōzō*), 271n.8, 275–77
Morning with the Ōsone Family (*Ōsone-ke no asa*; film), 306–7, 311
Mortality: differential, 73, 84–86, 87; household structure and, 80–84
Moses, Claire, 157
Mosk, Carl, 52
Mother-Child Protection Law (Boshi Hogo Hō), 272, 280
Motherhood, 65–70, 158, 190, 216, 247; in interest of state, 270n.7, 272–73, 275–77, 280; male experts on, 95n.26; and Meiji state, 158, 169, 174; in postwar Japan, 12; in prewar Japan, 39n.73; state protection of, 9, 11, 176, 189–98; and womanhood, 3–4, 7, 17, 40, 317; and women's factory work, 267–70
Mothering, 13, 30, 40, 94; "reliable," 95–96
Mothers, 65–70; and daughters, 99; and

sons, 65–66; working, 206, 213, 216. *See also* Motherhood; *ryōsai kenbo*
Mothers-in-law, 66, 70, 77, 80, 87, 95, 174
muko (daughter's husband), 23
mukoyōshi (adopted son-in-law), 136, 142, 144, 145
Murakami Nobuhiko, 209–10, 211, 258n.63, 259n.65
mura-okuri issatsu (passports), 42
musume yado (girls' rooms), 45
Myōjō, 179, 180n.12, 183n.17, 184

Nabeshima, Marchioness, 160
Nagy, Margit, 9–10, 11, 14, 238, 258n.61
naien (common-law) marriage, 210
Nakabayashi Chikutō, 115
Nakadai Tatsuya, 308
Nakajima Kuni, 287n.41
Nakano Hatsue, 177
Nakazawa Dōni, 103, 104, 105
namaiki (cheeky, bold), 263
"Narayama bushiko" (Fukazawa), 72
narikin (nouveau riche), 211
National Cooperation Council (Kokumin Chūō Kyōryoku Kaigi), 274
National Eugenics Law (Kokumin Yūsei Hō), 278, 280
National Mobilization Law (Kokka Sōdōin Hō), 272, 277–78
Neo-Confucianism, 108, 153. *See also* Confucianism
New Japanese Women's Alliance, 198
New Poetry Society, 179, 184
New Theater movement, 175n.1
New Woman, 9, 14, 247–48, 251n.41, 254, 255n.54
New Woman's Association (Shin Fujin Kyōkai), 259
Nightingale, Florence, 173–74
Nihongi, 131
Nihon joseishi (Japanese women's history), 20
Nihon shoki, 93
Nii Itaru, 241, 244, 256
Ninomiya Sontoku, 163, 168, 171
Ni Tsan, 124
Nolte, Sharon H., 7, 259, 317, 318
No Regrets for Our Youth (*Waga seishun ni kui nashi*; film), 303–4, 311, 312
Nōyaku kikō (observations of agricultural practices), 56

nuke-mairi (escape pilgrimages), 49
Nursing, 203–4, 211
Nyonin geijutsu (women's arts), 250, 251, 252, 253, 254, 256
nyoshi seki (females' place), 96

"Obasuteyama" (lit., "Old Woman–Abandoning Mountain"), 71, 87
obasuteyama (abandoned old women), 211
obōzu (woman who assumed male gender), 99n.37
Occupation of Japan, 293–94, 297, 303, 313; film censorship under, 303n.14, 310n.24
Odake Kōkichi, 177
Ōguchi Yujirō, 68
ohariya (needle shops), 45–46
Okada Yachiyo, 175
Ōkōchi Kazuo, 293n.67
oku (inner living quarters), 96, 142
Ōkubo Shibutsu, 109n.2
Oku Mumeo, 258
Okumura Ioko, 160
Ōkura Ryūzan, 115
omote (outer store), 96
omotemuki (outward facing, or public, matters), 96
onnagata (male Kabuki actors in female roles), 90, 106
Onna myōga kai (A treatise on female fate, 1776), 97
onna no waza (female work), 95, 96
onnarashisa (female-likeness), 89, 90, 91, 94, 96, 97, 98, 100, 106, 107, 316
Onoda, Governor, 167
ooku (innermost quarters), 96–97
"Ordinance on Women's Volunteer Corps" (Joshi Teishin kinrō rei), 288, 289
Organization of Women's Consumer Unions (Fujin Shōhi Kumai Kyōkai), 259–60
Osado Kanako, 63
Osaka jiji, 203
Osanai Kaoru, 175
Oshioki Reiruishū (Representative examples of punishments and executions, 1771–1852), 92
Ōsugi Sakae, 178
otoko wa futtei, onna wa fueru (male shortage, female increase), 203
otokorashisa (male-likeness), 90

"Outline for Establishing Population Growth Policy" (*Jinkō seisaku kakuritsu yōkō*), 277, 278–80
"Outline for Reinforcement of Women's Volunteer Corps" (*Joshi teishintai seido kyōka hōsaku*), 288
oyabun (patron; family head), 62, 63
oyakata (labor boss), 30
Ōyama, Marchioness, 160, 161
Ōya Sōichi, 249
Ozaki Hotsumi, 303

Parii yori (From Paris; Yosano Akiko and Yosano Tekkan), 184
Patriarchal system, 70, 98, 106, 151, 176n.4, 247n.27, 254, 266, 268n.3, 319; and Confucianism, 90n.6, 91, 100; rebellion against, 102, 155; threats to, 259n.64, 263
Patriotic associations, 272, 273–74
Peace Preservation Law (Chian Iji Hō), 279, 280
Peasants, 2, 4, 23n.19, 35, 42–70. *See also* Women: peasant
People's Rights movement, 155
Pilgrimages, 48, 66–67
The Pillow Book, 179
Plath, David W., 43
Politics, 259, 260, 261n.70, 264, 318; exclusion of women from, 8, 13–14, 40, 151, 152, 154–57, 163, 164, 170–71, 312–13; and feminist debates, 176, 189
Population registers. *See shūmon aratamechō*
Precepts for Women (Han dynasty), 93
Primogeniture, 6, 23n.21, 138
Productivity, cult of, 154, 172, 173

Rai San'yō, 113–15, 117, 120–21, 126, 128, 129; *Nihon gaishi* (An unofficial history of Japan), 113
Rakuhoku Shōko: *Shinsen onna Yamato daigaku* (The new greater learning for Japanese women), 94
rangaku (Dutch studies), 109
Red Wave Society (Sekirankai), 259
Reikiginsha (poetry society), 126
ren'ai (love), 242, 243n.11
ren'aishugi (free love), 183n.19
reppu (*teijo*; virtuous woman), 105

Rice: mystique of, 135n.5; polishing of, 138, 147; price of, 146
Rice Riots of 1917–18, 192n.38, 210
Richie, Donald, 300, 304
Rinji Hōsei Shingikai, 259
Robertson, Jennifer, 5, 316, 320
Rodd, Laurel Rasplica, 8, 9, 238
Russo-Japanese War (1904–5), 158–59, 163, 165, 167, 168, 207, 257n.59
ryōsai kenbo ("good wife, wise mother"), 9, 11, 13, 40, 174, 195, 263, 266, 269, 276n.16; and Bluestocking group, 9; criticisms of, 176, 178, 180, 194; and Meiji state, 7, 8, 38, 94, 95, 152, 158, 159, 200, 271n.8, 273n.14, 317
"Ryūryū shinkuroku" ("A painstaking record"), 57

Sado Take, 298–99
Said, Edward, 320
Saito Osamu, 52
Sake industry, 131–48; as family business, 134–35
Sakuma Shōzan, 89
Sakura Masamune, 134, 138, 139n.11
Samurai class, 2, 20, 88, 89, 95n.26, 96, 103, 108, 168; bureaucratization of, 91; and Confucianism, 30, 113; fathers of, 31, 32; households of, 8, 22, 34n.58, 35, 48; and peasants, 50, 55, 62, 63; women of, 27–28, 57, 61, 62, 136, 137, 151, 168, 171
Sanger, Margaret, 191n.36
Sanpō Association (Sangyō Hōkokukai), 286n.39
Sanwa Shuzo, 134
Sata Ineko, 251, 253–54, 263
Sato Tadao, 312
Satsuma Rebellion (1877), 203n.11
Schreiner, Olive: *Women and Work*, 189
Scott, Anne Firor, 217
Scott, Joan, 222, 224, 225
Security Police Law (Chian Keisatsu Hō; 1900), 155, 156
Segalen, Martine, 56
Seitō (Bluestockings), 8, 176, 177–78, 189, 192n.38. *See also* Bluestockings
Sekiguchi family, 43, 48, 66
Sekiguchi Toemon, 60, 66
Sex, 89n.5, 90, 91, 92, 93, 98, 256; pre

marital, 50–51. *See also* Gender: vs. sex; *moga*
Sexuality, 89n.5, 97, 98, 176, 228, 242, 243, 245, 250, 254, 263
shamoji (rice scoop), 25
Shibata Hana, 166–67
shikigin (dowry), 136
Shikitei Sanba: *Ukiyo buro* (Bathhouse of the floating world), 32
Shimai Sōshitsu, 33, 34
Shimamura Hogetsu, 175
Shimin (The subject), 163–64, 165, 167, 169, 170–71; articles in, 170nn. 59,61, 173
Shimoda Jirō, 172
Shinchō, 250
Shin Fujin Kyōkai (New Women's Association), 198
Shingaku colleges, 103, 104, 105
Shingaku (Heart Learning) movement, 5, 88–107, 317, 320; female disciples of, 99–106
Shingaku Woman, 93–107
Shinjō Tsunezō, 49
Shinkokinshū, 179
Shintō, 64, 89n.4, 100, 131, 132
Shirai Hanbei, 99
Shirakaba, 178
shiseiji (illegitimate births), 210
shojokai (associations of young girls), 261
shokugyō fujin (working women), 257
Shōwa period, 198, 202, 209, 215, 266, 292; family-state ideology in, 270–77, 318
shufu (housewife), 24, 26
Shufu no tomo (Housewife's friend), 256
shūmon aratamechō (population registers), 42, 73, 75, 86
shūtome (mother-in-law), 26n.31, 27
Silverberg, Miriam, 11, 238, 320, 321
Sino-Japanese War (1894–95), 38, 39, 144, 147, 162
Sister Goes to the Front (Ane no shuppei; film), 301, 311
Small Learning, 93
Smith, Thomas C., 20
Socialism, 176, 194, 259
Society of Working Women (Shokugyo Fujinsha), 260
Song of the Advancing Army (Shingun no uta; film), 300–301

Spivak, Gayatri, 319
Standing Committee on Women's Associations to Encourage Thrift (Kinben Shōrei Fujin Dantai Jōnin Iinkai), 215
A Story of Instruction (*Shidō monogatari*), 302
Sudermann, Hermann, 177
Suffrage, women's, 9, 14, 154, 170, 194, 198, 210, 227, 240, 251, 259, 261, 275
Sugimoto, Etsu: *A Daughter of the Samurai*, 72
Suidobashi Women's Employment Exchange, 210
Su Tung-p'o, 124
Suzuki Bokushi, 34, 43, 47, 55, 58, 61, 62, 63, 64, 65, 67, 69
Suzuki family, 47, 55, 62–63, 65
Suzuki Heikurō, 43, 66
Suzuki Jūkichi, 240n.3
Suzuki Kayo, 57
Suzuki Toyo, 48, 57, 66, 69

Tadano Makuzu, 90n.6
Tagami Tatsuko, 104, 106
Taishō period, 9, 11, 137, 198, 219, 258n.63, 272n.11, 275; children in, 36; divorce in, 199n.1; increase of urban middle class in, 201; working women in, 202, 204, 205, 208, 209, 210, 212, 215, 237, 238. *See also* Motherhood: state protection of; New Woman
Taiyō (Sun), 178, 186, 189, 194, 208
Takai Toshio, 31n.52, 227, 228n.40, 229–30, 230n.48
Takamine Hideko, 307
Takemure Itsue, 250
Takikawa Incident (1933), 303
Takizawa Eisuke, 301
The Tale of Genji, 179, 183, 194
Tanahashi Ayako, 169, 174
Tanaka Hisara, 242n.7
Tanaka Kinuyo, 305
Taniguchi Kiku, 167, 168
Tanino Setsu, 208, 282, 284, 285, 286
Tanizaki Junichirō: *A Fool's Love*, 244, 245, 246, 247, 254, 258
tanomo haha shiki mono (reliable mothering), 95–96
tanomoshikō (revolving credit association), 58
T'ao Yüan-ming, 120

taru-kaisen (sail-powered cask ship), 139, 146
Tasaka Tomotaka, 299
Tatsuenosuke, 142–44, 145, 146, 147
Tatsu'uma family, 140–48
Tatsu'uma Kiyo, 6, 131, 137, 138–48
Teaching, 203, 206, 209, 210, 211
teishuku (feminine modesty), 158
Tejima Toan, 89, 90, 91, 92, 93, 94, 95, 96, 97, 98, 101, 102, 104, 106
tenbun (mission in life), 200
terakoya (commoner's school), 31n.51, 46
Textile industry, Taishō, 10, 217–38, 246n.26, 282, 290; conditions in, 231–36, 237, 286, 289; farm women in, 221–25; Okinawans in, 227, 228, 230–31; postwar, 292, 293; recruitment in, 225–31; wages for women in, 226n.31
Tilly, Louise, 218, 222, 224, 225, 236
tofu (jealous wife), 105
Tōgō, Admiral, 161
Tohimondō (City-country dialogues, 1739; Ishida Baigan), 102
toji (brewer), 132
Tōkaidō hizakurige, 253
tokkō (thought police), 273
Tōkoku-ni, 101
Tokugawa (Edo) period, 2–6, 17–35, 74n.12, 90, 134; art in, 109; expansion of brewing in, 138–40; farm women in, 42–70; fiction in, 105; geronticide in, 72, 73; increase in nuns in, 100; men's household activities in, 30–34; misogyny in, 91; spread of literacy in, 30; woman's role in, 13, 99, 106–7, 153, 168, 316, 317; women's household activities in, 19–30; women in industry during, 12, 136
Tokugawa Tatsukō, Count, 164, 165
Tokyo Muslin, 227, 229–30, 232n.60
Tokyo Women's Reform Society, 170
Tolstoy, Leo, 189, 190
Tomeoka Kōsuke, 168, 171
tonari gumi (neighborhood associations), 272
"Torikaebaya Monogatari," 93
Toward the Decisive Battle in the Sky (*Kessen no ōzora e*; film), 302–3
Tōyō Muslin, 226, 230; 1930 strike of, 236, 253–54, 255, 260

Toyokawa Women's Volunteer Corps, 290–91
Tsurezuregusa, 93, 102
Turgenev, Ivan, 194
Twenty-four Eyes (Nijūshi no hitomi; film), 307–8, 311, 312

Uesugi Yozan, 89
Umehara Miki, 33
Umezu Hagiko, 228, 230
Unge, 115–17
United Nations International Year of Women (1985), 180n.15
United States: cotton textile industry in, 221, 222, 223, 233n.64; films in, 296n.1, 297; "flapper" in, 263n.71; mobilization of women in World War II, 268n.2, 281; women and industrialization in, 172, 260
Uno, Kathleen S., 3, 4, 317
Uno Chiyo, 256
Uragami Shunkin, 115, 117, 120, 126
Ushio Shigenosuke, 165

Varner, Richard, 53
The Victory of Women (Josei no shori; film), 305–6, 311, 312

waka (31-syllable poems), 179, 194
Wakita Osamu, 20
Walthall, Anne, 4, 319
ware (ego), 94
Wartime Factory Act, 286
warui asobi (bad play), 229
watakushi suru mi (privatizing one's entire being), 97
Watanabe Yōzō, 293n.67
What Made Her Do What She Did? (Nani ga kanojō wo sō saseta; film), 240
Widows, 94, 153, 172, 267; mortality rates of, 79–80, 84, 87
Wives, 52–64, 67–68, 94, 95, 316; attitude toward concubines, 97–98; expansion of rights of, 215; in Meiji period, 8, 164, 168, 174; post–World War II, 293n.67; Tokugawa, 3, 9, 106. See also *ryōsai kenbo*
Womanhood: bureaucratic ideals of, 163–74; definition of, 1–2, 7, 13, 14, 17, 18, 35–36, 38; and motherhood, 3–4, 7,

17, 40, 317; women's discussions of, 8–9
Women: activist, 10, 217–19, 226n.30, 233–38, 253–60; and capital accumulation, 167, 171, 172; Chinese, 67, 98; as civil servants, 7, 8, 11, 12, 13–14, 38, 157, 166–67, 171, 215, 271, 277, 280, 318; commodification of, 251; as consumers, 256n.55, 258, 260; crimes and punishments of, 92n.13; in early modern household, 22–30; economic independence of, 192–93, 194, 195, 198, 207, 209, 218; elderly, 4, 69, 71–87; empowerment of, 11, 137; in family business, 6, 10, 21, 28–29, 29n.44, 57–58, 134–35; farm, 220n.14, 221, 223–28, 280, 293n.67; in films, 12, 240, 256, 266, 296–313; "four virtues" of, 97; funerals for, 69–70; and government, 176; history of, 315–21; as household managers, 4, 8, 13, 171, 193n.38, 214; in industry, 136–38, 153, 217–38, 282–88, 292–95; inferiority of, 8, 30, 40, 91, 92–93, 275n.19, 276; literati, 108–30, 130n.19, 179–89; middle-class, during interwar years, 199–216; military conscription of, 288–92; mortality rates of, 73, 77–80; as mothers, 3–4, 7, 9, 11, 12, 40, 173, 272n.9, 273, 274; peasant, 4, 18, 20, 25, 27, 37, 38, 39n.74, 42–70, 153, 171, 172; and pollution, 131–32; and productive work, 26–30, 38, 57; as role models, 31n.51; in sake industry, 131–48; stereotypes of, 105–6; urban, 17, 37, 38, 39n.74, 95, 96; and war, 157–63, 267–92, 296–313; wealthy, 25, 27, 28, 57, 61, 62–63, 70, 164–65, 172; working, 9–11, 12, 13, 37n.68, 38, 57, 153, 169, 200–216, 257, 281nn. 25,27, 294–95. See also Entrepreneurs, female; *moga*; Politics: exclusion of women from; Shingaku Woman; Women, education of; Working women, middle-class
Women, education of: and equality, 251; and factory work, 226–27, 237; in Meiji era, 38, 40, 153, 157–58, 179; in Tokugawa era, 24n.27, 31, 46, 48, 91, 128; in twentieth century, 8, 9, 176, 193, 194, 198, 203, 207; and woman's role, 13

The Women of Suye Mura (Smith and Wiswell), 63, 64
Women's Alliance (Fujin Dōshikai), 261
Women's movement, 14, 151, 174, 180, 183, 190, 192, 194, 198, 206, 295n.71. *See also* Feminists
Women Suffragists League (Fusen Kakutoku Dōmei), 273
Work, productive, 25, 36, 37, 39, 269; women and, 10, 26–30, 38, 40, 76, 96, 269, 317
Work, reproductive, 25, 26–30, 36, 37, 39, 40, 41, 76, 96, 269, 277–81, 288n.47; men and, 33–34, 39
Working Woman, 257–58; vs. flapper, 261n.68, 266
Working Woman (*Shokugyō fujin*), 260
Working women, middle-class (*chūryū shokugyō fujin*), 10, 200–216; defined, 201–4; motivations of, 204–8; part-time, 295; postwar firing of, 292; and sexual harassment, 211; societal response to, 209–15; wages of, 209, 226n.31, 294
World War I, 8–9, 151, 203, 204, 209, 227, 237, 247, 257n.59, 258
World War II, 8, 36, 217, 219, 221n.15, 266, 267, 268, 275, 276, 281, 285, 296, 297

Yagi Akiko, 251, 253
Yaguchi Nakako, 104, 106
Yajima Kajiko, 170
Yamada Nishiki, 139–40
Yamada Waka, 176, 189–90, 194–95
Yamaga Sokō, 95
Yamakawa Kikue, 176, 193, 194, 195, 198, 235, 251, 257n.58, 260; "An Examination of Feminism," 251; "Modern Girls, Modern Boys," 248, 249; "Women's Problems Viewed by a Woman," 194
Yamamoto Baiitsu, 115
Yamana Bunsei, 65
Yamano Chieko, 260
Yamanouchi Mina, 226, 227, 228, 230

Yamasaki Ichi, 165, 168
Yamasaki Toyoko: *Bonchi*, 137; *Hana noren*, 137
Yamato monogatari, 93
Yamauba (Mountain witch; Nō play), 102
Yanagawa Seigan, 124
Yana Kunio, 51
yobai (night visits), 50, 51, 52, 56
Yokohama bōeki shinpō (Yokohama trade news), 195
yome (brides), 23, 26, 27, 30. *See also* Daughters-in-law
Yomiuri (newspaper), 205
Yosano Akiko, 9, 175, 176, 178, 179–98; *Akarumi e* (Toward the light), 183; on childbirth, 195, 197; children of, 191n.35, 198; *Hitosumi yori* (From my little corner), 180, 187; journal articles by, 179n.10, 180, 189; *Karasu to ame* (Crows and rain), 186n.22; lectures of, 179n.11, 194; *Midaregami* (Tangled hair), 179; on motherhood, 190; "Records of the Purple Shadows" (*Shieiroku*), 192; "Women's Complete Independence" (*Joshi no tettei shita dokuritsu*), 192; *Zakkichō* (Miscellaneous notes), 187, 188
Yosano Tekkan, 179, 182, 184, 186, 187, 188, 191; children of, 191n.35; *Rira no hana* (Lilac flowers), 184
Yoshida Shōin, 90, 91, 93n.16
Yoshida Shūran, 115
Yoshimoto Osei, 137
Yoshimura family, 60
Yoshimura Kimisaburō, 306
Yüan Mei (Sui-yüan), 108n.2
Yuri Takahashi, 199n

Zeami, 72
zendō inkan (teaching permits), 104
Zenkun (lectures for women), 93, 94, 95, 96, 97, 98, 102, 105, 106
zuihutsu ("following the brush") poems, 180n.13, 192

Compositor: Princeton University Press
Text: 10/12 Baskerville
Display: Baskerville
Printer: Princeton University Press
Binder: Princeton University Press